SMITHSONIAN INSTITUTION

UNITED STATES NATIONAL MUSEUM

BULLETIN 225

WASHINGTON, D.C.

1963

MUSEUM OF HISTORY AND TECHNOLOGY

Papers 12–18
On History

CONTRIBUTIONS FROM THE MUSEUM OF HISTORY AND TECHNOLOGY

SMITHSONIAN INSTITUTION WASHINGTON, D.C. 1963

Publications of the United States National Museum

The scholarly publications of the United States National Museum include two series, *Proceedings of the United States National Museum* and *United States National Museum Bulletin*.

In these series are published original articles and monographs dealing with the collections and work of the Museum and setting forth newly acquired facts in the fields of Anthropology, Biology, Geology, History, and Technology. Copies of each publication are distributed to libraries and scientific organizations and to specialists and others interested in the different subjects.

The *Proceedings*, begun in 1878, are intended for the publication, in separate form, of shorter papers. These are gathered in volumes, octavo in size, with the publication date of each paper recorded in the table of contents of the volume.

In the *Bulletin* series, the first of which was issued in 1875, appear longer, separate publications consisting of monographs (occasionally in several parts) and volumes in which are collected works on related subjects. *Bulletins* are either octavo or quarto in size, depending on the needs of the presentation. Since 1902 papers relating to the botanical collections of the Museum have been published in the *Bulletin* series under the heading *Contributions from the United States National Herbarium*.

The present collection of Contributions from the Museum of History and Technology, Papers 19–30, comprises *Bulletin* 228.

Frank A. Taylor
Director, United States National Museum

For his wise, thoughtful, and sympathetic guidance in developing the Museum of History and Technology and its programs of research and publication, the authors respectfully dedicate this volume to

Dr. A. Remington Kellogg
Director of the United States National Museum
1948 to 1962

Papers

Contributions from

The Museum of History and Technology

Paper 12

Hermann Stieffel, Soldier-Artist of the West

Edgar M. Howell

1

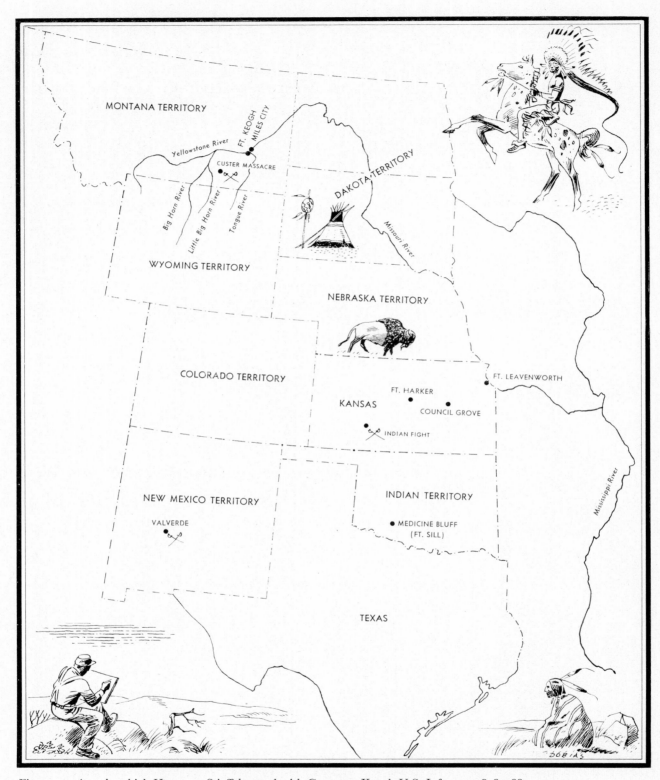

MONTANA TERRITORY

FT. KEOGH
MILES CITY

Yellowstone River

CUSTER MASSACRE

Big Horn River

Little Big Horn River

Tongue River

WYOMING TERRITORY

DAKOTA TERRITORY

Missouri River

NEBRASKA TERRITORY

COLORADO TERRITORY

KANSAS

FT. HARKER

COUNCIL GROVE

FT. LEAVENWORTH

INDIAN FIGHT

NEW MEXICO TERRITORY

VALVERDE

INDIAN TERRITORY

MEDICINE BLUFF
(FT. SILL)

Mississippi River

TEXAS

DOBIAS

Figure 1.—Area in which Hermann Stieffel served with Company K, 5th U.S. Infantry, 1858–1882.

By Edgar M. Howell

Hermann Stieffel,
Soldier Artist
of the West

A number of gifted artists painted the West and the colorful Indian-fighting army of the post-Civil-War period, but since none of these were military men their work lacked the viewpoint that only a soldier could provide.

German-born Hermann Stieffel, for 24 years a private in the U.S. Infantry, painted a series of water colors while serving in the Indian country in the 1860's and 1870's. Although Stieffel could never be called talented, and certainly was untutored as an artist, his unusually canny eye for the colorful and graphic and his meticulous attention to detail have given us valuable pictorial documentaries on the West during the Indian wars.

The Author: Edgar M. Howell is curator of military history in the United States National Museum, Smithsonian Institution.

THE AMERICAN WEST has never wanted for artists with a high sense of the documentary. Through the talented hands of men like George Catlin, Carl Bodmer and Alfred Jacob Miller, Frederick Remington, and the cowboy painter Charles M. Russell the trans-Mississippi regions have been pictured as have few other areas on earth.[1] From historical and ethnological standpoints these men made tremendous and timeless contributions to our American heritage. But the West held an esthetic fascination for the untutored and less talented as well, and not a few soldiers, miners, stage drivers, and just plain adventurers recorded their impressions on paper

[1] For George Catlin, Gustavus Sohon, and George Gibbs, see: John C. Ewers, "Gustavus Sohon's Portraits of Flathead and Pend d'Oreille Indians, 1854," *Smithsonian Miscellaneous Collections*, vol. 110, no. 7, 1948; "George Catlin, Painter of Indians and the West," in *Annual Report of the . . . Smithsonian Institution . . . 1955*, 1956, pp. 483–528; Marvin C. Ross, *George Catlin, Episodes from Life Among the Indians and Last Rambles*, Norman, Okla., Univ. Oklahoma Press, 1959; Harold McCracken, *George Catlin and the Old Frontier*, New York, Dial Press, 1959; David I. Bushnell, Jr., "Drawings by George Gibbs in the Far Northwest, 1849–1851," *Smithsonian Miscellaneous Collections*, vol. 97, no. 8, 1938.

For Alfred Jacob Miller, see: Bernard DeVoto, *Across the Wide Missouri*, Boston, Little, Brown and Co., 1947; Marvin C. Ross, editor, *The West of Alfred Jacob Miller*, Norman, Okla., Univ. Oklahoma Press, 1951.

For Frederick Remington and Charles Russell, see: Harold McCracken, *Frederick Remington, Artist of the Old West*, Philadelphia, Lippincott, 1947, and *The Charles M. Russell Book; the Life and Work of the Cowboy Artist*, Garden City, Doubleday, 1957.

Figure 2.—Attack on General Marcy's train near Pawnee Fort, Kansas, September 23, 1867. The train was escorted by Company K, 5th U.S. Infantry, Brevet Major D. H. Brotherton commanding. (*USNM 384185; Smithsonian photo 38986–A.*)

and canvas. Crude though many of these works are, they are nonetheless significant, for they are a graphic record of what these men saw, where they lived, and what they did, in many cases the only record of particular places and events, for the camera of L. A. Huffman and his colleagues did not come into its own until the late 1870's.[2] Without them we would have no description, graphic or otherwise, of much of the West both before and after the Civil War—the early trading posts and forts, the Oregon, Santa Fe, and Overland Trails, the Bozeman Trail, the stage stations, all of which played a part in the opening and development of the West.[3]

[2] See: Mark H. Brown and W. R. Felton, *The Frontier Years. L. A. Huffman, Photographer of the Plains,* New York, Henry Holt and Co., 1955; Martin F. Schmitt and Dee Brown, *Fighting Indians of the West,* New York, Charles Scribner's Sons, 1948.

[3] An excellent group of these crude on-the-spot drawings and paintings is reproduced in Grace Raymond Hebard and E. A. Brininstool, *The Bozeman Trail,* 2 vols., Cleveland, The Arthur H. Clark Co., 1922.

In 1946 the heirs of Lt. Col. David H. Brotherton, U.S. Army, an Indian-fighting officer of many years experience on the frontier, donated to the United States National Museum a collection [4] comprising a number of Sioux Indian specimens, including a Model 1866 Winchester carbine said to have been surrendered in 1881 to Colonel Brotherton by the Sioux chief, Sitting Bull, and ten water colors by a German-born private soldier, Hermann Stieffel of Company K, 5th U.S. Infantry. Nine of these paintings (the tenth being a view of Rattenberg in the Tyrol Alps) are photographically reproduced herein. They constitute an unusually graphic and colorful, if somewhat unartistic, series of documentaries on the West of the post-Civil-War Indian fighting period.

It can be surmised that Brotherton obtained the paintings from Stieffel, for from 1861 to 1879 he

[4] No. 173740 in the U.S. National Museum.

commanded the infantry company in which the latter spent the entire 24 years of his Army career. Brotherton's career itself is an interesting sidelight on the West of the period and an excellent if somewhat sad commentary on the promotion system in the Army during a period when the development of the West was so heavily dependent on the Army's curbing Indian depredations.

Brotherton was graduated from the U.S. Military Academy with the class of 1854 along with several officers who later distinguished themselves in the Confederate States Army, including George Washington Custis Lee, son of Robert E. Lee, John Pegram, J. E. B. Stuart, Stephen D. Lee, and William Dorsey Pender.[5] Assigned to the 5th Infantry, Brotherton by 1861 had risen to the rank of captain and had acquired considerable experience against the Comanches and Apaches in the Southwest, the Seminoles in Florida, and the Mormons in Utah. Electing to remain with his regiment at the outbreak of the Civil War rather than resign and enter a volunteer or militia unit where he easily might have risen to general rank as did so many of his contemporaries, he remained a captain in the Army until 1879 when a vacancy occurred and he was promoted to major. He was promoted to lieutenant colonel in 1883 after 29 years of service, but only at the expense of transferring from his old regiment to the 7th Infantry, where there was a vacancy at that rank. He retired for disability in 1885 after 30 years of almost constant service in the field.

We know little of Stieffel the man. He was born in Wiesbaden, Germany, in 1826, and became a printer by trade, indicating a fair amount of education. He emigrated to this country at an unknown date and in December 1857 at New York City enlisted in the Army as a private of infantry. He was 31 years old at the time, and was described as being five feet five and one-half inches tall with blue eyes, sandy hair, and a fair complexion.[6] He remained a private for the entire time of his military service. After recruit training at a general depot, he was assigned to Company K, 5th Infantry, joining that unit late in August 1858 at Camp Floyd (later Fort Crittenden), Utah Territory, where the regiment was an element of Col. Albert Sidney Johnston's "Army of Utah" sent westward to police the recalcitrant Mormons.[7]

Stieffel's record shows nothing of note until December 1859 when he was court-martialed and fined.[8] This court-martial seemed to set the pace for him. Although the precise charge on which he was tried is not stated, in view of his later record it can be surmised that it was for drunkenness—a very common offense in the frontier army—for in October 1861 Stieffel owed a sutler $27.95, a heavy debt for a day when a private's net pay was less than $11.00 a month.[9] The debt remained unpaid through 1862 and even increasing an additional $15.00. During this period Stieffel also was in confinement on a number of occasions for crimes or misdemeanors unspecified.[10]

In 1860 the 5th Infantry was transferred from Utah southward to the Department of New Mexico. It was here in 1862 that Stieffel saw his first combat in Col. E. R. S. Canby's[11] Union force, which frustrated the wild Confederate attempt under Brig. Gen. H. H. Sibley to invade the present states of New Mexico and Arizona and conquer California.[12] Captain Brotherton, Private Stieffel, and the remainder of Company K fought in the sharp action at Valverde, New Mexico, on February 21, 1862, and evidently

[5] The information on Brotherton's career has been culled from: *Register of Graduates and Former Cadets United States Military Academy, 1802–1946*, New York, The West Point Alumni Foundation, Inc., 1946; Francis B. Heitman, *Historical Register and Dictionary of the United States Army*, Washington, Government Printing Office, 1903, vol. 1; George W. Cullum, *Biographical Register of the Officers and Graduates of the U.S. Military Academy*, Boston, 1891–1930, vol. 3.

[6] Enlistment papers of Hermann Stieffel dated December 17, 1857, Adjutant General's Records, National Archives, Washington.

[7] Theo F. Rodenbough and William L. Haskin, *The Army of the United States*, New York, Maynard, Merrill & Co., 1896, pp. 471–472; Remarks on Muster Roll, Company K, 5th Infantry (hereinafter cited as Muster Roll, Co. K), August 31, 1858, Adjutant General's Records, National Archives, Washington.

[8] Muster Roll, Co. K, *op. cit.* (footnote 7), December 31, 1859.

[9] In 1861 a private's pay was $13.00 per month with $2.00 withheld until expiration of his enlistment and $.12½ withheld for support of the U.S. Soldiers' Home at Washington. (*U.S. Army Regulations*, 1861.)

[10] Muster Roll, Co. K, *op. cit.* (footnote 7), October 31, 1861; December 31, 1861; April 30, 1862; June 30, 1862; December 31, 1862; February 28, 1863; April 30, 1863; February 28, 1864; June 30, 1864.

[11] Canby was murdered by the Modoc Captain Jack in 1873 while engaged in a peace conference.

[12] For details of these operations, see: *The War of the Rebellion: Official Records of the Union and Confederate Armies*, 130 vols., Washington, War Department, 1880–1901, ser. 1, vol. 9, pp. 487–522.

Figure 3.—Satanta addressing the peace commissioners at Council Grove, Medicine Lodge Creek, Kansas. (*USNM 384183; Smithsonian photo 38298.*)

with some distinction as Brotherton was breveted major for gallantry as a result of his unit's performance.[13] Unfortunately for posterity, Stieffel did not record his impressions of this little-known sideshow of the Civil War.

The Battle of Valverde was Stieffel's only experience in formal combat so far as the record shows. After the final withdrawal of Sibley's force into Texas whence it had come, the 5th Infantry turned its hand to policing the Indians and was almost constantly in the field during the period 1863–1866.[14] Stieffel, however, was seldom with his unit during this time. When not on one of his frequent stays in the stockade,

he was on extra duty at the closest army hospital.[15] He continued on such duty for most of the remainder of his service,[16] except for confinements, a period of desertion, and necessary changes of station.

Stieffel's exact unofficial status in Company K over the years is difficult to account for. It is possible, though hardly probable, that Captain Brotherton had developed a friendship with the German, which might account for both his acquisition of the paintings and Stieffel's extra-duty tours. But such is doubtful. Brotherton was a hardened professional officer in an era when there was a far wider gap between officer and enlisted man than exists today. There is no evidence that Stieffel was a shirker. At the end of

[13] *Ibid.*, ser. 1, vol. 47, pt. 2, p. 1246.
[14] Rodenbough and Haskin, *op. cit.* (footnote 7), p. 472; Muster Roll, Co. K, *op. cit.* (footnote 7), April 30, 1863; June 30, 1864; October 31, 1865.

[15] The first note of such duty is in Muster Roll, Co. K, *op. cit.* (footnote 7), February 28, 1863.
[16] See Muster Roll, Co. K, *op. cit.* (footnote 7), 1863–1882. The muster rolls were submitted bimonthly.

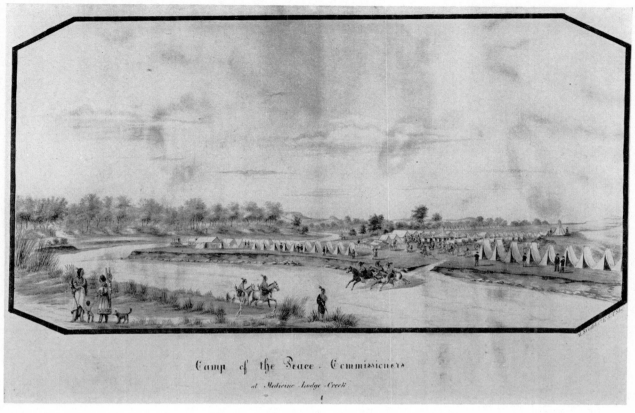

Figure 4.—Camp of the peace commissioners at Medicine Lodge Creek, Kansas.
(*USNM 384184; Smithsonian photo 38298–A.*)

each enlistment he reenlisted and always in Company K, and such reenlistment was subject to the company commander's veto. It is probable that he was not a particularly good soldier. But after the Civil War an army career in the ranks held little glamor for the average young man and recruiting officers were hard put to keep the ranks even partially filled, too often being forced to take what they could get. The most plausible explanation is that since every unit in the Army, then as today, was constantly called on for extra-duty men, the company first sergeant just as constantly selected the apparently agreeable Stieffel as the person whose absence was least likely to weaken the combat readiness of the company. The arrangement must have suited Brotherton, for he allowed it to continue for years. It obviously suited Stieffel, for once he was placed more or less permanently on such detail his periods of confinement ceased. Hospital duty in that day and age was hardly arduous, and the discipline was light. Also, it provided 25 cents a day extra pay. Thus, this duty gave Stieffel time to paint and, if our surmise is correct, both the time and the money for him to indulge his thirst. In any case, we are indebted to this light duty that gave him the opportunity to paint.

In September 1867 Company K left New Mexico for Fort Harker, Kansas, in the Department of the Missouri, as escort for Brig. Gen. R. B. Marcy, an old member of the 5th Infantry who was acting as inspector general for troop units west of the Mississippi. On that march of something more than 500 miles the column was sharply attacked near Fort Dodge on the Arkansas River by a large force of Cheyenne believed led by Black Kettle, and Stieffel had his second and last taste of combat. The action must have impressed him, for it furnished the subject of the first of his paintings (fig. 2). From Fort Harker, Company K escorted the Indian peace commissioners to Council Grove on Big Medicine Lodge Creek for their treaty meeting with the Kiowas, Apaches, Comanches, Chey-

The Wicheta Mountains from the Medicine Bluffs. In. Ter.

Figure 5.—The Wichita Mountains from Medicine Bluffs, Indian Territory.
(*USNM 384188; Smithsonian photo 42880.*)

enne, and Arapahoes in October. This historic meeting Stieffel witnessed and depicted with considerable color and attention to detail (figs. 3, 4).

After another period of hospital duty at Fort Harker (figs. 6, 7), Stieffel went in the field, for what appears to have been the last time, as a member of a wagon-train escort to Medicine Bluff, Indian Territory (present day Oklahoma), where General Sheridan was establishing Fort Sill on the southern edge of the Wichita Mountains.[17] This picturesque overhang of Medicine Bluff Creek, a small tributary of the Red River, was the subject of one of Stieffel's landscapes and perhaps his finest single work (fig. 5).

After this brief interlude in the wilderness, Stieffel went back to his hospital work. Then in September

1873, following a change of station for Company K from Harker to Fort Leavenworth, he went in desertion until the following May, being restored to duty upon his return, rather strangely, without trial but with loss of pay for the period of his absence.[18] The only possible explanation for this leniency in a period when court-martial sentences tended to severity could be that since extra-duty men had to be furnished, Stieffel was worth more to the company out of the stockade than in. With Indian unrest increasing every man counted.[19]

[17] *Ibid.*, June 30, 1868; February 28, 1869; April 30, 1869.

[18] *Ibid.*, December 31, 1869; September 30, 1873; June 30, 1874.

[19] Company K was almost at full strength at the time, mustering 58 enlisted men of the 60 authorized. *Ibid.*, September 30, 1873; *Official Army Register for January 1874*, Washington, Adjutant General's Office, 1874, p. 260B.

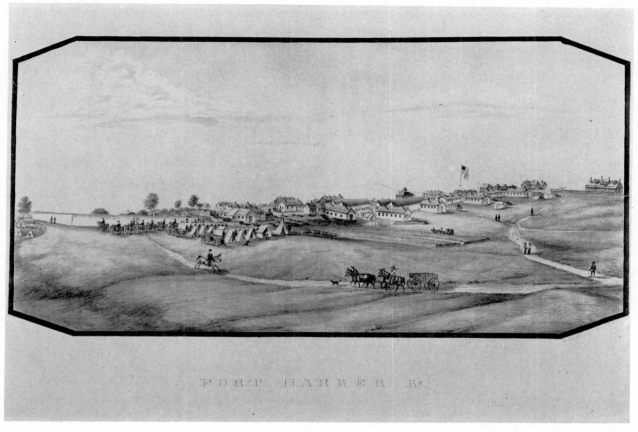

Figure 6.—Fort Harker, Kansas; east side. (*USNM 384187; Smithsonian photo 42895.*)

Following the Custer massacre on June 25, 1876, all posts in the Department of the Missouri were virtually stripped of troops, among them the 5th Infantry, and dispatched to the Department of Dakota in an all-out attempt to bring the rampaging Sioux under control. But Stieffel saw no action in the campaigns that followed. He was sick [20] and was left behind on July 12 when Company K left Leavenworth for the northwest for five years of almost continuous campaigning including numerous actions with the Sioux and the campaign against the gifted Indian tactician, Chief Joseph, and his Nez Percé. We could wish that Stieffel had been present during the Nez Percé campaign, for he might have pictured for us Nelson Miles and the 5th Infantry taking the surrender of Joseph in the Bear Paw Mountains at the end of his

epochal 1,600-mile running fight.[21]

Stieffel remained at Fort Leavenworth until 1877 when he rejoined his regiment at Cantonment Tongue River, Montana Territory, renamed Fort Keogh in 1879. At Keogh he was again placed on hospital extra-duty and so remained until he was discharged June 23, 1882,[22] on a surgeon's certificate of disability. After his discharge he retired to the Soldier's Home in Washington where he died on December 14, 1886, at the age of 60. He was buried in the National

[20] Muster Roll, Co. K, *op. cit.* (footnote 7), August 31, 1876.

[21] Frederick Remington has pictured this surrender for us, but he was not an eye witness.

[22] Muster Roll, Co. K, *op. cit.* (footnote 7), August 31, 1878, to June 30, 1882; Certificate of Disability for Discharge, Private Hermann Stieffel, April 8, 1882, Adjutant General's Records, National Archives. The date of June 23, given on the Muster Roll, was apparently that on which the discharge received final approval in Washington.

Cemetery on the Soldiers' Home grounds.[23]

Stieffel painted three scenes of Fort Keogh and vicinity—one of the fort itself, one of Miles City across the Tongue River, and a landscape of the Yellowstone River near Miles City (figs. 8–10).

The Paintings

Chronologically, the first of the paintings (fig. 2) is that of the Indian attack on General Marcy's train escorted by Company K on September 23, 1867. This attack took place on the Arkansas River about nine miles west of Cimarron Crossing, Kansas. It was an insignificant action as such, similar to hundreds of other such fights in the West, but, in the days of wet-plate photography and low-speed camera shutters, the painting is significant as a rare eye-witness drawing and tells us far more than might any written description. General Marcy's report is somewhat cursory:

Yesterday at about 9 o'clock a.m. as we were approaching a bluff near the Arkansas River thirty-five miles above here we suddenly discovered a great many Indians approaching us from various different directions. I immediately halted our train and after arranging our escort in proper order for action went forward. The Indians circled around us at full speed firing as they ran but did not come very near us. I would not allow our men to fire at the long range, believing that the Indians would come nearer but they did not. Some of the men fired and it is believed that two were wounded as groups collected around them. They wounded Lt. Williams severely in the leg and one soldier who has since died.

Near the point where the affair occurred was a large train of wagons en route to New Mexico with valuable freight. The train had two hundred mules driven off by the Indians about twelve days ago, and it had been guarded by twenty-five men since, and it is probable that the Indians were there for the purpose of capturing the train as they had been firing into it previous to our arrival.[24]

Stieffel tells us much more in his painting. Upon being attacked the train has pulled off the road, visible in the left foreground, and corralled. The

horses remain hitched, witness to the suddenness of the attack. That the Indians did not venture overly close, as stated by Marcy, is indicated by the fact that Brotherton's men have not been forced to take cover behind the wagons. That the Indians appear closer than Marcy indicates is due to the artist's lack of perspective. They are firing muzzle-loading rifles, several men being in the act of ramming home charges. Stieffel is doubtless correct in this detail. The Chief of Ordnance reported in October 1867 that nearly all the infantry in the Departments of the Missouri and the Platte had been issued breech-loaders.[25] It seems more than probable that Company K, in transit as it was from the distant Department of New Mexico, had never seen the new weapons.

In the matter of uniform, Stieffel may have been indulging his fancy somewhat when he pictured the men as wearing the long frock coat and black campaign hat. A miscellany of dress with the short fatigue jacket and kepi predominating would seem far more reasonable for an outfit which had just finished six rough years in the desert Southwest and was even then nearing the end of a 500-mile march. The artist, as did most observers of the period, has patently overestimated the number of Indians who must have carried firearms in the attack. Fully 50 percent or more of the Indians are pictured as so armed, a point which—understandable as it may be in the case of an observer participating in what may well have been his first Indian fight—is not borne out by the record. In the Fetterman Massacre of the previous December, of the 81 white men killed only six bore gunshot wounds,[26] and the best evidence indicates that the force which overwhelmed Custer on the Little Big Horn River in 1876 was at least 50 percent armed with bow and arrow.[27] Then again, General Marcy's report would seem to bear this out. Had the Indians been well armed, the freight wagon train, which Stieffel pictures corralled in the right background, could hardly have held out for twelve days against a force estimated at 300 or more warriors

[23] There is no record of Stieffel's ever having been a member of the Soldiers' Home, but the Home's records for the 1880's are very incomplete. However, his discharge gives his forwarding address as that institution, and there is definite record of the date of his death and interment there.

[24] Report of Brig. Gen. R. B. Marcy, September 24, 1867, document no. 1,000, AGO, Department of Missouri, vol. 4, 1867, Civil War Branch, National Archives.

[25] Report of Chief of Ordnance, 1867, Washington, War Department, 1868.

[26] George Bird Grinnell, The Fighting Cheyenne, New York, Charles Scribner's Sons, 1915, p 235.

[27] Frazier and Robert Hunt, I Fought With Custer: The Story of Sergeant Windolph, New York, Charles Scribner's Sons, 1947, p 92. For an excellent discussion of Indian armament at this period, see John E. Parsons and John S. DuMont, Firearms in the Custer Battle, Harrisburg, The Stackpole Company, 1953.

Figure 7.—Fort Harker, Kansas; south side. (*USNM 384186; Smithsonian photo 38986.*)

defended by only 25 men, at least a part of whom were Mexicans described by Marcy as badly frightened.[28] The soldier in the center background making a dash for the corralled wagons is probably a flanker cut off by the sudden attack, possibly the Lt. Williams who was wounded, since only officers in the infantry were mounted. The group of Indians around the fire (in the right centerground) cannot be accounted for.

Stieffel's two pictures of the meeting of the Government's peace commissioners with the Indians at the general tribal rendezvous on Big Medicine Lodge Creek in October 1867 (figs. 3, 4) are his most important from a historical standpoint, especially the one of Satanta, the Kiowa chief, addressing the meeting.[29]

Indian unrest during and immediately after the Civil War caused by the ever-increasing white migration to the West had grown to such proportions that in 1867 the Congress launched an all-out effort to establish a lasting peace on the frontier. The plan was to persuade the warring tribes to sign treaties whereby they would move onto reservations where they would be undisturbed by the whites and, in turn, would cease to molest the frontier settlements.[30] The Indians concerned with the Medicine Lodge treaty were the Kiowa, Comanche, Apache, Cheyenne, and Arapahoe. This treaty is unusually important, as it changed the entire status of these tribes from that of independence with free and unrestricted range over the entire plains area to that of dependence on the Government with confinement to the limits of a

---

[28] Marcy's report, *op. cit.* (footnote 24).

[29] Jack Howland, artist for *Harper's Weekly*, also pictured Satanta speaking to the commissioners, and with more accuracy in that all the civilian commissioners are visible, but his pictures lack the color and drama of Stieffel's work. See: *Harper's Weekly*, November 16, 1867.

[30] The records of this treaty meeting are contained in the Office of Indian Affairs, Record Group 75, National Archives. The final treaties are reproduced in *Indian Affairs: Laws and Treaties*, vol. 2, Washington, Government Printing Office, 1903, pp 754–764.

Figure 8.—Fort Keogh, Montana. (*USNM 384189; Smithsonian photo 37925.*)

reservation with constant civilian and military super-vision. For the Indians it was the beginning of the end.

Upon its arrival at Fort Harker following the action of September 23, Company K had been assigned as escort for the commissioners, thus Stieffel's presence at Council Grove. It was a colorful gathering, with some 5,000 Indians on hand. First came a series of speeches. Then the treaty was drawn up and ex-plained to the Indians. They were to retire to assigned reservations, cease attacking the whites, and permit railroads to be built across the plains. In return the reservations were to be closed to the white buffalo hunters and the tribes were to be issued certain annuities and provided with farming imple-ments, seeds, churches, and schools. In short, the Indians were to be forced to "walk the white man's road."

When the turn came for the Indians to reply, sev-eral chiefs responded, the most notable being the Kiowa chief, Satanta, or "White Bear" (fig. 11), one

of the most remarkable individuals in his tribe's history. Speaking for all, Satanta made an unusually strong impression on most of those present, Stieffel among them, for this is the incident which he chose to depict [31] (fig. 3).

Satanta is pictured in the act of speaking to the commissioners, three of whom can be identified as the military members, Generals Terry, Augur, and Harney from left to right, [32] plus one of the civilian commissioners, possibly N. G. Taylor, Commissioner of Indian Affairs. A daring and successful warrior, Satanta's eloquence and vigor of expression had already won for him the title "Orator of the Plains." Every feature on his strong face, every line, showed

[31] There are several accounts of this. The best, in the opinion of the writer, is in James Mooney's "Calendar History of the Kiowa Indians," *17th Annual Report of the Bureau of American Ethnology*, Washington, Government Printing Office, 1898, pp 181–186, 206–210.

[32] See photo taken at later date by Alexander Gardner, Still Picture Branch, National Archives.

Miles City Montana

Figure 9.—Miles City, Montana. (*USNM 384190; Smithsonian photo 37925–B.*)

his character—a forceful, untamable savage of a tribe as well known for its lack of honor, gratitude, and general reliability as for its bravery. [33] With great dignity and impact he first denounced bitterly and scornfully the killing for mere sport of a number of buffalo near the council site by some troopers of the 7th Cavalry:

Has the white man become a child, that he should recklessly kill and not eat? When the red men slay game, they do so that they may live and not starve.

In direct relation to the treaty, he continued with obvious sincerity:

I love the land and the buffalo . . . . I don't want any of the medicine lodges [schools and churches] within the country. I want the children raised as I was . . . . I have heard that you intend to settle us on a reservation near the mountains. I don't want to settle. I love to roam over the prairies. There I am free and happy, but when

we settle down we grow pale and die . . . . A long time ago this land belonged to our fathers; but when I go up to the river I see camps of soldiers on its banks. These soldiers cut down my timber; they kill my buffalo; and when I see that my heart feels like busting.

Little wonder Stieffel and all those present were impressed. It is appropriate to add that neither the Indians nor the Government of the United States observed the provisions of this treaty.

The remainder of Stieffel's paintings have no such impact as the earlier ones, but nonetheless they are important, especially for their almost meticulous detail of camp and post life and terrain in the West. In that of the camp of peace commissioners he accurately depicts the various types of tentage of the Army at the time—the small slanting wall tents of the enlisted men, the wall tents of the individual officers, the large wall headquarters and officers' mess tents, and the familiar Sibleys, one of which is obviously being used for the guard. The escort wagons and ambulances are regulation transport of the period. The artist has even included a sentry walking post at the ration dump with fixed bayonet, a sound precaution against sticky

---

[33] An interesting sidelight on Satanta: In the spring of 1867 he accepted a complete general officer's uniform from General Hancock at Fort Dodge and reciprocated shortly afterwards by attacking the post while decked out in his new dress.

The Yellowstone River near Ft. Keogh, Montana

Figure 10.—The Yellowstone River near Fort Keogh, Montana. (*U.S.NM 384191; Smithsonian photo 37925–A.*)

red fingers. Two Indian camps are shown in the background, and the Indians, as would befit the atmosphere of a treaty council, are moving freely through the military camp to the apparent unconcern of the military.

The landscape of the Wichita Mountains from Medicine Bluffs (fig. 5) on the present-day Fort Sill reservation is noteworthy as a terrain sketch to anyone who has served at that post. I have ridden over this country many times, and the undulating prairie, the meandering of Medicine Creek, the Bluffs themselves—over the highest of which (left centerground) the Apache Geronimo did *not* ride his horse with the 7th Cavalry in full cry behind—Mount Hinds and lofty Mount Scott are remarkable in their accuracy when one considers that the painting must have been done from sketches made when Stieffel was on escort detail to the Indian Territory in 1869.[34]

---

[34] Detail and orientation check closely with map of Fort Sill, Oklahoma, sheet 6353 III NW, scale 1:25,000, Army Map Service.

The two views of Fort Harker, Kansas (figs. 6, 7), now Ellsworth, must have been painted during 1870 and 1871 while Stieffel was on extra duty as a hospital attendant there. From an artistic standpoint they are the poorest of his work. His detail, however, more than compensates for any deficiencies as a draftsman and gives us an excellent concept of the physical layout and daily routine of a small post in the Southern Plains. The two views are from the east and south, and complement one another nicely. Headquarters, officers' quarters, and barracks, all of typical clapboard construction, are readily discernible, as are the stables, the latter being the long unfenestrated buildings. Even the barrack privies, an outdoor bake oven alongside a mess hall, and earth-covered powder magazines can be easily identified. The long rows of cordwood for cooking and heating were to be seen on any post of the period. In the view from the east (fig. 6) may be seen a detail of cavalrymen with led horses moving out for animal exercise past the camp of a transient unit with its standard tentage and transport. The high white

Figure 11.—Kiowa Chief Satanta, or White Bear. (*Smithsonian photo BAE 1380–A.*)

paling fence is difficult to place, being either an animal corral, in which case it would be much too high, or a forage yard, since no hay piles are visible elsewhere. Stieffel seems to have been considerably fascinated by the railroad (fig. 7) with its accompanying telegraph line running southwest of the fort, for again he paints in some detail, although this time with an almost childish conception. The "U.P.R.W.E.D." which he so carefully letters in identifies the line as the Union Pacific Railway, Eastern Division.[35] The naming of the engine "Osage"

[35] This was identified in Engineer Files, Cartographic Branch, National Archives.

was as typical of the period as the naming of individual commercial aircraft is today.

The last three paintings (figs. 8–10) fall in the period of Stieffel's service at Fort Keogh in the Department of Dakota. The fort, named for Captain Miles Keogh (who died with Custer in the Little Big Horn massacre) and originally called Cantonment Tongue River, was located at the confluence of the Tongue and Yellowstone Rivers near present-day Miles City, Montana.

The pictures of both the fort (fig. 8) and Miles City (fig. 9) are subject to check against extant photographs; they are amazing in their detail and accuracy.

The over-all layout of the fort conforms, and such minute details as the gable windows and chimneys of the officers' quarters on the left of the parade ground and the two-story verandas on the enlisted barracks opposite are absolutely correct.[36] The familiar stables, corral, wood piles, and hay piles—the latter surrounded by a stone wall as protection against grass fire in the dry months—are readily discernible (fig. 8). The low stone buildings and corral in the right centerground probably are part of the original structures of Cantonment Tongue River. The small shacks to the left of them probably are the homes of the civilian hangers-on who founded Miles City in 1876 after being ejected from the post by Col. Nelson Miles, the commander of the 5th Infantry. The first site of Miles City can be seen in the upper right corner on the banks of the Tongue. The town was moved across the river in 1877. The mounted drill in the foreground is difficult to explain in a period when and in an area where the troops were almost constantly in the field under combat conditions. Perhaps it is mere window dressing by the artist. It is entirely possible, however, that Stieffel has pictured elements of his own regiment, which was mounted from 1877 until after the surrender of Sitting Bull in 1881. Being basically infantry they would be most in need of training in mounted tactics. Then again, these could be legitimate cavalry whose commander thought had wandered too far from regulation movements during the unorthodox winter warfare they had been waging against the Indians.

The view of Miles City (fig. 9) has little importance in a military sense, but it is a fine contemporary view of a frontier town of the period. It is probably the product of a spring afternoon Stieffel spent along the banks of the Tongue. It was painted before 1880—a wooden bridge had replaced the ferry by that year[37]—and probably as early as 1878, for the town grew rapidly and Stieffel pictures only two streets, Main and Park, running at right angles. The town is correctly placed in a grove of cottonwoods, and low to the river as evidenced by the almost annual flooding of the streets.[38] Structures which can be readily identified, reading from left to right on Main Street, are the Diamond D corral visible near the ferry landing; the town stockade which Stieffel has either misplaced or which was later moved; Major Bochardt's store, the white two-story building; Broadwater, Hubbel and Co., the brown two-story structure next right; the Cottage Saloon at the corner of Main and Park Streets, just to the right of the flag pole; and Morris Cahn's drygoods emporium on Park Street, in the right centerground, that can be identified by Cahn's name on the false front.[39]

A Note on Stieffel's Indians

In seven of his nine paintings Stieffel has executed his Indian subjects in colorful detail and with some care. Although he apparently did not know his subjects well enough to distinguish them by tribe, he does depict them in typical dress of the period. Many of them are wearing German silver ornaments of various designs about their necks, on strips of flannel attached to their hair pigtail-like, or as arm bands. At least four are wearing hair-pipe breast plates, a fact of interest to ethnologists,[40] and several wear the comical, Puritan style, tall black hats issued as annuity goods. The red and blue robes are of trades-good flannel, as probably are the leggings. Two wear buffalo robes with the skin side out and the hair side rolled over at the shoulder.[41] Two, in the Fort Keogh picture (fig. 8) and the Yellowstone River landscape (fig. 10), wear robes of the familiar, colorfully striped Hudson Bay blanketing material. Arms are conventional—bows, quivered arrows, and pipe tomahawks, with a scattering of firearms. In the Yellowstone River landscape one discrepancy should be pointed out—the canoe; the Northern Plains Indians seldom used water transport, and then generally only in the form of rafts.

---

[36] An over-all photographic view of the post is in Still Picture Branch, National Archives. For photos of the officers' quarters and barracks, see Brown and Felton, op. cit. (footnote 2), pp 98, 128.

[37] See photo in Brown and Felton op. cit. (footnote 2), p 135.

[38] Ibid., pp. 137, 140.

[39] Ibid., pp. 157, 163, and end paper map.

[40] Ewers, op. cit. (footnote 1), pp. 58–61, 1948.

[41] Lower right in the Council Grove scene and in the foreground of the Fort Keogh picture.

Contributions from

The Museum of History and Technology:

Paper 13

North Devon Pottery and Its Export
To America in the 17th Century

C. Malcolm Watkins

FIGURE 1.—North Devon sgraffito cup, deep dish, and jug restored from fragments excavated from fill under brick drain at May-Hartwell site, Jamestown, Virginia. The drain was laid between 1689 and 1695. Colonial National Historical Park.

By C. Malcolm Watkins

NORTH DEVON POTTERY
AND ITS EXPORT TO AMERICA
IN THE 17th CENTURY

Recent excavations of ceramics at historic sites such as Jamestown and Plymouth indicate that the seaboard colonists of the 17th century enjoyed a higher degree of comfort and more esthetic furnishings than heretofore believed. In addition, these findings have given us much new information about the interplay of trade and culture between the colonists and their mother country.

This article represents the first work in the author's long-range study of ceramics used by the English colonists in America.

THE AUTHOR: *C. Malcolm Watkins is curator of cultural history, United States National Museum, Smithsonian Institution.*

POTTERY SHERDS FOUND ARCHEOLOGICALLY in colonial sites serve a multiple purpose. They help to date the sites; they reflect cultural and economic levels in the areas of their use; and they throw light on manufacture, trade, and distribution.

Satisfying instances of these uses were revealed with the discovery in 1935 of two distinct but unidentified pottery types in the excavations conducted by the National Park Service at Jamestown, Virginia, and later elsewhere along the eastern seaboard. One type was an elaborate and striking yellow sgraffito ware, the other a coarse utilitarian kitchen ware whose red paste was heavily tempered with a gross water-worn gravel or "grit." Included in the latter class were the components of large earthen baking ovens. Among the literally hundreds of thousands of sherds uncovered at Jamestown between 1935 and 1956, these types occurred with relatively high in-

cidence. For a long time no relationship between them was noted, yet their histories have proved to be of one fabric, reflecting the activities of a 17th-century English potterymaking center of unsuspected magnitude.

The sgraffito pottery is a red earthenware, coated with a white slip through which designs have been incised. An amber lead glaze imparts a golden yellow to the slip-covered portions and a brownish amber to the exposed red paste. The gravel-tempered ware is made of a similar red-burning clay and is remarkable for its lack of refinement, for the pebbly texture caused by protruding bits of gravel, and for the crude and careless manner in which the heavy amber glaze was applied to interior surfaces. Once seen, it is instantly recognizable and entirely distinct from other known types of English or continental pottery. A complete oven (fig. 10), now restored at

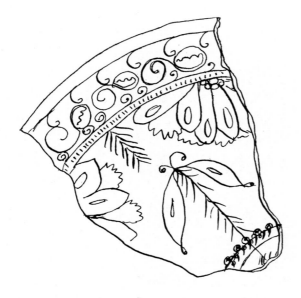

FIGURE 2.—Sketch of sherd of sgraffito-ware dish, dating about 1670, that was found during excavations of C. H. Brannam's pottery in Barnstaple. (*Sketch by Mrs. Constance Christian, from photo.*)

Jamestown, is of similar paste and quality of temper. It has a roughly oval beehive shape with a trapezoidal framed opening in which a pottery door fits snugly.

Following the initial discoveries at Jamestown there was considerable speculation about these two types. Worth Bailey, then museum technician at Jamestown, was the first to recognize the source of the sgraffito ware as "Devonshire."[1] Henry Chandlee Forman, asserting that such ware was "undoubtedly made in England," felt that it "derives its inspiration from Majolica ware . . . especially that of the early Renaissance period from Faenza."[2]

Bailey also noted that the oven and the gravel-tempered utensils were made of identical clay and temper. However, in an attempt to prove that earthenware was produced locally, he assumed, perhaps because of their crudeness, that the utensils were made at Jamestown. This led him to conjecture that the oven, having similar ceramic qualities, was also a local product. He felt in support of this that it was doubtful "so fragile an object could have survived a perilous sea voyage."[3]

Since these opinions were expressed, much further archeological work in colonial sites has revealed widespread distribution of the two types. Bailey himself noted that a pottery oven is intact and in place in the John Bowne House in Flushing, Long Island. A fragment of another pottery oven recently has been identified among the artifacts excavated by Sidney Strickland from the site of the John Howland House, near Plymouth, Massachusetts; and gravel-tempered utensil sherds have occurred in many sites. The sgraffito ware has been unearthed in Virginia, Maryland, and Massachusetts.

Such a wide distribution of either type implies a productive European source for each, rather than a local American kiln in a struggling colonial settlement like Jamestown. Bailey's attribution of the sgraffito ware to Devonshire was confirmed in 1950 when J. C. Harrington, archeologist of the National Park Service, came upon certain evidence at Barnstaple in North Devon, England. This evidence was found in the form of sherds exhibited in a display window of C. H. Brannam's Barnstaple Pottery that were uncovered during excavation work on the premises. These are unmistakably related in technique and design to the American examples. A label under a fragment of a large deep dish (fig. 2) in the display is inscribed: "Piece of dish found in site of pottery. In sgraffiato. About 1670." This clue opened the way to the investigation pursued here, the results of which relate the sgraffito ware, the gravel-tempered ware, and the ovens to the North Devon towns and to a busy commerce in earthenware between Barnstaple, Bideford, and the New World.

This study, conducted at first hand only on the American side of the Atlantic, is admittedly incomplete. Later, it is planned to consider sherd collections in England, comparative types of sgraffito wares, and possible influences and sources of techniques and designs. For the present, it is felt the immediate evidence is sufficient to warrant the conclusions drawn here.

The author is under special obligation to J. C. Harrington, chief of interpretation, Region I, National Park Service, who discovered the North Devon wares

[1] Worth Bailey, "Concerning Jamestown Pottery—Its Past and Present," *Ceramic Age*, October 1939, pp. 101–104.

[2] H. C. Forman, *Jamestown and Saint Mary's*, Baltimore, 1938, p. 133.

[3] Worth Bailey, "A Jamestown Baking Oven of the Seventeenth Century," *William and Mary College Quarterly Historical Magazine*, 1937, ser. 2, vol. 17, no. 4, pp. 496–500.

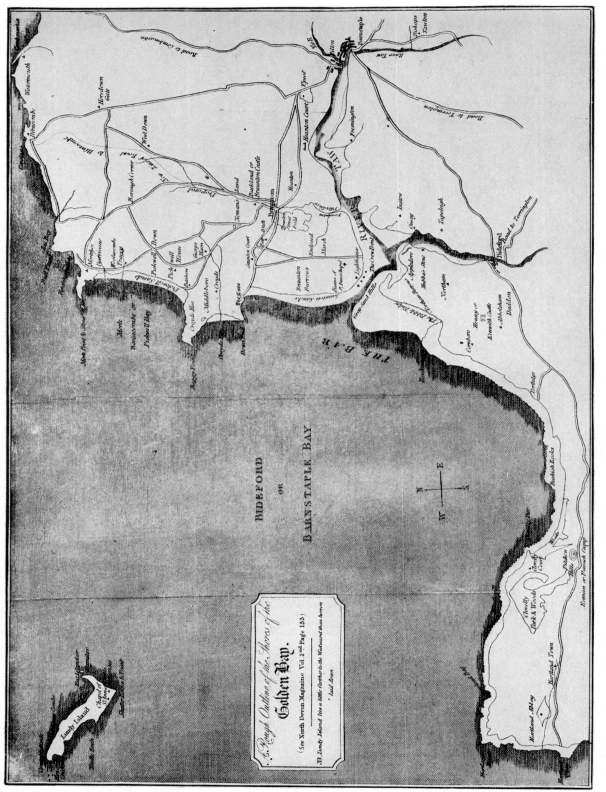

FIGURE 3.—Map of the area around Bideford and Barnstaple. Reproduced from J. B. Gribble, *Memorials of Barnstaple*, 1830.

and whose warm encouragement led to this paper. Also, the author is greatly indebted to the following for their help and cooperation: E. Stanley Abbott, superintendent, J. Paul Hudson, curator, and Charles Hatch, chief of interpretation, Colonial National Historical Park; Worth Bailey, Historic American Buildings Survey; Robert A. Elder, Jr., assistant curator, division of ethnology, U.S. National Museum; Miss Margaret Franklin of London; Henry Hornblower II and Charles Strickland of Plimoth Plantation, Inc.; Ivor Noel Hume, chief archeologist, Colonial Williamsburg, Inc.; Miss Mildred E. Jenkinson, librarian and curator, Borough of Bideford Library and Museum; Frederick H. Norton, professor of ceramics, Massachusetts Institute of Technology; and Mrs. Edwin M. Snell of Washington.

Historical Background

Barnstaple and its neighbor Bideford are today quiet market centers and summer resorts. In the 17th and early 18th centuries, by contrast, they were deeply involved in trade with America and with the whole West of England interest in colonial settlement. Bideford was the home of Sir Richard Grenville, who, with Sir Walter Raleigh, was one of the first explorers of Virginia. As the leading citizen of Bideford, Grenville obtained from Queen Elizabeth a modern charter of incorporation for the town. Consequently, according to the town's 18th-century chronicler, "Bideford rose so rapidly as to become a port of importance at the latter end of Queen Elizabeth's reign . . . when the trade began to open between England and America in the reign of King James the First, Bideford early took a part in it."[4] Its orientation for a lengthy period was towards America, and the welfare of its inhabitants was therefore largely dependent upon commerce with the colonies.

In common with other West of England ports, Barnstaple and Bideford engaged heavily in the Newfoundland fishing trade. However, "the principal part of foreign commerce that Bideford was ever engaged in, was to Maryland and Virginia for tobacco. . . . Its connections with New England were also very considerable."[5]

During the first half of the 18th century Bideford's imports of tobacco were second only to London's, but the wars with France caused a decline about the year 1760.[6] Barnstaple, situated farther up the River Taw, followed the pattern of Bideford in the rise and decline as well as the nature of its trade. Although rivals, both towns functioned in effect as a single port; Barnstaple and Bideford ships sailed from each other's wharves and occasionally the two ports were listed together in the Port Books. As early as 1620 seven ships, some of Bideford and some of Barnstaple registry, sailed from Barnstaple for America,[7] but the height of trade between North Devon and the colonies occurred after the Restoration and lasted until the early part of the 18th century. In 1666, for example, the *Samuel* of Bideford and the *Philip* of Barnstaple sailed for Virginia, despite the dangers of Dutch warfare.[8] The following year, on August 13, 1667, it was reported that 20 ships of the Virginia fleet, "bound to Bideford, Barnstaple, and Bristol have passed into the Severn in order to escape Dutch men-of-war."[9] Later, in 1705, we find that the *Susanna* of Barnstaple, as well as the *Victory, Zunt,*

[4] John Watkins, *An Essay Towards a History of Bideford in the County of Devon*, Exeter, 1792, p. 56.

[5] *Ibid.*, pp. 65, 67–68.

[6] *Ibid.*, p. 70.

[7] Port Book, Barnstaple, 1620, Public Record Office, London (hereinafter referred to as *Port Book*), E 190/947.

[8] *Virginia Magazine of History and Biography*, 1911, vol. 19, p. 31.

[9] *Ibid.*, quoting Sainsbury Abstracts, p. 184.

Devonshire, *Laurell, Blackstone,* and *Mary and Hannah,*
all of Bideford, were anchored in Hampton Roads
off Kecoughtan. They comprised one-ninth of a
fleet of 63 ships from various English ports.[10]

Aside from such indications of a well-established
mercantile trade, the entrenchment of North Devon
interests in the colonies is repeatedly shown in other
ways. Before 1645, Thomas Fowle, a Boston merchant, was doing business with his brother-in-law,
Vincent Potter, who lived in Barnstaple.[11] In 1669,
John Selden, a Barnstaple merchant, died after con-
signing a shipment of goods to William Burke, a
merchant of Chuckatuck, Virginia. John's widow
and administratrix, Sisely Selden, brought suit to
recover these goods, which were "left to the sd.
Wm Burke, &c, for the use of my late husband."[12]

FIGURE 4.—Old pottery in Torrington Lane (formerly Potter's Lane), East-the-Water section of
Bideford. The photo was taken in 1920, just before
the buildings were razed. (*Courtesy of Miss M. E.
Jenkinson.*)

Burke was evidently an agent, or factor, who acted in
Virginia on Selden's behalf. In Northampton County,
alone, there resided six Bideford factors, remarkable
when one considers the isolated location of this Virginia Eastern Shore county and the sparseness of its
population in the 17th century.[13] John Watkins, the
Bideford historian, adds further evidence of mercantile involvement with the colonies, stating of Bideford
that "some of its chief merchants had very extensive
possessions in Virginia and Maryland."[14] Both in
New England and the southern colonies, local merchants acted as resident agents for merchants based
in the mother country. Often tied to the latter by

[10] *Virginia Magazine of History and Biography,* 1901, vol. 9, pp.
257–258.

[11] Bernard Bailyn, *The New England Merchants in the Seventeenth
Century,* Cambridge, Massachusetts, 1955, p. 87.

[12] Isle of Wight County (Virginia) records, quoted in *William and Mary College Quarterly Historical Magazine,* 1899, ser. 1,
vol. 7, p. 228.

[13] P. A. Bruce, *Economic History of Virginia in the Seventeenth
Century,* New York, 1895, vol. 2, p. 334.

[14] Watkins, *op. cit.* (footnote 4), p. 65.

bonds of family relationship, the factors arranged the exchange of American raw materials for the manufactured goods in which their English counterparts specialized.

That there was a large and important commerce in North Devon earthenware to account for many of the relationships between Bideford, Barnstaple, and the colonies seems to have remained unnoticed. Indeed, the fact that the two towns comprised an important center of earthenware manufacture and export in the 17th century has hitherto received little attention from ceramic historians, and then merely as sources of picturesque folk pottery. Yet in the excavations of colonial sites and in the British Public Records Office are indications that the North Devon potters, for a time at least, rivaled those of Staffordshire.

The earliest record of North Devon pottery reaching America occurs in the Port Book entry for Barnstaple in 1635, when the *Truelove*, Vivian Limbry, master, sailed on March 4 for New England with "40 doz. earthenware," consigned to John Boole, merchant.[15] The following year the same ship sailed for New England with a similar amount. After the Stuart restoration larger shipments of earthenware are recorded, as illustrated by sample listings (below) chosen from Port Books in the British Public Records Office.

TYPICAL SHIPMENTS OF EARTHENWARE FROM NORTH DEVON

(Sample entries from Port Books, verbatim)

BARNSTAPLE 1665 [16]

Date	Ship	Master	For	In Cargo	Subsidy
					s d
26 Aug 1665	Exchange of Biddeford	Wᵐ Titherly	New England	150 doz. of Earthenware	7 – 6
4 Sept 1665	Philipp of Biddeford	Edmond Prickard	Virginia	30 doz. of Earthenware	1 – 6
28 Nov 1665	Providence of Barnstaple	Nicholas Taylor	Virginia	20 doz. of Earthenware	1 – 0

BARNSTAPLE AND BIDEFORD, 1680 [17]

Date	Ship	Master	Shipment
Aug 6ᵗʰ 1680	Forester of Barnstaple, for Maryland	Christopher Browning	Twenty dozen of Earthenware Subsidy 1/
Sept 6	Loyalty of Barnstaple	Philip Greenslade	30 dozen Earthenware Andrew Hopkins, merchant Subsidy 1/6

[15] *Port Book*, E 190/959/6.

[16] *Ibid.*, E 190/954/6.

[17] *Ibid.*, E 190/959/6.

Date	Ship	Master	To	Goods & Merchants
May 30 1681	Seafare of Bideford	Bartholomew Shapton	New England	Forty-two hundred [weight] parcells of Earthenware Subsidy 7/
28 June	Hopewell of Bideford	Peter Prust	Virginia	30 cwt. parcells of Earthenware Peter Luxeron Merchant Subsidy 5/
Aug. 12	Beginning of Bideford	John Limbry	Virginia	15 cwt. parcells of Earthenware Subsidy 2/6 Richard Corkhill Merchant [19]

BIDEFORD, 1681 [20]

Date	Ship	Master	To	Goods
21 June	Beginning of Bideford	Thomas Phillips	Virginia	Thirty hundred pclls of Earthenware Joseph Conor merchant Subsidy 5/
19 July	John & Mary of Bideford	Thomas Courtis	Maryland	750 parcells of Earthenware John Barnes, Merchant Subsidy 1/3
14 Aug	Exchange of Bideford	George Ewings	Maryland	40 dozen earthenware William Titherly Merchant Subsidy 2/
Aug. 22	Merchants Delight of Bideford	William Britten	Virginia	1500 parcells Earthenware Henry Guiness Merchant Subsidy 2/6
Aug. 23	Hart of Bideford	Henry Penryn	Virginia	1500 parcells of Earthenware John Lord Merch[t] Subsidy 2/6

[18] *Ibid.,* E 190/960/10.

[19] Richard Corkhill was one of the six Bideford factors residing in Northampton County. Bruce, *op. cit.* (see footnote 13).

[20] *Port Book,* E 190/959/6.

Date	Ship	Master	To	Cargo, etc.
Michaelmas Quarter	Robert & William of North^am	John Esh	Maryland	30 dozen Earthenware Subsidy 1/6 William Bishop merchant

BIDEFORD 1682—OUTWARDS [22]

Date	Ship	Master	To	Cargo, etc.
May 15	Seafare of Bideford	John Titherley	New England	42 cwt. parcells of Earthenware Barth. Shapton Merchant Subsidy 7/
July 9	John & Mary of Bideford	Thomas Courtis	Maryland	9 cwt parcells of Earthenware John Barnes Merchant Subsidy 1/6
July 20	Merchant's Delight of Bideford	William Bruston	Maryland	6 cwt parcells of Earthenware Samuel Donnerd merchant
Sept. 11	Exchange of Bideford	Mark Chappell	Maryland	30 cwt. parcells of earthenware Subsidy 5/ William Titherly Merchant

BARNSTAPLE/BIDEFORD OUTWARDS 1690 [23]

Date	Ship	Master	To	Cargo, etc.
Aug. 23	Yarmouth of Bideford	Roger Jones	Maryland	300 parcells of Earthenware Subsidy 6^d
Sept. 11	Expedition of Bideford	Humphrey Bryant	Maryland	1,200 parcells of Earthenware Subsidy 2/
Sept. 23	Integrity of Bideford	John Tucker	Maryland	300 parcells of Earthenware Subsidy 6^d
Sept. 23	Happy Return of Bideford	John Rock	Maryland	750 parcells of Earthenware Subsidy 1/3
Sept. 23	Sea Faire of Bideford	Tym. Brutton	Maryland	1800 parcells of Earthenware Subsidy 3/

[21] *Ibid.*, E 190/960/8.

[22] *Ibid*, E 190/960/3.

[23] *Ibid.*, E 190/966/10.

Date	Ship	Master	To	Cargo, etc.	Subsidy
Dec. 6	Happy Returne	John Hartwell	Maryland	450 parcels of Earthen ware	9d

Another source shows that the *Eagle* of Bideford arrived at Boston from her home port on October 11, 1688, with a cargo consisting entirely of 9,000 parcels of earthenware, while on July 28, 1689, the *Freindship* (sic) of Bideford landed 7,200 parcels of earthenware and one hogshead of malt. On August 24 of the same year the *Delight* brought a cargo of "9,000 parcels of earthenware and 2 fardells of dry goods" from Bideford.[25]

It will be noted that there was a close relationship between vessel, shipmaster, and factor, suggesting that there may have been an equally close connection between all of them and the owners of the potteries. The *Exchange*, for instance, seems to have been regularly employed in the transport of earthenware. In 1665, according to the listings, she sailed to New England under command of William Titherly. By 1681 Titherly had become a Maryland factor to whom the Exchange's earthenware was consigned then and in 1682. In the same way Bartholomew Shapton in 1681 sailed as master on the *Sea Faire* with earthenware to New England, becoming in the following year the factor for earthenware sent on the same ship under command of John Titherly.

The proportion of earthenware cargo to the carrying capacity of the usual 17th-century ocean-going ship, which ranged from about 30 to 50 tons, is difficult to estimate. A ton and a half of milk pans nested in stacks would be compact and would occupy only a small amount of space. A similar weight of ovens might require a much larger space. When earthenware shipments are recorded in terms of parcels, we are again left in doubt, since the sizes of the parcels are not indicated. We know, however, that the *Eagle*, which was a 50-ton ship, carried 9,000 parcels

of earthenware as her sole cargo in 1688, in contrast to the much smaller amounts shown in the sample listings where the parcel standard is used. Yet even a typical shipment of 1,500 parcels, with each parcel containing an indeterminate number of pots, must have filled the needs of many kitchens when delivered in Virginia in 1681. Certainly a shipment such as this suggests a vigorous rate of production and an active trade.

The export of earthenware from North Devon was not solely to America. As early as 1601 there were shipped from Barnstaple to "Dublyn—100 dozen Earthen Pottes of all sorts." In later years, selected at random, we find the following shipments to Ireland from Barnstaple listed in the Public Record Office Port Books: 1617, 290 dozen; 1618, 320 dozen; 1619, 322 dozen; 1620, 508 dozen; 1632, 260 dozen; 1635, 300 dozen; 1636, 480 dozen; 1639, 660 dozen. Typical of the destinations were Kinsale, Youghal, Limerick, Cork, Galway, Coleraine, and Waterford. As the century advanced, this trade increased enormously. In 1694, 17 separate earthenware shipments totaling 50,400 parcels were made from Barnstaple and Bideford to Dublin, Wexford, and Waterford.[26] It is possible that some of these cargoes were shipped to America, since it was necessary to list only the first port of entry. However, the rapid turn-around of many of the ships shows this was not usually the case.

Besides Ireland, Bristol and Exeter were destinations in a busy coastwise trade. In 1681, for example, large quantities of earthenware, tobacco pipes, and pipe clay were sent to these places.[27] Bristol merchants probably re-exported some of the earthenware to America.

The coastwise trade appears to have diminished very little as time passed. In 1755, *The Gentlemen's*

---

[24] *Ibid.*, E 190/968/10.

[25] Colonial office shipping records relating to Massachusetts ports, typescript in Essex Institute, Salem, Massachusetts, 1931, vol. 1, p. 78.

[26] *Port Book*, E 190/939/14; 942/13; 944/8; 951.

[27] *Ibid.*, E 190/959/5.

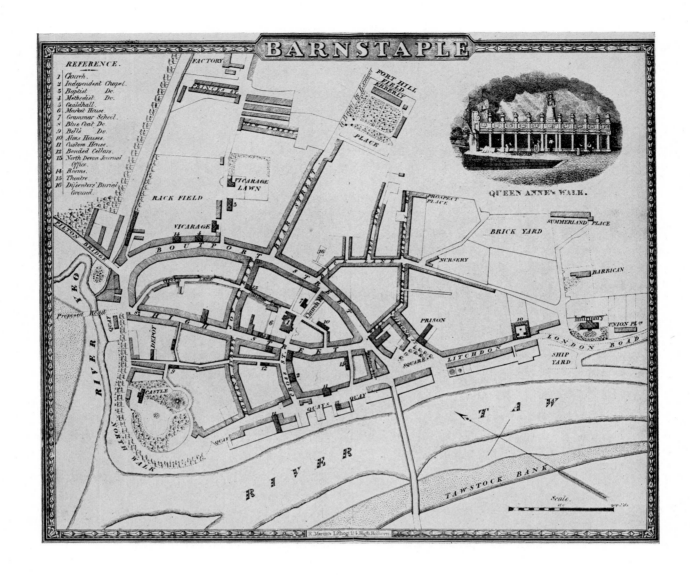

FIGURE 5.—Map of Barnstaple. Reproduced from J. B. Gribble, *Memorials of Barnstaple*, 1830.

Magazine carried an account of Bideford, stating:[28]

Great quantities of potters ware are made, and exported to Wales, Ireland, and Bristol . . . . In the parish of Fremington are great quantities of reddish potters' clay, which are brought and manufactured at Biddeford, whence the ware is sent to different places by sea.

John Watkins, in 1792, wrote:[29]

The potters here, for making coarse brown earthenware, are pretty considerable, and the demand for the articles of their manufacture in various parts of the kingdom, is constantly great . . . The profits to the manufacturers of this article are very great, which is evidenced by several persons having risen within a few years, from a state of the greatest obscurity and poverty, to wealth and consequence of no small extent.

---

[28] "Some Account of Biddeford, in Answer to the Queries Relative to a Natural History of England," *The Gentlemen's Magazine*, 1755, vol. 25, p. 445.

[29] Watkins, *op. cit.* (footnote 4), pp. 74–75.

FIGURE 6.—Gravel-tempered oven of the 17th or early 18th century, acquired in Bideford. (*USNM 394505.*)

FIGURE 7.—Gravel-tempered oven from 17th-century house on Bideford Quay. Borough of Bideford Public Library and Museum. (*Photo by A. C. Littlejohns.*)

Not only was coastwise trade in earthenware maintained throughout the 18th century but it was continued, in fact, until the final decline of the potteries at the turn of the present century.

Although great antiquity attaches to the origins of North Devon pottery manufacture—Barnstaple has had its Crock Street for 450 years [30]—the principal evidence of early manufacture falls into the second half of the 17th century. We have seen that a growing America provided an increasing market for North Devon's ceramic wares. In 1668 Crocker's pottery was established at Bideford, and it is in the period following that Bideford's importance as a pottery center becomes noticeable. Crocker's was operated until 1896, its dated 17th-century kilns then still intact after producing wares that varied little during all of the pottery's 228 years of existence.[31]

In Barnstaple the oldest pottery to survive until modern times was situated in the North Walk. When it was dismantled in 1900, sherds dating from the second half of the 17th century were found in the surroundings, as was a potter's guild sign, dated 1675, which now hangs in Brannam's pottery in Litchdon Street, Barnstaple. A pair of fire dogs, dated 1655 and shaped by molds similar to one from the North Walk site, was excavated near the North Walk pottery.

Both Bideford and Barnstaple had numerous potteries in addition to Crocker's and Brannam's. One, in Potter's Lane in the East-the-Water section of Bideford, was still making "coarse plain ware" in 1906;[32] its buildings were still standing in 1920. We have already observed that the Litchdon Street works of C. H. Brannam, Ltd., remains in operation in a modern building on the site of its 17th-century forerunner. Outside the limits of the two large towns there were "a number of small pot works in remote districts," including the parish of Fremington, where Fishley's pottery, established in the 18th century, flourished until 1912.[33] Jewitt states that the remains of five old potteries were found in the location of Fishley's.[34]

The clay with which all the potters worked came from three similar deep clay deposits in a valley run-

[30] T. M. Hall, "On Barum Tobacco-Pipes and North Devon Clays," *Report and Transactions of the Devonshire Association for the Advancement of Science, Literature, and Art*, Devon, 1890, vol. 22, pp. 317–323.

[31] T. Charbonnier, "Notes on North Devon Pottery of the Seventeenth, Eighteenth, and Nineteenth Centuries," *Report and Transactions of the Devonshire Association for the Advancement of Science, Literature, and Art*, Devon, 1906, vol. 38, p. 255.

[32] *Ibid.*, p. 256.

[33] Bernard Rackham, *Catalogue of the Glaisher Collection of Pottery and Porcelain in the Fitzwilliam Museum*, Cambridge, 1950, ed. 2, vol. 1, pp. 10–11.

[34] Llewellyn Jewitt, *The Ceramic Art of Great Britain*, London, 1883, ed. 2, pp. 206–207.

FIGURE 8.—Views of opening of oven in figure 7, photographed before its removal from house. This illustrates how oven was built into corner of fireplace and concealed from view. At right, the oven door is in place. (*Photos by A. C. Littlejohns.*)

ning parallel with the River Taw in the parishes of Tawstock and Fremington between Bideford and Barnstaple. A geologist in 1864 wrote that the clay is "perfectly homogeneous . . . exceedingly tough, free from slightest grit and soft as butter."[35] When fired at too high a temperature, he wrote, the clay would become so vesicular that it would float on water. The kilns were bottle-shaped and, according to tradition, originally were open at the top, like lime kilns; the contents were roofed over with old crocks.[36]

Apparently all the potteries made the same types of wares, "coarse" or common earthenware having comprised the bulk of their product. The utilitarian redware was indeed coarse, since it was liberally tempered with Bideford gravel in order to insure hardness and to offset the purity and softness of the Fremington clay. An anonymous historian wrote in 1755:[37]

Just above the bridge [over the River Torridge] is a little ridge of gravel of a peculiar quality, without which the potters could not make their ware. There are many other ridges of gravel within the bar, but this only is proper for their use.

John Watkins wrote that Bideford earthenware "is generally supposed to be superiour to any other of the kind, and this is accounted for, from the peculiar excellence of the gravel which this river affords, in binding the clay." His claim that "this is the true reason, seems clear, from the fact that though the potteries at Barnstaple make use of the same sort of clay, yet their earthenware is not held in such esteem at Bristol, &c. as that of Bideford"[38] is scarcely supportable, since the Barnstaple potters also used the same Bideford gravel. The fire dogs found in Barnstaple with the date 1655, referred to above, were tempered with this gravel, as were "ovens, tiles, pip-

[35] George Maw, "On a Supposed Deposit of Boulder-Clay in North Devon," *Quarterly Journal of the Geological Society of London,* 1864, vol. 20, pp. 445–451.

[36] Charbonnier, *op. cit.* (footnote 31), pp. 255, 259.

[37] "Supplement to the Account of Biddeford," *The Gentlemen's Magazine,* 1755, vol. 25, p. 564.

[38] Watkins, *op. cit.* (footnote 4), p. 74. However, the "bye-laws" of Barnstaple for 1689 indicate that tempering materials were also obtained locally: "Every one that fetcheth sand from the sand ridge, shall pay for each horse yearly 1ᵈ, and for every boat of Crock Sand 1ᵈ., according to the antient custome." (Joseph B. Gribble, *Memorials of Barnstaple,* Barnstaple, 1830, p. 360.)

FIGURE 9.—Gravel-tempered oven made at Crocker pottery, Bideford, in the 19th century. Borough of Bideford Public Library and Museum. (*Photo by A. C. Littlejohns.*)

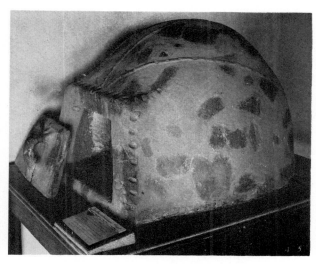

FIGURE 10.—Restored gravel-tempered oven from Jamestown. Colonial National Historical Park. (*National Park Service photo.*)

kins, etc.," in order "to harden the ware," according to Charbonnier, who also observed that "The ware generally was very badly fired. . . . From the fragments it can be seen that the firing was most unequal, parts of the body being grey in colour instead of a rich red, as the well-fired portions are." He noted that the potters applied "the galena native sulphide of lead for the glaze, no doubt originally dusted on to the ware, as with the older potters elsewhere." [39] A sherd of gravel-tempered ware is displayed in the window of Brannam's Barnstaple pottery, while a small pan from Bideford, probably of 19th-century origin, is in the Smithsonian collections (USNM 394440).

The most remarkable form utilizing gravel-tempered clay is found in the baking ovens which remained a North Devon specialty for over two centuries. These ovens vary somewhat in shape, and were made in graduated sizes. Most commonly they are rectangular with domed superstructures, having been molded or "draped" in sections, with their parts joined together, leaving seams with either tooled or thumb-impressed reenforcements. An oven obtained in Bideford has a flat top, without visible seams (USNM 394505; fig. 6).

An early example occurs in Barnstaple, where, in a recently restored inn, an oven was found installed at the side of a fireplace which is "late sixteenth century in character." Pipes and a pair of woman's shoes, all dating from the first half of the 18th century, were found in the fireplace after it had been exposed, thus indicating the period of its most recent use.[40] An oven discovered intact behind a wall during alteration of a Bideford house is believed to date from between 1650 and 1675.[41] That oven (figs. 7, 8) is now exhibited in the Bideford Museum.

At the other extreme, C. H. Brannam of Barnstaple in 1890 was still making ovens in the ancient North Walk pottery.[42] The following year H. W. Strong wrote of Fishley's Fremington pottery that "shiploads of the big clay ovens in which the Cornishman bakes his bread . . . meet with a ready sale in

---

[39] Charbonnier, *op. cit.* (footnote 31), p. 258.

[40] B. W. Oliver, "The Three Tuns, Barnstaple," *Report and Transactions of the Devonshire Association for the Advancement of Science, Literature, and Art,* Torquay, Devon, 1948, vol. 80, pp. 151–152.

[41] Mildred E. Jenkinson in personal correspondence from Bideford, April 20, 1955.

[42] Hall, *op. cit.* (footnote 30), p. 319.

the fishing towns on the rugged coast of North Cornwall."[43] Fremington ovens also were shipped to Wales,[44] and, according to Jewitt, those made in the Crocker pottery in Bideford "are, and for generations have been, in much repute in Devonshire and Cornwall, and in the Welsh districts, and the bread baked in them is said to have a sweeter and more wholesome flavour than when baked in ordinary ovens."[45]

Of ovens made at Barnstaple there is much the same kind of evidence. In 1851, Thomas Brannam

---

[43] H. W. Strong, "The Potteries of North Devon," *Report and Transactions of the Devonshire Association for the Advancement of Science, Literature, and Art*, Devon, 1891, vol. 23, p. 393.

[44] Charbonnier, *op. cit.* (footnote 31), p. 257.

[45] Jewitt, *op. cit.* (footnote 34), vol. 1, pp. 205–206.

FIGURE 11.—Sgraffito-ware platters from Jamestown. The platter shown above has a diameter of 15 inches; the others, 12 inches. Colonial National Historical Park.

"Staffordshire, Broseley, and Glass Warehouse." [47] Thirty-six years earlier, in 1750, Dr. Pococke, who indefatigably entered every sort of observation in his journal, noted that in Devonshire and Cornwall "they make great use here of Cloume ovens,[48] which are of earthen ware of several sizes, like an oven, and being heated they stop 'em up and cover 'em over with embers to keep in the heat." [49] Pococke visited Calstock, "where they have a manufacture of coarse earthenware, and particularly of earthenware ovens." [50]

exhibited an oven at the Crystal Palace, where it was described as "generally used in Devonshire for baking bread and meat." [46] In 1786, "Barnstaple ovens" were advertised for sale in Bristol at M. Ewers'

---

[46] *Great Exhibition 1851. Official, Descriptive, and Illustrated Catalogue*, London, 1851, p. 776, no. 131.

[47] W. J. Pountney, *Old Bristol Potteries*, Bristol, n.d., pp. 153–154.

[48] Cloume=cloam: "In O. E. Mud, clay. Hence, in mod. dial. use: Earthenware, clay . . . b. *attr.* or *adj.*" (J. A. H. Murray, ed., *A New English Dictionary on Historic Principles*, Oxford, 1893, vol. 2, p. 509.)

[49] J. J. Cartwright, ed., *The Travels through England of Dr. Richard Pococke*, Camden Society Publications, 1888, new ser., no. 42, vol. 1, p. 135.

[50] *Ibid.*, vol. 1, p. 131.

We have encountered only one other instance of ovens having been made at any place other than the North Devon communities around the Fremington clay beds. Calstock lies some 35 miles below Bideford in the southeast corner of Cornwall, just over the Devonshire boundary.

As for evidence concerning the manner in which these ovens were used in England, we have already seen that they were built into houses. Jewitt wrote that they "are simply enclosed in raised brickwork, leaving the mouth open to the front." They were heated until red hot by sticks or logs, which were then raked out with long iron tongs.[51] A bundle of gorse, or wood, according to Jewitt,[52] was sufficient to "thoroughly bake three pecks of dough." Pococke's remarks to the effect that the ovens were covered over with embers to keep in the heat suggests that they were sometimes freestanding. However, this could also have been the practice when ovens were built into fireplaces.

From an esthetic point of view, the crowning achievement of the North Devon potters was their sgraffito ware, examples of which in Brannam's window display have already been noted. Further evidence in the form of 17th-century sherds was found by Charbonnier around the site of the North Walk pottery in Barnstaple. These consisted of "plates and dishes of various size and section . . . . Extensive as the demand for these dishes must have been, judging from the heap of fragments, not a single piece has to my knowledge been found above ground." [53] The apparently complete disappearance of the sgraffito table wares suggests that they ceased to be made about 1700. They were apparently forced from the market by the refinement of taste that developed in the 18th century and by the delftware of Bristol and London and Liverpool that was so much more in keeping with that taste.

However, certain kinds of sgraffito ware continued to be made without apparent interruption until early in the present century. Instead of useful tableware, decorated with symbols and motifs characteristic of 17th-century English folk ornament, we find after 1700 only presentation pieces, particularly in the form of large harvest jugs. The harvest jugs were made for annual harvest celebrations, when they were passed around by the farmers among their field hands in a folk ritual observed at the end of harvest.[54] Unlike the sgraffito tablewares, where style and taste were deciding factors in their survival, these special jugs were intended to be used only in annual ceremonies. Thus they were carefully preserved and passed on from generation to generation, with a higher chance for survival than that which the sgraffito tablewares enjoyed.

The style of the harvest jugs is in sharp contrast to that of the tablewares, the jugs having been decorated in a pagan profusion of fertility and prosperity symbols, mixed sometimes with pictorial and inscriptive allusions to the sea, particularly on jugs ascribed to Bideford. The oldest dated examples embody characteristics of design and techniques that relate them unmistakably to the tablewares, while later specimens made throughout the 18th and 19th centuries show an increasing divergence from the 17th-century style. An especially elaborate piece was made for display at the Great Exhibition of 1851 in the Crystal Palace.[55]

Less complicated pieces, with a minimum of incising, were made for ordinary use, as were plain pieces whose surfaces were covered with slip without decoration. The trailing and splashing of slip designs on the body of the ware, practiced in Staffordshire and many of our colonial potteries, apparently was not followed in North Devon.[56]

Sites Yielding North Devon Types

Excepting the Bowne House oven and a 1698 jug (see p. 45), no example of North Devon pottery used in America is known to have survived above ground. Archeological evidence, however, provides a sufficient record of North Devon wares and the tastes and customs they reflected. Following are descriptions of the principal sites in which these wares were found.

JAMESTOWN, VIRGINIA: MAY-HARTWELL SITE.

The site of Jamestown, first permanent English settlement in North America, has been excavated at intervals by the National Park Service. The early excavations were under the supervision of several

[51] Jenkinson correspondence (see footnote 41).

[52] Jewitt, op. cit. (footnote 34), pp. 206–207.

[53] Charbonnier, op. cit. (footnote 31), p. 258.

[54] Jenkinson correspondence (footnote 41).

[55] Made in Devon. An Exhibition of Beautiful Objects Past and Present, Dartington Hall, 1950, p. 9.

[56] Charbonnier, op. cit. (footnote 31), p. 258.

archeological technicians directing Civilian Conservation Corps crews. In September 1936, J. C. Harrington became supervising archeologist of the project, and until World War II he continued the work as funds permitted. Except for the privately sponsored excavation of the Jamestown glasshouse site by Harrington in 1947, no extensive archeological work was thereafter undertaken until 1954, when John L. Cotter was appointed chief archeologist. Thorough exploration of Jamestown was his responsibility until 1956.[57]

One of the most interesting subsites in the Jamestown complex was the two and one-half acres of lots which belonged successively to William May, Nicholas Merriweather, William White, and Henry Hartwell. The site was first explored in 1935. On this occasion there was disclosed a meandering brick drain that

FIGURE 12.—Sgraffito-ware cup and plate from Jamestown. The cup is 4 inches high; the plate is 7 inches in diameter. Colonial National Historical Park.

had been built on top of a fill of artifactual refuse, mostly pottery sherds. The richness of this yield was unparalleled elsewhere at Jamestown; from it comes our principal evidence about the North Devon types sent to America.

The May-Hartwell site was explored further and in far greater detail in 1938 and 1939 by Harrington, whose unpublished typescript report is on file with the National Park Service.[58] Harrington's excavation, in the light of historical documentation, led to the conclusion that the brick drain had been laid during Henry Hartwell's occupancy of the site

[57] John L. Cotter, *Archeological Excavations at Jamestown, Virginia*. Archeological Research Series, no. 4, National Park Service, U.S. Department of the Interior, Washington, 1958.

[58] J. C. Harrington, *Archeological Report, May-Hartwell Site, Jamestown: Excavations at the May-Hartwell site in 1935, 1938, and 1939 and Ditch Explorations East of the May-Hartwell Site in 1935 and 1938.*

FIGURE 13.—Sgraffito-ware jugs, about 8 inches high, from Jamestown. Colonial National Historical Park.

between 1689 and 1695. This was supported by the inclusion in the fill of many bottle seals bearing Hartwell's initials, "H. H." Hartwell married the widow of William White, who had purchased the property from Nicholas Merriweather in 1677. That was the year following Bacon's Rebellion, when Merriweather's house presumably was destroyed.

There were many hundreds of sherds in the fill under and around the brick drain, as well as in other ditches in the site. The North Devon types were found here in association with numerous classes of pottery. The most readily identifiable were sherds of English delftware of many forms and styles of decoration related to the second half of the 17th century. There were occasional earlier 17th-century examples, also, as might be expected. No 18th-century intrusions were noted in the brick drain area, and only a scattering in other portions; none was found in association with the North Devon sherds.

JAMESTOWN, VIRGINIA: OTHER SITES.

North Devon wares occur in the majority of sites at Jamestown, but it is not always possible to date them from contextual evidence because precise archeological records were not always kept in the early phases of the excavations. Nevertheless, narrow dating is easily possible in enough sites to suggest date horizons for the wares.

The earliest evidence occurs in material from a well (W–21)—excavated in 1956[59]—that contained an atypical sgraffito sherd described below (p. 43). The sherd lay beneath a foot-deep deposit that included Dutch majolica, Italian sgraffito ware, and tobacco pipes, all dating in form or decoration prior to 1650. This sherd is unique among all those found at Jamestown, but it is essentially characteristic of North Devon work. Presumably it is a forerunner of the typical varieties found in the May-Hartwell site and elsewhere.

No gravel-tempered sherds occur in contexts that can positively be dated prior to 1675. A sizable

[59] Cotter, *op. cit.* (footnote 57), p. 158.

FIGURE 14.—Sgraffito-ware jug and cups from Jamestown. Colonial National Historical Park.

deposit of gravel-tempered sherds was found between the depth of one foot and the level of the cellar floor of the mansion house site (Structure 112) located near the pitch-and-tar swamp. This house was built before 1650, but burned, probably during Bacon's Rebellion in 1676.[60] The sherds were doubtless part of the household equipment of the time. All other ceramic fragments, with one exception, were associated with objects dating earlier than 1660.

In sites dating from before about 1670, no North Devon wares are found, excepting the early sgraffito sherd mentioned above. Such was the case with a brick kiln (Structure 127) of early 17th-century date and two sites (Structure 110 and Kiln C) in the vicinity of the pottery kiln. In Structure 110 all the ceramics date from before 1650.[61]

The latest occurrence of gravel-tempered wares is in contexts of the early and middle 18th century. A pit

near the Ambler property (Refuse Pit 2)[62] yielded a typical early 18th-century deposit with flat-rimmed gravel-tempered pans of characteristic type. Associated with these were pieces of blue delft (before 1725), Staffordshire "combed" ware (made throughout the 18th century, but mostly about 1730–1760), Nottingham stoneware (throughout the 18th century), gray-white Höhr stoneware (last quarter, 17th century), Buckley black-glazed ware (mostly 1720–1770), and Staffordshire white salt-glazed ware (1740–1770).

HAMPTON, VIRGINIA: KECOUGHTAN SITE.

In 1941, Joseph B. and Alvin W. Brittingham, amateur archeologists of Hampton, Virginia, excavated several refuse pits on the site of what they believed to be an early 17th-century trading post located at the original site of Kecoughtan, an Indian village

[60] *Ibid.*, pp. 112–119.

[61] *Ibid.*, pp. 102–112.

[62] *Ibid.*, pp. 151–152.

FIGURE 15.—This sgraffito-ware chamber pot, from Jamestown, has incised on the rim *WR 16 ..*, probably in reference to the king. Height, 5½ inches. Colonial National Historical Park.

FIGURE 16.—Sgraffito-ware harvest jug made in Bideford, with the date "1795" inscribed. Borough of Bideford Public Library and Museum. (*Photo by A. C. Littlejohns.*)

and colonial outpost settlement which later became Elizabeth City, Virginia. Rich artifactual evidence, reflecting on a small scale what was found at Jamestown, indicates a continuous occupancy from the beginning of settlement in 1610 to about 1760.[63] The collection was given to the Smithsonian Institution in 1950.

JAMES CITY COUNTY, VIRGINIA: GREEN SPRING PLANTATION.

In 1642 Sir William Berkeley arrived in Virginia to be its governor. Seven years later he built Green Spring, about five miles north of Jamestown. The house remained standing until after 1800. Its site was excavated in 1954 by the National Park Service under supervision of Louis R. Caywood, Park Service archeologist.[64] The project, supported jointly by the

Jamestown-Williamsburg-Yorktown Celebration Commission and the Virginia 350th Anniversary Commission, was executed under supervision of Colonial National Historical Park at Yorktown, Virginia.

WILLIAMSBURG, VIRGINIA: EARLY 18TH-CENTURY DEPOSITS.

A small amount of North Devon gravel-tempered ware was found in sites excavated in Williamsburg by Colonial Williamsburg, Inc. These excavations have been carried out as adjuncts to the Williamsburg restoration program over a 30-year period. Few of the North Devon sherds found can be closely dated, having occurred primarily in undocumented ditches, pits, and similar deposits. However, it is unlikely that any of the material dates earlier than the beginning of the 18th century, since Williamsburg was not authorized as a town until 1699. It is significant, in the light of this, that North Devon pan sherds in the Williamsburg collection have characteristics like those of specimens from other 18th-century sites. Also sig-

---

[63] Joseph B. Brittingham and Alvin W. Brittingham, Sr., *The First Trading Post at Kicotan (Kecoughtan), Hampton, Virginia,* Hampton, 1947.

[64] Louis R. Caywood, *Excavations at Green Spring Plantation,* Yorktown, 1955.

FIGURE 17.—Views of North Devon harvest jug used in Sussex County, Delaware. This jug, 11 inches high and dated 1698, is in the collection of Charles G. Dorman. The inscription reads:

"Kind Sʳ: i com to Gratifiey youre Kindness Love and
and Courtisy and Sarve youre table with Strong beare for this
intent i was sent heare: or if you pleas i will supply youre workmen when in
harvist dry when they doe labour hard and swearᵉ good drinke is better far then Meat"

nificant is the fact that no sgraffito ware occurs here. A gravel-tempered pan (fig. 23) from the Coke-Garrett House site was found in a context that can be dated about 1740–1760.

WESTMORELAND COUNTY, VIRGINIA: SITE OF JOHN WASHINGTON HOUSE.

In 1930 the National Park Service became custodians for "Wakefield," the George Washington birthplace site on Pope's Creek in Westmoreland County. About a mile to the west of "Wakefield" itself, but within the Park area, is the site of Bridges Creek Plantation, purchased in 1664 by John Washington, the earliest member of the family in America. It was occupied by John at least until his death in 1677, and probably by Lawrence Washington until a few years later. Much artifactual material was dug from the plantation house site, including the largest deposits of North Devon types found outside of Jamestown.[65]

STAFFORD COUNTY, VIRGINIA: MARLBOROUGH SITE.

A short-lived town was built in 1691 at the confluence of Potomac Creek and the Potomac River on Potomac Neck. The town was abandoned by 1720, but six years later became the abode of John Mercer, who developed a plantation there. The site of his house was excavated by the Smithsonian Institution in 1956. Two small sherds of North Devon gravel-tempered ware were found there in a predominantly mid-18th-century deposit.

───────

[65] J. Paul Hudson, "George Washington Birthplace National Monument, Virginia," National Park Service Historical Handbook Series, no. 26, Washington, 1956.

FIGURE 18.—Gravel-tempered pan (top) and cooking pot with cover, all from Jamestown. The pan has a height of 4½ inches and a diameter of 15 inches. The pot is 6 inches high and 9½ inches in diameter; the diameter of its cover is 10 inches. Colonial National Historical Park.

CALVERT COUNTY, MARYLAND: ANGELICA KNOLL SITE.

Since 1954 Robert A. Elder, Jr., assistant curator of ethnology at the United States National Museum, has been investigating the site on the Chesapeake Bay of a plantation or small settlement known as Angelica Knoll. This investigation has revealed a generous variety of gravel-tempered utensil forms, including both 17th and 18th century styles. The range of associated artifacts points to a site dating from the late 17th century to about 1765.

KENT ISLAND, QUEEN ANNE COUNTY, MARYLAND.

A small collection of late 17th-century and early 18th-century material—gathered by Richard H. Stearns near the shore of Kent Island, a quarter-mile south of Kent Island Landing—includes both North

Devon types. The collection was given to the United States National Museum.

LEWES, SUSSEX COUNTY, DELAWARE: TOWNSEND SITE.

The Townsend site was excavated by members of the Sussex County Archeological Society in 1947. This was primarily an Indian site, but a pit or well contained European artifacts, including a North Devon gravel-tempered jar (fig. 25). The village of Lewes, originally the Dutch settlement of Zwaanandael, was destroyed by the British, who occupied the area in 1664.[66] The European materials from the Townsend site were given to the United States National Museum.

PLYMOUTH, PLYMOUTH COUNTY, MASSACHUSETTS: "R.M." SITE.

A site of a house believed to have been Robert Morton's, located south of the town of Plymouth, was excavated by Henry Hornblower II. It contained North Devon gravel-tempered sherds. The collection is now in the archeological laboratory of Plimoth Plantation, Inc., in Plymouth.

ROCKY NOOK, KINGSTON, PLYMOUTH COUNTY, MASSACHUSETTS: SITES OF JOHN HOWLAND HOUSE AND JOSEPH HOWLAND HOUSE.

The John Howland house was built between 1628 and 1630; it burned about 1675. The site was excavated between September 1937 and July 1938 under supervision of the late Sidney T. Strickland.[67] Several gravel-tempered utensil sherds were found here, as well as a piece of an oven (see fig. 26). Artifacts from this and the following site are at the Plimoth Plantation laboratory.

The foundations of the Joseph Howland house, adjacent to the John Howland house site, were excavated in 1959 by James Deetz, archeologist at Plimoth Plantation. This is the only New England site of which we are aware that has yielded North Devon sgraffito ware. Two successive houses apparently

[66] Virginia Cullen, *History of Lewes, Delaware*, Lewes, 1956; C. A. Bonine, "Archeological Investigation of the Dutch 'Swanendael' Settlement under de Vries, 1631–1632," *The Archeolog, News Letter of the Sussex Archeological Association*, Lewes, December 1956, vol. 8, no. 3.

[67] S. T. Strickland, *Excavation of Ancient Pilgrim Home Discloses Nature of Pottery and Other Details of Everyday Life*, typescript, n.d.

stood on the site. Statistical evidence of pipe-stem-bore measurements points to 1680–1710 as the first principal period of occupancy.[68]

MARSHFIELD, PLYMOUTH COUNTY, MASSACHUSETTS: WINSLOW SITE.

This site, excavated by Henry Hornblower II and tentatively dated 1635–1699, yielded considerable quantities of gravel-tempered ware. Cultural material is predominantly from about 1675.

FLUSHING, LONG ISLAND, NEW YORK: THE JOHN BOWNE HOUSE.

The John Bowne House is a historic house museum at Bowne Street and Fox Lane, Flushing, Long Island, maintained by the Bowne House Historical Society. Bowne was a Quaker from Derbyshire, who built his house in 1661. A North Devon oven is still in place, with its opening at the back of the fireplace.

YORKTOWN, VIRGINIA.

The National Park Service has excavated at various locations in Yorktown, both in the neighboring battle-field sites and the town itself. Yorktown, like Marlborough, was established by the Act for Ports in 1691. In several of the areas excavated, occasional sherds of North Devon gravel-tempered ware were found. In refuse behind the site of the Swan Tavern, opened as an inn in 1722 but probably occupied earlier, a single large fragment of a 15-inch sgraffito platter was discovered. No other pieces of this type were found, associated artifacts having been predominantly from the 18th century.

Descriptions of Types

NORTH DEVON SGRAFFITO WARE

Sites: Jamestown, Kecoughtan, Green Spring, John Washington House, Kent Island, Yorktown, Joseph Howland House.

PASTE

Manufacture: Wheel-turned, with templates used to shape collars of jugs and to shape edges and some-times ridges where plate rims join bezels.

---

[68] James Deetz, *Excavations at the Joseph Howland Site (C5), Rocky Nook, Kingston, Massachusetts, 1959: A Preliminary Report.* Supplement, *The Howland Quarterly,* 1960, vol. 24, nos. 2, 3. The Pilgrim John Howland Society, Inc.

FIGURE 19.—Gravel-tempered bowl (top) and pipkins from Jamestown. Colonial National Historical Park.

Temper: Fine, almost microscopic, water-worn sand particles.

Texture: Fine, smooth, well-mixed, sharp, regular cleavage.

Color: Dull pinkish red, with gray core usual.

Firing: Two firings, one before glazing and one after. Usually incomplete oxidation, shown by gray core. A few specimens have surface breaks or flakings incurred in the firing and most show warping (suggesting that "rejects," unsalable in England, were sent to the colonists, who had no recourse but to accept them).

SURFACES

Treatment: Inner surfaces of plates and bowls and outer surfaces of jugs, cups, mugs, chamber pots, and other utensils viewed on the exteriors are coated with white kaolin slip. Designs are scratched through the slip while wet and into the surface of the paste, exposing the latter. Undersides of plates and chargers are often scraped to make irregular flat areas of sur-

FIGURE 20.—Gravel-tempered chafing dish from Jamestown. Colonial National Historical Park. (*Smithsonian photo 43104.*)

Concave-sided mugs: Height about 4″. Slipped and decorated externally; glazed internally and externally. (Only complete specimen, at Jamestown, has incised band around rim.) (Fig. 14.)

Jugs: Height 6½″ and 8″–8½″. Globose bodies, vertical or slightly everted collars tooled in a series of ridged bands, with tooled rims at top. Some have pitcher lips, some do not. Slipped, decorated, and glazed externally above an incised line encircling the waist; glazed internally. (Figs. 13, 14.)

Eating bowls: Diameter, including handle, 9″–10″; depth 3¼″–4″. Straight, everted sides, flat rims, with slightly raised edges, one small flat loop handle secured to rim. Slipped, decorated, and glazed internally and on rim.

face. Slip-covered portions are coated with amber glaze by sifting on powdered galena (lead sulphide). Containers which are slipped externally are glazed externally and internally. Slip and glaze do not cover lower portions of jugs, but run down unevenly.

Color: Slipped surfaces are white where exposed without glaze. Unglazed surfaces are a dull terra cotta. The glaze varies in tone from honey color to a dark greenish amber. When applied over the slip, the glaze ranges from lemon to a toneless brown-yellow, or, at best, a sparkling butter color. When applied directly over the paste and over the incised and abraided designs, the glaze appears as a rich mahogany brown or dark amber.

FORMS

Plates, platters, and chargers:
  (a) Diameter 7″–7½″. Upper surface slipped, decorated, and glazed. (Fig. 12.)
  (b) Diameter 12″; depth 2″–3″. Upper surface slipped, decorated, and glazed. (Fig. 11.)
  (c) Diameter 14½″–15″; depth 2″–3″. Upper surface slipped, decorated, and glazed. (Fig. 11.)
All have wide rims, but of varying widths, raised bezels, and heavy, raised, curved edges.

Baluster wine cups: Height 3¾″–4″. Slipped and decorated externally; glazed internally and externally. (Figs. 12, 14.)

FIGURE 21.—Gravel-tempered baking pan from Jamestown. Length, 15 inches; width, about 12 inches. Colonial National Historical Park.

Chamber pots: Height 5½″. Curving sides, terminating at heavy, raised, rounded band surmounted by concave, everted rim. Rim 1″ wide and flat. Slipped, decorated, and glazed externally and internally. (Fig. 15.)

Candlestick: Unique specimen. Height 6″. Bell-shaped base with flange and shaft above with socket at top. Handle from bottom of socket to bottom of shaft. Upper portion slipped, decorated, and glazed.

Ripple-edged, shallow dish: Unique specimen. Diameter 9¼″. Concave, rimless dish or plate with edge crimped as for a pie or tart plate. Upper surface slipped, decorated, and glazed.

Technique: (1) Incising through wet slip into paste with pointed tool for linear effects. (2) Excising of small areas to reveal paste and to strengthen tonal qualities of designs. (3) Incising with multiple-pointed tools having three to five points, to draw multiple-lined stripes. (4) Stippling with same tools.

Motifs: The motifs are varied and never occur in any one combination more than once. There are two general categories of design, geometric and floral, although in some cases these are joined in the same specimen.

In the geometric category, the majority of plate rims are decorated with hastily drawn spirals and *guilloches.* The centers may have circles within squares, circles enclosing compass-drawn petals, circles within a series of swags embellished with lines. Triple-lined chevrons decorate the border of one plate. A chamber pot is decorated with diagonal stripes of multiple lines, between which wavy lines are punctuated by small excised rectangles. Some cups, jugs, and the candlestick are simply decorated with vertical stripes, between which are wavy lines, stippling, and excised blocks.

The floral category includes elaborate and intricate stylized floral and vine motifs: tulips, sunflowers, leaves, tendrils, hearts, four-petaled flowers. One plate (fig. 11) combines the geometric feeling of the first category with the floral qualities of the second in its swag-and-tassel rim and swagged band, which encloses a sunflower springing from a stalk between two leaves.

The design motifs are unique in comparison with those found on other English pottery of the 17th century. The geometrical patterns and spiral ornaments, which also occur in Hispanic majolica, have

FIGURE 23.—North Devon gravel-tempered pan with typical terra cotta paste and characteristic 18th-century flattened rim, slightly undercut on the interior. This pan, measuring 13¼ inches in diameter and 4⅜ inches high, was found at the Coke-Garrett house site in Williamsburg, Virginia, in a context attributed to the period about 1740–1760. Colonial Williamsburg, Inc. (*Colonial Williamsburg photo 59–DW–703–44.*)

a Moorish flavor. Christian symbols—especially tulips, sunflowers, and hearts—are recurrent, as they are on contemporary West-of-England furniture, pewter, and embroidery and on the carved chests, and crewel work of Puritan New England. There is considerable reason to believe that there was a connection between North Devon sgraffito-ware manufacture and design on the one hand and the influx of Huguenot and Netherlands Protestant artisans into southern and southwestern England on the other. Low Country immigrant potters were responsible for two other ceramic innovations elsewhere in England—stoneware and majolica.

ATYPICAL SPECIMEN

Already mentioned is a large fragment of a dish found in a context not later than 1640 and cruder and simpler in treatment than the remainder of North Devon sgraffito ware thus far seen. It nevertheless belongs to the same class. Its paste has the same

FIGURE 22.—Slip-coated porringers and drinking bowl (center). Colonial National Historical Park.

FIGURE 24.—Gravel-tempered pan sherds from Kecoughtan site, Hampton, Virginia. United States National Museum.

characteristics of color and fracture, while the firing has left the same tell-tale gray core found in a large proportion of North Devon sherds. Surface treatment techniques match those reflected in the typical dish sherds—glazed slip over the red paste on the interior; unglazed, scraped, and abraided surfaces on the underside. The yellow color is paler and the glazed surface is duller. The rim has a smaller edge and omits the heavy raised bezel usually occurring on the typical plates and chargers. The design motifs—crude and primitive in comparison with those described above—consist of a series of stripes on the rim, drawn at right angles to the edge with a four-pointed tool, and crude hook-like ornaments traced with the same tool in the bowl of the plate. This may be regarded as a forerunner of the developed sgraffito ware made in the second half of the 17th century.

UNIQUE FEATURE

The flat rim of a chamber pot from Jamestown (fig. 15) has "WR 16 . . " scratched through the slip. It is probable that the initials indicate "William Rex," for William III, who became king in 1688. Why the king should be memorialized in such an undignified fashion could be explained by the fact that Barnstaple and Bideford were strongly Puritan and also Huguenot centers. Although William was a popular monarch, he was, nevertheless, head of the Church of England, and an anti-royalist, Calvinist potter might well have expressed an earthy contempt in this way. Later, in the 18th century, George III appears to have been treated with similar disrespect by Staffordshire potters, who made saltglazed chamber pots in the style of Rhenish Westerwald drinking jugs, flaunting "GR" emblems on the sides. Owners' initials or names do not occur on any of the North Devon wares found in American sites, nor do the initials of the potters. Otherwise, it would seem unlikely that the only exception would appear on the rim of a chamber pot.

Sherds owned by C. H. Brannam, Ltd., and excavated at the site of the Litchdon Street pottery in Barnstaple.—The largest of these is part of a deep dish (fig. 2). Its border design seems to be a degenerate form of a beetle-like device found on Portuguese majolica of the period. From a crude oval with a stippled line running the length of it, extends a spiral scroll, terminating in a heavy dot, reminiscent of the tendrils found on the Portuguese examples. From incised lines near the rim and on the edge of the bezel are small linear "hooks." The interior has sunflower petals flanking a short, stylized palmette, with another stalk and pair of leaves above, reaching up to what may have been an elaborate floral center, now missing. This decoration resembles closely the interiors of the floral-type plates and chargers found at Jamestown. A section of plate rim is similar to typical rims found in American sites. The surface color is the butter yellow found on the best Jamestown pieces. Paste color also matches.

Sherds from the North Walk pottery in Barnstaple, described by Charbonnier.—These were found near the site, on the banks of the Yeo and in a pasture. They include plates and dishes, some finished and others thrown out in the biscuit state. Charbonnier illustrates a plate with a zig-zag or chevron border and an incised bird in the center. The chevron appears on Jamestown specimens but the bird does not.

Harvest jugs.—18th-century North Devon harvest jugs examined by the writer display the same characteristics of paste, slip, and glaze as the Jamestown sherds. However, the jugs differ stylistically to a marked degree, suggesting that later potters were not affected by the influences that appear in the earlier work (fig. 16). The earliest harvest jug of which we are aware is a hitherto unrecorded example, dated 1698, that is in the collection of Charles G. Dorman. This is the only harvest jug yet encountered with a history of use in America and the only North Devon sgraffito piece known to have survived above ground on this continent. It is a remarkably vigorous pot, having a great rotund body, a high flaring collar, and a lengthy inscription (see fig. 17). A female figure under a wreath of pomegranates forms the central motif. The head is turned in left profile, with hair cascading to the shoulders. The bust is highly stylized in an oval shape, within which are intersecting curved lines forming areas decorated with diagonal incising or with rows of short dashes. The design

Figure 25.—Gravel-tempered food-storage jar from Townsend site, Lewes, Delaware. Height, 12 inches; diameter at base, 9 inches. (*USNM 60.1188; Smithsonian photo 38821.*)

here is strongly reminiscent of the geometrical decoration on Jamestown plates and deep dishes. A pair of unicorns flanks the central figure, and behind each unicorn are a dove and swan, at left and right respectively. Under these are sunflowers and tulips, while a tulip stands above rows of leaves on a stem below the handle. Feather-like leaves flank the lower attachment of the handle. At the junction of the shoulder and collar is a narrow band of incised tulips. Above this is a heavy ridge from which springs the flaring collar. Under the spout is a male head, wearing a wig which is depicted in the same manner as the pomegranates on the wreath, and a

FIGURE 26.—Gravel-tempered sherds from Plymouth, Massachusetts: fragment of oven (left) and rim sherd (upper right), from John Howland house site; and pan-rim sherd from "R. M." site. Plimoth Plantation, Inc., Plymouth. (*Smithsonian photo 45008–B.*)

stylized hat and stock-like collar. One suspects that the man is a clergyman, although his eyes are cast down in a most worldly manner upon the lady below. He is flanked by a pair of doves; behind each dove is a vertical tulip with stem and leaves.

Some of the shading is applied with a four-pointed tool, as in many of the Jamestown pieces, although the tool was smaller. The handle bears the same characteristics as those on jugs found at Jamestown— the same carelessly formed ridge, the same spreading, up-thrust reinforcement at the base of the handle.

Unlike the Jamestown jugs, this one is covered completely on the exterior with slip and glaze. However, since this was a presentation piece, we could expect more careful treatment than was usual on pots made for commercial sale.

The jug descended in a Sussex County, Delaware, family—on the distaff side, curiously. Family recollection traces its ownership back to the early 19th century, with an unsubstantiated legend that it was used by British soldiers during the Revolutionary War. We may conclude at least that the jug is not a recent import and surmise that it was probably brought to America as an heirloom by an emigrating Devon family, perhaps before the Revolution. Sussex County has a stable population, mostly of old-stock English descent. It was settled during the second half of the 17th and first half of the 18th centuries. There is a strong possibility, therefore,

FIGURE 27.—Gravel-tempered sherds from Angelica Knoll site, Calvert County, Maryland. United States National Museum. (*Smithsonian photo 45008–A.*)

that the jug was introduced into Delaware at a comparatively early date.

Many other harvest jugs have been similarly cherished in England. An almost exact counterpart of the Delaware jug, and obviously by the same potter, is in the Glaisher collection in Cambridge. This jug, dated "1703/4," [69] displays such variations as absence of the male head and a different inscription. Another jug, with a hunting scene but with a similar neck and collar treatment, seems again to be by the same hand; it is dated "1703." [70]

From the standpoint of identifying and dating the archeologically recovered sgraffito ware, these jugs are important in showing certain traits similar

[69] Rackham, *op. cit.* (footnote 33), vol. 2, p. 11, fig. 8D, no. 58.

[70] John Eliot Hodgkin and Edith Hodgkin, *Examples of Early English Pottery, Named, Dated, and Inscribed.* London, 1891, p. 59.

to those found in the sherds, while displaying other characteristics that are distinctly different. They support the archeological evidence that the Jamestown pieces are earlier than the jugs and that new design concepts were appearing by the turn of the century in a novel type of presentation piece.

North Devon Plain Slip-Coated Ware

This is a plain variant of the sgraffito ware, differing only in the absence of decoration and in some of the forms.

Site: Jamestown.

Forms

Plates: Diameter 7″–11½″. Profiles as in sgraffito plates. Upper surface slipped and glazed.

Eating bowls: Diameter 9″; height 3½″. Profile and handle same as in sgraffito bowls. Slipped and glazed on interior and over rim.

Porringers: Diameter 5½″; height 2¾″. Ogee profiles. Horizontal loop handle applied ¾″ below rim on each. Slipped and glazed on interiors. (Fig. 22.)

Drinking bowls: Diameter of rim, including handle, 5″; height 2¾″–3″; diameter of base 2″. In shape of mazer bowl, these have narrow bases and straight sides terminating in raised tooled bands at the junctions with vertical or slightly inverted rims 1″ in height. Each has a horizontal looped handle attached at bottom of rim. Slipped and glazed on interiors. (Fig. 22.)

Wavy-edge pans: Diameter 9″–10″; height 2″. Flat round pans with vertical rims distorted in wide scallops or waves. Purpose not known. Slipped and glazed on interiors.

North Devon Gravel-Tempered Ware

Sites: Jamestown, Kecoughtan, Green Spring, Williamsburg, Marlborough, John Washington House, Kent Island, Angelica Knoll, Townsend, John Bowne House, "R. M.," Winslow, John Howland House.

Paste

Manufacture: Wheel-turned, except ovens and rectangular pans, which are "draped" over molds. (See "Forms," below.)

Temper: Very coarse water-worn quartz and feldsparthic gravel up to one-half inch in length; also occasional sherds. Proportion of temper 15–25 percent, except in ovens, which were about 30 percent.

Texture: Poorly kneaded, bubbly, and porous, with temper poorly mixed. Temper particles easily rubbed out of matrix. Very irregular and angular cleavage because of coarse temper. Hard and resistant to blows, but crumbles at fracture when broken.

Color: Dull pinkish red to deep orange-red. Almost invariably gray at core, except in ovens.

Firing: Carelessly fired, with incomplete oxidation of paste.

Surface

Treatment: Glazed with powdered galena on interiors of containers, never externally. Glaze very carelessly applied, with much evidence of dripping, running, and unintentional spilling.

Texture: Very coarse and irregular, with gravel temper protruding.

Color: Unglazed surfaces range from bright terra cotta to reddish buff. Glazed surfaces on well-fired pieces are transparent yellow-green with frequent orange splotches. Overfired pieces become dark olive-amber, sometimes approaching black. Rare specimens have slipped interiors subsequently glazed, with similar butter-yellow color effect as in sgraffito and plain slip-coated types.

Forms

All forms are not completely indicated, there being many rims not represented by complete or reconstructed pieces. The following are established forms.

Round, flat-bottomed pans: Diameter 16″, height 4″; diameter 16″, height 5″; diameter 18″, height 4″; diameter 15″, height 4½″; diameter 13¼″, height 4⅞″. Heavy rounded rims. Glazed internally below rims. These were probably milk pans, but may also have served for cooking and washing. Those lined with slip may have functioned as wash basins. (Figs. 18, 23.)

Round, flat-bottomed pans: Diameter approximately 19″, height unknown. (No complete specimen.) Heavy rims, reinforced with applied strips of clay beneath external projection of rim. Reinforcement strips are secured with thumb impressions or square impressions made by end of flat tool. (Figs. 28, 29.)

Cooking pots: Diameter 12″, height 6″; diameter 8″, height 5″. Curving sides, terminating at tooled concave band with flattened, slightly curving rim above. Glazed inside.

Bowls: Diameter 8″, height 5″. Sides curved, with flattened-curve rims, tooled bands below rims. Glazed internally. (Fig. 19.)

FIGURE 28.—Exteriors (left) and interiors of gravel-tempered sherds. Top to bottom: bowl; pan; heavy pan with reinforced rim; and pan with 18th-century-type rim. Colonial National Historical Park. (*From Smithsonian photos 43039–A, 43041–A.*)

Cooking pots: Diameter (including handles) 9½″, height 6″. Profile a segmented curve, with rim the same diameter as base. Exterior flange to receive cover. Small horizontal loop handles. Band of three incised lines around waist. (Fig. 18.)

Cooking pot covers: Diameters 7″, 10″, 10½″, 11″. Flat covers, with downward-turned rims. Off-center loop handles, probably designed to facilitate exam-

FIGURE 29.—Exteriors (left) and interiors of gravel-tempered sherds. Pan (top) with 18th-century-type rim, and handle of heavy pan with reinforced rim. Colonial National Historical Park. (*From Smithsonian photos 43039–C, 43039–D.*)

ination of contents of pot by permitting one to lift up one edge of cover. Covers are sometimes numbered with incised numerals. Unglazed. (Fig. 18.)

Pipkins: Diameter 7″, height 3″; diameter 8½″, height 3½″; diameter 8¼″, height 4″; diameter 8″, height 5″. Curving sides, terminating at tooled concave band with flattened, slightly curved rim above. Three stubby legs. Stub handle crudely shaped and casually applied at an upward angle. Glazed inside. Used as a saucepan to stand in the coals. (Fig. 19.)

Rectangular basting or baking pans: Length 15″, width 11¾″ (dimensions of single restored specimen at Jamestown; many fragments in addition at Jamestown and Plymouth). Drape-molded. Reinforced scalloped rim. Heavy horizontal loop handles are sometimes on sides, sometimes on ends. Glazed inside. (Fig. 21.)

Storage jars: Various sizes. The one wholly restored specimen (Lewes, Delaware) has a rim diameter of 8″ and a height of 12½″. Rims of largest examples (diameters 7″, 10″, 12″) have reinforcement strips applied below external projection. Heavy vertical loop handles, with tops attached to rims.

Most have interior flanges to receive covers. Glazed inside. Such jars were essential for preserving and pickling foods and for brewing beer. (Fig. 25.)

Plate warmer or chafing dish: Unique specimen. Diameter (including handle) 11″, height 7″. Heavy, flaring pedestal foot supports wide bowl, glazed inside. Flat rim with slight elevation on outer edge. Protruding vertically from rim are three lugs or supports for holding plates. Vertical loop handles extend from rim to lower sides of bowl. "Spirits of wine" were probably burned in the bowl to heat the plate above. (Fig. 20.) Fragmentary pedestals, similar in profile to the one here (but smaller, having step turnings around base) may have been parts of smaller chafing dishes). (Fig. 31.)

Ovens: (1) One wholly reconstructed oven at Jamestown. Made in sections on drape molds: base, two sides, two halves of top, opening frame, and door. Side and top sections are joined with seams, reinforced by finger impressions, meeting at top of trapezoidal opening. The opening was molded separately and joined with thumb-impressed reinforcements. A

FIGURE 30.—Exteriors (left) and interiors of gravel-tempered sherds. Top to bottom: rim of small bowl; rim of small jar with internal flange to receive cover; and pipkin handle. Colonial National Historical Park. (*From Smithsonian photos 43039–C, 43039–D.*)

flat door with heavy vertical handle, round in section, fits snugly into opening. Thickness varies from ¾″ to 1½″. Unglazed, although smears of glaze dripped during the firing indicate that the oven was fired with glazed utensils stacked above it. (Fig. 10.)

(2) Oven in place in Bowne House, Flushing, Long Island. Similar in shape to Jamestown oven. Opening is arched.

(3) Body sherd and handle sherds at Jamestown, from additional oven or ovens.

(4) Body sherd from dome-top oven similar to those at Jamestown and Flushing. John Howland House site, Rocky Nook, Kingston, Plymouth County, Massachusetts. (Fig. 26.)

Paste color, temper, and texture are consistent when examined microscopically. Resemblance is very close between oven sherds from the Jamestown and Howland house sites, and between these and a large chip obtained from the Smithsonian's oven purchased in Bideford. Except for a somewhat lower proportion of temper, utensil sherds from various sites are consistent with the oven fragments. The Smithsonian's 19th-century Bideford pan also closely resembles these, except for the proportion of temper, which is somewhat less. Further close resemblance of form exists between the Jamestown and Flushing ovens and those in the Bideford Museum. (Figs. 7, 9.)

In 1954 comparative tests were made by Frederick H. Norton, professor of ceramics at Massachusetts Institute of Technology. Jamestown clay was used for a control. Thin sections, made of sherds found at Jamestown, were fired at several temperatures and the results recorded in photomicrographs. Of the gravel-tempered sherd submitted in these tests, Professor Norton commented, "The clay mass looks quite dissimilar from the Jamestown clay."

No other identifiable English ware of this period compares with the gravel-tempered pottery, the use of gravel for temper apparently being restricted to North Devon. Gravel is found in red earthenware sherds from Spanish colonial sites and in olive oil jars of Hispanic origin, but both the quality and proportion of temper differs, as do the paste characteristics, so that no possibility exists for confusion between them and the North Devon ware.

The North Devon potteries produced gravel-tempered ovens that probably were unique in England. Ceramic ovens were made elsewhere, to be sure; Jewitt describes and illustrates an oven made in Yearsley by the Yorkshire Wedgwoods in 1712, but it is in no way related to the North Devon form. We have mentioned Dr. Pococke's allusion to "earthenware ovens" made in the mid-18th century at Calstock on the Cornish side of the Devonshire border, about 35 miles from Bideford; however, one may suppose that these were the products of diffusion from the North Devon center, if, indeed, they even resembled the North Devon ovens.

The closest comparisons with the North Devon ovens are to be found in Continental sources. A woodcut in Ulrich von Richental's *Concilium zu Constancz* (fig. 35), printed at Augsburg in 1483, shows an oven whose shape is similar to that of the Jamestown specimen. The oven in the woodcut is mounted on a two-wheeled cart drawn by two men. A woman is removing a tart from the flame-licked opening while a couple sits nearby at a table in front of a shop. Le Moyne, a century later, depicted the Huguenot Fort Caroline in Florida.[71] Just outside the stockade, on a raised platform under a thatched lean-to appears an oven whose form is similar to that of typical North Devon examples (fig. 36). It is a safe assumption that the ovens in both Richental's and Le Moyne's scenes were ceramic ovens, for both were used outdoors in a portable or temporary manner. No other material would have been suitable for such use.

This portable usage gives support to Bailey's conjecture that the Jamestown oven may have been used indoors in the winter and outdoors in the summer. He noted that carbon had been ground into the base, as though the oven had lain on a fireplace hearth.[72] Sidney Strickland, writing about his excavation of the John Howland House site, noted that the stone fireplace foundation there had no provision for a built-in brick oven of conventional type.[73] Not having recognized the earthen oven sherd, he assumed that bread was baked on the stone hearth. The pottery oven may well have been placed on the hearth or have been set up in an outbuilding. That ovens of some sort, whether ceramic or brick, were used away from houses is borne out by occasional documentary evidence. In 1662 John Andrews of Ipswich, Massachusetts, bequeathed a "bake house" worth 2 pounds, 10 shillings. In 1673, Henry Short of Newbury provided in his will that his widow should have "free egress and regress into the Bakehouse for baking & washing." In 1679 the inventory of Lt. George Gardner's estate in Salem listed his "dwelling house, bake house & out housing."[74] Bailey quotes the records of Henrico County, Virginia, to show a similar usage in the South.[75]

---

[71] J. Le Moyne, *Brevis Narratio corum quae in Florida . . .*, Frankfort, 1591, pl. 10.

[72] Bailey, *op. cit.* (footnote 3), pp. 497–498.

[73] Strickland, *op. cit.* (footnote 67).

[74] The probate records of Essex County, Massachusetts, Salem, Massachusetts, 1916, vol. 1, p. 378; vol. 2, p. 346; vol. 3, p. 328.

[75] Bailey, *op. cit.* (footnote 3), p. 498.

FIGURE 31.—Pedestal bases of small chafing dishes or standing salts. Top, exterior and interior of one sherd; bottom, exterior and top view of another sherd. Colonial National Historical Park. (*From Smithsonian photos 43039–C, 43030–D.*)

The only unquestionable evidence of how these ovens were used remains in the Bowne House, where the oven is built into the fireplace back. Originally, the oven protruded outdoors from the back of the chimney.[76]

Conclusions

Archeological, documentary, and literary evidences indicate that yellow sgraffito ware, gravel-tempered earthenware utensils, and gravel-tempered pottery ovens were made in several potteries in and around Barnstaple and Bideford in North Devon. Clay from the Fremington clay beds was used.

The North Devon potteries manufactured for export, sending their wares to Ireland as early as 1600 and to America by 1635. The trade was particularly heavy in the years following the Stuart Restoration and was tied to the influential 17th-century West-of-England commerce with America. New England,

Maryland, and Virginia received many shipments of North Devon pottery, an entire cargo of it having been delivered in Boston in 1688.

Sgraffito ware found in colonial sites in Virginia and Maryland is from a common source. The style of decoration is unique to English pottery and reflects Continental elements of design. It is reminiscent of decoration found on English and colonial New England furniture and embroideries. The only counterparts of this ware—matching it in style, paste color, and technique—are found among 17th-century sherds excavated from the sites of two potteries in Barnstaple. The 18th-century and 19th-century North Devon sgraffito ware surviving above ground differs considerably in style and form but in other respects it is the same as the ware found archeologically in Virginia and Maryland. The stylistic differences, noticeable on a piece in the Glaisher collection dated as early as 1704 (in which traces of the earlier style remain), were introduced by the turn of the century, thus strengthening the conclusion that the sgraffito tablewares found archeologically in this country must date from before 1700.

---

[76] *Bowne House; A Shrine to Religious Freedom*, Flushing, New York. Pamphlet of The Bowne House Historical Society, Flushing, N.Y., n.d.

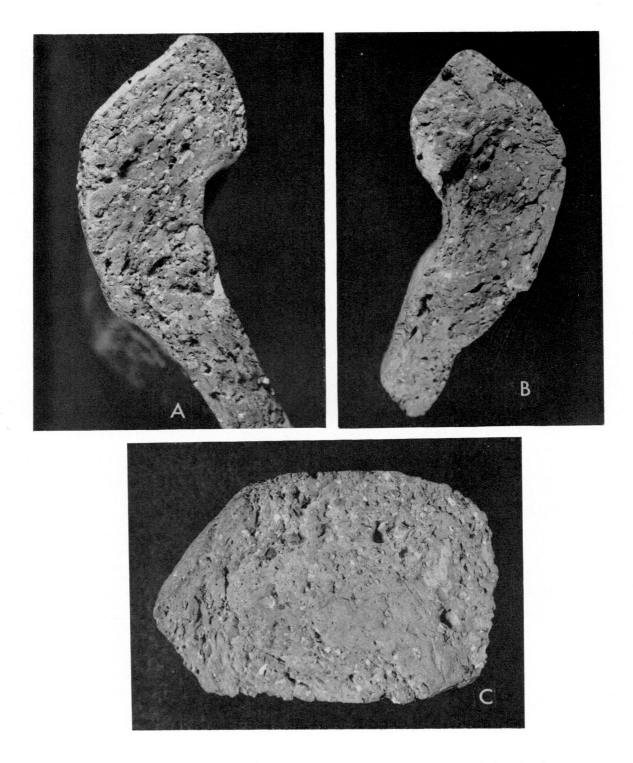

FIGURE 32.—Photomicrographs of gravel-tempered sherds enlarged twice natural size, showing cross-sectional fractures. Top left, pan sherd from Jamestown (Colonial National Historical Park); top right, pan sherd from Angelica Knoll site, Calvert County, Maryland (United States National Museum); and oven sherd from Bideford (United States National Museum).

FIGURE 33.—Photomicrographs of gravel-tempered sherds enlarged three times natural size, showing cross-sectional fractures. Top, pan sherd from "R. M." site, Plymouth, Massachusetts (Plimoth Plantation, Inc.); lower left, oven sherd from Jamestown (Colonial National Historical Park); and oven sherd from John Howland house site, Rocky Nook, Plymouth, Massachusetts (Plimoth Plantation, Inc.).

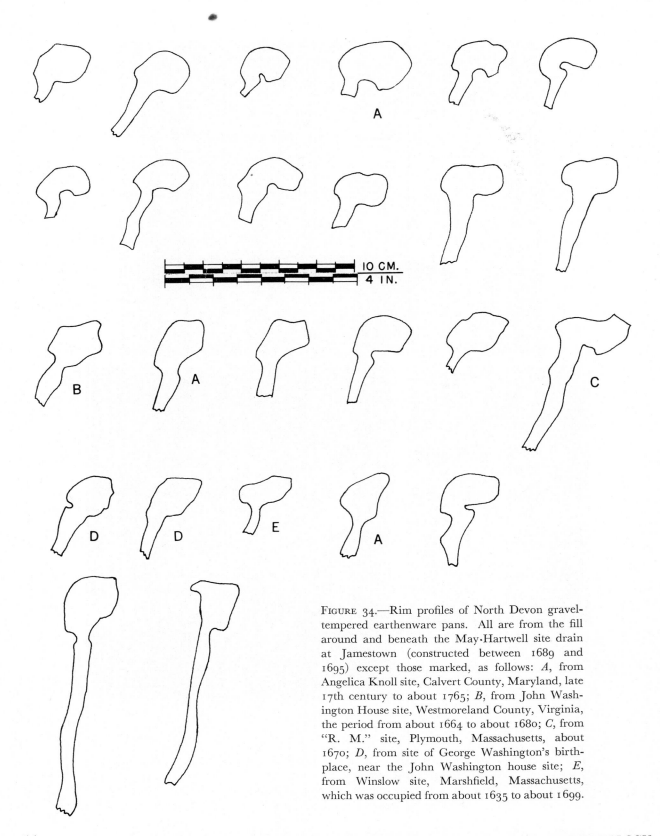

FIGURE 34.—Rim profiles of North Devon gravel-tempered earthenware pans. All are from the fill around and beneath the May·Hartwell site drain at Jamestown (constructed between 1689 and 1695) except those marked, as follows: A, from Angelica Knoll site, Calvert County, Maryland, late 17th century to about 1765; B, from John Washington House site, Westmoreland County, Virginia, the period from about 1664 to about 1680; C, from "R. M." site, Plymouth, Massachusetts, about 1670; D, from site of George Washington's birthplace, near the John Washington house site; E, from Winslow site, Marshfield, Massachusetts, which was occupied from about 1635 to about 1699.

mit vifchen gebachen wie die einer geren wolt haben dc
to fand man genůg in geleichem vnd gůtem kauff· vñ
darnach fy dañ kestlich warent vñ einer kauffen wolt·
vnd ift dife figur ꞓ·•

ꞓ Wie man bafteten in der ftat coftencz·
vmbfüret vnnd die fail het•

For kitchen utensils, tiles, and other objects subject
to heat or breakage, the same Fremington clay
received an admixture of fine pebbles, or gravel,
secured at a special place in the bed of the River
Torridge in Bideford. The use of gravel was described
by 18th-century writers as well as by later historians.
As found in America, the gravel-tempered ware
apparently is unique among the products of either
English or colonial American potters.

A specialty of the North Devon potteries was the
manufacture of ovens made of the same gravel-tempered clay as the kitchen utensils. The appearance of
these ovens and the method of making them remained
virtually the same from the 17th through the 19th
centuries. At Jamestown, a wholly reconstructed
oven reveals typical North Devon traits throughout,

FIGURE 35.—Baker's portable oven in a woodcut
from Ulrich von Richenthal's *Concilium zu Constancz*,
printed at Augsburg, Germany, in 1483. Lessing
J. Rosenwald Collection, Library of Congress.

while a fragment of an oven from the John Howland
House site near Plymouth displays, under a micro-
scope, the same qualities of paste and temper as in a
fragment of an oven obtained in Bideford by the
Smithsonian Institution. Sherds of gravel-tempered
utensils from several American sites also match the
oven fragments. Paste characteristics, exclusive of
the temper, are the same in the sgraffito ware, the
gravel-tempered ware, and the ovens. Furthermore,

FIGURE 36.—Detail from De Bry's engraving of Le Moyne's painting of Fort Caroline, depicting an oven on a raised platform under a crude shed. Fort Caroline was a French Hugenot settlement established in Florida in 1564. Rare Book Room, Library of Congress.

the gravel-tempered ware occasionally is found with a plain coating of slip, which, under the glaze, has the same yellow color as the sgraffito ware, while an undecorated variant of the sgraffito ware also occurs with a similar plain slip.

All these wares, including the ovens, are interrelated—the specimens found in America having been shipped in a busy North Devon-North American trade. The North Devon towns, moreover, were an important pottery-making center for export markets in the West of England, Ireland, and North America. Thousands of parcels of earthenware were shipped to the American colonies from Bideford and Barnstaple during the 17th century. Any doubts that ovens were among these overseas shipments are dispelled by the knowledge that they continually were being shipped in the English coastwise trade, and also by intrinsic and comparative evidence that oven sherds found on American sites are of North Devon origin.

The only known counterparts of the North Devon ovens are Continental. A 15th-century example appears in an Augsburg woodcut, and a 16th-century specimen is depicted in De Bry's engraving after Le

Moyne's painting of Fort Caroline, the Huguenot settlement in Florida. There are many suggestions of Huguenot and Low Country influences on North Devon pottery. Bideford and Barnstaple both were Puritan strongholds in the 17th century, and both became French Huguenot centers, especially after the revocation of the Edict of Nantes in 1685.

The style of sgraffito decoration changed radically after about 1700. After that date, decoration was confined mainly to harvest jugs and presentation pieces. Gravel-tempered utensils and ovens continued to be made, but the North Devon trade with America ceased by 1760.

Archeological evidence indicates that gravel-tempered ware was used in America between about 1675 and about 1760. An isolated example of sgraffito pottery, distinguished by crude design and glaze, dates from before 1640. The typical sgraffito ware is illustrated by specimens found in the fill under and around the brick drain in the May-Hartwell site at Jamestown. This ware dates between 1677 and 1695. No other sites provide a more certain dating than this. Sgraffito ware found at Bridge's Creek, Virginia (John

Washington house site), may date as early as 1664, but may be as late as 1677 or a few years thereafter.

The May-Hartwell oven was also found in the drain fill, so presumably it also was used before 1695. The oven fragment from the site of the John Howland house dates between about 1630 and about 1675, the lifetime of the house. The oven in the Bowne House is no earlier than 1664, the date of construction.

Typical sgraffito ware, therefore, dates from 1664 to 1695, plus or minus a few years. Gravel-tempered ware predominates in the same period, but extends well into the 18th century, probably to about 1760. Ovens date from between 1664 and 1695. The concentrations of wares within the limits of the May-Hartwell drain site correspond roughly with records of heavy shipments of the wares between 1681 and 1690. The earliest shipment recorded was to New England in 1635.

The sgraffito ware probably served as much for decoration as for practical use. Each piece was decorated differently, with elaborate designs, and in such a manner that it could provide a colorful effect on a court cupboard or a dresser, matching in style the carved woodwork or crewel embroidery of late 17th-century furnishings. Although sgraffito ware represented a degree of richness and dramatic color, it did not match the elegance of contemporary majolica, decorated after the manner of Chinese porcelain. Heavy and coarse, the sgraffito ware essentially was a variant of English folk pottery, reflecting the less sophisticated tastes of rural West of England. It did not occur in the colonies after 1700, by which time it was supplanted in public taste by the more refined majolica.

Gravel-tempered ware apparently was esteemed as a kitchen ware, much as is the modern "ovenware" or Pyrex in the contemporary home. Since gravel-tempered ovens were widely used in the West of England, they were accepted by settlers in America, especially where built-in brick ovens were lacking.

Unlike those of Staffordshire or Bristol, the North Devon potteries failed to develop new techniques or to change with shifts in taste. The delftware of London and Bristol and the yellow wares of Bristol and Staffordshire became preferable to the soft and imperfect sgraffito ware. In the same way, the kitchen ware of Staffordshire and the adequate red-wares of American potters made obsolete the heavy, ugly, and incomparably crude gravel-tempered ware, while American bricklayers, having adopted the custom of building brick ovens into fireplaces, outmoded the portable ovens from North Devon after 1700. Any chance of a renaissance of North Devon's potteries was killed by the blockading of its ports in the mid-18th century. From then on the potteries continued traditionally, their markets gradually shrinking at home in the face of modern production elsewhere. Today, only Brannan's Litchdon Street Pottery in Barnstaple has survived.

OTHER REFERENCES CONSULTED

BEMROSE, GEOFFREY, *Nineteenth-Century English Pottery and Porcelain*, New York, n.d. (about 1952).

BLACKER, J. F., *Nineteenth-Century English Ceramic Art*, London, 1911.

CHAFFERS, WILLIAM, *Marks and Monograms on Pottery and Porcelain*, 14th issue, London, 1932.

GRIBBLE, JOSEPH B., *Memorials of Barnstaple*, Barnstaple, 1830.

HAGGAR, REGINALD, *English Country Pottery*, London, 1950.

HONEY, W. B., *European Ceramic Art from the end of the Middle Ages to about 1815*, London, n.d. (about 1952).

MANKOWITZ, WOLF, AND HAGGAR, REGINALD G., *The Concise Encyclopedia of English Pottery and Porcelain*, London, 1957.

METEYARD, ELIZA, *The Life of Josiah Wedgwood*, London, 1865.

U.S. GOVERNMENT PRINTING OFFICE: 1960

CONTRIBUTIONS FROM

THE MUSEUM OF HISTORY AND TECHNOLOGY

PAPER 14

TEA DRINKING IN 18TH-CENTURY AMERICA:
Its ETIQUETTE AND EQUIPAGE

Rodris Roth

An English Family at Tea. Detail from an oil painting attributed to Joseph Van Aken, about 1720. In collection of Victoria and Albert Museum. Crown Copyright. (Color plate courtesy of the *Saturday Book*.)

Tea Drinking in 18th-Century America: Its Etiquette and Equipage—

By Rodris Roth

In 18th-century America, the pleasant practice of taking tea at home was an established social custom with a recognized code of manners and distinctive furnishings. Pride was taken in a correct and fashionable tea table whose equipage included much more than teapot, cups, and saucers.

It was usually the duty of the mistress to make and pour the tea; and it was the duty of the guests to be adept at handling a teacup and saucer and to provide social "chitchat." Because of the expense and time involved, the tea party was limited to the upper classes; consequently, such an affair was a status symbol. The cocktail party of the 20th century has, perhaps, replaced the tea party of the 18th century as a social custom, reflecting the contrast between the relaxed atmosphere of yesterday with the hurried pace of today.

THE AUTHOR: *Miss Roth is assistant curator of cultural history in the United States National Museum, Smithsonian Institution.*

THE AMERICANS "use much tea," noted the Abbé Robin during his visit to this country in 1781. "The greatest mark of civility and welcome they can show you, is to invite you to drink it with them."[1]

Tea was the social beverage of the 18th century; serving it was a sign of politeness and hospitality, and drinking it was a custom with distinctive manners and specific equipment. Most discussions of the commodity have dealt only with its political, historical, or economic importance; however, in order to understand the place tea holds in this country's past, it also is important to consider the beverage in terms of the social life and traditions of the Americans. As the Abbé Robin pointed out, not only was tea an important commodity on this side of the Atlantic, but the imbibing of it was an established social practice.

An examination of teatime behavior and a consideration of what utensils were used or thought appropriate for tea drinking are of help in reconstructing and interpreting American history as well as in furnishing and re-creating interiors of the period, thus bringing into clearer focus the picture of daily life in 18th-century America. For these reasons, and because the subject has received little attention, the present study has been undertaken.

Tea had long been known and used in the Orient before it was introduced into Europe in the early part of the 17th century. At about the same time

---

[1] Claude C. Robin, *New Travels through North America: in a Series of Letters . . . in the Year 1781*, Boston, 1784, p. 23.

two other new beverages appeared, chocolate from the Americas and coffee from the Near East. The presence of these commodities in European markets is indicative of the vigorous exploration and active trade of that century, which also witnessed the successful settlement of colonies in North America. By about mid-17th century the new beverages were being drunk in England, and by the 1690's were being sold in New England. At first chocolate was preferred, but coffee, being somewhat cheaper, soon replaced it and in England gave rise to a number of public places of refreshment known as coffee houses. Coffee was, of course, the primary drink of these establishments, but that tea also was available is indicated by an advertisement that appeared in an English newspaper in 1658. One of the earliest advertisements for tea, it announced:

That Excellent, and by all Physitians approved, *China Drink*, called by the *Chineans*, *Tcha*, by other nations *Tay alias Tee*, is sold at the *Sultaness-head*, a *Cophee-house* in *Sweetings* Rents by The Royal Exchange, London. [2]

For a time tea was esteemed mainly for its curative powers, which explains why it was "by all Physitians approved." According to an English broadside published in 1660, the numerous contemporary ailments which tea "helpeth" included "the headaches, giddiness, and heaviness." It was also considered "good for colds, dropsies and scurvies and [it] expelleth infection. It prevents and cures agues, surfeits and fevers." [3] By the end of the 17th century, however, tea's medicinal qualities had become secondary to its fashionableness as a unique drink. Tea along with the other exotic and novel imports from the Orient such as fragile porcelains, lustrous silks, and painted wallpapers had captured the European imagination. Though the beverage was served in public pleasure gardens as well as coffee houses during the early 1700's in England, social tea drinking in the home was gradually coming into favor. The coffee houses continued as centers of political, social, and literary influence as well as of commercial life into the first half of the 19th century, for apparently Englishmen preferred to drink their coffee in public rather than private houses and among male rather than mixed company. This was in contrast to tea, which was drunk in the home with breakfast or as a morning beverage and socially at afternoon gatherings of both sexes, as we see in the painting *An English Family at Tea* (frontispiece). As tea drinking in the home became fashionable, both host and hostess took pride in a well-appointed tea table, for a teapot of silver or fragile blue-and-white Oriental porcelain with matching cups and saucers and other equipage added prestige as well as elegance to the teatime ritual.

At first the scarcity and expense of the tea, the costly paraphernalia used to serve it, and the leisure considered necessary to consume it, limited the use of this commodity to the upper classes. For these reasons, social tea drinking was, understandably, a prestige custom. One becomes increasingly aware of this when looking at English paintings and prints of the early 18th century, such as *Family Group* (fig. 1), painted by Gawen Hamilton about 1730. Family members are portrayed in the familiar setting of their own parlor with its paneled walls and comfortable furnishings. Their pet, a small dog, surveys the scene from a resting place on a corner of the carpet. Teatime appears to have just begun, for cups are still being passed around and others on the table await filling from the nearby porcelain teapot. It seems reasonable to assume, since the painting is portraiture, that the family is engaged in an activity which, although familiar, is considered suitable to the group's social position and worthy of being recorded in oil. That tea drinking was a status symbol also is indicated by the fact that the artist has used the tea ceremony as the theme of the picture and the tea table as the focal point.

Eighteenth-century pictures and writings are basic source materials for information about Anglo-American tea drinking. (See the chronological list of pictures consulted, on page 90.) A number of the pictures are small-scale group or conversation piece paintings of English origin in which family and friends are assembled at tea, similar to *Family Group*, and they provide pictorial information on teatime modes and manners. The surroundings in which the partakers of tea are depicted also reveal information about the period and about the gracious living enjoyed in the better homes. Paneled walls and comfortable chairs, handsome chests and decorative curtains, objects of ceramic and silver and glass, all were set down on canvas or paper with painstaking care, and sometimes with a certain amount of artistic license. A careful study of these paintings provides an excellent guide for furnishing and reconstructing period rooms and ex-

---

[2] *Mercurius Politicus*, September 23–30, 1658.
[3] Edward Wenham, "Tea and Tea Things in England," *Antiques*, October 1948, vol. 54, p. 264.

Figure 1.—*Family Group*, by Gawen Hamilton, about 1730. In collection of Colonial Williamsburg, Inc. The tea set, undoubtedly of porcelain, includes cups and saucers, a cream or milk container, and a sugar container with tongs. (*Photo courtesy of Colonial Williamsburg, Inc.*)

hibits, even to the small details such as objects on mantels, tables, and chests, thus further documenting data from newspapers, journals, publications, and writings of the same period.

In America, as in England, tea had a rather limited use as a social beverage during the early 1700's. Judge Samuel Sewall, the recorder-extraordinary of Boston life at the turn of the 17th century, seems to have mentioned tea only once in his copious diary. In the entry for April 15, 1709, Sewall wrote that he had attended a meeting at the residence of Madam Winthrop where the guests "drunk Ale, Tea, Wine." [4] At this time ale and wine, in contrast to tea, were fairly common drinks. Since tea and the equipment used to serve it were costly, social tea drinking was restricted to the prosperous and governing classes who could afford the luxury. The portrayal of the rotund silver teapot and other tea-drinking equipment

---

[4] Samuel Sewall, *Diary of Samuel Sewall, 1674–1729*, reprinted in *Collections of the Massachusetts Historical Society*, 1879, ser. 5, vol. 6, p. 253.

in such an American painting as *Susanna Truax* (fig. 2), done by an unknown painter in 1730, indicates that in this country as in England not only was the tea ceremony of social importance but also that a certain amount of prestige was associated with the equipage. And, the very fact that an artist was commissioned for a portrait of this young girl is suggestive of a more than ordinary social status of the sitter and activity depicted.

English customs were generally imitated in this country, particularly in the urban centers. Of Boston, where he visited in 1740, Joseph Bennett observed that "the ladies here visit, drink tea and indulge every little piece of gentility to the height of the mode and neglect the affairs of their families with as good grace as the finest ladies in London." [5] English modes and manners remained a part of the social behavior after the colonies became an independent nation. Visitors to the newly formed United States were apt to remark about such habits as tea drinking, as did Brissot de Warville in 1788, that "in this, as in their whole manner of living, the Americans in general resemble the English." [6] Therefore, it is not surprising to find that during the 18th century the serving of tea privately in the morning and socially in the afternoon or early evening was an established custom in many households.

The naturalist Peter Kalm, during his visit to North America in the mid-18th century, noted that tea was a breakfast beverage in both Pennsylvania and New York. From the predominantly Dutch town of Albany in 1749 he wrote that "their breakfast is tea, commonly without milk." At another time, Kalm [7] stated:

With the tea was eaten bread and butter or buttered bread toasted over the coals so that the butter penetrated the whole slice of bread. In the afternoon about three o'clock tea was drunk again in the same fashion, except that bread and butter was not served with it.

This tea-drinking schedule was followed throughout the colonies. In Boston the people "take a great deal of tea in the morning," have dinner at two o'clock, and "about five o'clock they take more tea,

some wine, madeira [and] punch," [8] reported the Baron Cromot du Bourg during his visit in 1781. The Marquis de Chastellux confirms his countryman's statement about teatime, mentioning that the Americans take "tea and punch in the afternoon." [9]

During the first half of the 18th century the limited amount of tea available at prohibitively high prices restricted its use to a proportionately small segment of the total population of the colonies. About mid-century, however, tea was beginning to be drunk by more and more people, as supplies increased and costs decreased, due in part to the propaganda and merchandising efforts of the East India Company. According to Peter Kalm, tea, chocolate, and coffee had been "wholly unknown" to the Swedish population of Pennsylvania and the surrounding area before the English arrived, but in 1748 these beverages "at present constitute even the country people's daily breakfast." [10] A similar observation was made a few years later by Israel Acrelius: [11]

Tea, coffee, and chocolate are so general as to be found in the most remote cabins, if not for daily use, yet for visitors, mixed with Muscovado, or raw sugar.

America was becoming a country of tea drinkers. Then, in 1767, the Townshend Act imposed a duty on tea, among other imported commodities. Merchants and citizens in opposition to the act urged a boycott of the taxed articles. A Virginia woman, in a letter [12] to friends in England, wrote in 1769:

. . . I have given up the Article of Tea, but some are not quite so tractable; however if wee can convince the good folks on your side the Water of their Error, wee may hope to see happier times.

In spite of the tax many colonists continued to indulge in tea drinking. By 1773 the general public, according to one Philadelphia merchant, "can afford

[5] John Marshall Phillips, *American Silver*, New York, 1949, p. 76.

[6] Jacques Pierre Brissot de Warville, *New Travels in the United States of America Performed in 1788*, London, 1794, p. 80.

[7] Peter Kalm, *The America of 1750. Peter Kalm's Travels in North America*, edited and translated by Adolph B. Benson, New York, 1937, vol. 1, p. 346, vol. 2, p. 605.

[8] Baron Cromot du Bourg, "Journal de mon Séjour en Amérique," *Magazine of American History* (1880–1881), quoted in Charles H. Sherrill, *French Memories of Eighteenth-Century America*, New York, 1915, p. 155.

[9] Marquis de Chastellux, *Voyages de M. le Marquis de Chastellux dans l'Amérique Septentrionale*, Paris, 1788, quoted in Sherrill, *op. cit.* (footnote 8), p. 190.

[10] Kalm, *op. cit.* (footnote 7), vol. 1, p. 195.

[11] Israel Acrelius, *A History of New Sweden; or, The Settlements on the River Delaware*, translated and edited by William M. Reynolds, Philadelphia, 1874, p. 158.

[12] Letter from M. Jacquelin, York, Virginia, to John Norton, London, August 14, 1769. In, *John Norton and Sons, Merchants of London and Virginia, Being the Papers from Their Counting House for the Years 1750 to 1795*, edited by Frances Norton Mason, Richmond, 1937, p. 103.

Figure 2.—*Susanna Truax*, an American painting dated 1730. In collection of Edgar William and Bernice Chrysler Garbisch, National Gallery of Art. On the beige, marble-like table top beside Susanna—who wears a dress of red, black, and white stripes—are a fashionable silver teapot and white ceramic cup, saucer, and sugar dish. (*Photo courtesy National Gallery of Art.*)

to come at this piece of luxury" while one-third of the population "at a moderate computation, drink tea twice a day." [13] It was at this time, however, that efforts were made to enforce the English tea tax and the result was that most famous of tea parties, the "Boston Tea Party."

Thereafter, an increasing number of colonists abstained from tea drinking as a patriotic gesture. Philip Fithian, a tutor at Nomini Hall, the Virginia plantation of Col. Robert Carter, wrote in his journal on Sunday, May 29, 1774:

After dinner we had a Grand & agreeable Walk in & through the Gardens—There is great plenty of Strawberries, some Cherries, Goose berries &c.—Drank Coffee at four, they are now too patriotic to use tea.

And indeed they were patriotic, for by September the taste of tea almost had been forgotten at Nomini Hall, as Fithian vividly recounted in his journal: [14]

Something in our palace this Evening, very merry happened—Mrs. *Carter* made a dish of Tea. At Coffee, she sent me a dish—& the Colonel both ignorant—He smelt, sipt—look'd—At last with great gravity he asks what's this?—Do you ask Sir—Poh!—And out he throws it splash a sacrifice to Vulcan.

Other colonists, in their own way, also showed their distaste for tea (see fig. 3). Shortly before the outbreak of the American Revolution there appeared in several newspapers an expression of renouncement in

[13] Letter from Gilbert Barkly to directors of the East India Company, May 26, 1773. *Tea Leaves: Being a Collection of Letters and Documents . . .*, edited by Francis S. Drake, Boston, 1884, p. 200.

[14] Philip Vickers Fithian, *Journal and Letters of Philip Vickers Fithian, 1773–1774; a Plantation Tutor of the Old Dominion*, edited by Hunter Dickinson Farish, Williamsburg, 1957, pp. 110, 195–196.

rhyme, "A Lady's Adieu to Her Tea-Table" [15] (below), which provides a picture of contemporary teatime etiquette and equipage.

Many people gave up tea for the duration of the war and offered various substitute beverages such as

de St. Méry observed in 1795, during his residence in Philadelphia, that "the whole family is united at tea, to which friends, acquaintances and even strangers are invited." [17] That teatime hospitality was offered to the newest of acquaintances or "even strangers" is

A Lady's Adieu to Her Tea-Table

FAREWELL the Tea-board with your gaudy attire,
Ye cups and ye saucers that I did admire;
To my cream pot and tongs I now bid adieu;
That pleasure's all fled that I once found in you.
Farewell pretty chest that so lately did shine,
With hyson and congo and best double fine;
Many a sweet moment by you I have sat,
Hearing girls and old maids to tattle and chat;
And the spruce coxcomb laugh at nothing at all,
Only some silly work that might happen to fall.
No more shall my teapot so generous be
In filling the cups with this pernicious tea,
For I'll fill it with water and drink out the same,
Before I'll lose LIBERTY that dearest name,
Because I am taught (and believe it is fact)
That our ruin is aimed at in the late act,
Of imposing a duty on all foreign Teas,
Which detestable stuff we can quit when we please.
LIBERTY'S The Goddess that I do adore,
And I'll maintain her right until my last hour,
Before she shall part I will die in the cause,
For I'll never be govern'd by tyranny's laws.

coffee and dried raspberry leaves, "a detestable drink" which the Americans "had the heroism to find good," remarked a postwar visitor, Léon Chotteau.[16] Although the colonists had banished tea "with enthusiasm," the tea habit was not forgotten. Chotteau further noted that "they all drink tea in America as they drink wine in the South of France." Tea drinking continued to be an important social custom in the new nation well into the 19th century.

The tea ceremony, sometimes simple, sometimes elaborate, was the very core of family life. Moreau

verified by Claude Blanchard. He wrote of his visit to Newport, Rhode Island, on July 12, 1780, that "in the evening there was an illumination. I entered the house of an inhabitant, who received me very well; I took tea there, which was served by a young lady." And while staying in Boston, Blanchard mentioned that a new acquaintance "invited us to come in the evening to take tea at his house. We went there; the tea was served by his daughter." [18]

---

[17] Médéric Louis Elie Moreau de Saint-Méry, *Moreau de St. Méry's American Journey*, translated and edited by Kenneth Roberts and Anna M. Roberts, Garden City, 1947, p. 266.

[18] Claude Blanchard, *The Journal of Claude Blanchard, Commissary of the French Auxiliary Army Sent to the United States During the American Revolution, 1780–1783*, translated by William Duane and edited by Thomas Balch, Albany, 1876, pp. 41, 49.

---

[15] R. T. H. Halsey and Charles O. Cornelius, *A Handbook of the American Wing*, New York, 1924, pp. 111–112.

[16] Léon Chotteau, *Les Français en Amérique*, Paris, 1876, quoted in Sherrill, *op. cit.* (footnote 8), p. 96.

A SOCIETY of PATRIOTIC LADIES.

Figure 3.—*A Society of Patriotic Ladies* at Edenton in North Carolina pledging to drink no more tea, 1775, an engraving published by R. Sayer and J. Bennet, London. In Print and Photograph Division, Library of Congress. (*Photo courtesy of Library of Congress.*)

In the daily routine of activities when the hour for tea arrived, Moreau de St. Méry remarked that "the mistress of the house serves it and passes it around."[19] In the words of another late-18th-century diarist, the Marquis de Barbé-Marbois, those present might

"seat themselves at a spotless mahogany table, and the eldest daughter of the household or one of the youngest married women makes the tea and gives a cup to each person in the company." *Family Group* (fig. 1) provides an illustration of this practice in the early part of the century. During the tea hour social and economic affairs were discussed, gossip exchanged, and, according to Barbé-Marbois, "when

---

[19] Moreau de Saint-Méry, *op. cit.* (footnote 17), p. 266.

PAPER 14: TEA DRINKING IN 18TH-CENTURY AMERICA

544609—60——2

there is no news at all, they repeat old stories." [20]
Many entries in Nancy Shippen's journal [21] between
1783 and 1786 indicate that this Philadelphian passed
many such hours in a similar manner. On March
11, 1785, she wrote: "About 4 in the Afternoon
D[r] Cutting came in, & we spent the afternoon in the
most agreable chit-chat manner, drank a very
good dish of Tea together & then separated." Part
of an undated entry in December 1783 reads: "This
Afternoon we were honor'd with the Company of
Gen[l] Washington to Tea, M[rs] & Major Moore,
M[rs] Stewart M[r] Powel M[r] B Washington, & two or
3 more." If acquaintances of Nancy's own age were
present or the company large, the tea hour often
extended well into the evening with singing, con-
versing, dancing, and playing of whist, chess, or
cards. Of one such occasion she wrote: [21]

M[rs] Allen & the Miss Chews drank Tea with me & spent
the even'g. There was half a dozen agreable & sensible
men that was of the party. The conversation was carried
on in the most sprightly, agreable manner, the Ladies
bearing by far the greatest part—till nine when cards was
proposed, & about ten, refreshments were introduced which
concluded the Evening.

Obviously, young men and women enjoyed the
sociability of teatime, for it provided an ideal occasion
to get acquainted. When the Marquis de Chastellux
was in Philadelphia during the 1780's he went one
afternoon to "take tea with Madam Shippen," and
found musical entertainment to meet with his approval and a relationship between the sexes which
had parental sanction. One young miss played on
the clavichord, and "Miss Shippen sang with timidity
but a very pretty voice," accompanied for a time by
Monsieur Otto on the harp. Dancing followed,
noted the Marquis, "while mothers and other grave
personages conversed in another room." [22] In New
York as in Philadelphia teatime was an important
part of the younger set's social schedule. Eliza
Bowne, writing to her sister in January 1810, reported
that "as to news—New York is not so gay as last

Winter, few balls but a great many tea-parties." [23]
The feminine interest and participation in such gatherings of personable young men and attractive young
women was expressed by Nancy Shippen [24] when she
wrote in her journal after such a party:

"Saturday night at 11 o'clock. I had a very large company at Tea this Evening. The company is but just broke
up, I dont know when I spent a more merry Even[g]. We
had music, Cards, &c &c."

A masculine view of American tea parties was openly
voiced by one foreign visitor, Prince de Broglie, who,
upon arrival in America in 1782, "only knew a few
words of English, but knew better how to drink
excellent tea with even better cream, how to tell a
lady she was pretty, and a gentleman he was sensible,
by reason whereof I possessed all the elements of
social success." [25] Similar feelings were expressed by
the Comte de Segur during his sojourn in America
in the late 18th century when, in a letter to his wife
in France, he wrote: "My health continues excellent,
despite the quantity of tea one must drink with the
ladies out of gallantry, and of madeira all day long
with the men out of politeness." [26]

Festive tea parties such as the ones described above
are the subject of some of the group portraits or
conversation pieces painted about 1730 by the English
artist William Hogarth. *The Assembly at Wanstead
House*, now in the Philadelphia Museum of Art,
illustrates quite an elegant affair taking place in a
large, richly decorated, English interior. The artist
has filled the canvas with people standing and con-
versing while a seated group plays cards at a table in
the center of the room. To one side near the fireplace
a man and two women drinking tea are seated at an
ornately carved, square tea table with a matching
stand for the hot water kettle. On a dish or circular
stand in the center of the table is a squat teapot with
matching cups and saucers arranged in parallel rows
on either side.

Tea-drinking guests seem to have been free to sit
or stand according to their own pleasure or the num-

[20] François, Marquis de Barbé-Marbois, *Our Revolutionary Fore-
fathers. The Letters of François, Marquis de Barbé-Marbois During
His Residence in the United States as Secretary of the French Legation
1779–1785*, translated and edited by Eugene Parker Chase,
New York, 1929, p. 123.
[21] Nancy Shippen, *Nancy Shippen, Her Journal Book*, edited by
Ethel Armes, Philadelphia, 1935, pp. 167, 229, 243.
[22] Chastellux, *op. cit.* (footnote 9), quoted in Sherrill, *op. cit.*
(footnote 8), p. 40.

[23] Eliza Southgate Bowne, *A Girl's Life Eighty Years Ago. Selections from the Letters of Eliza Southgate Bowne*, edited by Clarence
Cook, New York, 1887, p. 207.
[24] Shippen, *op. cit.* (footnote 21), p. 167.
[25] Prince de Broglie, "Journal du Voyage," *Mélanges de la
Société des Bibliophiles Français*, Paris, 1903, quoted in Sherrill,
op. cit. (footnote 8), p. 13.
[26] Comte de Ségur, *Mémoires, ou Souveniers et Anecdotes*, Paris,
1826, quoted in Sherrill, *op. cit.* (footnote 8), p. 78.

ber of chairs available, and Barbé-Marbois noted that at American tea parties "people change seats, some go, others come." The written and visual materials offer little in the way of evidence to suggest that in general men stood and women sat during teatime. In fact, places at the tea table were taken by both sexes, even at formal tea parties such as the one depicted in *The Assembly at Wanstead House*.

A less formal but more usual tea scene is the subject of another Hogarth painting, *The Wollaston Family*, now in the Leicester Art Gallery, England. The afternoon gathering has divided into two groups, one playing cards, the other drinking tea. An atmosphere of ease and comfort surrounds the party. The men and women seated at the card table are discussing the hand just played, while the women seated about the square tea table in front of the fireplace are engaged in conversation. A man listens as he stands and stirs his tea. Each drinker holds a saucer with a cup filled from the teapot on a square tile or stand in the center of the table. One woman is returning her

cup, turned upside down on the saucer, to the table. More about this particular habit later.

The same pleasant social atmosphere seen in English paintings seems to have surrounded teatime in America, as the previously cited entries in Nancy Shippen's journal book suggest. Her entry for January 18, 1784,[27] supplies a description that almost matches *The Wollaston Family*:

A stormy day, alone till the afternoon; & then was honor'd with the Company of Mr Jones (a gentleman lately from Europe) M^r Du Ponceau, & Mr Hollingsworth at Tea—We convers'd on a variety of subjects & play^d at whist, upon the whole spent an agreable Even^g ."

Tea was not only a beverage of courtship; it also was associated with marriage. Both Peter Kalm, in 1750, and Moreau de St. Méry, in the 1790's, report the Philadelphia custom of expressing good wishes to a newly married couple by paying them a personal visit soon after the marriage. It was the duty of the

---

[27] Shippen, *op. cit.* (footnote 21), p. 175.

CONVERSAZIONI.

Figure 4.—*Conversazioni*, by W. H. Bunbury, published 1782. In Print and Photograph Division, Library of Congress.

bride to serve wine and punch to the callers before noon and tea and wine in the afternoon.[28]

No doubt, make-believe teatime and pretend tea drinking were a part of some children's playtime activities. Perhaps many a little girl played at serving tea and dreamed of having a tea party of her own, but few were as fortunate as young Peggy Livingston who, at about the age of five, was allowed to invite "by card . . . 20 young misses" to her own "Tea Party & Ball." She "treated them with all good things, & a violin," wrote her grandfather. There were "5 coaches at ye door at 10 when they departed. I was much amused 2 hours."[29]

Tea seems to have been the excuse for many a social gathering, large or small, formal or informal. And sometimes an invitation to drink tea meant a rather elegant party. "That is to say," wrote one cosmopolitan observer of the American scene in the 1780's, the Marquis de Chastellux, "to attend a sort of assembly pretty much like the *conversazioni* [social gathering] of Italy; for tea here, is the substitute for the *rinfresco* [refreshment]."[30] A view of such an event has been depicted in the English print *Conversazioni* (fig. 4), published in 1782. It is hoped that the stiffly seated and solemn-faced guests became more talkative when the tea arrived. However, this tea party may have been like the ones Ferdinand Bayard attended in Bath, Virginia, of which he wrote: "The only thing you hear, while they are taking tea, is the whistling sound made by the lips on edges of the cups. This music is varied by the request made to you to have another cup."[31] At tea parties, cakes, cold pastries, sweetmeats, preserved fruits, and plates of cracked nuts might also be served, according to Mrs. Anne Grant's reminiscences of pre-Revolutionary America.[32] Peter Kalm noted during his New York sojourn in 1749 that "when you paid a visit to any home" a bowl of cracked nuts and one of apples were "set before you, which you ate after

drinking tea and even at times while partaking of tea."[33] Sometimes wine and punch were served at teatime, and "in summer," observed Barbé-Marbois, "they add fruit and other things to drink."[34] Coffee too might be served. As the Frenchman Claude Blanchard explained:[35]

They [the Americans] do not take coffee immediately after dinner, but it is served three or four hours afterwards with tea; this coffee is weak and four or five cups are not equal to one of ours; so that they take many of them. The tea, on the contrary, is very strong. This use of tea and coffee is universal in America.

Dealing with both food and drink at the same time was something of an art. It was also an inconvenience for the uninitiated, and on one occasion Ferdinand Bayard, a late-18th-century observer of American tea ritual, witnessed another guest who, "after having taken a cup [of tea] in one hand and tartlets in the other, opened his mouth and told the servant to fill it for him with smoked venison!"[36]

While foreign visitors recognized that the "greatest mark of courtesy" a host and hostess could offer a guest was a cup of tea, hospitality could be "hot water torture" for foreigners unless they understood the social niceties not only of holding a cup and tartlet, but of declining without offending by turning the cup upside down and placing a spoon upon it. The ceremony of the teaspoon is fully explained by the Prince de Broglie who, during his visit to Philadelphia in 1782, reported the following teatime incident at the home of Robert Morris:[37]

I partook of most excellent tea and I should be even now still drinking it, I believe, if the [French] Ambassador had not charitably notified me at the twelfth cup, that I must put my spoon across it when I wished to finish with this sort of warm water. He said to me: it is almost as ill-bred to refuse a cup of tea when it is offered to you, as it would [be] indiscreet for the mistress of the house to propose a fresh one, when the ceremony of the spoon has notified her that we no longer wish to partake of it.

Bayard reports that one quick-witted foreigner,

[28] Kalm, *op. cit.* (footnote 7), vol. 2, p. 677; Moreau de Saint-Méry, *op. cit.* (footnote 17), p. 286.

[29] Shippen, *op. cit.* (footnote 21), p. 248.

[30] François Jean, Marquis de Chastellux, *Travels in North America in the Years 1780-81-82*, New York, 1827, p. 114.

[31] Ferdinand Marie Bayard, *Travels of a Frenchman in Maryland and Virginia, with a Description of Philadelphia and Baltimore in 1791*, translated and edited by Ben C. McCary, Ann Arbor, 1950, p. 48.

[32] Mrs. Anne Grant, *Memoirs of an American Lady, with Sketches of Manners and Scenery in America, as They Existed Previous to the Revolution*, New York, 1846, p. 54.

[33] Kalm, *op. cit.* (footnote 7), vol. 2, p. 611.

[34] Barbé-Marbois, *op. cit.* (footnote 20), p. 123.

[35] Blanchard, *op. cit.* (footnote 18), p. 78.

[36] Ferdinand M. Bayard, *Voyage dans l'Intérieur des Etats-Unis*, Paris, 1797, quoted in Sherrill, *op. cit.* (footnote 8), p. 93.

[37] Claude Victor Marie, Prince de Broglie, "Narrative of the Prince de Broglie," translated by E. W. Balch in *Magazine of American History*, April 1877, vol. 1, p. 233.

Figure 5.—*Tea Party in the Time of George I*, an English painting of about 1725. In collection of Colonial Williamsburg, Inc. The silver equipage includes (left to right) a sugar container and cover, hexagonal tea canister, hot water jug or milk jug, slop bowl, teapot, and (in front) sugar tongs, spoon boat or tray, and spoons. The cups and saucers are Chinese export porcelain. (*Photo courtesy of Colonial Williamsburg, Inc.*)

uninformed as to the teaspoon signal, had had his cup filled again and again until he finally "decided after emptying it to put it into his pocket until the replenishments had been concluded." [38]

---

[38] Bayard, *op. cit.* (footnote 36), quoted in Sherrill, *op. cit.* (footnote 8), p. 93.

The gracious art of brewing and serving tea was as much an instrument of sociability as was a bit of music or conversation. This custom received the attention of a number of artists, and it is amazing what careful and detailed treatment they gave to the accessories of tea. We are familiar with the journals, newspaper advertisements, and other writings that provide contemporary reports on this custom, but it is to the artist we turn for a more clearly defined view. The painter saw, arranged, and gave us a visual image—sometimes richly informative, as in *Tea Party in the Time of George I* (fig. 5)—of the different teatime items and how they were used. The unknown artist of this painting, done about 1725, has carefully illustrated each piece of equipment considered appropriate for the tea ceremony and used for brewing the tea in the cups held with such grace by the gentleman and child.

Throughout the 18th century the well-equipped tea table would have displayed most of the items seen in this painting: a teapot, slop bowl, container for milk or cream, tea canister, sugar container, tongs, teaspoons, and cups and saucers. These pieces were basic to the tea ceremony and, with the addition of a tea urn which came into use during the latter part of the 18th century, have remained the established tea equipage up to the present day. Even a brief investigation of about 20 inventories—itemized lists of the goods and property of deceased persons that were required by law—reveal that in New York between 1742 and 1768 teapots, cups and saucers, teaspoons, and tea canisters were owned by both low and high income groups in both urban and rural areas.

The design and ornament of the tea vessels and utensils, of course, differed according to the fashion of the time, and the various items associated with the beverage provide a good index of the stylistic changes in the 18th century. The simple designs and unadorned surfaces of the plump pear-shaped teapot in *Tea Party in the Time of George I* (fig. 5) and the spherical one seen in the portrait *Susanna Truax* (fig. 2) mark these pieces as examples of the late baroque style popular in the early part of the 18th century. About mid-century, teapots of inverted pear-shape, associated with the rococo style, began to appear. A pot of this shape is depicted in the portrait *Paul Revere* painted about 1765 by John Singleton Copley and owned by the Museum of Fine Arts, Boston. The fact that a teapot was chosen as an example of Revere's craft, from all of the objects he made, indicates that such a vessel was valued as highly by its maker as by its owner. The teapot was a mark of prestige for both craftsman and hostess. Apparently the famous silversmith and patriot was still working on the piece, for the nearby tools suggest that the teapot was to have engraved and chased decoration, perhaps of flowers, scrolls, and other motifs typical of the rococo style.

The restrained decoration and linear outlines of the teapot illustrated in the print titled *The Old Maid* (fig. 14) and the straight sides and oval shape of the teapot belonging to a late 18th-century child's set (fig. 6) of Chinese export porcelain are characteristics of the neoclassic style that was fashionable at the end of the century. Tea drinkers were extremely conscious of fashion changes and, whenever possible, set their tea tables with stylish equipment in the prevailing fashion. Newspaper advertisements, journals, letters, and other written materials indicate that utensils in the "best and newest taste" were available, desired, purchased, and used in this country.

Further verification of the types and kinds of equipage used is supplied by archeological investigations of colonial sites. For instance, sherds or fragments of objects dug from or near the site of a dwelling at Marlborough, Virginia, owned and occupied by John Mercer between 1726 and 1768, included a silver teaspoon made about 1735 and two teapot tops—one a pewter lid and the other a Staffordshire salt-glaze cover made about 1745—as well as numerous pieces of blue-and-white Oriental porcelain cups and saucers (fig. 7). Such archeological data provides concrete proof about tea furnishings used in this country. A comparison of sherds from colonial sites with wares used by the English and of English origin indicates that similar types of equipage were to be found upon tea tables in both countries. This also substantiates the already cited American practice of following English modes and manners, a practice Brissot de Warville noted in 1788 when he wrote that in this country "tea forms, as in England, the basis of the principal parties of pleasures. [39]

Tea furnishings, when in use, were to be seen upon rectangular tables with four legs, square-top and circle-top tripods, and Pembroke tables. Such tables were, of course, used for other purposes, but a sampling of 18th-century Boston inventories reveals that in some households all or part of the tea paraphernalia was prominently displayed on the tea table rather than being stored in cupboards or closets. A "Japan'd tea Table & China" and "a Mahog[any] Do. & China," both in the "Great Room," are listed in Mrs. Hannah Pemberton's inventory recorded in Boston in 1758. The inventory of Joseph Blake of Boston recorded in 1746 lists a "tea Table with a Sett of China furniture" in the back room of the

---

[39] Brissot de Warville, *op. cit.* (footnote 6), p. 129.

Figure 6.—Part of a child's tea set of Chinese export porcelain, or "painted China," made about 1790. The painted decoration is of pink roses and rose buds with green leaves; the border is orange, with blue flowers. At one time this set probably included containers for cream or milk and sugar, as did the adult "tea table setts complete." (*USNM 391761; Smithsonian photo 45141–B.*)

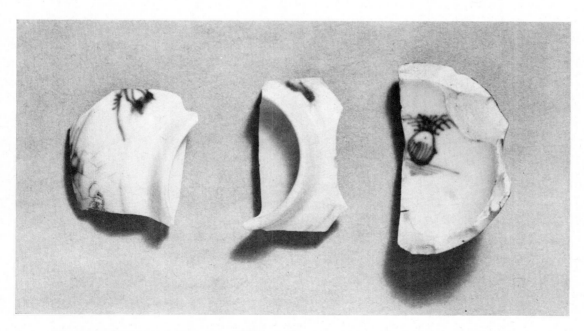

Figure 7.—Fragments of teacups of Chinese export porcelain with blue decoration on white, excavated at the site of John Mercer's dwelling at Marlborough, Virginia, 1726–1768. These sherds, now in the United States National Museum, are from cups similar in shape and decoration to the ones depicted in figures 1 and 5. (*USNM 59.1890, 59.1969, 59.1786; Smithsonian photo 45141–G.*)

house, while in the "closett" in the front room were "6 Tea Cups & Saucers" along with other ceramic wares.[40]

The most popular type of tea table apparently was the circular tripod; that is, a circular top supported on a pillar with three feet. This kind of table is seen again and again in the prints and paintings (figs. 1, 2, 9, 14), and is listed in the inventories of the period. These tables, usually of walnut or mahogany, had stationary or tilt tops with plain, scalloped, or carved edges. Square or round, tripod or four-legged, the tables were usually placed against the wall of the room until teatime when, in the words of Ferdinand Bayard, "a mahogany table is brought forward and

[40] Suffolk County [Massachusetts] Probate Court Record Books (hereinafter cited as Suffolk County Record Books), vol. 53, p. 444, inventory of Mrs. Hannah Pemberton, Boston, June 22, 1758; vol. 39, p. 185, inventory of Joseph Blake, Boston, September 18, 1746. Among other inventories in Suffolk County Record Books listing tea tables with tea equipment thereon were those of Sendal Williams, Boston, March 13, 1747 (vol. 43, p. 407); Revd. Dr. Benja. Colman, Boston, September 1, 1747 (vol. 40, p. 266); Mr. Nathl. Cunningham, February 6, 1748 (vol. 42, p. 156); Joseph Snelling, Boston, December 8, 1748 (vol. 42, p. 60); Eliza. Chaunay, Boston, May 28, 1757 (vol. 52, p. 382); Gillam Tailer, Boston, October 18, 1757 (vol. 52, p. 817); Jon. Skimmer, Boston, October 30, 1778 (vol. 77, p. 565).

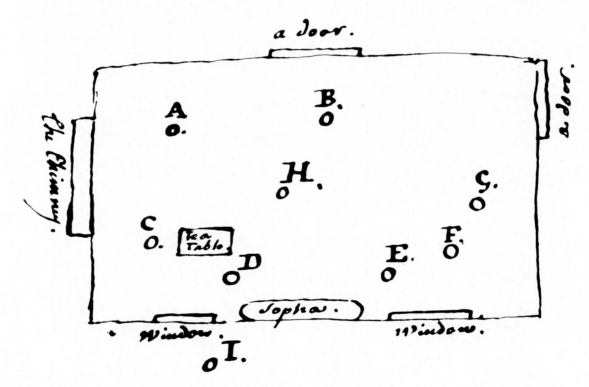

Figure 8.—A sketch by Louis Guillaume Otto that was enclosed in a letter to Nancy Shippen of Philadelphia about 1780. The sketch indicates the placement of the furniture in the Shippen parlor and the location of the tea-party participants. The "Explication" accompanying the drawing reads in part: "A. Old Dr Shippen sitting before the Chimney. . . . B. Mr Lee walking up and down, speaking and laughing by intervalls. . . . C. Miss Nancy [Shippen] before the tea table. . . . D. Mrs Shippen lost in sweet meditations. E. F. G. Some strangers which the Spy [Mr. Otto] could not distinguish. H. Cyrus [the butler] standing in the middle of the room—half asleep. I. Mr Otto standing before the window. . . ." From Shippen Papers, Manuscripts Division, Library of Congress.

Figure 9.—*The Honeymoon*, by John Collett, about 1760. In the midst of a domestic scene replete with homey details, the artist has depicted with care the tea table and its furnishing, including a fashionable tea urn symbolically topped with a pair of affectionate birds. (*Photo courtesy of Frick Art Reference Library*.)

placed in front of the lady who pours the tea." [41] This practice is depicted in a number of 18th-century pictures, with the tea table well out in the room, often in front of a fireplace, and with seated and standing figures at or near the table (fig. 1). Evidence of such furniture placement in American parlors is recorded in a sketch and note Nancy Shippen received from one of her beaus, who wrote in part: [42]

. . . this evening I passed before Your house and seeing Company in the parlour I peep'd through the Window and saw a considerable Tea Company, of which by their situation I could only distinguish four persons. You will see the plan of this Company upon the next page.

In the sketch (fig. 8), a floor plan of the Shippen parlor, we can see the sofa against the wall between the windows, while chairs and tea table have been moved out in the room. The table is near the fireplace, where Miss Shippen served the tea. In the 18th century such an arrangement was first and foremost one of comfort, and perhaps also one of taste. The diary of Jacob Hiltzheimer indicates that in 1786 the first signs of fall were felt on August 1, for the Philadelphian wrote: "This evening it was so cool that we drank tea by the fire." [43] In the south

---

[41] Bayard, *op. cit.* (footnote 31), p. 47.

[42] Letter from [Louis Guillaume] Otto [to Nancy Shippen], undated, Shippen Papers, box 6, Manuscripts Division, Library of Congress. The letter is dated about 1780 by Ethel Armes, *op. cit.* (footnote 21), p. 8.

[43] Jacob Hiltzheimer, *Extracts from the Diary of Jacob Hiltzheimer of Philadelphia, 1765–1798*, edited by Jacob Cox Parsons, Philadelphia, 1893, p. 94.

Figure 10.—Pieces of a tea set of Crown-Derby porcelain, dating about 1790. The cups and saucers, covered sugar bowl, container for cream or milk, plate, and bowls are ornamented with gilt borders and a scattering of blue flowers on a white ground. (*USNM 54089–54095; Smithsonian photo 45541–A.*)

as in the north, tea—or, at the time of the American Revolution its patriotic substitute, coffee—was served by the fire as soon as the first winter winds were felt. Philip Fithian, while at Nomini Hall in Virginia, wrote in his journal on September 19, 1774: "the Air is clear, cold & healthful. We drank our Coffee at the great House very sociably, round a fine Fire, the House and Air feels like winter again." [44]

Table cloths—usually square white ones (as in fig. 9) that showed folds from having been stored in a linen press—were used when tea was served, but it is difficult to say with any certainty if their use depended upon the whim of the hostess, the type of table, or the time of day. A cloth probably was used more often on a table with a plain top than on one with scalloped or carved edges. However, as can be seen in *Family Group* (fig. 1) and *An English Family at Tea* (frontispiece), it was perfectly acceptable to serve tea on a plain-top table without a cloth. Apparently such tables were also used at breakfast or morning tea, because Benjamin Franklin, in a letter from London dated February 19, 1758, gave the following

directions for the use of "six coarse diaper Breakfast Cloths" which he sent to his wife: "they are to spread on the Tea Table, for nobody breakfasts here on the naked Table, but on the Cloth set a large Tea Board with the Cups." [45] Some of the 18th-century paintings depicting tea tables with cloths do deal with the morning hours, as indicated by their titles or internal evidence, as in *The Honeymoon* (fig. 9) painted by John Collett about 1760. In this scene of domestic confusion and bliss, a tray or teaboard has been placed on the cloth, illustrating Franklin's comment about English breakfast habits. Cloths may also be seen in pictures in which the time of day cannot be determined. Therefore, the use of a cloth at teatime may in truth have depended upon the hostess's whim if not her pocketbook.

In addition, trays or teaboards of various sizes and shapes were sometimes used. They were usually circular or rectangular in form, occasionally of shaped or scalloped outline. Some trays were supported

---

[44] Fithian, *op. cit.* (footnote 14), p. 193.

[45] Benjamin Franklin, letter to Mrs. Deborah Franklin, dated February 19, 1758, London. *The Writings of Benjamin Franklin*, edited by Albert Henry Smyth, New York, 1905, vol. 3, p. 432.

Figure 11.—Silver tea set consisting of teapot, sugar bowl, container for cream or milk, and waste bowl, made by John McMullin, of Philadelphia, about 1800. Matching coffee and hot water pot made by Samuel Williamson, also of Philadelphia. The letter "G," in fashionable script, is engraved on each piece. (*USNM 37809; Smithsonian photo 45541*.)

upon low feet; others had pierced or fretwork galleries or edges to prevent the utensils from slipping off. Wood or metal was the usual material, although ceramic trays were also used. At large gatherings a tray was often employed for passing refreshments (fig. 4). "A servant brings in on a silver tray the cups, the sugar bowl, the cream jugs, pats of butter, and smoked meat, which are offered to each individual," explained Ferdinand Bayard.[46] The principal use of the tray was, of course, to bring the tea equipage to the table. Whether placed on a bare or covered table, it arrived with the various pieces such as cups and saucers, spoons, containers for sugar and cream or milk, tongs, bowls, and dishes arranged about the teapot.

Such tea furnishings of ceramic were sold in sets; that is, all pieces being of the same pattern. Newspaper advertisements in the 1730's specifically mention "Tea Setts," and later in the century ceramic imports continue to include "beautiful compleat Tea-Setts" (fig. 10). In the early 18th century, tea sets of silver were uncommon if not actually unique, though pieces were occasionally made to match existing items, and, in this way, a so-called set similar to the pieces seen in *Tea Party in the Time of George I* (fig. 5) could be formed. However, by the latter part of the century the wealthier hostesses were able to purchase from among a "most elegant assortment of Silver Plate . . . compleat Tea and Coffee services, plain and rich engraved." [47] When of metal, tea sets (fig. 11) usually consisted of a teapot, containers for sugar and cream or milk, and possibly a slop bowl, while ceramic sets, such as the one seen in *Family Group* (fig. 1), included cups and saucers as well.

[46] Bayard, *op. cit.* (footnote 36), quoted in Sherrill, *op. cit.* (footnote 8), p. 93.

[47] *Boston Gazette*, April 25, 1737; *Boston News-Letter*, June 24, 1762; *The New-York Gazette*, January 8, 1799. These and other newspaper references have been taken variously from the following sources: George Francis Dow, *The Arts and Crafts in New England, 1704–1775*, Topsfield, Massachusetts, 1927; Rita Susswein Gottesman, *The Arts and Crafts in New York, 1726–1776*, New York, 1938, and *The Arts and Crafts in New York, 1777–1799*, New York, 1954; and Alfred Coxe Prime, *The Arts and Crafts in Philadelphia, Maryland, and South Carolina, 1721–1785*, Topsfield, Massachusetts, 1929.

While the tea set illustrated in *Family Group* appears to have all the basic pieces, it can hardly be considered a "complete" tea set when compared with the following porcelain sets listed in the 1747 inventory of James Pemberton of Boston:

One sett Burnt [china] Cont[aining]12 Cups & Saucers   Slop Bowl   Tea Pot   Milk Pot boat [for spoons]   tea Cannister   Sugar Dish 5 Handle Cups   plate for the Tea Pot & a wh[i]t[e] Tea Pot   Value } [£]20

One set Blue & white do. contg. 12 Cups & saucers   Slop Bowl   2 plates   Sugr. Dish Tea Pot   6 Handle Cups & white tea Pot Value } [£]10

In addition, the Pemberton inventory lists a silver tea pot and "1 pr. Tea Tongs & Strainer," items that were undoubtedly used with the ceramic sets.[48]

Tea sets were even available for the youngest hostess, and the "several compleat Tea-table Sets of Children's cream-colored [ceramic] Toys" mentioned in a Boston advertisement of 1771 no doubt added a note of luxury to make-believe tea parties during playtime.[49] The pieces in children's tea sets, such as the ones pictured from a child's set of Chinese export porcelain (fig. 6), usually were like those of regular sets and differed only in size. Little Miss Livingston must have been happy, indeed, when her uncle wrote [50] that he had sent

. . . a compleat tea-apparatus for her Baby [doll]. Her Doll may now invite her Cousins Doll to tea, & parade her teatable in form. This must be no small gratification to her. It would be fortunate if happiness were always attainable with equal ease.

The pieces of tea equipage could be purchased individually. For instance, teacups and saucers, which are differentiated in advertisements from both coffee and chocolate cups, regularly appear in lists of ceramic wares offered for sale, such as "very handsome Setts of blue and white China Tea-Cups and Saucers," or "enamell'd, pencill'd and gilt (fig. 12), red and white, blue and white, enamell'd and scallop'd (fig. 13), teacups and saucers." [51] These adjectives used by 18th-

Figure 12.—Cup and saucer of Chinese export porcelain with scalloped edges and fluting. The painted decoration of black floral design on the side of the cup is touched with gold; the borders are of intersecting black vines and ribbons. (*USNM 284499; Smithsonian photo 45141–D.*)

century salesmen usually referred to the types and the colors of the decorations that were painted on the pieces. "Enameled" most likely meant that the decorations were painted over the glaze, and "penciled" may have implied motifs painted with a fine black line of pencil-like appearance, while "gilt," "red and white," and "blue and white" were the colors and types of the decoration. Blue and white china was, perhaps, the most popular type of teaware, for it regularly appears in newspaper advertisements and inventories and among sherds from colonial sites (fig. 7).

Concerning tea, the Abbé Robin went so far as to say that "there is not a single person to be found, who does not drink it out of china cups and saucers." [52] However exaggerated the statement may be, it does reflect the popularity and availability of Chinese export porcelain in the post-Revolutionary period when Americans were at last free to engage in direct trade with

[48] Suffolk County Record Books, vol. 39, p. 499, inventory of James Pemberton, Boston, April 8, 1747.

[49] *Boston News-Letter*, November 28, 1771.

[50] Shippen, *op. cit.* (footnote 21), p. 215.

[51] *Boston News-Letter*, October 4, 1750; *Maryland Journal*, November 20, 1781.

[52] Robin, *op. cit.* (footnote 1), p. 23.

Figure 13.—Hand-painted Staffordshire creamware teacup excavated at the site of a probable 18th-century and early 19th-century china shop in Newburyport, Massachusetts. Decoration consists of a brown band above a vine border with green leaves and blue berries over orange bellflowers. The spiral fluting on the body and the slight scalloping on the edge of this cup are almost identical with that on the cup held by Mrs. Calmes in figure 15. (*USNM 397177–B; Smithsonian photo 45141–C.*)

the Orient. Porcelain for the American market was made in a wide variety of forms, as well as in complete dinner and tea sets, and was often decorated to special order. Handpainted monograms, insignia of various kinds, and patriotic motifs were especially popular. A tea set decorated in this way was sent to Dr. David Townsend of Boston, a member of the Society of the Cincinnati, by a fellow member of the Society, Maj. Samuel Shaw, American consul at Canton. In a a letter to Townsend from Canton, China, dated December 20, 1790, Shaw wrote:

Accept, my dear friend, as a mark of my esteem and affection, a tea set of porcelain, ornamented with the Cincinnati and your cypher. I hope shortly after its arrival to be with you, and in company with your amiable partner, see whether a little good tea improves or loses any part of its flavor in passing from one hemisphere to the other.

Appended to the letter was the following inventory,[53] which provides us with a list of the pieces deemed essential for a fashionably set tea table:

> 2 tea pots & stands
> Sugar bowl & do
> Milk ewer
> Bowl & dish
> 6 breakfast cups & saucers
> 12 afternoon do

Porcelain, however, had long been a part of China-trade cargos to Europe and from there to America. The early shipments of tea had included such appropriate vessels for the storage, brewing, and drinking of the herb as tea jars, teapots, and teacups. The latter were small porcelain bowls without handles, a form which the Europeans and Americans adopted and continued to use throughout the 18th century for tea, in contrast to the deeper and somewhat narrower cups, usually with handles, in which chocolate and coffee were served. Even after Europeans learned to manufacture porcelain early in the 18th century, the ware continued to be imported from China in large quantities and was called by English-speaking people, "china" from its country of origin. Porcelain also was referred to as "India china ware," after the English and continental East India Companies, the original traders and importers of the ware. "Burnt china" was another term used in the 18th century to differentiate porcelain from pottery.

Whatever the ware, the teacups and saucers, whether on a tray, the cloth, or a bare table, were usually arranged in an orderly manner about the teapot, generally in rows on a rectangular table or tray and in a circle on a round table or tray. In the English conversation piece painting titled *Mr. and Mrs. Hill in Their Drawing Room*, by Arthur Devis about 1750, the circular tripod tea table between the couple and in front of the fireplace is set in such a way. The handleless teacups on saucers are neatly arranged in a large semicircle around the rotund teapot in the center that is flanked on one side by a bowl and on the other by a jug for milk or cream and a sugar container. Generally, cups and saucers were not piled one upon the other but spread out on the table

---

[53] W. Stephen Thomas, "Major Samuel Shaw and the Cincinnati Porcelain," *Antiques*, May 1935, vol. 27, p. 178. The letter and tea set are exhibited at Deerfield, Massachusetts, by the Heritage Foundation.

THE OLD MAID

The Lady here you see display'd,
By some is still'd an ancient maid,
But if her inward thoughts you'd view,
She thinks herself as young as you,
Oh! Puss forbear to lick the cream,
Your Mistress longs to do the same.

Pub.ᵈ Nov.ʳ 12 1777. by J. Walker. N.ᵒ 13. Parliament Street.

Figure 14.—*The Old Maid*, an English cartoon published in 1777. In Print and Photograph Division, Library of Congress. Although the Englishwoman apparently is defying established tea etiquette by drinking from a saucer and allowing the cat on the table, her tea furnishings appear to be in proper order. The teapot is on a dish and the teakettle is on its own special stand, a smaller version of the tripod tea table.

or tray where they were filled with tea and then passed to each guest.

Pictures show male and female guests holding both cup and saucer or just the cup. An English satirical print, *The Old Maid* (fig. 14), published in 1777, was the only illustration found that depicted an individual using a dish for tea, or, to be exact, a saucer. In the 18th century a dish of tea was in

Figure 15.—*Mrs. Calmes*, by G. Frymeier, 1806. In Calmes-Wright-Johnson Collection, Chicago Historical Society. The cup and saucer (or bowl), possibly hand-decorated Staffordshire ware or Chinese export porcelain, are decorated with dark blue bands and dots, wavy brown band, and a pink rose with green foliage. (*Photo courtesy of Chicago Historical Society.*)

reality a cup of tea, for the word "dish" meant a cup or vessel used for drinking as well as a utensil to hold food at meals. A play on this word is evident in the following exchange reported by Philip Fithian between himself and Mrs. Carter, the mistress of Nomini Hall, one October forenoon in 1773: "Shall I help you, Mr. Fithian, to a Dish of Coffee?—I choose a deep Plate, if you please

Figure 16.—Silver tongs in the rococo style, made by Jacob Hurd, of Boston, about 1750.
(*USNM 383530; Smithsonian photo 45141.*)

Ma'am, & Milk." [54] The above suggests that the practice of saucer sipping, while it may have been common among the general public, was frowned upon by polite society. The fact that Americans preferred and were "accustomed to eat everything hot" further explains why tea generally was drunk from the cup instead of the saucer. According to Peter Kalm, "when the English women [that is, of English descent] drank tea, they never poured it out of the cup into the saucer to cool it, but drank it as hot as it came from the teapot." [55] Later in the century another naturalist, C. F. Volney, also noted that "very hot tea" was "beloved by Americans of English descent." [56] From this it would appear that "dish of tea" was an expression rather than a way of drinking tea in the 18th century. On the table a saucer seems always to have been placed under the cup whether the cup was right side up or upside down.

Teaspoons, when in use, might be placed on the saucer or left in the cups. The portrait titled *Mrs. Calmes* (fig. 15), painted by G. Frymeier in 1806, indicates that handling a cup with the spoon in it could be accomplished with a certain amount of grace. Teaspoons also were placed in a pile on the table or in a

silver "Boat for Tea Spoons," or more often in such ceramic containers as "Delph Ware . . . Spoon Trays," or blue-and-white or penciled china "spoon boats." [57]

Tongs were especially suited for lifting the lumps of sugar from their container to the teacup. During the 18th century both arched and scissor type tongs were used. Instead of points, the latter had dainty flat grips for holding a lump of sugar (fig. 16). The early arched tongs were round in section, as are the pair illustrated in *Tea Party in the Time of George I* (fig. 5), while tongs made by arching or bending double a flat strip of silver (fig. 17) date from the second half of the 18th century. These articles of tea equipage, variously known as "tongs," "tea tongs," "spring tea tongs," and "sugar tongs," were usually made of silver, though "ivory and wooden tea-tongs" were advertised in 1763. [58] According to the prints and paintings of the period, tongs were placed in or near the sugar container. Teaspoons were also used for sugar, as illustrated in the painting *Susanna Truax* (fig. 2). Perhaps young Miss Truax is about to indulge in a custom favored by the Dutch population of

[54] Fithian, *op. cit.* (footnote 14), p. 133.

[55] Kalm, *op. cit.* (footnote 7), vol. 1, p. 191.

[56] C. F. Volney, *Tableau du Climat et du Sol des Etats-Unis,* Paris, 1803, quoted in Sherrill, *op. cit.* (footnote 8), p. 95.

[57] *Boston News-Letter*, March 24, 1774, November 18, 1742, and April 4, 1771; *New-York Journal*, August 3, 1775.

[58] *New-York Gazette*, April 3, 1727; *Boston Gazette*, June 4, 1759; *Boston News-Letter*, January 9, 1772; *Maryland Gazette*, May 13, 1773; *Pennsylvania Journal*, December 15, 1763.

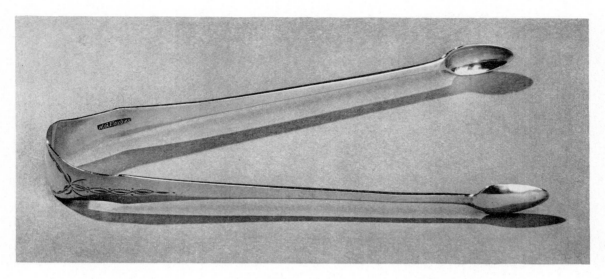

Figure 17.—Silver tongs made by William G. Forbes, of New York, about 1790. In the United States National Museum. The engraved decoration of intersecting lines is typical of the neoclassic style. A variant of this motif appears as the painted border on a porcelain cup and saucer of the same period (fig. 12). (*USNM59.474; Smithsonian photo 45141–A.*)

Albany as reported by Peter Kalm in 1749: "They never put sugar into the cup, but take a small bit of it into their mouths while they drink." [59]

Shallow dishes, such as the one seen in the portrait *Susanna Truax*, and hemispherical bowls were used as containers for sugar. Often called "sugar dishes" or just "sugars," they were available in delftware, glass (fig. 18), and silver as well as in blue-and-white, burnt, enameled, and penciled china. Some containers were sold with covers, and it has been suggested that the saucer-shaped cover of the hemispherical sugar dish or bowl, fashionable in the first half of the 18th century, also served as a spoon tray. However, in the painting *Tea Party in the Time of George I* (fig. 5) the cover is leaning against the bowl and the spoons are in an oval spoon tray or boat. Another possibility, if the lid was multipurpose, is that it was used as a dish or stand under the teapot to protect the table top. Silver sugar boxes, basins, and plated sugar baskets were other forms used to hold sugar,[60] which,

in whatever container, was a commodity important to the Americans. As Moreau de St. Méry noted, they "use great quantities in their tea." [61]

Containers for cream or milk may be seen in many of the 18th-century teatime pictures and are found in the advertisements of the period under a variety of names. There were cream pots of glass and pewter and silver (figs. 19 and 20), jugs of penciled and burnt china, and in the 1770's one could obtain "enameled and plain three footed cream jugs" from Mr. Henry William Stiegel's glass factory at Manheim, Pennsylvania. There were cream pails, urns, and ewers of silver plate, and plated cream basins "gilt inside." [62] Milk pots, used on some tea tables instead of cream containers, were available in silver, pewter, ceramic, and "sprig'd, cut and moulded" glass.[63] Although contemporary diarists and observers of American customs seem not to have noticed whether cream was

[59] Kalm, *op. cit.* (footnote 7), vol. 1, p. 347.

[60] *Boston News-Letter*, April 4, 1771, November 18, 1742, and January 9, 1772; *New-York Gazette*, February 14, 1757; *Pennsylvania Gazette*, January 25, 1759; *Rivington's New York Gazeteer*, January 13, 1774; *New-York Journal*, August 3, 1775; *Boston Gazette*, September 11, 1758; *New-York Daily Advertiser*, January 21, 1797.

[61] Moreau de Saint-Méry, *op. cit.* (footnote 17), p. 38.

[62] *New-York Gazette*, February 14, 1757; *Boston Gazette*, May 14, 1764; *Maryland Gazette*, January 4, 1759; *New-York Journal*, August 3, 1775; *Pennsylvania Gazette*, July 6, 1772, and October 31, 1781; *Boston News-Letter*, April 4, 1771, and January 9, 1772; *New-York Daily Advertiser*, January 21, 1797.

[63] *New-York Mercury*, October 30, 1758; *Pennsylvania Journal*, April 25, 1765; *Boston News-Letter*, January 17, 1745; *New-York Gazette*, December 6, 1771.

Figure 18.—Stiegel-type, cobalt-blue glass sugar dish with cover, made about 1770. (*USNM 38922; Smithsonian photo 42133–D.*)

ished, the remaining tea and dregs were emptied into the slop bowl. Then the cup might be rinsed with hot water and the rinsing water discarded in the bowl. The slop basin may also have been the receptacle for the mote or foreign particles—then inherent in tea but now extracted by mechanical means—that had to be skimmed off the beverage in the cup. In England this was probably done with a small utensil known to present day collectors as a mote spoon or mote skimmer. Although the exact purpose of these spoons remains unsettled, it seems likely that they were used with tea. It has been suggested that the perforated bowl of the spoon was used for skimming foreign particles off the tea in the cup and the tapering spike-end stem to clear the clogged-up strainer of the teapot spout. The almost complete absence of American-made mote spoons suggests that these particular utensils were seldom used here. Possibly the "skimmer" advertised in 1727 with other silver tea

served cold and milk hot, or if tea drinkers were given a choice between cream and milk, the Prince de Broglie's comment already cited concerning his ability to drink "excellent tea with even better cream" and the predominance of cream over milk containers in 18th-century advertisements would seem to indicate that in this country cream rather than milk was served with tea in the afternoon.

While the Americans, as the Europeans, added cream or milk and sugar to their tea, the use of lemon with the beverage is questionable. Nowhere is there any indication that the citrus fruit was served or used with tea in 18th-century America. Punch seems to have been the drink with which lemons were associated.

Often a medium-sized bowl, usually hemispherical in shape, is to be seen on the tea table, and it is most likely a slop bowl or basin. According to advertisements these bowls and basins were available in silver, pewter, and ceramic.[64] Before a teacup was replen-

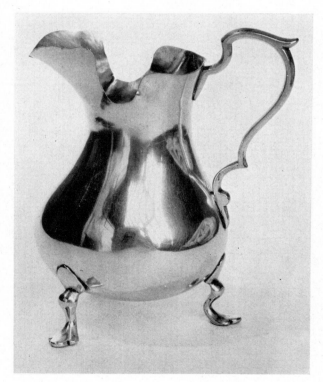

Figure 19.—Silver creamer made by Myer Myers, of New York, about 1750. The fanciful curves of the handle and feet are related to the rococo design of the sugar tongs in figure 16. (*USNM 383553; Smithsonian photo 45141–F.*)

---

[64] *Pennsylvania Gazette*, January 25, 1759; *Pennsylvania Journal*, April 25, 1765; *Independent Journal* [New York], July 23, 1785.

pieces was such a spoon.[65] No doubt, tea strainers (fig. 21) were also used to insure clear tea. The tea dregs might then be discarded in the slop bowl or left in the strainer and the strainer rested on the bowl. However, only a few contemporary American advertisements and inventories have been found which mention tea strainers.[66] Punch strainers, though generally larger in size, seem to have doubled as tea strainers in some households. The 1757 inventory of

---

[65] *New-York Gazette*, April 3, 1727.

[66] *Maryland Gazette*, January 4, 1759; *Pennsylvania Chronicle*, January 29, 1770; Suffolk County Record Books, vol. 52, p. 324, inventory of John Procter, May 13, 1757.

Figure 20.—Silver creamer made by Simeon A. Bayley, of New York, about 1790. The only ornamentation is the engraving of the initials "R M" below the pouring lip. (*USNM 383465; Smithsonian photo 45141–E.*)

Figure 21.—Silver strainer made by James Butler, of Boston, about 1750. The handle's pierced pattern of delicate, curled vines distinguishes this otherwise plain strainer. (*USNM 383485; Smithsonian photo 44828–J.*)

Charles Bockwell of Boston includes a punch strainer which is listed not with the wine glasses and other pieces associated with punch but with the tea items: "1 Small Do. [china] Milk Pot 1 Tea Pot 6 Cups & 3 Saucers & 1 Punch Strainer." [67] Presumably, the strainer had last been used for tea.

The teapot was, of course, the very center of the social custom of drinking tea; so, it usually was found in the center of the tray or table. At first, only teapots of Oriental origin imported with the cargos of tea were available, for the teapot had been unknown to Europeans before the introduction of the beverage. However, as tea gained acceptance as a social drink and the demand for equipage increased, local craftsmen were stimulated to produce wares that could compete with the Chinese imports. Teapots based on Chinese models and often decorated with Chinese

---

[67] Suffolk County Record Books, vol. 52, p. 327, inventory of Revd. Charles Brockwell, May 13, 1757.

motifs were fashioned in ceramic and silver. No doubt many an 18th-century hostess desired a silver teapot to grace her table and add an elegant air to the tea ceremony. A lottery offering one must have raised many a hope, especially if, as an advertisement of 1727 announced, the "highest Prize consists of an Eight Square Tea-Pot," as well as "six Tea-Spoons, Skimmer and Tongs." By the end of the century "an elegant silver tea-pot with an ornamental lid, resembling a Pine-apple" would have been the wish of a fashion-conscious hostess. Less expensive than silver, but just as stylish according to the merchants' advertisements were "newest fashion teapots" of pewter or, in the late 18th century, Britannia metal teapots. The latest mode in ceramic ware also was to be found upon the tea table. In the mid-18th century it was "English brown China Tea-Pots of Sorts, with a rais'd Flower" (probably the ceramic with a deep, rich brown glaze known today as Jackfield-type ware), "black," "green and Tortois" (a pottery glazed with varigated colors in imitation of tortoise shell), and "Enameled Stone" teapots. At the time of the American Revolution, teaware imports included "Egyptian, Etruscan, embossed red China, agate, green, black, colliflower, white, and blue and white stone enamelled, striped, fluted, pierced and plain Queen's ware tea pots." [68]

Sometimes the teapot, whether ceramic, pewter, or silver, was placed upon a dish or small, tile-like stand with feet. These teapot stands served as insulation by protecting the surface of the table or tray from the damaging heat of the teapot. Stands often were included in tea sets but also were sold individually, such as the "Pencil'd China . . . tea pot stands," advertised in 1775, and the "teapot stands" of "best London plated ware" imported in 1797.[69] The stands must have been especially useful when silver equipage was set on a bare table top; many of the silver teapots of elliptical shape with a flat base, so popular in the latter part of the 18th century, had matching stands raised on short legs to protect the table from the expanse of hot metal. On occasion

the teapot was placed on a spirit lamp or burner to keep the beverage warm.

In most instances it was the hot water kettle that sat upon a spirit lamp or burner rather than a teapot. Kettles were usually related to the form of contemporary teapots, but differed in having a swing handle on top and a large, rather flat base that could be placed over the flame. Advertisements mention teakettles of copper, pewter, brass, and silver, some "with lamps and stands." [70] The actual making of tea was part of the ceremony and was usually done by the hostess at the tea table. This necessitated a ready supply of boiling water close at hand to properly infuse the tea and, as Ferdinand Bayard reported, it also "weakens the tea or serves to clean up the cups." [71] Thus, the kettle and burner on their own individual table or stand were placed within easy reach of the tea table. According to 18th-century pictures the kettle was an important part of the tea setting, but it seldom appeared on the tea table. Special stands for kettles generally were made in the same form as the tea tables, though smaller in scale (fig. 14). The square stands often had a slide on which to place the teapot when the hot water was poured into it.

Both pictures and advertisements reveal that by the 1770's the tea urn was a new form appearing at teatime in place of the hot water kettle. Contrary to its name, the tea urn seldom held tea. These large silver or silver-plated vessels, some of which looked like vases with domed covers, usually had two handles on the shoulders and a spout with a tap in the front near the bottom. "Ponty pool, japanned, crimson, and gold-striped Roman tea urns" imported from Europe were among the fashionable teawares advertised at the end of the 18th century.[72] The urn might be placed on a stand of its own near the table or on the tray or table in the midst of the other equipage as it is in the painting titled *The Honeymoon* (fig. 9). Wherever placed, it signified the newest mode in teatime furnishings. One Baltimorean, O. H. Williams, in a letter dated April 12, 1786, to a close friend, enthusiastically explained that "Tea

---

[68] Quotations variously from *New-York Gazette*, April 3, 1727, August 2, 1762; *Commercial Advertiser* [New York], Oct. 10, 1797; *Boston Gazette*, July 26, 1756; *New-York Daily Advertiser*, May 7, 1793; *Boston News-Letter*, October 18, 1750; *Pennsylvania Evening Post*, July 11, 1776.

[69] *New-York Journal*, August 3, 1775; *New-York Daily Advertiser*, January 21, 1797.

[70] *Pennsylvania Packet*, May 29, 1775; *American Weekly Mercury* [Philadelphia], January 1736; *Boston Gazette*, May 3, 1751, and September 11, 1758; *Pennsylvania Journal*, August 1, 1771.

[71] Bayard, *op. cit.* (footnote 36), quoted in Sherrill, *op. cit.* (footnote 8), p.92.

[72] *New-York Daily Advertiser*, May 7, 1793.

& Coffee Urns plated (mine are but partially plated and are extremely neat) are the genteelest things of the sort used now at any House & tables inferior to the first fortunes." [73]

The tea canister (fig. 22), a storage container for the dry tea leaves, was yet another piece of equipment to be found on the table or tray. Ceramic canisters of blue and white, and red and gold, could be purchased to match other tea furnishings of the same ware, and silver tea canisters often were fashioned to harmonize with the silver teapots of the period. Individual canisters were produced, as well as canisters in sets of two or three. A set of canisters usually was kept in the box in which it came, a case known as a tea chest or tea caddy, such as the "elegant assortment of Tea-caddies, with one, two and three canisters" advertised in 1796.[74] Canister tops if dome-shaped were used to measure out the tea and transfer it to the teapot. Otherwise, small, short-handled spoons with broad, shallow bowls known as caddy spoons and caddy ladles were used. However handled, the tea could have been any one of the numerous kinds available in the 18th century. Although Hyson, Soughong, and Congo, the names inscribed on the canister in figure 22, may have been favored, there were many other types of tea, as the following advertisement from the *Boston News-Letter* of September 16, 1736, indicates:[75]

To be Sold . . . at the Three Sugar Loaves, and Cannister . . . very choice Teas, viz: Bohea Tea from 22 s. to 28 s. per Pound, Congou Tea, 34 s. Pekoe Tea, 50 s. per Pound, Green Tea from 20 s. to 30 s. per Pound, fine Imperial Tea from 40 s. to 60 s. per Pound.

In the 18th century tea drinking was an established social custom with a recognized etiquette and distinctive equipage as we know from the pictures and writings of the period. At teatime men and women gathered to pursue leisurely conversations and enjoy the sociability of the home.

A study of *An English Family at Tea* (frontispiece) will summarize the etiquette and equipage of the ritual—

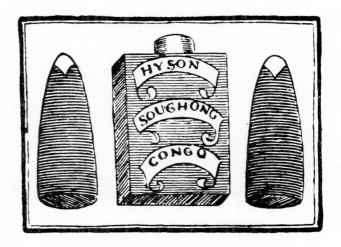

Figure 22.—The sign of "The Tea Canister and Two Sugar Loaves" used by a New York grocer and confectioner in the 1770's. Other "tea" motifs for shop signs in the 18th century included "The Teapot," used by a Philadelphia goldsmith in 1757, and "The Tea Kettle and Stand," which marked the shop of a Charleston jeweller in 1766.

On the floor near the table is a caddy with the top open, showing one canister of a pair. The mistress of the house, seated at the tea table, is measuring out dry tea leaves from the other canister into its lid. Members of the family stand or sit about the square tea table while they observe this first step in the ceremony. A maidservant stands ready with the hot water kettle to pour the boiling water over the leaves once they are in the teapot. In the background is the tripod kettle stand with a lamp, where the kettle will be placed until needed to rinse the cups or dilute the tea.

Not seen in this detail of the painting is the entry of a male servant who is carrying a tall silver pot, which may have contained chocolate or coffee. These two other social beverages of the 18th century were served in cups of a deep cylindrical shape, like the three seen on the end of the table. The shallow, bowl-shaped, handleless teacups and the saucers are arranged in a neat row along one side of the table. The teapot rests on a square tile-like stand or dish that protects the table from the heat. Nearby is a bowl to receive tea dregs, a pot for cream or milk, and a sugar bowl.

The teatime ritual has begun.

[73] Letter from O[tho] Holland Williams to Dr. Philip Thomas, April 12, 1786, Williams Papers, vol. 4, letter no. 320. Manuscript, Maryland Historical Society, Baltimore, Maryland.

[74] *Boston News-Letter*, April 4, 1771; *Pennsylvania Gazette*, October 31, 1781; *Minerva, & Mercantile Evening Advertiser* [New York], August 4, 1796.

[75] *Boston News-Letter*, September 16, 1736.

CHRONOLOGICAL LIST OF PICTURES CONSULTED

1700 ca. *Portrait Group of Gentlemen and a Child.* Believed to be English or Dutch. Reproduced in Ralph Edwards, *Early Conversation Pictures from the Middle Ages to about 1730*, London, 1954, p. 117, no. 73.

1710 ca. *The Tea-Table.* English. Reproduced in *The Connoisseur Period Guides: The Stuart Period, 1603–1714*, edited by Ralph Edwards and L. G. G. Ramsey, New York, 1957, p. 30.

1720 ca. *A Family Taking Tea.* English. Reproduced in Edwards, *Early Conversation Pictures*, p. 132, no. 95.

Two Ladies and a Gentleman at Tea. Attributed to Nicolaas Verkolje, Dutch. Reproduced in Edwards, *Early Conversation Pictures*, p. 96, no. 42.

An English Family at Tea (frontispiece). Joseph Van Aken(?). Reproduced in Percy Macquoid and Ralph Edwards, *The Dictionary of English Furniture*, revised and enlarged by Ralph Edwards, London, 1954, vol. 1, p. 10, fig. 16.

1725 ca. *Tea Party in the Time of George I* (fig. 5). English. Reproduced in *Antiques*, November 1955, vol. 68, p. vi following p. 460.

1730 ca. *The Assembly at Wanstead House.* By William Hogarth, English. Reproduced in Edwards, *Early Conversation Pictures*, p. 125, no. 87.

Family. By William Hogarth, English. Reproduced in R. H. Wilenski, *English Painting*, London, 1933, pl. 11a.

Family Group (fig. 1). By Gawen Hamilton, English. Reproduced in *Antiques*, March 1953, vol. 63, p. 270.

A Family Party. By William Hogarth, English. Reproduced in *English Conversation Pictures of the Eighteenth and Early Nineteenth Century*, edited by G. C. Williamson, London, 1931, pl. 10.

1730 *Susanna Truax* (fig. 2). American. Reproduced in *Art in America*, May 1954, vol. 42, p. 101.

The Wollaston Family. By William Hogarth, English. Reproduced in Edwards, *Early Conversation Pictures*, p. 126, no. 88.

1731 Painting on lobed, square delft tea tray. Dutch. Reproduced in C. H. De Jonge, *Oud-Nederlandsche Majolica en Delftsch Aardewerk*, Amsterdam, 1947, p. 241, fig. 209.

1732 *A Tea Party at the Countess of Portland's.* By Charles Philips, English. Reproduced in Edwards, *Early Conversation Pictures*, p. 132, no. 94.

Thomas Wentworth, Earl of Strafford, with His Family. By Gawen Hamilton, English. Reproduced in Edwards, *Early Conversation Pictures*, p. 130, no. 92.

1735 ca. *The Western Family.* By William Hogarth, English. Reproduced in Sacheverell Sitwell, *Conversation Pieces*, New York, 1937, no. 14.

1736 ca. *The Strode Family.* By William Hogarth, English. Reproduced in Oliver Brackett, *English Furniture Illustrated*, New York, 1950, p. 168, pl. 140.

1740 ca. *The Carter Family.* By Joseph Highmore, English. Reproduced in *Connoisseur*, Christmas 1934, vol. 94, p. xlv (advertisement).

1743 Painting on lobed, circular Bristol delft tea tray. English. Reproduced in F. H. Garner, *English Delftware*, New York, 1948, pl. 54.

1744 ca. *Burkat Shudi and His Family.* English. Reproduced in Philip James, *Early Keyboard Instruments from Their Beginnings to the Year 1820*, New York, 1930, pl. 48.

1744 *Shortly after Marriage*, from *Marriage a la Mode* series. By William Hogarth, English. Reproduced in *Masterpieces of English Painting*, Chicago, 1946, pl. 3.

1745 ca. *The Gascoigne Family.* By Francis Hayman, English. Reproduced in *Apollo*, October 1957, vol. 66, p. vii (advertisement).

1750 ca. *Mr. and Mrs. Hill in Their Drawing Room.* By Arthur Devis, English. Reproduced in *The Antique Collector*, June 1957, vol. 28, p. 100.

1760 ca. *The Honeymoon* (fig. 9). By John Collett, English. Photograph courtesy of Frick Art Reference Library, New York.

1765 ca. *Paul Revere.* By John Singleton Copley, American. Reproduced in John Marshall Phillips, *American Silver*, New York, 1949, frontispiece.

1770 ca. *Lord Willoughby and Family.* By John Zoffany, English. Reproduced in Lady Victoria Manners and Dr. G. C. Williamson, *John Zoffany, R. A.*, London, 1920, plate preceding p. 153.

Mr. and Mrs. Garrick at Tea. By John Zoffany, English. Reproduced in Manners and Williamson, *John Zoffany, R. A.*, plate facing p. 142.

Sir John Hopkins and Family. By John Zoffany, English. Reproduced in Manners and Williamson, *John Zoffany, R. A.*, second plate following p. 18.

The Squire's Tea. By Benjamin Wilson, English. Reproduced in *Antiques*, October 1951, vol. 60, p. 310.

1775 *A Society of Patriotic Ladies* (fig. 3). Engraving published by R. Sayer and J. Bennet, London. Print and Photograph Division, Library of Congress.

1777 *The Old Maid* (fig. 14). English. Print and Photograph Division, Library of Congress.

1780 ca. *The Tea Party.* By William Hamilton, English. Reproduced in *Art in America*, May 1954, vol. 42, p. 91 (advertisement).

1782 *Conversazioni* (fig. 4). By W. H. Bunbury, English. Print and Photograph Division, Library of Congress.

1785 ca. *The Auriol Family* [*in India*]. By John Zoffany, English. Reproduced in Manners and Williamson, *John Zoffany, R. A.*, plate facing p. 110.

1786 *Dr. Johnson Takes Tea at Boswell's House.* By Thomas Rowlandson, English. Reproduced in Charles Cooper, *The English Table in History and Literature*, London, 1929, plate facing p. 150.

1790 ca. *Black Monday or the Departure for School.* Engraved by J. Jones after Bigg, English. Reproduced in *Antiques*, September 1953, vol. 64, p. 163 (advertisement).

1792 *Tea at the Pantheon.* By Edward Edwards, English. Reproduced in William Harrison Ukers, *The Romance of Tea*, New York, 1936, plate facing p. 214.

1806 *Mrs. Calmes* (fig. 15). By G. Frymeier, American. Reproduced in *Antiques*, November 1950, vol. 58, p. 392.

For sale by the Superintendent of Documents, U.S. Government Printing Office
Washington 25, D.C. — Price 40 cents

U.S. GOVERNMENT PRINTING OFFICE. 1961

CONTRIBUTIONS FROM

THE MUSEUM OF HISTORY AND TECHNOLOGY:

PAPER 15

ITALIAN HARPSICHORD-BUILDING

IN THE 16TH AND 17TH CENTURIES

John D. Shortridge

93

Figure 1.—Outer case of Albana harpsichord. (*Smithsonian photo 46794*)

Italian Harpsichord-Building
in the 16th and 17th Centuries

By John D. Shortridge

The making of harpsichords flourished in Italy throughout the 16th and 17th centuries. The Italian instruments were of simpler construction than those built by the North Europeans, and they lacked the familiar second manual and array of stops.

In this paper, typical examples of Italian harpsichords from the Hugo Worch Collection in the United States National Museum are described in detail and illustrated. Also, the author offers an explanation for certain puzzling variations in keyboard ranges and vibrating lengths of strings of the Italian harpsichords.

THE AUTHOR: *John D. Shortridge is associate curator of cultural history in the United States National Museum, Smithsonian Institution.*

PERHAPS the modern tendency to idealize progress has been responsible for the neglect of Italian harpsichords and virginals during the present day revival of interest in old musical instruments. Whatever laudable traits the Italian builders may have had, they cannot be considered to have been progressive. Their instruments of the mid-16th century hardly can be distinguished from those made around 1700. During this 150 years the pioneering Flemish makers added the four-foot register, a second keyboard, and lute and buff stops to their instruments. However, the very fact that the Italian builders were unwilling to change their models suggests that their instruments were good enough to demand no further improvements. Anyone who has heard a properly restored Italian harpsichord or an accurately made reproduction will agree that the tone of such instruments is of exceptional beauty.

This paper consists of a description of the structural features of two typical Italian instruments and a general discussion of the stringing and tuning of Italian harpsichords and virginals that is based on certain measurements of 33 instruments housed in various museums in the United States. To the curators and other staff members of these institutions I express my sincere gratitude for making it possible for me to measure valuable instruments entrusted to their care or for supplying similar information by mail.

The first type of instrument described below usually has been designated in modern books about musical instruments and in catalogs of instrument collections as a spinet, the term virginal being applied to the rectangular instruments having the keyboard along the long side. Since both of these types have basically the same arrangement of keyboard, wrest plank, hitch

Figure 2.—POLYGONAL VIRGINAL IN OUTER CASE. (*Smithsonian photo 46792.*)

pins, strings and jacks, and since both types were known as virginals in 17th-century England, it is logical to reserve the term spinet for another kind of instrument, namely the one with the wrest plank and tuning pins in front over the keyboard, and with the strings stretched diagonally. Such instruments were popular in England in the late 17th and early 18th centuries and were known in English as spinets during the period of their popularity. By using the term polygonal virginal we can distinguish, when necessary, the five-sided Italian model from the rectangular instruments usually produced in northern Europe. Some rectangular virginals were made in Italy; one Flemish polygonal virginal, made by the elder Hans Ruckers in 1591, survives. Long instruments, resembling the grand piano in shape, are called harpsichords. Of course it is understood that both types of virginals as well as the spinet and the harpsichord were keyed chordophones employing the plucking action of jacks and plectra.

Throughout this paper the different octaves are indicated according to the following system:

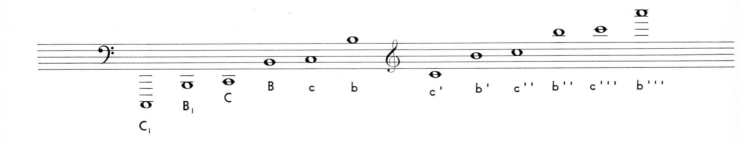

Figure 3.—Polygonal virginal removed from outer case. (*Smithsonian photo MNH 283.*)

The Typical Italian Polygonal Virginal

To give a clear idea of the construction of the Italian polygonal virginal, a detailed description of one particular example is presented here. This virginal is included in the Hugo Worch collection at the U.S. National Museum. The maker's name is not known, but the instrument is believed to have been built around 1600.

As is true of the great majority of Italian virginals and harpsichords of the 16th and 17th centuries, the instrument proper is removable from its outer case. The outer case (fig. 2), of sturdier construction than the virginal which it was designed to protect, is made of wood about ½″ thick and is decorated with paintings of female figures and garlands. The original legs are missing.

Our main interest is in the virginal proper (fig. 3), the construction of which is comparable in some ways to that of the violin. The very thin sides of the virginal are held together at the corners by blocks, and the soundboard is supported by a lining.

The cross section drawing (fig. 4) shows the ⁹⁄₁₆″ thick bottom and the sides which are ⅛″ thick. The lining, ½″ by 1⅛″, runs around four sides of the instrument, the wrest plank replacing it on the fifth side. The soundboard thickness, measured inside the

holes through which the jacks pass, varies from ¹⁄₁₆″ in the bass to ⅛″ in the treble. The manner in which variations in thickness are distributed over the entire soundboard has not been determined. The cross section drawing also shows the beautifully executed mouldings that make the sides appear to be thicker than they really are.

The positions of the knee braces, the shape of which can be seen in figure 4, are shown along either side of the keyboard in figure 5. These braces are ¾″ thick. The positions of the blocks, small pieces with the grain running perpendicular to the bottom, and the wrest plank, which is 1¼″ thick, are also shown. The two ribs are attached to the underside of the soundboard in the positions indicated. The jack guide, built up of separate pieces held together by long strips down either side, is glued to the underside of the soundboard and extends as far as the lining in the treble but stops a little short of it in the bass (fig. 5). The jack guide is ¹⁵⁄₁₆″ thick.

The layout of the soundboard in figure 6 gives the relative positions of the bridges, tuning pins, hitch pins, strings, jacks, and jack rail. There is, of course, one jack and one string per key. The jacks presently in this virginal, not being original, will not be described. Typical Italian jacks will be described later. The bridges are ⁵⁄₁₆″ wide and vary in height from ⁷⁄₁₆″ in the bass to ⅜″ in the treble. A cross

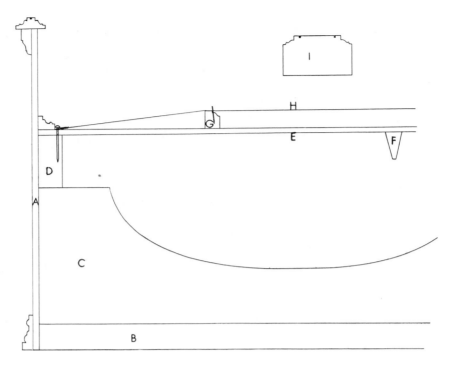

Figure 4.—CROSS SECTION OF POLYGONAL VIRGINAL. A, side; B, bottom; C, knee; D, liner; E, soundboard; F, rib; G, bridge; H, string; I, jack rail. Scale, 1:2.

section of one of the bridges appears in figure 4. The jack rail, also shown in figure 4, extends over the jacks 1⅛″ above the soundboard. It serves not only to prevent the jacks from flying out during play but also to terminate the downward fall of the fronts of the keys. The keys do not drop far enough to touch the key frame, but instead are stopped by the jacks striking the jack rail.

The keyboard has an apparent compass of four octaves and one note from *E* to *f′′′*. Short octave tuning would have extended the compass down a major third to *C* in the bass, with the *E* key sounding *C*, the *F♯* key sounding *D*, the *G♯* key sounding *E*, and the remaining keys sounding their proper pitches. These three keys will hereafter be referred to as *C/E*, *D/F♯* and *E/G♯*.

The lowest eight keys have small wire eyes attached to their undersides near the front. A corresponding slot is cut through the inner and outer cases, allowing the eyes to be connected to a short pedal keyboard which has not survived.

The keys themselves vary in length from 10″ in the bass to 18½″ in the treble; they are mounted on a trapezoidal key frame which is removable from the instrument. The balance rail and balance rail pins are on a diagonal, resulting in a gradual but noticeable change in the touch from one end of the keyboard to the other. The rack, ½″ thick and 1¾″ high, is fastened along the back of the key frame and has one vertical saw cut for each key. Projecting from the back of each key is a small sliver of wood which rides in its proper saw cut and serves to guide the key. The natural keys are veneered with boxwood and have arcaded boxwood fronts. The sharps are small blocks of hardwood stained black.

The sides, soundboard, ribs, jacks, guide, jackrail, and mouldings are made of cypress, the wrest plank and bridges are of walnut, and the framework, bottom, keys, and key frame are of pine.

The photographs (figs. 2, 3) show the decorative use of ivory studs. On the soundboard appears the Latin inscription *Vita brevis, ars longa.* A laminated parchment rose, 3⁵⁄₁₆″ in diameter, is placed in the soundboard in the position indicated in figure 6. A typical example of this decorative device is shown in figure 12.

The above-described virginal is typical of Italian practice. Other examples studied generally have differed from it only in small details, except in the case of compass and vibrating lengths of strings. These factors will be discussed in detail in a following section.

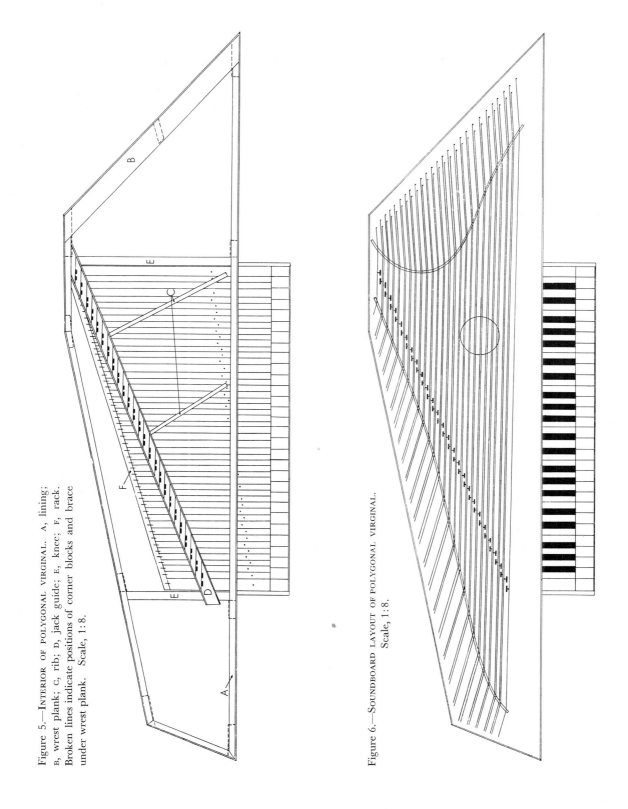

Figure 5.—Interior of polygonal virginal. A, lining; B, wrest plank; C, rib; D, jack guide; E, knee; F, rack. Broken lines indicate positions of corner blocks and brace under wrest plank. Scale, 1:8.

Figure 6.—Soundboard layout of polygonal virginal. Scale, 1:8.

Figure 7.—RIDOLFI HARPSICHORD REMOVED FROM CASE. (*Smithsonian photo MNH 238–A.*)

The Typical Italian Harpsichord

The instrument chosen to illustrate the stylistic features of the Italian harpsichord is also in the collection of the U.S. National Museum. This harpsi-

Figure 8.—CROSS SECTION OF RIDOLFI HARPSICHORD.
A, bottom; B, knee; C, lining; D, soundboard. Scale, 1: 2.

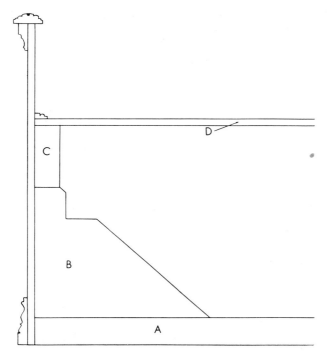

chord, purchased for the Museum in 1892 by Dr. G. Brown Goode, was made in 1665 by Giacomo Ridolfi, who claimed Girolamo Zenti as his teacher. The inscription on the nameboard reads "Jacobus Rodolphus Hieronymi de Zentis Discipulus MDCLXV Facieba."

Like the virginal described above, this harpsichord is separable from its outer case. The outer case rests on a separate stand consisting of three gilt cupids and a floral garland. Since the painted decoration of this case is not original, another outer case, belonging to a harpsichord made by Horatius Albana in 1633, was selected for the illustration (fig. 1).

Two unison strings per key and two registers of jacks are provided. The apparent compass of the keyboard is from C/E to c'''. The remains of pedal connections can be seen on the lowest eight keys.

The sides of the harpsichord are $\frac{5}{32}''$ thick; the bottom is $\frac{9}{16}''$ thick. The sides and lining are supported by knees that do not extend clear across the bottom of the instrument as they do in the virginal.

The knees are small triangular pieces, as shown in figure 8. Since the added tension of the second set of strings demands a somewhat more substantial framework than that employed in the virginal, a series of braces are attached to the floor. These are connected to the lining by several diagonal braces (fig. 9). This produces a remarkably strong but very light structure. The keys (not shown) are of more constant length than those of the virginal; therefore, the touch is much more uniform.

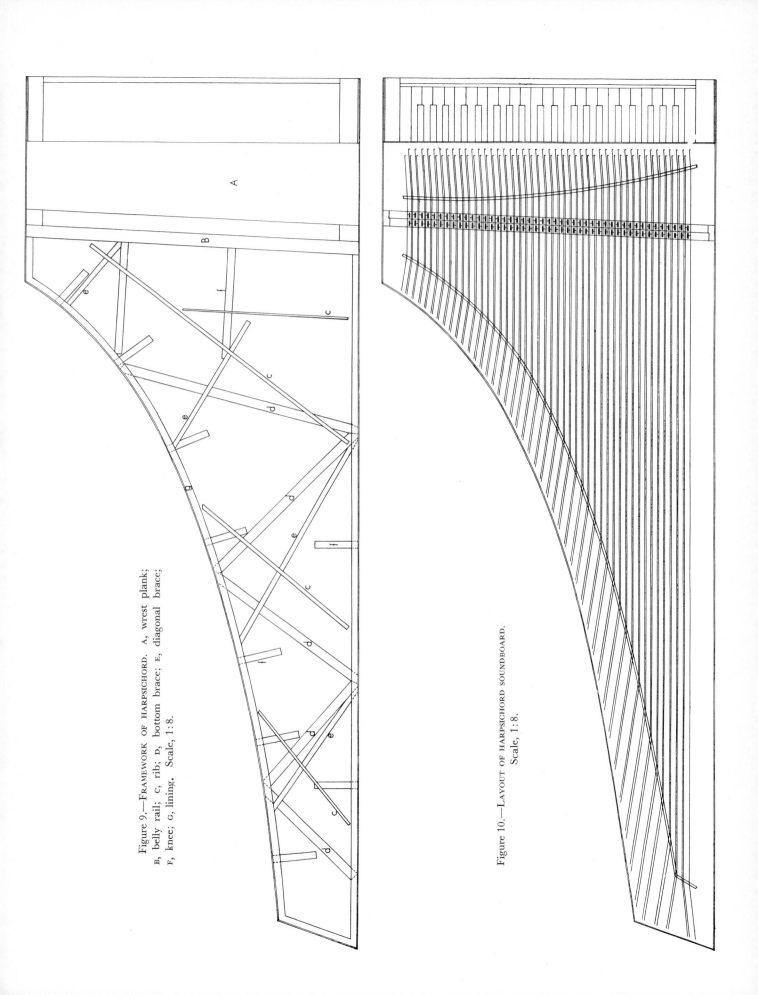

Figure 9.—FRAMEWORK OF HARPSICHORD. A, wrest plank; B, belly rail; C, rib; D, bottom brace; E, diagonal brace; F, knee; G, lining. Scale, 1:8.

Figure 10.—LAYOUT OF HARPSICHORD SOUNDBOARD. Scale, 1:8.

The wrest plank is supported by two end blocks, against which the partition behind the action (called the belly rail) is also placed. The soundboard is glued to the top of the belly rail. The wrest plank is veneered with cypress, giving the appearance that the soundboard extends over it. The jack guides also rest on the end blocks in the space between the wrest plank and the belly rail. Figures 8 and 11 clarify the arrangement of these structural features.

Figure 10 shows the layout of ribs, bridges, and strings on the soundboard. The soundboard is about ⅛″ thick. The bridge on the wrest plank tapers in height from ⅜″ in the treble to $^{7}/_{16}$″ in the bass and in width from $^{5}/_{16}$″ to $^{7}/_{16}$″. The soundboard bridge measures about ⅜″ by ¼″ and has virtually no taper. The soundboard does not have a rose, although that decorative device is fairly common on Italian harpsichords.

The jack guides are built up of spacer blocks held together by thin strips along the sides. There is now no provision for moving the guides, although plugged-up holes visible in the right end of each guide suggest that they originally could be disengaged. In Italian harpsichords generally, the jack guides were controlled by knobs projecting through the sides of the case. Sometimes these harpsichords had levers pivoted on the wrest plank and attached to the guides. The Ridolfi case has not been patched and there are no holes in the wrest plank where levers could have been attached; so, the guides probably were not intended to be movable.

The jacks are simple slips of walnut measuring about $^{3}/_{16}$″ by $^{7}/_{16}$″ by 3⅛″. The arrangement of the tongue, spring, plectrum, and damper are shown in figure 11. The dampers are small pieces of buckskin held in slots at the tops of the jacks. The plectra, perhaps not original, are of leather. Of course, there are no adjusting screws or capstans of any variety.

The direction in which the plectra of each row of jacks should be pointing is not known. Two clavicytheria having two registers of strings and a single row of double tongue jacks have been examined by the author. Each of these jacks has two plectra, one pointing to the right and one to the left. Turning these jacks around does not alter the order of direction. The plectra nearest the keyboard points the same way whether the jack is upside down or not. In the clavicytherium at the Smithsonian Institution the plectra nearest the keyboard points to the player's left. In a clavicytherium at the Boston Museum of Fine

Arts the opposite is true. Probably both arrangements were used in harpsichords also.

String Lengths and Pitch Standards

The vibrating lengths of the strings of the polygonal virginal and of the Ridolfi harpsichord can be roughly determined from the drawings. For purposes of comparison, a tabulation of the vibrating lengths (in inches) of the C strings on both instruments follows:

	Polygonal virginal	Harpsichord
c ′ ′ ′	6⅝	5$^{1}/_{16}$
c ′ ′ (pitch C)	12$^{15}/_{16}$	10
c ′ (middle C)	25$^{9}/_{16}$	20½
c	43$^{5}/_{16}$	42$^{1}/_{16}$
C/E	50$^{5}/_{16}$	61¼

The lengths shown for the harpsichord represent the shorter of the two strings with which each key is provided.

In order to produce a uniform tone color throughout the compass of a stringed instrument, it is necessary, among other things, to have the tension of all the strings reasonably uniform. In the treble this is accomplished by varying the string lengths. Since the length of a vibrating string is inversely proportional to its frequency, each string is made about half as long as the string an octave below, two thirds as long as the string a fifth below, etc. This principle cannot be carried all the way into the bass since the lowest strings would be inconveniently long, so somewhere below middle C the strings are gradually shortened and the diameters of the wires are increased in compensation.

As the above comparison shows, the string lengths are approximately doubled at each descending octave down to c′ on the virginal and c on the harpsichord. The shape of the case allows the harpsichord to have longer bass strings than the virginal; between c′ and c the string length is doubled in the harpsichord. However, in the virginal the c string is considerably less than twice as long as the string an octave above. In fact, the bass strings of the virginal are shortened to such an extent that the lowest string of the harpsichord is much longer than the lowest string of the virginal, although in the treble the virginal has longer strings than the harpsichord.

If the length of one treble string of an instrument of this sort is known, the lengths of all but the bass strings can be readily inferred; we can approximately describe the lengths of two-thirds to three-fourths of the strings of either of the above instruments by giving the length of one string. It has become customary to use *c ''* for this purpose, and to refer to it in such cases as pitch *C*.

In examining a number of Italian harpsichords and virginals dating from 1540 to 1694, lengths for pitch *C* ranging from 8'' to 13¾'' have been found. This seems to be a great discrepancy for instruments that are otherwise so standardized. Since a uniform standard of pitch did not yet exist in the 16th and 17th centuries, we would expect the string lengths employed to be varied somewhat in order to accommodate the instruments to higher or lower tunings. Also, a preference for the sound of thinner, longer wires or shorter, thicker ones may have caused some builders to increase or decrease the string lengths on their instruments in proportion to the string diameters chosen. We have no precise evidence concerning the original wire gauges of the strings of Italian harpsichords and virginals. Although the variety of pitch *C* lengths encountered on the instruments studied can partially be accounted for by these two factors, a third and more important cause existed.

Among the 33 instruments about which information has been secured, a correlation is discernible between the apparent manual compass and the pitch *C* string lengths. Sixteen of the instruments ascend to *f ' ' '*. For these, the length of the pitch *C* string varies from 10¼'' to 13¾''. The remaining instruments, with either *a ' '* or *c ' ' '* as the highest notes, have pitch *C* strings ranging from 8'' to 11⅜'' in length. If the average tension and wire diameter of the two groups are assumed to have been about equal, the difference in string lengths would suggest a corresponding difference in pitch, the instruments having the compass extended to *f ' ' '* sounding somewhat lower than the others.

There is some historical evidence that this actually was the case. In his *Theatrum Instrumentorum* Michael Praetorius[1] pictures a polygonal virginal, which appears to be very much like the many Italian examples that survive today, and a rectangular virginal that seems to be Flemish. He specifies that both are *so recht Chor-Thon* (at regular choir pitch). Praetorius also shows a harpsichord[2] that looks like a typ-

---

[1] Michael Praetorius, *Theatrum Instrumentorum*, Wolfenbüttel, 1620, pl. 14.
[2] *Ibid.*, pl. 6.

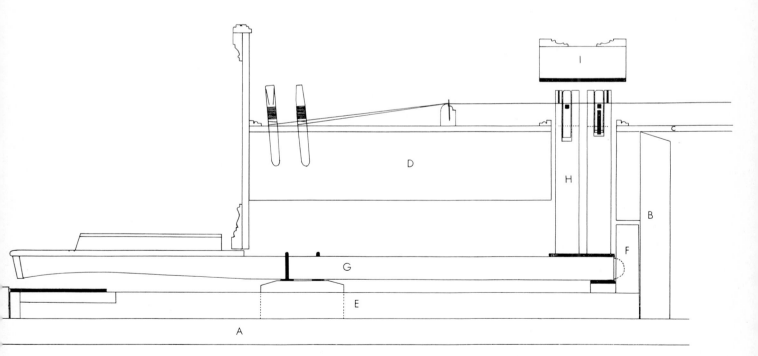

Figure 11.—ACTION OF HARPSICHORD. A, bottom; B, belly rail; C, soundboard; D, wrest plank; E, key frame; F, rack; G, key; H, jack; I, jack rail. Scale, 1:2.

ical Italian instrument except for the presence of a set of strings tuned an octave above unison pitch, a rare feature on Italian harpsichords. This harpsichord is described as *so eine Quart tieffer alss Chor-Thon* (a fourth lower than choir pitch), clearly indicating that single manual keyboard instruments a fourth apart in pitch were in existence. Since no reason is given for the harpsichord being tuned a fourth lower than the two virginals, we may assume that the author considered the matter commonplace enough as to demand no further elaboration and that instruments a fourth apart in pitch were not rare.

Praetorius does not state that the harpsichord in his illustration was tuned to a low pitch standard, which was actually used for certain purposes or in particular localities. He discussed the numerous pitches in use before and during his time, but the only one that he mentioned as being a fourth below choir pitch he considered obsolete and suitable only for plainsong. If the harpsichord was not intended to be tuned to this standard and used for this purpose, it must have been tuned to choir pitch and treated as a transposing instrument.

Querinus van Blankenburg,[3] writing in 1739, states:

At that time [the beginning of the 17th century], men had so little experience in transposition that in order to be able to transpose a piece a fourth downwards they made a special second keyboard in the harpsichord for this purpose. This seems incredible, but the very remarkable proof is the fact that the famous Ruckers from the beginning of the last century for a period of more than thirty years made harpsichords only in this way.[4]

That the second manual of the two-manual harpsichord originated as a device for transposition is well known. In an article titled "Transposing Keyboards on Extant Flemish Harpsichords," Sibyl Marcuse [5] discusses surviving examples that show how the second keyboard was arranged. The upper keyboard was the principal one, with the lower keyboard sounding a fourth below. The strings acted upon by a *c* key on the upper manual were sounded by an *f* key on the lower; so, in changing from the upper manual to the lower, the player would have to move his hands to the left the distance of a perfect fourth in order to

strike the same keys, thus producing the downward transposition. The compass of the upper manual was *E/C* to *c′′′*. Since the lower keyboard was shifted to the left, space was provided for five additional keys at its treble end. The apparent treble range of the lower keyboard was therefore extended to *f′′′*, although the lower *f′′′* and upper *c′′′* keys worked on the same strings and produced the same pitch. Room was also made for five extra bass keys at the lower end of the upper manual. However, since short octave tuning was employed and it was desirable to be able to use the same fingering in the bass on both manuals, the tails of the *C/E*, *D/F♯* and *E/G♯* keys of the upper manual had to be bent to the left in order to work on the strings played by the *F*, *G*, and *A* keys respectively of the lower manual. The vacant space to the left of the upper manual *C/E* was filled by a block of wood. Hence the five extra bass strings not used by the upper manual were those played by the *C/E*, *D/F♯*, *E/G♯*, *B*, and *c♯* keys of the lower keyboard.

Of the 16 Italian harpsichords and virginals studied that ascend in the treble to *f′′′*, 13 range to *C/E* in the bass, thus having exactly the same compass as the lower (transposing) keyboard of the Flemish two-manual instruments. Twelve of the 14 Italian examples having *c′′′* as the highest key stop on *C/E* in the bass and are identical in apparent compass to the Ruckers upper manual.

The correlation of compass and string length of the Italian instruments, the statements of Praetorius, and the similarity of the Italian keyboard ranges to those of the Ruckers transposing harpsichords have been considered. A plausible conclusion is that the Italian instruments extending to *f′′′* were transposing instruments sounding a perfect fourth lower than the prevailing pitch standard. Adopting the terminolgy used for orchestral wind instruments, these could be referred to as harpsichords in *G*.

The evidence of the correlation between string length and compass becomes much more convincing if we assume that the Italian builders abandoned the practice of making transposing harpsichords about the same time that the Ruckers family stopped employing the transposing lower manual. In the quotation previously given, Querinus van Blankenburg tells us that the Ruckers did not make transposing instruments later than the 1630's. Of the 10 dated Italian instruments with the keyboard extended to *f′′′*, only three were made after the third decade of the 17th

[3] Querinus van Blankenburg, *Elementa Musica*, The Hague, 1739.

[4] Translation by Arthur Mendel in "Devices for Transposition in the Organ before 1600," *Acta Musicologica*, 1949, p. 33.

[5] Sibyl Marcuse, "Transposing Keyboards on Extant Flemish Harpsichords," *Musical Quarterly*, July 1952.

Figure 12.—Typical decorative device, known as rose, that appeared in soundboards of virginals and harpsichords (*Smithsonian photo 46795*.)

century. Each of these has a shorter pitch *C* string than any of the seven earlier instruments. These three harpsichords, dated 1654, 1658, and 1666, are accordingly considered nontransposing instruments, with the extra treble keys representing an actual extension of the upward range. The six undated instruments with *f′′′* in the treble are classified as transposing instruments because of their pitch *C* lengths and are accordingly believed to have been made before about 1635.

The 33 instruments on which this study is based are classified in the list on page 107. They are grouped according to whether the highest key is *f′′′* or *c′′′*, with the exceptions of the three harpsichords mentioned in the preceding paragraph and three instruments that go only to *a′′*. That the three instruments ending on *a′′* belong with the nontransposing group is indicated by their string lenghts.

The listing gives additional information about each example. String lengths of instruments having two registers are for the shorter of the two pitch *C* strings.

Information has been secured on two Italian virginals which were not included in the tabulation. Their measurements are completely at variance with the pattern consistently set by the other 33 examples studied. One, made by Giovanni Domenico in 1556, is in the Skinner collection; it has a pitch *C* string 14¹⁄₁₆″ in length and an apparent compass of *C/E* to *c′′′*. The other, with the same apparent compass and a 7½″ pitch *C* string, is at Yale University. Whether these instruments are exceptional in terms of the pitch to which they were tuned, the tension which was applied to the strings, or the thickness and weight of the strings themselves, has not been determined.

The average of the pitch *C* lengths of the transposing instruments in the list is 12.78″; that of the nontransposing group is 10.45″. This suggests a separation between the two groups of about a major third since the first average is roughly ⅘ of the second. However, the fact that the separation of the two averages is not great enough to positively indicate a perfect fourth—the first average would have to be $\frac{4}{3}$ of the second to do so—does not disprove the theory of transposition by a fourth. In the first place, a considerable variety of pitches is no doubt represented in both groups since a universal pitch standard did not exist in the 16th and 17th centuries. Also, a margin of error of only a semitone is as good as could be expected considering the small number of examples on which the averages are based.

A further possible justification for the relationship of the two averages is found in Praetorius' discussion of the pitch standards with which he was familiar.[6] He states that choir pitch was a major second lower than chamber pitch and that *tertiam minorem* was a minor third lower than chamber pitch. Praetorius says of *tertiam minorem:* [7]

But in Italy and in various Catholic choirs in Germany, the said lower pitch is much in use. For some Italians, not unjustly, take no pleasure in high singing, and maintain it is not beautiful, and the words cannot be properly under-

stood, and it sounds like crowing, yelling, singing at the top of one's voice . . .

Possibly some of the nontransposing instruments were tuned to choir pitch and others to *tertiam minorem*, while the transposing instruments were set a fourth lower than choir pitch.

Three of the instruments listed are ottavinas, small instruments tuned an octave higher than usual. Ottavinas correspond to a four-foot register. Mersenne [8] mentions that they existed in two sizes, one a fifth above the usual pitch and the other an octave above. The three ottavinas included in the table are considered to be of the size sounding an octave above the usual pitch because they have C/E to c''' ranges and pitch C string lengths about half the average length of the other instruments in the nontransposing group. Although no examples were found for inclusion in this study, it is probable that some ottavinas a fifth above the usual pitch—and therefore an octave higher than the transposing instruments in our listing—survive. Such instruments would be expected to have apparent ranges of C/E to f''' and pitch C strings between $5\frac{3}{4}''$ and $6\frac{3}{4}''$ in length.

[6] Michael Praetorius, *Syntagma Musicum*, Wolfenbüttel, 1614–1620, vol. 2 (Organographia), chapter 2.

[7] Translation by Arthur Mendel in "Pitch in the 16th and early 17th Centuries, Part II," *Musical Quarterly*, April 1948.

[8] Marin Mersenne, *Harmonie Universelle*, Paris, 1636, p. 101.

Date	Pitch C length (in inches)	Apparent compass	Type	Registers	Maker	Present location
			TRANSPOSING INSTRUMENTS			
1540	11¹¹⁄₁₆	C/E–f′′′	Polygonal virginal	8′	Vi . . . ies	Metropolitan Museum of Art
1569	13¼	C/E–f′′′	Polygonal virginal	8′	Annibale Rossi	Juilliard School of Music
1602	13¼	C/E–f′′′	Rectangular virginal	8′	Ioannes Baptista Bononien	Smithsonian Institution
1610	13½	C/E–f′′′	Polygonal virginal	8′	Pasquino Querci	Harding Museum, Chicago
1613	11½	C/E–f′′′	Harpsichord	8′8′	Pasquino Querci	Smithsonian Institution
1617	13¾	C/E–f′′′	Polygonal virginal	8′	Giovanni Battista Boni	Yale University, New Haven, Conn.
1620	13⁹⁄₁₆	C/E–f′′′	Polygonal virginal	8′	Francesco Poggio	Rhode Island School of Design, Providence
	11¹⁵⁄₁₆	C/E–f′′′	Polygonal virginal	8′	Anonymous	Skinner Collection, Holyoke, Mass.
	12¹⁵⁄₁₆	C/E–f′′′	Polygonal virginal	8′	Anonymous	Smithsonian Institution
	13″	C/E–f′′′	Polygonal virginal	8′	Anonymous	Boston Museum of Fine Arts
	11½	C–f′′′	Polygonal virginal	8′	Anonymous	Folger Library, Washington, D.C.
	12¾	C/E–f′′′	Polygonal virginal	8′	Anonymous	Cincinnati Art Museum
	13⅝	C/E–f′′′	Polygonal virginal	8′	Anonymous	Smithsonian Institution
			NONTRANSPOSING INSTRUMENTS			
1548	11	C/E–c′′′	Polygonal virginal	8′	Domenicus Pesaurensis	Metropolitan Museum of Art
1554	[a] 10½	C/E–c′′′	Harpsichord	8′8′	Padre Stoppacio	Vassar College, Poughkeepsie, New York
1585	[b] 11½	C/E–a′′	Ottavina	4′	Franciscus Bonafinis	Metropolitan Museum of Art
1602	10½	C/E–c′′′	Harpsichord	. . . . . .	Christoforus Rigunini	Stearns Collection, Ann Arbor, Mich.
1615	[b] 9¾	C/E–a′′	Ottavina	4′	Pasquino Querci	Metropolitan Museum of Art
1625	10⅛	C/E–c′′′	Harpsichord	8′	Valerius Peres	Skinner Collection, Holyoke, Mass.
1633	11⅜	C/E–c′′′	Harpsichord	8′8′	Horatius Albana	Smithsonian Institution
1645	11	C/E–c′′′	Harpsichord	8′8′	Horatius Albana	Vizcaya, Miami, Fla.
1654	10¼	C/E–f′′′	Harpsichord	8′8′	Anonymous	Smithsonian Institution
1658	11⅛	C–f′′′	Harpsichord	8′8′	Hieronymus de Zentis	Metropolitan Museum of Art
1665	10	C/E–c′′′	Harpsichord	8′8′	Giacomo Ridolfi	Smithsonian Institution
1666	10¹⁵⁄₁₆	A₁–f′′′	Harpsichord	8′8′	Hieronymus de Zentis	Metropolitan Museum of Art
1682	10⅞	C/E–c′′′	Harpsichord	8′8′	Giacomo Ridolfi	Rhode Island School of Design, Providence
1683	8	C/E–c′′′	Polygonal virginal	8′	B. Obici	Harding Museum, Chicago
1690	10¹³⁄₁₆	C/E–c′′′	Harpsichord	8′	Giovanni Andrea Menegoni	Smithsonian Institution
1693	10⁵⁄₁₆	G₁–c′′′	Harpsichord	8′8′	Anonymous	Smithsonian Institution
1694	9⅞	C–c′′′ (minus C♯)	Harpsichord	8′8′4′	Nicolaus de Quoco	Smithsonian Institution
	9¾	C/E–a′′	Clavicytherium	8′8′	Anonymous	Smithsonian Institution
	[b] 10⅜	C/E–c′′′	Clavicytherium (Ottavina)	4′	Anonymous	Boston Museum of Fine Arts
	11	C/E–c′′′	Polygonal virginal	8′	Anonymous	Smithsonian Institution

[a] This length is approximate. It is double the length of the shortest string on the instrument.

[b] In order to arrive at a meaningful average value for the string lengths of the nontransposing group, it was necessary to double the measured lengths of the pitch C strings of the three instruments tuned an octave higher.

U.S. GOVERNMENT PRINTING OFFICE: 1960

CONTRIBUTIONS FROM

THE MUSEUM OF HISTORY AND TECHNOLOGY

PAPER 16

DRUG SUPPLIES IN THE AMERICAN REVOLUTION

George B. Griffenhagen

by George B. Griffenhagen

DRUG SUPPLIES
IN THE
AMERICAN REVOLUTION

At the start of the Revolution, the Colonies were cut off from the source of their usual drug supply, England. A few drugs trickled through from the West Indies, but by 1776 there was an acute shortage.

Lack of coordination and transportation resulted in a scarcity of drugs for the army hospitals even while druggists in other areas resorted to advertising in order to sell their stocks. Some relief came from British prize ships captured by the American navy and privateers, but the chaotic condition of drug supply was not eased until the alliance with France early in 1778.

THE AUTHOR: *George Griffenhagen—formerly curator of medical sciences, United States National Museum, Smithsonian Institution—is director of communications, American Pharmaceutical Association, and managing editor, Journal of the American Pharmaceutical Association.*

As ONE HISTORIAN has reminded us, "few fields of history have been more intensively cultivated by successive generations of historians; few offer less reward in the shape of fresh facts or theories" than does the American Revolutionary War.[1] This is true to some extent even in the medical history of the Revolution. The details of the feud within the medical department of the army have been told and retold.[2] Even accounts of the drugs employed and pharmaceutical services have been presented, primarily in the form of biographies and as reviews of the *Lititz Pharmacopoeia* of 1778. However, practically nothing has been published on the actual availability of medical supplies. Furthermore, the discovery of several significant but unrecorded account books of private druggists who furnished sizable

---

[1] John C. Miller, *Triumph of Freedom, 1775-1783*, Boston, 1948, preface.

[2] Louis C. Duncan, *Medical Men in the American Revolution, 1775–1783*, Carlisle Barracks, Pa., 1931; William O. Owen, *The Medical Department of the United States Army during the Period of the Revolution*, New York, 1920; James E. Gibson, *Dr. Bodo Otto and the Medical Background of the American Revolution*, Springfield, Ill., 1937; James Thomas Flexner, *Doctors on Horseback*, New York, 1939.

[3] Lyman F. Kebler, "Andrew Craigie, the First Apothecary General of the United States," *Journal of the American Pharmaceutical Association*, 1928, vol. 17, pp. 63–74, 167–178; Frederick Haven Pratt, "The Craigies," *Proceedings of the Cambridge Historical Society* (1941), 1942, vol. 27, pp. 43–86; Edward Kremers and George Urdang, *A History of Pharmacy*, Philadelphia, 1951 edition, chap. 11; Edward Kremers, "The Lititz Pharmacopoeia," *The Badger Pharmacist*, nos. 22–25, June–December 1938; J. W. England, ed., *The First Century of the Philadelphia College of Pharmacy*, Philadelphia, 1922, pp. 84–94; *American Journal of Pharmacy*, 1884, vol. 56, pp. 483–491.

quantities of drugs to the Continental Army and a careful re-evaluation of the unusually significant papers[4] of Dr. Jonathan Potts, Revolutionary War surgeon, justify a review of the drug supplies during the early years of the war.

Continental Medicine Chests

As early as February 21, 1775, the Provincial Congress of Massachusetts appointed a committee to determine what medical supplies would be necessary should colonial troops be required to take the field. Three days later the Congress voted to "make an inquiry where fifteen doctor's chests can be got, and on what terms"; and on March 7 it directed the committee of supplies "to make a draft in favor of Doct. Joseph Warren and Doct. Benjamin Church, for five hundred pounds, lawful money, to enable them to purchase such articles for the provincial chests of medicine as cannot be got on credit."[5]

A unique ledger of the Greenleaf apothecary shop of Boston[6] reveals that this pharmacy on April 4, 1775, supplied at least 5 of the 15 chests of medicines. The account, in the amount of just over £247, is listed in the name of the Province of the Massachusetts Bay, and shows that £51 was paid in cash by Dr. Joseph Warren. The remaining £196 was not paid until August 10, after Warren had been killed in the Battle of Bunker Hill.

The 15 medicine chests, including presumably the five supplied by Greenleaf, were distributed on April 18—three at Sudbury and two each at Concord, Groton, Mendon, Stow, Worcester, and Lancaster.[7] No record has been found to indicate whether or not the British discovered the medical chests at Concord, but, inasmuch as the patriots were warned of the British movement, it is very likely that the chests were among the supplies that were carried off and hidden.

Figure 1.—Medicine scales and oval box of medicinal herbs used by Dr. Solomon Drowne during the Revolution. Preserved at Fort Ticonderoga Museum, New York.

The British destroyed as much of the remainder as they could locate.[8]

Two days after the battles at Lexington and Concord, the Provincial Congress ordered that a man and horse be made available to transport medicines. On April 30, Andrew Craigie was appointed to take care of these medical stores and deliver them as ordered.

Medical supplies were an early source of anxiety to the Provincial Congress of Massachusetts. The supply of drugs in Boston must have been largely controlled by the British after Lexington-Concord, and the limited supply in the neighboring smaller towns was soon exhausted. Four days before the Battle of Bunker Hill the Congress "Ordered that Doct. Whiting, Doct. Taylor and Mr. Parks, be a committee to consider some method of supplying the several surgeons of the army with medicines," and further "Ordered that the same committee bring in a list of what medicines are in the medical store."[9]

On June 10 the responsibility of furnishing medical supplies to the army at Cambridge shifted to Philadelphia when the Continental Congress accepted the

---

[4] Jonathan Potts Papers, four volumes of miscellaneous manuscripts at The Historical Society of Pennsylvania, Philadelphia (hereinafter referred to as Potts Papers).

[5] Journals of the Provincial Congress of Massachusetts Bay, quoted in Owen, *op. cit.* (footnote 2), pp. 22–23.

[6] Greenleaf Ledger, 1765–1778, at the American Antiquarian Society, Worcester, Mass. (The Greenleaf pharmacy was established by Elizabeth Greenleaf in 1726 or 1727. See J. L. Sibley, *Biographical Sketches of Graduates of Harvard University, in Cambridge, Massachusetts*, Cambridge, 1920, vol. 5, pp. 472–476; Jonathan Greenleaf, *A Genealogy of the Greenleaf Family*, New York, 1854, pp. 89, 91, 205, 207; *Boston Post-Boy* and *Boston Gazette*, November 8, 1762, obituary of Elizabeth Greenleaf.)

[7] Owen, *op. cit.* (footnote 2), p. 23.

[8] J. R. Alden, *The American Revolution*, New York, 1954 p. 23.

[9] Owen, *op. cit.* (footnote 2), pp. 12–13.

request of the Massachusetts Provincial Congress to assume control and direction of the forces assembled around Boston. The Continental Congress established a Continental Hospital Plan on July 27, but it was not until September 14 that the Congress appointed a "committee to devise ways and means for supplying the Continental Army with medicines." On this same day, the deputy commissary general was directed to pay Dr. Samuel Stringer for the medicines he purchased,[10] which, as we learn later, were the initial supply for the Canadian campaign.

The first recorded purchase of drugs made directly by Congress, on September 23, was "a parcel of Drugs in the hands of Mr. Rapalje, which he offers at the prime cost."[11] Then, on November 10, Congress ordered that the medicine purchased in Philadelphia for the army at Cambridge be sent there by land.[12] But difficulties of supply commenced early. On January 1, 1776, Eliphalet Dyer wrote Joseph Trumbull asking "how could the cask of Rhubarb which was sent by order of Congress and was extremely wanted in the Hospital lye by to this time. After you came way I wrote to Daniel Brown to see it delivered."[13]

In the fall of 1775 there must have been a reasonably good stock of drugs in the hands of private Philadelphia druggists, and until the end of summer there were still a number of ships from Jamaica, Bermuda, Antigua, and Barbados putting in at Philadelphia with supplies, much of which originally came from England. Philadelphia druggists included William Drewet Smith, "Chemist and Druggist at Hippocrates's Head in Second Street";[14] Dr. George Weed in Front Street;[15] Robert Bass, "Apothecary in Market-Street"; Dr. Anthony Yeldall "at his Medicinal Ware-House in Front-Street";[16] and the

firm of Sharp Delaney and William Smith.[17] The largest pharmacy in Philadelphia was operated by the Marshall brothers—Christopher Jr. and Charles. This pharmacy had been established in 1729 at Front and Chestnut Streets by Christopher Marshall, Sr., a patriot who took an active part in the care of the sick and wounded in Philadelphia hospitals during the Revolution.[18]

As the plans progressed for raising troops from New Jersey, Maryland, Delaware, Pennsylvania, Virginia, North Carolina, and South Carolina, Congress called on the committee on medicines "to procure proper medicine chests for the battalions . . . ."[19] The journal of the Continental Congress fails to indicate the source of these medicine chests, but the Marshall brothers' manuscript "waste book" (daily record) for the period February 21 to July 6, 1776,[20] indicates that the Marshall apothecary shop was the primary supplier. The records show that the Marshalls furnished 20 medicine chests to the following battalions from February to June:[21]

February 1776: Pennsylvania 1st Battalion
March 1776: Jersey 3d Battalion
April 1776: Pennsylvania 2d, 3d, and 6th Battalions
May 1776: Six Virginia battalions
Jersey 1st Battalion
Pennsylvania 4th Battalion
June 1776: Six North Carolina battalions
Virginia 9th Battalion

The exact contents of each chest are indicated in the Marshalls' waste book. The chest furnished to the Pennsylvania 4th Battalion is an example of the ones supplied by Congress in the spring of 1776; its contents are listed on page 130.

Congress intended that all chests be substantially the same, but the amount of medicines demanded exceeded the stock of even the largest druggists. The first several chests were complete as ordered, but as early as April the Marshalls were running out of

[10] *Journals of the Continental Congress, 1774–1789*, edited by Worthington C. Ford, Washington, D.C., 1905, vol. 2, p. 250. Nearly all excerpts from Ford also appear in Owen, *op. cit.* (footnote 2).

[11] *Ibid.*, vol. 3, p. 261. The Samuel Ward diary for September 23 records that "a parcel of medicines for the hospital" was "to be bought" (E. C. Burnett, *Letters of Members of the Continental Congress*, Washington, D.C., 1921, vol. 1, p. 205).

[12] Ford, *op. cit.* (footnote 10), vol. 3, p. 344.

[13] Burnett, *op. cit.* (footnote 11), vol. 1, p. 292.

[14] *Pennsylvania Ledger*, May 6, 1775. [William Smith in Philadelphia was selling drugs in 1772 (Potts Papers, vol. 1, folio 52).]

[15] *Pennsylvania Evening Post*, December 26, 1775.

[16] *Pennsylvania Packet*, September 11, 1775; *Pennsylvania Journal*, September 6, 1775; *Pennsylvania Gazette*, October 4, 1775.

[17] The Marshalls sold drugs to Sharp Delaney and William Smith in April 1776 (Marshall Waste Book, see footnote 20).

[18] E. T. Ellis, "The Story of a Very Old Philadelphia Drug Store," *American Journal of Pharmacy*, 1908, vol. 75, p. 57; England, *op. cit.* (footnote 3), pp. 348–350; Parke, Davis & Co., *A History of Pharmacy in Pictures*, undated booklet edited by George Bender.

[19] Ford, *op. cit.* (footnote 10), vol. 3, p. 442; vol. 4, pp. 188, 197.

[20] Christopher Jr. and Charles Marshall Waste Book, February 21 to July 6, 1776, at The Historical Society of Pennsylvania, Philadelphia.

[21] Ford, *op. cit.* (footnote 10), vol. 3, p. 442; vol. 4, pp. 188, 197; Burnett, *op. cit.* (footnote 11), vol. 1.

certain drugs. Gum opium and nitre "found by Congress" was included in the chest for the Pennsylvania 4th Battalion, and by May 11 the Marshalls were out of Peruvian bark, ipecac, cream of tartar, gum camphor, and red precipitate of mercury. The chests outfitted after June 1 also failed to include Epsom salts, and the last chest lacked jalap as well. Thus the majority of the battalions traveling north were already without some of the most necessary drugs in their chests. Blithely their medical officers thought they could obtain the missing drugs when they arrived at the general hospital.

Treason, Poison, and Siege

After the Battle of Bunker Hill, the forces around Boston settled down for a 9-month siege. Two days after General Washington arrived in Cambridge on July 2, 1775, to take command of the army, the Provincial Congress of Massachusetts ordered a committee to prepare a letter informing him of the provisions that had been made for the sick and wounded of the army. On the very same day, July 4, the Provincial Congress appointed Andrew Craigie medical commissary and apothecary for the Massachusetts army.[22]

Following a personal inspection by Washington on July 21 and the establishment of the general hospital plan on July 27, the Continental Congress elected Dr. Benjamin Church as director general of the newly created medical department. Soon after this, Church conferred with several Massachusetts officials regarding the appointment of apothecaries for the medical store at Watertown. On August 3, a committee of the Provincial Congress advised "that the Medical Store in Watertown be continued where it now is, and that Mr. Andrew Craigie, appointed by the late Congress Apothecary to the Colony, be directed to take charge thereof, and prepare the necessary compositions; and that Mr. James Miller Church be appointed Assistant Apothecary to put up and distribute said Medicines. . . ."[23]

The medical supplies were slow in coming from Philadelphia, as we have already noted. On the other hand, troops were arriving daily, placing an increased demand on all types of supplies, including drugs. One event which undoubtedly resulted in delays in establishing proper supply depots was the

startling discovery that Director General Church was guilty of holding treasonable correspondence with the enemy. On October 16, Congress elected Dr. John Morgan to replace Church.[24]

On December 2, by order of Morgan, Apothecary Craigie made an inventory of the medical supplies in the general hospital at Cambridge. The inventory included 120 different items, but only limited quantities of the essential drugs.[25] There were 52 pounds of Jesuits' bark, 18 pounds of cream of tartar, 76 pounds of purging salts, 1 pound of camphor, 5 pounds of jalap, 1 pound of ipecac, and ½ pound of tartar emetic. The 44 pounds of gum ammoniac was reported "damaged," and the 86 pounds of rhubarb was described as "bad."[26] An inventory of medicines held by the different regimental surgeons in Massachusetts indicated that all regiments had "but few medicines" except for Colonel Hand's, which reported "a good supply."[27]

However, this rather meager inventory of drugs probably was not inadequate. The siege of Boston resulted in few wounded soldiers, and there was a surprisingly small amount of sickness in the army during the winter of 1775–76; furthermore, towns not too distant still had a limited supply of drugs on hand. Smith and Coit, of Hartford, Connecticut, informed "their good Customers, and the public in general, that notwithstanding the entire stop to Importation which hath long since taken place, they still have on hand, small Quantities of most Articles of the Apothecary Way . . . which they mean to sell at a reasonable retailing Price."[28] Jacob Isaacks of Newport, Rhode Island, similarly advertised "a complete assortment of genuine Medicines, with furniture for containing the same, to the amount of about 300 pounds sterling; which medicines were purchased with cash, and will be sold, at the prime cost and charges, without any advance. Any of the lawful or Continental bills now current will be taken in pay for the above medicines."[29]

Drug supplies also were quite adequate in Boston during the British occupation. Sylvester Gardiner at "The Sign of the Unicorn and Mortar in Marlborow Street" reported that "all kinds of the best and

[22] Owen, *op. cit.* (footnote 2), pp. 18–19.

[23] *American Archives* . . . Peter Force, ed., Washington, ser. 4, vol. 1–6, 1837–46; ser. 5, vol. 1–3, 1848–53. Ser. 4, vol. 3, p. 306.

[24] Duncan, *op. cit.* (footnote 2), pp. 62–64.

[25] *Pennsylvania Packet*, June 24, 1779.

[26] It is quite possible that the designation "bad" was a typographical error for "rad[ix]."

[27] *American Archives*, ser. 4, vol. 5, p. 115.

[28] *Connecticut Courant*, February 12, 1776.

[29] *Newport Mercury*, January 15, 1776.

freshest drugs and medicines . . . are continued to be sold as usual." However a cautionary note was added that drugs and medicines had been "constantly imported every fall and spring to June last." Implicit in the advertising is the suggestion that the securing of new supplies was highly uncertain.[30]

A letter dated December 2, 1775, from a British officer in Boston to a friend in Edinburgh observed that "many of our men are sick, and fresh provisions very dear." However, the officer added, "but the Rebels must be in a much worse condition. . . ."[31] Drugs were imported into Boston during the siege as evidenced by an advertisement on February 22, 1776, announcing "just imported from LONDON and to be sold at Mr. Dalton's Store, on the Long-Wharf, a proper assortment of Drugs and Medicines of the Best quality in Cases."[32]

By the end of February 1776, Washington had decided to try to end the siege of Boston by seizing Dorchester Heights and placing his artillery there in a position to bombard the town. General Howe believed it was time to leave, and the British evacuated on March 17.

As the Continental Army moved into Boston, there was an outcry that the British had poisoned a supply of drugs left behind. On April 15 the *Boston Gazette* reported that "it is absolutely fact that the Doctors of the diabolical ministerial butcher when they evacuated Boston, intermixed and left 26 weight of Arsenick with the medicines which they left in the Alms House."[33] Then, a week later, on April 22, appeared a series of testimonials that had been made by Joseph Warren, Daniel Scott, and Frederick Ridgley at Watertown on April 3d "by order of the Director-General of the Continental Hospital." Warren swore under oath that on or about March 29 he had gone into the workhouse [almshouse] "lately improved as an hospital by the British troops stationed in said town" and upon examining the state of "a large quantity of Medicine" left in the medicinal storeroom had found about 12 or 14 pounds of arsenic intermixed with the drugs, which were found "to be chiefly capital articles and those most generally in demand."[34]

Despite this incident, we have the word of Morgan that "a large, though unassorted stock of medicines" was collected in Boston when the British evacuated.[35] Hospital Surgeons Ebenezer Crosby and Frederick Ridgley reported that "at the evacuation of Boston . . . all the Mates of the Hospital that could be spared from Cambridge . . . were employed in packing up and sending off [to Cambridge] drugs, medicines and other hospital stores, collected by order of Dr. Morgan, the quantity of which appeared great."[36]

Inasmuch as few medicines were listed in the inventory of stores left by the British on the wharfs and in the scuttled ships in the harbor,[37] it appears that most of these drugs obtained in Boston were confiscated from the homes, offices, and shops of the Loyalists who fled when the British evacuated. Morgan reported that he had taken possession of the medicines and furniture of Dr. Sylvester Gardiner's shop, and a small stock of drugs from the office of Dr. William Perkins, a private practitioner.[38] No inventory of these supplies has been located thus far, but a contemporary biographer of Sylvester Gardiner records that the confiscated drugs from his shop "filled from 20 to 25 wagons."[39] This is not unlikely because Gardiner's apothecary shop was one of the largest and most prosperous in the Colonies prior to the Revolution.[40]

Soon after the British evacuated Boston, the Greenleaf apothecary shop in Boston was again supplying medicines to the Continental Army. The Greenleaf ledger[41] shows that on May 25 the shop sold nearly £4 worth of "Sundry Medicines . . . [to] the Committee of War, State of Massachusetts Bay." Then, on June 20, the Massachusetts Assembly resolved that "Dr. John Greenleaf of Boston be requested to supply the Chief Surgeon of . . . Colonels Marshall's, Whitney's and Craft's Regi-

[30] *Massachusetts Gazette*, September 7, 1775.

[31] *American Archives*, ser. 4, vol. 4, p. 159.

[32] *Massachusetts Gazette*, February 22, 1776.

[33] *Boston Gazette*, April 15, 1776.

[34] *Ibid.*, April 22, 1776. It is worth noting that Morgan did not think this important enough to include in his *Vindication* (see footnote 35).

[35] John Morgan, *A Vindication of His Public Character in the Station of Director-General of the Military Hospital, and Physician in Chief of the American Army; Anno, 1776*, Boston, 1777.

[36] *Pennsylvania Packet*, June 24, 1779.

[37] *American Archives*, ser. 4, vol. 5, p. 488.

[38] Morgan, *op. cit.* (footnote 35), pp. 102, 144; and *Independent Chronicle*, April 10, 1777.

[39] James Thacher, *American Medical Biography*, Boston, 1828, vol. 1, pp. 270–273.

[40] For biographies of Sylvester Gardiner see *Dictionary of American Biography*, New York, 1931, vol. 8, pp. 139–140; *Appleton's Cyclopedia of American Biography*, New York, 1887, vol. 2; H. A. Kelly and W. L. Burrage, *Dictionary of American Medical Biography*, New York, 1928, pp. 450–452; James H. Stark, *The Loyalists of Massachusetts*, Boston, 1910, pp. 313–315.

[41] Greenleaf Ledger (see footnote 6).

ments . . . with medicines as may be necessary . . . ." [42] A short time later the Assembly advanced "up to £50 to Greenleaf for purchasing such medicines "as he cannot supply from his own store." [43]

The Greenleaf ledger shows that over £32 worth of medicines were sold for Colonel Whitney's regiment and over £36 worth for Colonel Marshall's regiment between June 13 and November 20, 1776. Thus, drugs were available; but until the fall of '76, Greenleaf was having difficulty in obtaining an abundant supply.

From Bad to Worse

General Washington, correctly foretelling that New York City would be the next British objective, marched there from Boston with as much of his army as could be induced to stay under the colors. Had it not been for the presence of Washington's forces in New York, that colony would certainly have remained Loyalist; as it was, the Patriot committees had the greatest difficulty in keeping the Tories quiet by strong-arm methods. [44]

The availability of drugs in New York prior to the arrival of Washington's forces did not seem to be particularly affected by the war. Thomas Attwood "at his store in Dock-Street" offered for sale a wide assortment of drugs and medicines, [45] while William Stewart offered "a fresh supply of Genuine Drugs and Medicines . . . on the most reasonable terms either for cash or at the usual credit." [46] The citizens of New York did not even have to do without their popular English patent medicines. [47]

Washington, however, had to provide for his own medical supplies in New York. In a letter dated April 3 he ordered Director General Morgan to remove the general hospital to New York with "all convenient speed. . . ." [48] The fixing and completing of the regimental chests was to be deferred until Morgan arrived at New York.

Morgan remained behind in Boston for another six weeks collecting medicines, furniture, and hospital stores worth thousands of pounds. "The like quantity . . . could not be procured," so Morgan later claimed, "in any [other] part of America." He was also able to purchase drugs from Salem, Newport, and Norwich, and before departing for New York he completed a medicine chest for each of the five regiments at Boston, Salem, and Marblehead, as ordered by Washington. [49]

Morgan arrived in New York about June 3 and purchased some additional drugs there. By June 17 his staff had made up 30 medicine chests for the regiments at New York as well as for "the branches of the General Hospital at New-York, in the bowry and neighborhood and at Long-Island." But the number of regiments requiring medical supplies exceeded Morgan's expectations, particularly since he had been advised that "the Southward regiments" would be supplied by Congress in Philadelphia. [50]

By the middle of June, Morgan must have realized that the supply of drugs available was inadequate despite the sizable quantity brought from Boston and the small stock he was able to obtain in New York. It appears that many of the New York druggists were Loyalists, and somehow they and their stock of drugs disappeared when needed by Washington's army. For example, druggist Thomas Attwood "removed his store consisting of a general assortment of Drugs and Medicines" to Newark in May only to reappear in New York again under British occupation with a good stock of "Drugs and Medicines." [51]

The New York Committee of Safety had attempted to develop a stock of drugs early in the year when they were plentiful, [52] but in June this supply was valued at only £30. Even this small stock was not available to Morgan because when he asked permission to purchase the medicines at "a reasonable price . . . for use of the Continental Hospital" the New York Provincial Congress rejected his plea on June 26 with the explanation that this medicine was to be "reserved

[42] *American Archives*, ser. 5, vol. 1, pp. 282, 284.

[43] *Ibid.*, p. 314.

[44] S. E. Morison and H. S. Commager, *The Growth of the American Republic*, New York, 1950, vol. 1, p. 210.

[45] *New-York Journal*, July 13, 1775.

[46] *Ibid.*, May 11, 1775.

[47] *New-York Gazette*, January 1 and January 29, 1776. For a history of the English patent medicines in America, see G. B. Griffenhagen and J. H. Young in *The Chemist and Druggist*, 1957, vol. 167, pp. 714–722, and in *U.S. National Museum Bulletin 218*, 1959, pp. 155–183 (Contributions from the Museum of History and Technology, Paper 10).

[48] George Washington, *The Writings of George Washington*, edited by John C. Fitzpatrick, Washington, 1931, vol. 4, pp. 464–465.

[49] Morgan, *op. cit.* (footnote 35), pp. 4, 9, 68; *Pennsylvania Packet*, June 19, 1779; and Washington, *op. cit.* (footnote 48), vol. 4, pp. 464–465.

[50] Duncan, *op. cit.* (footnote 2), p. 135; Morgan, *op. cit.* (footnote 35), p. 11.

[51] *New-York Gazette*, May 6 and December 23, 1776.

[52] *American Archives*, ser. 4, vol. 4, p. 1026.

for the use of the poor and other inhabitants of this city." [53]

With increasing demands to supply the troops in the Northern Department, Morgan turned to Philadelphia and the Continental Congress. Morgan owned a small stock of drugs in Philadelphia, and knew of another supply in the possession of the firm of Delaney and Smith, [54] so he sent Dr. Barnabus Binney to Philadelphia to forward "with all dispatch" what medicines he had there and whatever could be obtained from Congress.[55] Congress resolved on July 17 "to purchase the Medicines (now in Phila) belonging to Doctor Morgan," [56] but for nearly a month Binney was unable to obtain any additional supplies either from Congress or from private sources.

On June 25 Morgan wrote to Samuel Adams asking for power "to demand a proportion of the Continental medicines left in care of Messrs. Delaney & Smith," and he repeated the request in July. However, Morgan's only reply from Adams, dated August 5, made no mention of the Delaney and Smith drug stock. Instead Adams wrote only: "I have received several letters from you, which I should have sooner acknowledged, if I could only have found leisure. I took however, the necessary steps to have what you requested effected in Congress." [57]

Finally, on August 8, Congress directed the committee for procuring medicines "to supply the director general of the Hospital with such medicines as he may want." [58] By this time, such a resolution was hardly much consolation to Morgan. Evidence of the status of the supplies in the general hospital at New York can be gleaned from an advertisement in the *New-York Gazette* of July 29 signed by Thomas Carnes, "Steward and Quarter-Master to the General Hospital":

WANTED immediately . . . a large quantity of dry herbs, for baths, fomentations, &c. &c. particularly baum hysop, wormwood and mallows, for which a good price will be given. The good people of the neighboring towns, and even those who live more remote from this city, by carefully collecting and curing quantities of useful herbs will greatly promote the good of the Army, and considerably benefit themselves.

The retreat from Long Island on August 27 and the subsequent loss of New York City to the British certainly did not help the medical supply problem. Despite the fact that part of the medical stores were shipped to Stamford, Connecticut, and another stock of supplies removed to Newark, Morgan admits that "the most valuable part was still left in New-York when the enemy had effected a landing, drawn a line across the island, and were entering New-York." [59] General Knox later told how "late in the day of the 15th of September, 1776, after the enemy had beat back part of the American troops," Morgan "came over from Powles Hook in a pettiauger, and had her loaded with Hospital stores." [60] Washington personally reported on September 16 that "the retreat was effected with but little loss of Men, tho' a considerable part of our Baggage . . . part of our Stores and Provisions, which we were removing, was unavoidably left in the City . . ." [61]

One small bundle of private drug supplies saved from the British is reported [62] by "Doct. Prime, A Refuge from Long Island," who announced the opening of a shop in Wethersfield. The newspaper advertisement reported that Prime

. . . has saved from the enemy a parcel of medicines, part of which he would barter for such articles as he wants, especially shop utensils of which he had unfortunately lost the most of his own . . . .

The medical supply problem went from bad to worse as Washington's army retreated from Harlem Heights to White Plains and then finally into New Jersey. Morgan again turned to Philadelphia for drugs, but obtained "none or next to none." Instead of ten pounds of tartar emetic which Morgan requested from Philadelphia druggist Robert Bass and the newly appointed Continental Druggist, William Smith, four ounces was all that he received, but with "a proper apology." [63]

On September 21, the supply of bark was completely exhausted, and Washington was furious. On September 24 in a letter to the President of the Congress, Washington charged that the regimental surgeons were aiming "to break up the Genl. Hospital" and that they had "in numberless Instances

[53] *Ibid.*, vol. 6, p. 1431.
[54] Morgan misspelled Delaney as "Delancey" in his letter of June 25 to Adams.
[55] Morgan, *op. cit.* (footnote 35), p. 128.
[56] Ford, *op. cit.* (footnote 10), vol. 5, p. 570.
[57] *American Archives*, ser. 4, vol. 6, p. 1069.
[58] Ford, *op. cit.* (footnote 10), vol. 5, p. 633.

[59] Morgan, *op. cit.* (footnote 35), p. 12.
[60] *Pennsylvania Packet*, June 26, 1779.
[61] Washington, *op. cit.* (footnote 48), vol. 6, pp. 58–59.
[62] *Connecticut Courant*, January 6, 1777.
[63] Morgan, *op. cit.* (footnote 35), pp. 13, 136, 146. William Smith was appointed Continental Druggist on August 20; see Ford, *op. cit.* (footnote 10), vol. 4, pp. 292–293.

drawn for Medicines, Stores, &c. in the most profuse and extravagent manner for private purposes." [64]

To make matters worse, new troops continued to arrive without medical supplies. For example, those from Maryland arrived at White Plains with their regimental surgeons fully expecting Morgan to supply them with medicines, even though the Maryland Convention on October 4 had ordered that these troops be supplied with medicines by the Maryland Council of Safety before their departure. [65]

Morgan thought he had at least one small but safe stock of drugs. Barnabas Binney, who was sent to Philadelphia in July for medical supplies, was successful in obtaining "a reasonable good order" about the middle of August, including "30 lb. Camphor; 10 lb. Ipecac; 7 lb. Opium; 50 lb. Quicksilver; 40 lb. Jalap; 68 lb. Manna; 186 lb. Nitre; 200 lb. Cream of Tartar; 269 lb. Bark; and other important articles." [66] However, since these supplies arrived at Newark just as Washington was beginning to pull out of Long Island, they were deposited at a newly established hospital under Cutting, the assistant apothecary. [67]

When Morgan finally began drawing on these supplies, Dr. William Shippen had been placed in charge of the hospitals in New Jersey and the medicines had been turned over to him by a vote of Congress. [68] Finally, on January 9, 1777, Congress dismissed Morgan as director general without giving any reasons except to indicate indirectly that it was due to his inability to provide adequate medical supplies. [69] To add insult to injury, on February 5 Congress asked "what is become of the medicines which Dr. Morgan took from Boston . . ." and resolved to "take measures to have them secured, and applied to the use of the army." [70]

Meanwhile, in New York City the supply of drugs had returned to normal or near normal within a few weeks after the British occupation. On September 30, 1776, Thomas Brownejohn announced the opening "of his medicinal store at the corner of Hanover-Square . . . where gentlemen of the army and navy can be supplied at the shortest notice with all kinds of medicines on the most reasonable terms." On December 16 Richard Speaight announced that he "has once again opened his Shop at the sign of the Elaboratory in Queen-Street," and a week later

---

[64] Washington, *op. cit.* (footnote 48), vol. 6, pp. 86, 113.

[65] *American Archives*, ser. 5, vol. 3, pp. 116, 837.

[66] *Pennsylvania Packet*, June 24, 1779.

[67] Morgan, *op. cit.* (footnote 35), p. 129.

[68] *Ibid.*, p. xxv. [For details of the manner in which Shippen moved in on Morgan to replace him eventually as director general, see Flexner, *op. cit.* (footnote 2), pp. 3–53.]

[69] *Ibid.*, p. xxxv; Owen, *op. cit.* (footnote 2), p. 55.

[70] Ford, *op. cit.* (footnote 10), vol. 7, p. 91.

Figure 2.—Set of surgical instruments used by Dr. Benjamin Treadwell during the Revolution. Included are three amputation knives, forceps, a ball extractor, and two surgical hooks. Preserved at the Medical Museum of the Armed Forces Institute of Pathology. (*Photo courtesy of Armed Forces Institute of Pathology.*)

Thomas Attwood returned from Newark to open "his store of Drugs and Medicines in Dock-Street." To touch upon the sympathy of the Loyalists, Donald McLean, "Surgeon of the late Seventy-Seventh Regiment," reported in January 1777 that he was "now happily delivered from his late capitivity" and again opening a shop in Water-Street for drugs and medicines. [71]

Importations from London commenced as early as December 1776 when "the Brig Friendship lying at Beaches Wharf" offered for sale "An Assortment of Drugs, Consisting of Bark, Opium, Rhubarb, &c." In April 1777 Speaight advertised "a fresh Importation . . . from the original ware-houses in London," and, in June, Attwood advertised "A large and general Assortment of Drugs and Medicines freshly imported . . . . Several Medicine Chests complete. fitted up in London, with printed Directions." [72]

Importation by the British was not without its problems, however. Joseph Gurney Bevan, owner of the Plough Court Pharmacy in London, wrote Dr. Traser in Jamaica on October 25, 1777:

I hope thou will be pleased with the Bark. It is very good and the best I have seen this year, but I do not think any Bark in town is equal to what I have seen in former years. Thou wilt note the snake root to be very dear. The cause is the stoppage of the American trade. Opium is also much higher than I ever knew it. The insurance is raised on account of the American privateers.

Answering a letter from William Stewart of New York, Bevan wrote on March 5, 1777:

I wish it were yet in my power to . . . forward the medicines and utensils thou hast written for. But on inquiry I am informed that it is not permitted that anything shall yet be sent to New York in a mercantile way. Therefore I must defer till the wanted intercourse between us and you is re-established . . . . I want to advise thee to buy what snake root thou cans't pick up which I believe if sent hither at the first opening of the trade, will turn to good Account."

Bevan was still reluctant to make any shipments in April because the "ships and cargoes on their arrival at New York will be at the mercy of the persons in command there," but on September 4 he shipped a large order to McLean. [73] During the

remainder of the war, the Plough Court Pharmacy continued regular shipments to McLean as well as to Stewart and to Brownejohn.

"Medicines—None"

Morgan's chaotic situation at New York was mild compared to the conditions at Fort George and Ticonderoga in the Northern Department. Dr. Samuel Stringer, medical director of the Northern Department, wrote General Washington on May 10, 1776, that the majority of the regimental surgeons had neither medicines nor instruments, and that there was no possibility of getting them in Canada Washington replied that he would direct Dr. Morgan to send the required supplies, and ask for additional help from Congress. [74] However, until early in June, Morgan was in no position to outfit medicine chests for any of the troops at New York, much less for the army in the north; and Congress didn't even get around to directing "the committee appointed to provide medicines . . . to send a proper assortment of medicine to Canada" until June 17. [75]

After Morgan had established the general hospital at New York, he wrote to Samuel Adams on June 25 that

. . . the state of the Army in Canada . . . for a supply of medicines is truly deplorable. General Gates sets out to-morrow to take command of the Army in Canada. Dr. Potts will accompany him. I have therefore given orders to supply him from the General Hospital with a large chest of such medicines as I can best spare, and which can be got ready to-morrow before his departure. [76]

Until July 24, the only medicines to arrive at Fort George were the "few that Dr. Potts brought with him" even though Morgan had, according to Stringer, promised to send "by the first sloop twenty half-chests of medicines" put up at New York for ten battalions in the north. Stringer therefore asked permission of General Gates at Ticonderoga to "go forth to York and see the medicines forthwith forwarded by land, until they can be safely conveyed by water." Permission was granted on July 29 and Stringer departed for New York. [77] Meanwhile, Morgan had written Potts on July 28 that he had sent Dr. James McHenry to Philadelphia for drugs, and that he was

[71] New-York Gazette, September 30, December 16, 23, 1776, January 20, 1777.

[72] Ibid., December 9, 1776, April 28, June 9, 1777.

[73] Plough Court Pharmacy letterbook dated April 7, 1778, through December 8, 1779, in possession of Allen and Hanburys, London. See also Chapman-Huston and Ernest C. Gripps, Through a City Archway; The Story of Allen and Hanburys, 1715–1954, London, 1954.

[74] Duncan, op. cit. (footnote 2), p. 97.

[75] Owen, op. cit. (footnote 2), p. 39.

[76] American Archives, ser. 4, vol. 6, p. 1069.

[77] American Archives, ser. 5, vol. 1, pp. 651–652, 1114.

sending Andrew Craigie to Fort George to "act as an Apothecary." Morgan also asked for an inventory of drugs on hand in the Northern Department. [78]

Stringer spent only a day or two in New York with Morgan—just long enough to intensify their personal feud over responsibilities and authority. Stringer determined that the "twenty half-chests" apparently were a figment of someone's imagination, because supplies in New York were almost as bad as they were in the north. Also, he learned that Morgan was sending a box of medicine northward "under the care of the Surgeon of Col. Wayne Regt." [79] that was undoubtedly intended to serve only as a regimental chest. Stringer then hurried on to Philadelphia just in time to intercept McHenry, who had obtained "an order from the Committee of Congress for 40 lb. Bark, 10 [lb.] Camphire and some other articles." [80]

Stringer wrote Potts on August 17 that at last he had obtained an order for medicines that would be packed in two days, but added "when you'll receive them God knows." He also reported that "there will also arrive another Box under the care of Doct. McHenry containing only 5 articles of which there is but 30 lbs. Bark and I think not a purgative except some few pounds of Rhubarb and a little Fol. Senae." [81] McHenry, however, only got as far as New York with his meager supplies, because Stringer discharged him from the service in an attempt to show both Morgan and Potts who had the most authority. [82]

Stringer's inexcusably long absence from his hospital post and failure to send the needed medicines so aroused General Gates that he wrote the President of the Congress on August 31 as follows: [83]

The Director of the General Hospital in this department, Doctor Stringer, was sent to New-York three and thirty days ago, with positive orders to return the instant he had provided the drugs and medicines so much wanted. Since then, repeated letters have been wrote to New-York and

Philadelphia, setting forth in the strongest terms the pressing necessity of an immediate supply of these articles.

Finally, almost a month after his arrival in Philadelphia, Stringer set out for Albany with a small stock of drugs. On September 7 he wrote Potts from Albany that he hoped the small supply that he obtained and the chest of medicines that Morgan had just sent would hold out until he could obtain additional supplies in New England, where he was then headed "to ransack that Country of those articles we want." [84]

Meanwhile, Potts at Fort George had started making the desired inventory of medicines. It came as no surprise to anyone that the situation was deplorable— indeed, it was worse than that. On August 31 a committee of surgeons at Ticonderoga prepared at General Gates' order "A Catalogue of Medicines Most Necessary for the Army." This list, undoubtedly representing the minimum requirements of each battalion, called for 20 pounds of bark, 4 pounds of gum camphor, 2 pounds of gum opium, 3 pounds of powdered ipecac, 4 pounds of powdered jalap, 2 pounds of powdered rhubarb, 15 pounds of Epsom salts, and 3 pounds of tartar emetic among two dozen different medicines. [85] Instead of these minimum requirements, regimental surgeons at Ticonderoga, Crown Point, Mount Independence, and Fort George presented inventories (mostly dated September 8) that clearly emphasized their destitute condition.

The first New Jersey battalion at Ticonderoga reported "No Jallap, Rhubarb, Salts, or Ipecac"; while Colonel Whilocks' regiment at Ticonderoga reported "No medicines exclusive of private property." The five companies of artillery at Fort George reported "Medicines—None," as did the 24th Regiment at Mount Independence. Others reported small or "tollerable" assortments of medicine. A close examination of the inventory of the Pennsylvania 6th Battalion at Crown Point shows it to have been

---

[78] Potts Papers, vol. 1, folio 77; Morgan to Potts, July 28, 1776.

[79] *Ibid.*, folio 89; Stringer to Potts, August 17, 1776. See also Gibson, *op. cit.* (footnote 2), pp. 108–109. Washington mentions Stringer's visit with Morgan in a letter to Gates dated August 14 (Washington, *op. cit.* footnote 48, vol. 5, pp. 433–435).

[80] *Ibid.*; McHenry to Potts, August 3, 1776. [Stringer arrived in Philadelphia on the evening of August 2.]

[81] *Ibid.*; Stringer to Potts, August 17, 1776.

[82] *Ibid.*; McHenry to Potts, August 21, 1776.

[83] *American Archives*, ser. 5, vol. 1, p. 1271. For a similarly worded letter to Egbert Benson dated August 22, see Gibson, *op. cit.* (footnote 2), p. 112.

[84] Potts Papers, vol. 1, folio 98; Stringer to Potts, September 7, 1776. Stringer arrived in Albany on September 5 (Potts Papers, vol. 1, folio 97).

[85] *American Archives*, ser. 5, vol. 1, p. 1266. Other items included "Acet. Com. six barrels; Alo. Hepta. 3 lb.; Calomel 2 lb.; Emp. Diachyl 10 lb.; Cantharid. 2 lb.; Gm. Guiac 1 lb.; Myrrh 1 lb.; Hord. Com. 100 lb.; Jerc. Precip. Rub. ½ lb.; Merc. Cor. Sublim. 1 lb.; Rad. Serpent. Virg. 3 lb.; Sal. Nit. 5 lb.; Spirit Sal. Ammo. 4 lb.; Ung. Diath. 3 lb.; Elix. Asthmat. 5 lb.; and Elix. Vitriol. 10 lb." Also included were six gross of vials and corks and three reams of wrapping paper.

lacking bark, ipecac, rhubarb, camphor, and salts; and only one-half ounce of jalap and 2 ounces of gum opium remained in the chest outfitted by Christopher and Charles Marshall on April 25 in Philadelphia. The 15th Regiment of Foot at Mount Independence claimed 2 ounces of bark and 1½ ounces of gum opium, while the 6th Regiment at Ticonderoga was as well off as any with one-half pound of bark and 4 ounces of gum opium.[86] Compared with the minimum need of 20 pounds of bark and 2 pounds of gum opium, even this was not of much comfort.

The inventory "of the Medicines in the Continental Store at Fort George" dated September 9 was not very comforting either. While the store included 137 different items, including equipment and containers of all the capital medicines, only Epsom salts appeared to be available in a sufficient quantity. Seven pounds of rhubarb were also on hand, but conspicuous by their absence were bark, ipecac, jalap, gum camphor, and gum opium.[87]

With their continuous requests and demands, the regimental surgeons made life miserable for Potts. Surgeon Mate of the Pennsylvania 1st wrote that the "Chest of Medicine . . . is not yet arrived but expect it hourly. . . ." Trumbull asked: "Have your Medicines arriv'd? Have Stringer or McHenry made their appearance yet? Our people fall sick by Dozens. I not a Pennys worth of Medicine have for them, even in the most virulent disorders." Surgeon Johnston begged: "Pray if possible send me 4 pounds Pulv. Cort. Peruv. [Bark] and 3 ounces Tart[ar] Emet[ic]. With those medicines I think I could restore a number of our best Men to perfect Health."[88]

In those instances where some drugs were on hand, the shortage of pharmaceutical equipment hampered, if not prevented, the preparation of proper dosage forms. Surgeon McCrea on board the *Royal Savage* wrote on September 2 that he "found a great inconvenience for want of scales & waits,"[89] and the surgeon at Crown Point wrote on September 19 that "the Medicines which I rec'd a few days ago will be of very little Benefit as I have no fit Mortar &c to prepare them with & must use them in Decoction."[90]

It wasn't until October that any relief arrived, and even then there were disappointments. Andrew Craigie, at Fort George, received a wagonload of herbs on October 3, but, as Craigie reported to Potts, "one half the load is enitrely useless, containing Saffron, Pink flower, and whole H[eade]d Pennyroyal, &c. &c. Dr. Brown thinks his broad shoulders would carry all the articles that are worth anything." Craigie recommended to Potts that payment should not be made for all the useless articles.[91]

The long-lost Stringer finally arrived at Albany from Boston on October 5 and reported to Gates that he had met the greatest success in procuring £5,000 of medicines.[92] Ten days later, Stringer wrote Potts that he was now forwarding "by waggon two Barrels & 1 Box of Medicines . . . [which] will suffice for the present, not thinking it prudent to send up the whole, especially as we can always get them up as they are wanted."[93]

Even after the long delay, most of the supplies were still held in Albany instead of being distributed among the surgeons who needed them. This infuriated Potts to a point that even Stringer found it necessary, on October 25, to explain:

I received yesterday a letter from you . . . before this time you will have rec'd such of the articles you desired as we had to spare [from] the Medicines I purchased at Boston . . . I thought [it] not proper to risque [them] up here; neither were any of them in powder, and all that were so at this place we sent you, and have two hands busy in preparing more for our own use. I hope that [the shipment] sent will be sufficient for your purpose.[94]

Andrew Craigie had sent three barrels and four boxes of supplies to Ticonderoga on October 22,[95] but the shipment obviously did not suffice. On November 7 Stringer wrote that "as soon as possible the Medicines you wrote for shall be prepared and sent, but they are chiefly to be pulverized." In his typical style he added, "I cannot conceive what use you will have for five sieves when you have no large mortar."[96]

The November 27 report of the committee of Congress on the conditions in the general hospital

---

[86] Potts Papers, vol. 1, folios 102–106, 108–111, 114, 119.

[87] *Ibid.*, folio 99. There was a listing for 170 pounds of "Cathart: Am" (Epsom salts). The 7 pounds of rhubarb was listed as "3 lb. Rad. Rhaei and 4 lb. Pul. Rhaei." Also on hand were 1½ pounds of "Mithridat" (opium).

[88] *Ibid.*, folios 73, 94, 124.

[89] *Ibid.*, folio 4; McCrea to Potts, September 2, 1776.

[90] *Ibid.*, folio 124; Johnston to Potts, September 19, 1776.

[91] *Ibid.*, folio 125; Craigie to Potts, October 3, 1776.

[92] *American Archives*, ser. 5, vol. 2, p. 923. Stringer also wrote Potts on October 6 to advise him of the stock (Potts Papers, vol. 1, folio 126).

[93] Potts Papers, vol. 1, folio 131; Stringer to Potts, October 15, 1776.

[94] *Ibid.*, folio 133; Stringer to Potts, October 25, 1776.

[95] *Ibid.*, folio 132; Craigie to Potts, October 22, 1776.

[96] *Ibid.*, folio 138; Stringer to Potts, November 7, 1776.

at Fort George indicates that the supply situation was at last reasonably good,[97] but by this time the season was far advanced and the forces had to retire to winter quarters. Stringer was relieved of his command along with Morgan early the following year. Unlike that of Morgan, Stringer's dismissal appears to have been based on reasonably good grounds.

Privateers to the Rescue

Despite Congress' slow start in providing medical supplies, its members realized as early as December 1775 that additional sources of supply outside the Colonies would be required. On December 23 they heard that £2,000 of medicines, surgeon's instruments, and lint and bandages were required by the army, and on January 3, 1776, the Secret Committee reported to Congress that these supplies should be imported as soon as possible.[98]

In September 1775 Congress had created the Secret Committee to supervise the export and import of vital materials required for the war. Licenses to leave port were given shipmasters on the condition that they would return with vital military stores. Under this dispensation, American ships set out for Europe, Africa, and the West Indies in search of essential supplies.[99] Many months were required, however, to establish such importation as a significant source of supply, and this was especially true with regard to medical supplies.

The delay in initiating importation can hardly be charged as the only or even the main reason for medical supply shortages in 1776. For example, in August of that year, when at least a half-dozen medical supply officers were pleading for drugs from Congress in Philadelphia, John Thomson of Petersburg, Virginia, advertised that he had for sale "Rhubarb and Jalap, Glauber and Epsom Salts, Jesuits Bark" and a host of other supplies.[100] Whether or not Thomson's supplies constituted any significant amount, the very fact that he had to advertise them indicates a lack of coordination and communication between those urgently seeking supplies and those selling them.

Even more frustrating were those suppliers right under Congress's nose advertising essential drugs. Suppliers like Dr. Anthony Yeldall at "his Medicinal

Ware-House" were still advertising "Bark, Camphire, Rhubarb, &c" in July of '76.[101] Philadelphia was second only to New York for Loyalists, and Yeldall was later proven to be a strong Tory. Then there were those who were neither Patriot nor Loyalist; they were just indifferent to the cause for American independence, and thus insisted on cash, even though six months' credit was the common practice just prior to the war. In 1771 in Philadelphia one druggist regularly gave a 15 percent discount on all purchases if paid within six months and 7½ percent discount was allowed for payments between six and nine months, but interest was expected on all debts over a year's standing.[102]

The business-minded members of Congress tried to follow prewar methods by seeking credit. Merchants who sold on credit found that, when they finally were paid, they received paper money backed only by a promise to exchange for gold and silver at some future time. Furthermore, they were caught in a spiraling inflation, and often found that when they finally received their money from Congress it then would cost them twice as much to replenish their stocks. Medical supply officers therefore found it necessary to pay ready cash for merchandise out of their own pocket, and sometimes they had to wait six months for reimbursement from Congress.

As we have noted, by the fall of 1776 Boston had become a better source of supply of drugs than Philadelphia, although it had been occupied by the British for nine months and Morgan had removed most of the drugs left there the previous May. This was primarily due to a single factor—the American privateer. British shipping was vulnerable to the American privateers, which were fast vessels well suited to this kind of enterprise. Well over 1,000 captures were made during the war by Massachusetts privateers alone, and the arrivals of rich prize ships at New England ports became frequent.[103]

The Greenleaf ledger confirms that drugs were included in some of these prize ships. On December 14, 1776, Greenleaf records the receipt of £62 from the Massachusetts government in payment for "an invoice of Druggs taken from the prize ship Julius Caesar." Greenleaf received an even larger stock "of druggs taken in the prize Brig Three Friends" in

---

97 Duncan, *op. cit.* (footnote 2), p. 110.
98 Ford, *op. cit.* (footnote 10), vol. 3, p. 453, vol. 4, pp. 24–25.
99 Miller, *op. cit.* (footnote 1), pp. 103–113.
100 *Virginia Gazette*, August 24, 1776.

101 *Pennsylvania Evening Post,* July 18, 1776.
102 G. B. Griffenhagen, "The Day-Dunlap 1771 Pharmaceutical Catalogue," *American Journal of Pharmacy,* 1955, vol. 127, pp. 296–302.
103 Miller, *op. cit.* (footnote 1), pp. 110–112.

March 1777. This was valued at over £170, and was also used by Massachusetts to pay on its account with Greenleaf, largely for outfitting its privateers.[104]

On June 30, 1777, J. G. Frazer of Boston wrote Dr. Potts, still at Ticonderoga, as follows:[105]

I have the pleasure to give you this Early notice of a prize ship being sent into Casco Bay last week with four tons of Jesuits Bark on board for one valuable article besides a great quantity of other stores for the British Army at New-York.

Brisk Business in Boston

A series of letters to Director General Potts from Apothecary Andrew Craigie, who was on a purchasing trip through New England, gives us an interesting glimpse into the situation. On August 29, 1777, Craigie wrote Potts from Springfield[106] that he had just arrived from Wethersfield where he purchased 222 pounds of bark of excellent quality. He saw it weighed and repacked, and left the necessary instructions for shipment to Albany. Having heard that "a quantity of Bark & other articles are arrived at some eastern ports" Craigie took off for Boston where he wrote Potts on September 1 as follows:[107]

I wrote you from Springfield acquainting you that I had engaged 222 lb. Bark at the Price [£5 per pound] Mr. Livingston mentioned to you; it being very dear induced me to engage a less quantity than you proposed 'til I should make enquiry here. I find to my great mortification that it is 40/ [shillings] less than that in Wethersfield. I wish we could get clear of that engagement, and at least think some adjustment should be made as I am informed it cost Mr. Livingston who bought it at publick sale only 3 Pounds at which price I expect to engage 1 or 200 lb. tomorrow . . . . In the morning I go to Cape Anne about 40 miles from this, after medicines that have lately arrived . . . .

Recalling Stringer's long absence of the previous year, Craigie concluded:

I shall pay particular attention to, and if to be had, procure the articles, but everything is very dear. I hope not to exceed the time you have limited.

Craigie returned to Albany on September 20 and advised Potts that he "succeeded in procuring medicines as expected" and that he had "on the road 2 covered waggons of capital medicines &c."[108] The shipment included 200 pounds of bark that Craigie bought at £3 a pound, and waiting for him in Albany were also the 222 pounds of bark, for which he was billed at £5 a pound plus £23/10 "Carting and Expenses."[109] Payment had not been made by November 10,[110] nor was there any evidence of an adjustment.

At the same time that Craigie was in Boston purchasing supplies for the Northern Department, Apothecary Jonathan B. Cutting of the Middle Department was also there, competing with him.[111] Furthermore, several agents for the Congress (Thomas Cushing, Daniel Tillinghast, and John Bradford) were purchasing drugs for the Continental Navy. Greenleaf's ledger records that between January 23 and May 28 over £500 worth of medicine chests and sundry medicines were sold to "The United American States" for the Continental frigates *Boston*, *Hancock*, *Providence*, and *Columbus*.

This competition among various branches of the army and navy led to a brisk business in Boston. Druggists in nearby communities chanced the British blockade to send supplies which they had on hand. For example, Jonathan Waldo, an apothecary at Salem, Massachusetts, recorded in his account book[112] on April 8, 1777, that "13 packages and 4 cases of medicines are ship'd on Board the Sloop called the Two Brothers Saml West Master. An Account and [illegible word] of Mr. Oliver Smith of Boston Apothecary and to him consigned." Evidence of the war appears in the footnote to the entry, however. It reads: "The cases are unmarked being ship'd at Night. Error Excepted. Jon. Waldo."

The Situation Improves

Oliver Smith, advertising in a Boston newspaper in October 1777, clearly emphasized the fact that "A Large and Valuable Assortment of Drugs and Medicines" were on hand. Included in the listing were bark, gum camphor, gum opium, jalap, rhubarb, and salts.[113]

Back in Philadelphia, the supply situation was also improving. William Smith, Continental Druggists, received over $5,000 from Congress for drug pur-

[104] Greenleaf Ledger, *op. cit.* (footnote 6).
[105] Potts Papers, vol. 2, folio 213.
[106] *Ibid.*, vol. 3, folio 305.
[107] *Ibid.*, folio 331.
[108] *Ibid.*, folio 346.

[109] *Ibid.*, folio 336.
[110] *Ibid.*, folio 369.
[111] *Ibid.*, folio 331; Craigie to Potts, September 1, 1777.
[112] Preserved at the Essex Institute, Salem, Massachusetts.
[113] *Independent Chronicle*, October 30, 1777.

chases, [114] and the Marshalls also continued to furnish Congress with a variety of medical supplies in amounts upwards of $4,000. [115] Drugs were occasionally being imported into Philadelphia despite the British blockade. In January 1777, Robert Bass, an apothecary in Market Street, advertised [116] "A Quantity of Peruvian Bark, just imported . . . together with Drugs and Medicines of most kinds." Bass was supplying the Northern Department with drugs in February 1777, but, according to a letter from John Warren to Potts, "he is determined not even to pack them untill he shall receive the money in payment for them." [117] In March, Bass wrote Potts directly that

. . . if in future you want any compositions let me know in time that I may have them ready. I cou'd not send a full quantity [of] fly Plasters, but am this week making a large quantity of most kinds and shall send of deficiency in your next order. [118]

In June, Christopher and Charles Marshall also received "a small assortment of valuable medicines, just imported and to be sold" [119] to replenish their stock. Even Congress purchased directly certain of the importations, on May 28, 1778, for example, ordering that "755 42/90 dollars be advanced to the Committee of Commerce, to enable them to pay Andrew and James Caldwell, the freight of sundry medicines imported in their sloop from Martinico." [120] Many of the British prize ships were carried to the French island of Martinique in the West Indies for trans-shipment of their cargoes.

These shipments however did not meet with the requirements for medical supplies. In March, Apothecary Cutting, then stationed at the "Continental Medicine Store in Fourth-Street," Philadelphia, advertised that "any price will be given for old sheets, or half worn linen proper for lint and bandages," while, in May, Commissary Hugh James advertised that "a handsome price will be given for

Vials and Corks." [121] The problems of medical supplies were often brought to the attention of the public. Thomas Carnes, "Quarter Master and Steward" of the American hospital in New England, advertised in several papers that he

is authorized to make known in this public manner, that no Expense shall be spared in future in making the most ample Provision for the sick and wounded of the Army . . . . Proper medicines will be prepared, not only by General Hospitals, but by Regimental Surgeons. The Difficulties the Sick and Wounded met with the last Campaign arose from the unsettled State of the Army, and the Distance Medicines, and other Necessaries used to be sent. [122]

The reorganization of the medical department by Congress, including the establishment of "two Apothecaries" and their duties, was published in the *Pennsylvania Packet* on April 15, and a front page account presenting "directions for preserving the Health of Soldiers" was featured in the next issue. [123]

Dr. Potts wrote the Medical Committee in Congress on April 3, 1777:

I have the Honour to enclose you a Return of the Medicines & Stores belonging to the General Hospital in the Department, which I have received from Doctor Samuel Stringer, these with what I brought with me from Philadelphia & some few I expect from Boston will be quite sufficient for this campaign.

In contrast to the time when stores were short in '76, the chairman of the Medical Committee, M. Thornton, was quick to reply on April 12 that

. . . we are highly pleased with your having the prospect of a sufficient supply of medicines in your Department for the ensuing Campaign, & approve of the returns you have made us. [124]

Valley Forge

Washington's forces were defeated at Brandywine on September 11, 1777, and on September 25 the British army occupied Philadelphia. Washington, after trying without success to dislodge them by a sudden attack at Germantown on October 4, retreated to Valley Forge.

Business in Philadelphia under British occupation continued much as it had under American control, except for a few missing suppliers and a few new ones.

---

[114] Ford, *op. cit.* (footnote 10), vol. 5, p. 748, vol. 7, p. 274, vol. 8, p. 538. (Smith received $2,490 on September 9, 1776, $2,952 on April 17, 1777, "for sundry medicines," and Caldwell & Co. received $666 on July 7, 1777, "for sundry medicine delivered William Smith.")

[115] *Ibid.*, vol. 7, p. 321. (Christopher and Charles Marshall received $4,151 on May 2, 1777, "for sundry medicines and chirurgical instruments supplied by them for the use of different battalions of continental forces.")

[116] *Pennsylvania Journal*, January 29, 1777.

[117] Potts Papers, vol. 2, folio 150.

[118] *Ibid.*, folio 153; Bass to Potts, March 17, 1777.

[119] *Pennsylvania Journal*, June 11, July 9, 23, 1777.

[120] Ford, *op. cit.* (footnote 10), vol. 11, p. 546.

[121] *Pennsylvania Evening Post*, March 18, May 27, 1777.

[122] *Boston Gazette*, February 3, 1777; *Connecticut Courant*, April 7, 1777.

[123] *Pennsylvania Packet*, April 15, 22, 1777. This anonymous article was written by Dr. Benjamin Rush and reprinted as a pamphlet.

[124] Potts Papers, vol. 2, folios 158, 159.

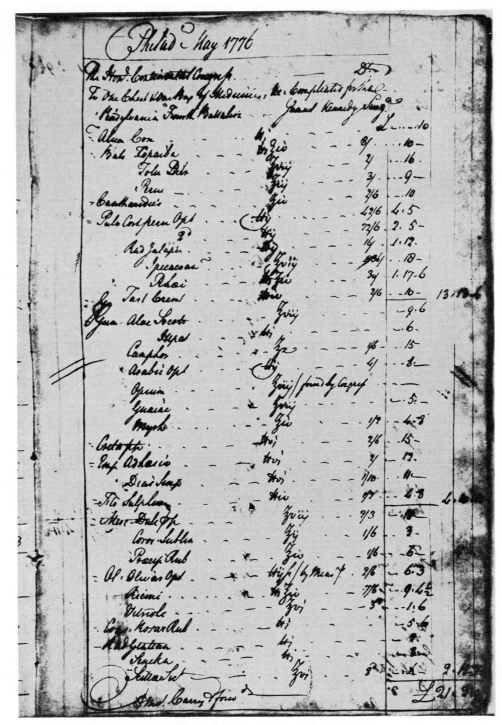

Figure 3.—Page from the Waste Book manuscript of the Christopher Marshall, Jr., and Charles Marshall apothecary shop in Philadelphia. This is the first page of the contents of a medicine chest furnished on order of the Continental Congress for the Pennsylvania 4th Battalion. Preserved at the Historical Society of Pennsylvania, in Philadelphia.

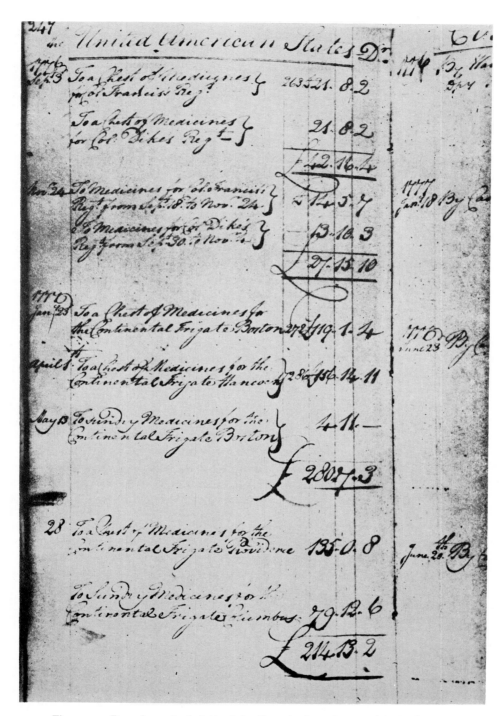

Figure 4.—Page from the ledger of the Greenleaf apothecary shop in Boston, showing the accounts between September 3, 1776, and May 28, 1777, with "the United American States" for outfitting ships of the Continental Navy. Preserved at the American Antiquarian Society, Worcester, Mass.

One druggist who was little in evidence after the war commenced was back in business advertising within two weeks after the British occupied Philadelphia. It was William Drewet Smith (not to be confused with William Smith) who advised "friends and customers . . . that they can be supplied with Medicine and Drugs as usual, at his shop in Second-Street." To indicate that he was expecting an active business, Smith also advertised for "a person who can be well recommended for honesty and sobriety . . . to attend a Druggist's Shop." [125]

During the British occupation there was a large number of thefts and losses—perhaps aided by the American patriots who remained in Philadelphia— that included drugs and surgical instruments. In November an advertisement reported the loss of "a sett of Surgeons Pocket instruments in a crimson chequered covering, with a silver clasp. Whoever will bring them to the bar of the coffee-house or to Mr. Allman, surgeons mate of the Royal Artillery, shall have a Guinea reward, and no questions asked." In April an unidentified druggist advertised: "Stolen yesterday afternoon out of an apothecary's shop Three Specie Glasses, with brass caps; one contained two pounds of native cinnabar. Whoever discovers the thief and goods shall have Twenty Shillings reward from the printer." [126]

A sign of the times is evident from the advertisement by Dr. Anthony Yeldall, who offered his "Anti-Venereal Essence at only Two Dollars." This nostrum, it was claimed, would not only cure the disease, but would "absolutely prevent catching the infection." Each bottle came with printed instructions "so that no questions need be asked." The fact that the advertisement appeared no less than 10 times from January through April speaks for its success. [127] It is interesting to note that, after the British evacuated Philadelphia, "Anthony Yeldall, Surgeon, late of the city of Philadelphia," was included among those who were charged as having "knowingly and willingly aided and assisted the enemies" and who would be brought to trial for high treason. [128]

While the British forces rested, well nourished, warm, and relatively secure in Philadelphia, Washington's troops, hardly more than 20 miles away, were tortured by cold, hunger, and disease. On December 23 there were 2,898 men at Valley Forge reported sick or unfit for duty because of lack of clothing. [129] Even so, the lack of medical supplies was nowhere near as bad as the conditions that existed in '76. Under the command of Director General Shippen and Purveyor General Potts, [130] the medical department operated a series of hospitals in such Pennsylvania communities as Easton, Bethlehem, Lancaster, Ephrata, and Lititz. The principal hospital for Valley Forge was established 10 miles away at Yellow Springs (now Chester Springs).

The largest drain on medical supplies appears not to have been during the height of winter but rather in the early spring when the medicine chests of various regiments and hospitals were being restocked for the expected spring offensive. The first step was to supplement the supply of medical supplies on hand. In late February or early March, Dr. William Brown sent Purveyor General Potts a list of needs of the entire medical department that included £20,000 worth of medicines, vials, corks, etc. [131] Dr. Brown supplemented this list with a letter to Potts dated March 11 in which he itemized the following equipment: [132]

3 doz. Boxes Small Apothecary's Weights & Scales
3 doz. Bolus knives
3 doz. Pot Spathulae
2 doz. Marble Mortars, of one pint, & Pestles
2 doz. Setts Measures, from ½ ounce to 1 [pint?]
6 doz. Earthen Vessels (deep) with handles—of different sizes, from 2 quarts to 2 galls, for boiling Decoctions, or 2 doz. copper Do. of one gallon—for that purpose.
6 doz. Delft Ware Tiles, for mixing Boluses &c. on.

While Dr. Brown was completing his report on medical supplies, he was also concluding his compila-

[125] *Pennsylvania Ledger*, October 10, 1777; *Pennsylvania Evening Post*, October 14, 18, 1777.

[126] *Pennsylvania Evening Post*, November 1, 8, 13, 1777, April 29, 1778. (A large number of advertisements announcing thefts appeared during the British occupation.)

[127] *Pennsylvania Evening Post*, January 10 through April 20, 1778, and *Pennsylvania Ledger*, April 4, 15, 1778. [Yeldall advertised his "Anti-Venereal Essence" only once under American occupation, but at $4.00 per bottle (*Pennsylvania Evening Post*, August 26, 1777).]

[128] *Pennsylvania Evening Post*, June 25, 1777.

[129] Gibson, *op. cit.* (footnote 2), p. 149.

[130] It was in February 1778 that Dr. Potts assumed his office as purveyor general for the hospital department of the Continental Army with the duty of purchasing and distributing all supplies and medicines (*ibid.*, p. 154).

[131] Potts Papers, vol. 1, folio 24. (This apparently is the list prepared by Brown, even though it is not signed by him. The item "Medicines, Vials, Cork &c £20,000" was added with the statement "The above enumerated articles should be purchased immediately," and both were in the handwriting of "W. Shippen, D.G." The document is undated.)

[132] *Ibid.*, vol. 4, folio 419; Brown to Potts, March 11, 1778.

tion of an emergency military hospital formulary which has become known as the *Lititz Pharmacopoeia*, so named because Brown was making Lititz his headquarters at the time. The preface is dated "Lititz, March 12, 1778." The actual title (translated from Latin) reads: "Formulary of simple and yet efficacious remedies for the use of the military hospital, belonging to the army of the Federated States of America. Especially adapted to our poverty and straitened circumstances, caused by the ferocious inhumanity of the enemy, and the cruel war unexpectedly brought upon our fatherland." This formulary was published by Styner & Cist of Philadelphia in 1778, which means that it was not actually printed until sometime after June 18, when the British evacuated Philadelphia.

In the preface Brown explained that there were two types of formulas contained in the *Lititz Pharmacopoeia;* one was the "medicaments which must be prepared and compounded in a general laboratory; the others are to be mixed, as needed, in our hospital dispensaries."

The main store of drugs was housed at Manheim until late March, when Shippen ordered Apothecary Cutting to pack the medical stores there and proceed on to Yellow Springs. [133] Cutting wrote Potts on March 30 that

. . . the articles that we have in store are now ready to put on board the waggons excepting the want of cases to contain them . . . . Paper, Twine, Square Snuff Bottles & Corks are so essentially necessary to take with us, to fit up the Regimental Chests that I wish your order to buy them at Lancaster immediately. I never heard what place in the vicinity of Camp has been chosen for our temporary Medicine Shop, nor what quantities the Regimental Surgeons are to be supply'd when we get there . . . . [134]

On April 16 Cutting [135] wrote that the

. . . dispensing store is open'd here [at Yellow Springs] and we have begun to supply the Regiments in Camp . . . . Dr. Cochran has given orders to the Division on the left to bring their Chests first, and we propose going through the whole Army in the order in which they lay . . . . The best method I can think of is to act immediately about preparing new Chests upon the Northern Plan at some convenient place for all such Battallions as did not get chests from Dr. Craigie [in the] last campaign. When these new parcels are ready, let us call all the large chests into the Stores . . . which are too compleat & capacious for Field Service, & in lieu of them give out our smaller

ones. By this exchange, the Genl. Hospital will be well supplied with standing Chests & acquire a great variety of useful articles which are not essential in Camp.

Apothecary Cutting was concerned, however, over supplies and

. . . very apprehensive that the several Hospitals in this vicinity will render a further reinforcement necessary before we shall be able to compleat the whole . . . . To give only a few of the Capitals to each will be a work of Time, & a much more intensive piece of business than I at first imagined.

Meanwhile, Potts had sent Apothecary Craigie to Baltimore to obtain a fresh stock of drugs, and probably to prevent further friction between Craigie and Cutting. This feud started early in 1777 when Apothecary Cutting, serving with Shippen in Philadelphia, was named, over his preceptor Craigie, to head the newly organized "Apothecary department" of the army. [136] On March 27 Craigie wrote from Annapolis advising Potts that he had been in Baltimore

. . . not long since and waited on Messrs. Lux & Bowly. The medicines were not come to hand but were expected . . . . I have engaged the whole invoice which contains several important medicines not mentioned in your list. I think the prices are full high, tho' somewhat less than Dr. Shippen affixed, and it was not in my power to procure them at a cheaper rate. They were offered £20 per lb. for all the Cantharides and much higher price for the Bark. They are not yet arrived from some place in Virginia where they were first landed. I shall examine them immediately on their arrival, and if good forward them on to Manheim, if they prove not good shall reject them, as the engagement is conditional. [137]

Then on April 4, Craigie wrote from Chester Town: [138]

I this day received a letter from Messrs. Lux & Bowley informing me, the waggons were arrived, but to their great surprise with only two packages of medicines, the others being seized near Williamsburg for the use of Virginia State. Those arrived contain but a very small share of any of the articles mentioned in your list and I believe none of the Bark and Cantharides. I shall immediately proceed to Baltimore and examine those two packages & if good send them on to Manheim, provided the price is agreeable . . . . I shall inquire into the circumstances of the seizure and endeavor to find out if there has been any unfair play which I can hardly suspect from the character of the Gentlemen.

[133] *Ibid.*, folio 428; Cutting to Potts, March 25, 1778.

[134] *Ibid.*, folio 432; Cutting to Potts, March 30, 1778.

[135] *Ibid.*, folio 441; Cutting to Potts, April 16, 1778.

[136] *Ibid.*, vol. 2, folio 151; Tillotson to Potts, February 22, 1777. [Cutting served as Assistant Apothecary under Craigie at Cambridge and Roxbury. The feud has not been explored in any of Craigie's biographies.]

[137] *Ibid.*, vol. 4, folio 429; Craigie to Potts, March 27, 1778.

[138] *Ibid.*, folio 437; Craigie to Potts, April 4, 1778.

Just prior to May 1, Craigie returned to Carlisle, where the "Elaboratory and Stores for the reception of the medicines &c. belonging to the military hospitals" was established,[139] and complained that he did not find the medicinal store in the order which he expected to find it:

We have many important medicines but by no means an assortment sufficient for the Army. I speak only of what is now in store. There are Medicines in different places of which I have no list.

Craigie further noted that Cutting had come up from Yellow Springs on May 1 to confer regarding plans for completing medicine chests, and would leave the following day for Baltimore where he obviously was going to try to purchase more drugs.

Craigie was puzzled by the establishment of a dispensing store at Yellow Springs, and asked whether or not the plan was

. . . to have the principle Store at Carlisle, where all the medicines shall be prepared, and the Chests compleated supposing the Genl. Hospitals will be more collected, and the number lessened. I would propose that an Apothecary attend each with a complete Chest of Medicines; that the Surgeon & Physician Genl of the Army be attended by an Apothecary with good Chest, and the Regiments supply'd upon the Northern Plan. I would have an Issuing Store established at a convenient distance from the Army, from which the Hospital and Regimental Chests might occasionally be replenished.[140]

A sizable stock of drugs was finally received from Baltimore,[141] and a fairly good stock was brought down from the stores in the Northern Department, which were left well supplied by Craigie and Potts.[142] An improved plan for obtaining lint from the Moravian Sisters at Bethlehem and Lititz was pro-

posed by Dr. Brown,[143] and "the propriety of setting the glass works at Manheim agoing" was offered as a solution by Craigie for obtaining much needed vials.[144] Local manufacturing at Carlisle[145] and "in the Jersies"[146] was used as a source of volatile and purging salts.

Gibson records[147] that between April 19 and May 3, 1778, the commands of Generals Patterson, Leonard, Poor, Glover, Scott, and Woodward turned in their medicine chests to Apothecary Cutting at Yellow Springs, and that every regiment received a standardized field box containing a definite list and quantity of necessary drugs and supplies. However, it appears likely that the project started by Cutting and continued by Craigie was not completed until late June at the earliest.[148] The "invoice of those things thought essential for the protection and health of soldiers in the field or camp" presented by Gibson[149] is actually an "Invoice of a Chest of medi-icines &c. compleated in the medicinal Store, N[orthern] D[epartmen]t for Thos. Tillotson Esq."[150] Inasmuch as the plan used in the Northern Department was employed by both Craigie and Cutting, the items on this invoice may serve as a reasonably good picture of the medicine chests of '78 as compared with those of '76 (see page 130).

One of the reasons for better supplies at a time when other conditions were even worse than they were in 1776 is the fact that Congress was advancing sizable, if not always completely adequate, amounts of money for the cash purchase of supplies instead of seeking credit or expecting those responsible to procure

[139] *Ibid.*, folio 411; Potts to Gates, February 24, 1778.

[140] *Ibid.*, folio 441; Craigie to Potts, May 1, 1778.

[141] *Ibid.*, vol. 1, folios 41, 44; undated invoices from Lux & Bowly that undoubtedly were supplied during the spring or summer of 1778. Also, vol. 4, folio 476; letter from James Caldwell to Potts advising "I sent forward from Baltimore a case of medicine & five cases of Bark . . . I have three cases more of Bark not yet up from Williamsburg where it arrived."

[142] *Ibid.*, vol. 4, folio 458; Craigie to Potts, May 1, 1778. Craigie advises: "Enclosed is a small List directed to Mr. Root [Israel Root or Josiah Root, both apothecaries from Connecticut] which I think may well be spared from the Northward, and are much wanted here. I wish therefore they may be ordered. Andrew Atekin our assistant there might come with them—he would make a good Hospital Apothecary." Also, vol. 4, folio 431, an undated "Invoice of Medicines &c. to be forwarded for Head Quarters to Compleat ye Regimental Assortments for the Army of the United States in the Middle Department for the Campaign 1778."

[143] *Ibid.*, folio 419; Brown to Potts, March 11, 1778.

[144] *Ibid.*, folio 458; Craigie to Potts, May 1, 1778.

[145] *Ibid.*, folio 428; Cutting to Potts, March 25, 1778. Cutting notes: "as to volatile salts, I expect a fine parcel manufactured at Carlisle by tomorrow."

[146] *Ibid.*, folio 471; Craik to Potts, May 24, 1778. Dr. Craik, a regimental surgeon, advises: "I wish you could procure some Cathartic salts. The Regimental surgeons complain greatly for want of them . . . You may engage any quantity at the salt works in the Jersies."

[147] Gibson, *op. cit.* (footnote 2), pp. 166–167.

[148] Potts Papers, vol. 4, folios 462, 467; Craik to Potts, May 2 and May 15. On May 2, Craik advises that "the medicine chests are much wanted in the Regiments. Doctr. Cutting had best have them filled up as soon as possible to prevent complaints." On May 15 Craik commented: "I am sorry Doctr. Cutting went away before the Regiment Chests were finished; there is great clamour about them tho Doctr. Layman is as busy as possible . . . I hope Doctr. Craig[ie] will soon have his chests ready."

[149] Gibson, *op. cit.* (footnote 2), pp. 167–168.

[150] Potts Papers, vol. 1, folio 25, undated.

supplies by using their personal money and waiting on Congress to reimburse them. During 1778, Congress advanced some $940,000 to Purveyor General Potts alone for the exclusive use of the hospital department, and these funds were in turn distributed to the proper medical procurement officers, including the apothecaries. It is significant to compare the sum of $1,095,000 provided by Congress in 1778 with £10,000 (about $27,000) which, according to Morgan, was the limit for medical and hospital supplies in 1776.[151] True, inflation had set in by 1778, and the value of money had declined greatly. For example, cantharides purchased from the Marshalls' apothecary shop in Philadelphia in 1776 cost 10 shillings per pound as compared with the cantharides Craigie purchased in Baltimore in 1778 at £20 per pound. However, the worst of the inflation was yet to come.[152]

In Summary

Initially the drug supplies for the American Revolutionary Army had come from stocks largely in the hands of private druggists. However, this source of supply was totally inadequate for a war that attained such proportions as the Revolution. Even if stocks of drugs in the Colonies had been far greater than they were, there is little reason to believe that shortages would not have developed. After all, a good many of the suppliers were Loyalists, and others were indifferent to the cause of American liberty. Even the most patriotic pharmacists were faced with a complete financial suicide, caught between a spiraling inflation and a Congress that had no money and only a promise for the future.

As if all these problems were not bad enough, the internal organization of the medical department of the army was so chaotic that, even if adequate supplies were available and if the almost insurmountable problems of communications and transportation were solved, it is almost certain that shortages would have developed at least during the campaign of 1776. Add to this the fact that any retreating army is subject to loss of supplies and the reasons for the shortages become very obvious.

The encouragement which Congress, through its Secret Committee, gave to private shippers for the importation of vital war materials offered little relief in the field of medical supplies. Importation was, of course, cut off from England, and France did not directly export any quantity of medical supplies, at least until 1778. American privateers found it much more profitable to prey on British shipping than initiating trade channels with countries which prior to the Revolution were prohibited from shipping directly to the Colonies. These channels of commerce did not develop extensively until well after the Revolution.

Hence the most immediate relief from medical supply shortages was provided by the American privateers. Drug cargoes from British prize ships, many of which were en route to New York, served as a most important source of supply, particularly in 1777 and 1778.

However, even with the most adequate supplies, competition between different branches of the army and navy and the confiscation of supplies destined for Continental troops by state militias further encouraged inflationary trends.

The number of individual drugs mentioned in various inventories was considerable, as evidenced by the listing on page 130. However, of these, only about a dozen constituted the really critical shortages. Heading the list of these "capital articles" was Peruvian or Jesuits' bark, the same cinchona from which quinine was later discovered. Tons of bark were used during the Revolutionary War, and the price more than quandrupled between June 1776 and September 1777.

The most prominent group of drugs on the list of capital articles consisted of cathartics and purgatives. Jalap, ipecac, and rhubarb were the botanical favorites, while bitter purging salts (Epsom salts) and Glauber's purging salts were the chemical choices for purging. Tartar emetic (antimony and potassium tartrate) was the choice for a vomit, and cantharides (Spanish flies) was the most important ingredient of blistering plasters. Gum opium was administered for its narcotic effects, while gum camphor, nitre (saltpetre or potassium nitrate), and mercury (pure metal as well as certain salts) were employed for a variety of purposes. Lint, a form of absorbent material made by scraping or picking apart old woven material, also often was short in supply.

Equipment shortages included surgical instruments and mortar and pestles for pulverizing the crude drugs. Glass vials for holding compounded medicines were also a supply problem, especially after essential drugs were again available.

[151] Gibson, op. cit. (footnote 2), p. 178, and Duncan, op. cit. (footnote 2), pp. 115–116, 275.

[152] Miller, op. cit. (footnote 1), pp. 425–477.

Some of the shortages were eased, if not solved, by local manufacture. Lint was produced in large quantities in the Colonies, and glass vials were manufactured in numerous glasshouses. Even local manufacture of the purging salts and nitre aided in eliminating shortages of these essential items, and at the same time initiated the first large-scale pharmaceutical manufacturing in America.

Numerous botanicals indigenous to the Colonies were widely employed in medicine of the period, and certain ones such as snakeroot (seneka), which was widely found growing in Virginia, would have been very scarce had not an adequate supply been immediately at hand. However, attempts to substitute other indigenous plants for scarce drugs like Peruvian bark were largely unsuccessful. There is no indication that hysop, wormwood, and mallows called for during the New York crisis were ever found to be suitable replacements for any of the capital articles. Wine apparently was more useful as a substitute for bark than the bark of butternut recommended by the *Lititz Pharmacopoeia*. Peruvian bark, jalap, ipecac, camphor, opium, cantharides—these are the drugs which the American army physicians wanted, and these constituted the most serious shortage problems.

The medical supply problem was placed on relatively firm ground by the summer of 1778, having been established on the principles proven in the Northern Department under the guidance of Drs. Potts and Craigie. Furthermore, the turning point in the war had been reached. Even before Washington's forces went into winter quarters at Valley Forge, Burgoyne [153] had surrendered at Saratoga, on October 17, 1777; and, before the cold bleak winter at Valley Forge was over, the treaty of French alliance was signed on February 6, 1778. The torments at Valley Forge proved to be the birth of a new Continental Army.

The War was still a long way from being over, and a variety of problems were yet to face the Continental Army. Inflation was yet to deal its hardest blow to the supply problem, but not even this could produce the chaos of 1776. The worst of the drug supply problem was over.

[153] An interesting account of the medical aspects of Burgoyne's campaign is recorded by R. M. Gorssline in *Canadian Defense Quarterly*, 1929, vol. 6, pp. 356–363.

Contents of Army Medicine Chests

The following listing is an example of the contents of medicine chests ordered by the Continental Congress. The chest for the Pennsylvania 4th Battalion was filled for "Samuel Kennedy Surgeon" by the pharmacy of Christopher Jr. and Charles Marshall of Philadelphia in May 1776. The medicines are listed on an invoice in the Marshalls' waste book in the possession of The Historical Society of Pennsylvania. The contents of the Northern Department chest, compiled in the Northern Department's "Medicinal Store" for "Thos. Tillotson Esq. Surgeon & Physician General to the Army," probably was filled by Andrew Craigie at Fort George in 1778. (*Italics* denote capital article; asterisk indicates that the drug is mentioned in *Lititz Pharmacopoeia*. Contemporary English names are in parentheses following the Latin listings.)

	Pennsylvania 4th Battalion Chest	Northern Department Chest
BOTANICALS		
Cort[ex] Peruv[ianum] (Peruvian bark; Jesuits' bark; or bark)		4 lb.
Pulv[is] Cort[icis] Peruv[iani] (Powdered Peruvian bark)	2 lb. Opt.; 2 lb. 2nd	6 lb.
Pulvis Rad[ix] Jalapii (Powdered jalap)	2 lb.	2 lb.
Pulv[is] Rad[ix] Ipecacuan[hae] (Powdered ipecac)	8 oz.	12 oz.
Pulv[is] Rad[ix] Rhaei (Powdered rhubarb)	1 lb. 4 oz.	4 lb.
Rad[ix] Rhaei (Rhubarb root)		2 lb.
*Fol[ia] Sennae (Sennae or sena)		2 lb.
*Rad[ix] Gentian[ae] (Gentian root)	1 lb.	2½ lb.
*Rad[ix] Seneka (Senega; rattlesnake root; or snake root)	1 lb.	
*Rad[ix] Scillae Sict. (Squill; or sea-onion)	6 oz.	
Cinnamomi (Cinnamon)		1 lb.

	Pennsylvania 4th Battalion Chest	Northern Department Chest
BOTANICALS—Continued		
Cort[ex] Aurant[orium] (Orange peel)		3 lb.
Fl[ores] Chamom[eli] (Camomile flower)		2 oz.
Mellisa[e Folia] (Balm)	½ lb.	
*Gum[mi] Camphor[a] (Camphor; or camphire)	10 oz.	2½ lb.
*Gum[mi] Opium [also] Opii (Opium)	8 oz.	1 lb.
*Gum[mi] Arabic[um] (Gum Arabic)	2 lb. Opt.	2 lb.
*Gum[mi] Aloe Socotr[ina] (Aloe; or aloes)	8 oz.	1 lb.
Gum[mi] Aloe Hepat[ica] (Aloe; or aloes)	1 lb.	
*Gum[mi] Ammon[iacum] (Gum ammoniac)		12 oz.
*Gum[mi] Guaiac[um] (Gum guaiac)	8 oz.	¾ lb.
*Gum[mi] Myrrh[ae] (Myrrh)	4 oz.	2 oz.
*Bals[amum] Capivi (Balsam of copaiba)	1 lb. 4 oz.	2 lb.
*Bals[amum] Peruvian[um] (Balsam of Peru)	3 oz.	
Bals[amum] Tolu[tanum] (Balsam of tolu)	8 oz.	
*Ol[eum] Olivar[um] (Olive oil)	2½ lb.	
*Ol[eum] Ricini (Castor oil)	1 lb. 4 oz.	2 lb.
DRUGS OF ANIMAL ORIGIN		
*Cantharides (Spanish flies; or flies)	4 oz.	¾ lb.
*Cera Flav[a] (Yellow beeswax)	1 lb.	4 lb.
*Mel[lis] Com[munis] (Honey)	3 lb.	
Pul[vis] Oc[uli] Canc[orum] (Powdered crabs' eyes)		1 lb.
*Sperm[atis] Ceti (Spermaceti)		3 lb.
CHEMICALS		
*Alum[en] Com[munis] or Credem (Alum or rock alum)	1 lb.	
*Creta ppt [precipitated or praeparata] (Chalk)	6 lb.	
*Pulv[is] Crem[or] Tartar[i] (Cream of tartar)	4 lb.	2 lb.
*Tart[arus] Emetic[um] (Tartar emetic)	6 oz.	½ lb.
*Sal Nitri [or] Nitrum (Nitre or saltpetre)	4 lb.	4 lb.
Sal Absinthii (Salt of wormwood)	8 oz.	
*Sal Cath[articus] Amar[us] (Epsom salts; bitter purging salts; or bitter cathartic salts)	10 lb.	
*Sal Cath[articus] Glauber[i] [or] Sal Mirabile Glauberi (Glauber's salts; Glauber's purging salts; or Glauber's wonderful salts).	10 lb.	
*Sal Tartar[isatus] (Salt of tartar)		2 lb.
*Sal Amm[oniacum] (Sal ammoniac)		½ lb Cd.
*Merc[urius] Corros[ivus] Sublim[atus] (Corrosive sublimate of mercury)	2 oz.	2 oz.
*Merc[urius] Praecip[itatus] Rub[er] (Red precipitate of mercury)	4 oz.	2 oz.
*Merc[urius] Dulc[is] Ppt. (Calomel)	8 oz.	
Flor[es] Sulphur[is] (Flowers of sulphur)	4 lb.	2 lb.
*Ol[eum] Vitriol[um] (Oil of vitriol)	6 oz.	
Ol[eum] Tereb[inthinae] (Oil of turpentine)		1½ lb.
Tereb[inthina] Venet[ian] (Turpentine)	1 lb. 4 oz.	
*Vitriol[um] Alb[um] (White vitriol)	4 oz.	2 oz.
*Elix[ir] Vitriol[i] (Elixir of vitriol)	3 lb.	2 lb.
Vitriol[um] Rom[anum] (Roman vitriol)	4 oz.	
Sacch[arum] Saturni (Sugar of lead)	4 oz	
Vitr[um] Antomon[ii] Cerat[um] (Cerated glass of antimony)	3 oz.	
*Extr[actum] Saturni [also] Acetum Lithargyrites (Litharge of lead; litharge vinegar; or extract of Saturn).	11 oz.	

	Pennsylvania 4th Battalion Chest	Northern Department Chest
TINCTURES		
*Tinc[tura] Thebaic[a] [or] Tinctura Opii [or] Laudani Liquidi (Tincture of opium; thebaic tincture; liquid laudanum; and Sydenham's laudanam).	12 oz.	2 lb.
*Tinct[ura] Myrrh[ae] & Aloes (Tincture of myrrh and aloes).		1 lb. 12 oz.
Tinct[ura] Cinnam[omi] (Tincture of cinnamon)		2 lb.
SPIRITS		
Sp[iritus] Sal[is] Ammon[iaci] (Spirit of sal ammoniac)	1 lb. 5 oz.	
Sp[iritus] Nitri Dulc[is] [also] Sal[is] Vol[atilis] (Sweet spirit of nitre)	2½ lb.	1 lb. 12 oz.
Sp[iritus] Lavend[ula] Co[mpositus] (Compound spirit of lavender)	1 lb. 4 oz.	1½ lb.
Sp[iritus] Vini Rect[ificatus] (Rectified spirit of wine)	1 lb. 4 oz.	
MISCELLANEOUS PREPARATIONS		
*Cons[erva] Rosar[um] Rub[rarum] (Conserves of red roses)	1 lb.	
Conf[ectio] Cardiac[a] (Cordial confection)		1 lb.
Elect[uarium] Asthmatic[um] (Asthmatic electuary)	1 lb. 1 oz.	
*Elix[ir] Paregor[icum] (Paregoric elixir)		2 lb.
Pill[ulae] Purgant (Purgative pills)	8 oz.	
Pulv[is] e Bol[o Compositus] (Compound powder of bole with opium)		2 lb.
Linim[entum] Sapo[naceum] (Soap liniment)		3½ lb.
Sapo[nis] Venet[ian] (Venetian soap)	2 lb.	6 lb.
OINTMENTS		
*Ung[euntum] Lap[ide] Calamin[ari] (Ointment from calamine stone)	10 lb.	4 lb.
*Ung[uentum] Basilic[um] Flav[um] (Yellow basilicon ointment)	10 lb.	
*Ung[uentum] Merc[urale] Fort[is] (Strong mercurial ointment)	6 lb.	
Ung[uentum] e Gum[mi] Elemi (Ointment of gum elemi)		3 lb.
Ung[uentum] Alb[um] Camp[horatum] (Camphorated white ointment)		3 lb.
PLASTERS		
*Emp[lastrum] Adhesiv[um] (Adhesive plaster)	6 lb.	
Emp[lastrum] Diach[ylon] (Simple diachylon plaster)	6 lb.	2 lb.
Emp[lastrum] Diach[ylon] c[um] G[ummi] (Diachylon plaster with gum)		1 lb.
*Emp[lastrum] Epispast[icum] [also] Epithema Vesicatorium (Blistering plaster; vesicatory plaster).		1 lb.
Emp[lastrum] Stomach[icum] Majest. (Stomach plaster)		1 lb.
SURGICAL DRESSINGS, ETC.		
*Linteum Praeparatum (Lint)	1 lb. fine	
Tow	12 lb. fine	
Sponge	4 oz. fine	
Twine	1 lb. fine	½ lb.
Tape	1 piece	2 pieces
Fracture pillows	2	
Splints	2 p. Sharps	34 doz.
Thread		4 oz.
Needles		7 common
Pins		½ thousand
Compresses		6 doz.
Bandages		700
Flannel		6 yds.
Shears		2 pr.
Rags		1 bundle

	Pennsylvania 4th Battalion Chest	Northern Department Chest
SURGICAL INSTRUMENTS		
Director	1	1 steel
Probe, silver	1	1
Forceps	1	
Catheters	1 silver	
Amputating instruments		1 set
Trepanning instruments	1 Trepan	1 set
Lancets	2 best crown, 4 common	
Tourniquets	1 Brass	8 common with ligatures
Syringe, pewter	4	2
Syringe, ivory	2	
Glyster pipe arm'd	6	
Tooth-drawing instument	1 Crow Bill	
PHARMACEUTICAL EQUIPMENT		
Scales and weights	1 box	1 set
Mortar and pestle	1 Brass, 1 Glass	
Tyles (pill tiles)	2	
Spatulas	1 wooden handle, 1 iron handle	1 large, 1 pocket
Bolus knife	1	
Plaister knife (plaster spatula)		1
Leather skins	2 lb.	
MISCELLANEOUS SUPPLIES		
Bottles	Assortment	Assortment
Gallypots	1 doz.	Assortment
Vials	6 doz. sorted	
Corks	10 doz.	
Pillboxes	1 pacg.	
Wrapp[ing] paper	4 quire	
Writing paper	1 quire	6 quire
Ink powder		2 papers
Quiles (quills)		14 hundred

U.S. Government Printing Office : 1961

Contributions from

The Museum of History and Technology:

Paper 17

The Effect of Bacon's Rebellion

on Government in England and Virginia

Wilcomb E. Washburn

FIGURE 1.—Virginia in 1676. This map, which appeared in John Speed's *A Prospect of the Most Famous Parts of the World* (London, 1676), is derived largely from Augustine Herman's important map of Virginia and Maryland in 1670. Photo courtesy of Virginia State Library, Richmond.

by Wilcomb E. Washburn

THE EFFECT OF BACON'S REBELLION ON GOVERNMENT IN ENGLAND AND VIRGINIA

Bacon's rebellion, familiar to all students of the history of 17th-century colonial Virginia, influenced both directly and indirectly governmental institutions in Virginia and in England.

The Virginia turmoil may well have influenced the change in English foreign policy whereby Charles II allied himself with the Dutch and broke his secret alliance with Louis XIV of France.

However, the evolution toward self-government in the Virginia colony is seen to be not a result of rebel striving during the uprising, but mainly a product of the loyalists' reaction, after the rebellion had been put down, to the heavy-handed policy of the commissioners sent by the King to investigate its causes.

THE AUTHOR: *Wilcomb E. Washburn is curator of political history in the United States National Museum, Smithsonian Institution.*

BACON'S REBELLION burst with a flash across the politics of 17th-century England and America. It had important effects on the executive, judicial, and legislative branches of government on both sides of the Atlantic. In the executive sphere it revealed the incompetence of kingly rule of a distant colony in crisis. It proved, furthermore, the inability of the King's governor-on-the-scene to command obedience among an armed, angered, and scattered populace.

NOTE.—This paper was read at a session of the American Committee of the International Commission for the History of Representative and Parliamentary Institutions, at the annual meeting of the American Historical Association in Washington, D.C., December 29, 1958.

In the judicial sphere it showed that the King's legal advisers were uncertain as to how the King could deal with rebellion by his colonial subjects. In Virginia the result of this uncertainty was judicial chaos and internal bitterness. In the legislative sphere the rebellion caused a financial pinch in England, which seriously weakened the position of Charles II in his dealings with Parliament. In Virginia the rebellion led to an assertion on the part of a loyalist, not rebel, House of Burgesses of the right of a colonial assembly to privileges identical to those enjoyed by Parliament.

In the past Bacon's Rebellion has been thought of as a revolution for independence and democracy that failed because it began too soon. Bacon has traditionally been the hero of the piece, and Governor Sir William Berkeley the oppressive villain against whom the freedom-loving Virginians were forced to rebel. I have tried to dissolve this illusion in my book *The Governor and the Rebel: A History of Bacon's Rebellion in Virginia* (Univeristy of North Carolina Press, 1958), and I will avoid repeating the documentation cited there. Briefly, my argument states that there is no evidence to show that Bacon was a democratic reformer, and no evidence to prove that Berkeley's intent was to frustrate the aim of reform.

The conflict actually arose over a difference of opinion on Indian policy: Bacon desired to raise volunteers to exterminate all Indians, while Berkeley tried to maintain a distinction between "foreign," enemy Indians and dependent, friendly ones. In the course of events Bacon and his followers stormed into Jamestown to force from the frightened Assembly of June 1676 a commission empowering the rebel to fight the Indians in his own way. A civil war ensued. At first Bacon had the upper hand. But Berkeley eventually succeeded in making the rebel leader, as the Governor put it, "acknowledge the lawes are above him."[1] Victory was not obtained, however, until after Bacon's death in October 1676.

This paper will take up the effects of Bacon's Rebellion first on the executive, then on the judicial, and finally on the legislative bodies of England and Virginia. The subjects will be discussed in the order given, for that was the order in which the rebellion affected governmental institutions on both sides of the Atlantic.

Effect on Executive Branches

Bacon's Rebellion showed that the Crown's representative in Virginia, 70 years after the first settlement, was able to lead or restrain the colonists in ordinary matters but could not control them when they became aroused. The race issue, precipitated by mutual Indian-white murders on the frontier, provided the "cause" that fired men who were already tired of poor crops, bad weather, and low prices and who were looking for an escape from their misery. After the Virginia colonists had been so roused, even Governor Berkeley, who enjoyed great popularity, was unable to control them. There is little doubt that Berkeley was a popular leader from 1641, when he was appointed Governor, until the time of the rebellion in 1676. Assertions of his declining popularity after 1660, following his unanimous election by Virginia's House of Burgesses and Council in the Parliamentary period, are based on very scanty evidence indeed.

This successful defiance of authority was made possible by the improved status of the individual Virginian, who, until the onset of economic depression and the Indian threat immediately prior to the rebellion, was enjoying security and affluence unknown in the shaky early years of settlement. The planters were favored by their number and location. There were 40,000 of them spread out from the ocean to the falls of the Potomac River and south from that river to Albemarle Sound. Another element in their favor was that their arms were equivalent to any that could be brought against them by the government. The situation was fully comprehended by the Governor, who wrote: "How miserable that man is that Governes a People wher six parts of seaven are Poore Endebted Discontented and Armed."[2]

The Governor's role was weakened not only by the growing power of the people but by the creation of rival authorities in the colonies. In 1673, by an "Act for the Encouragement of Trade," Parliament had introduced into the colonies customs collectors who were not responsible to the local government at all, but directly accountable to the Crown in England.[3] The customs collector for Virginia, Giles Bland, from the moment of his arrival was entangled in violent controversies with Governor, Council, and House of Burgesses. Bland finally died in a hangman's noose for helping Bacon initiate the rebellion.

The physical requirements of a Virginia governor's job were staggering. Early in June of 1676, even before the full effects of the rebellion had burst upon him, the 70-year-old Governor wrote to Secretary Coyentry asserting that "I am so over wearied with riding into al parts of the country to stop this violent rebellion that I am not able to support my selfe at this age six

[1] William Berkeley's "Declaration and Remonstrance" of May 29, 1676, in the Henry Coventry Papers (hereinafter cited as Longleat), vol. 77, folios 157–158. The Longleat papers are preserved at Longleat, estate of the Marquis of Bath. Microfilm copies of these papers are available in the Microfilm Reading Room, Library of Congress.

[1] William Berkeley [to Thomas Ludwell], July 1, 1676, Longleat, vol. 77, folio 145.

[3] Archibald P. Thornton, *West-India Policy Under the Restoration*, Oxford, 1956, p. 164.

FIGURE 2.—Charles II.   From portrait by J. M. Wright in National Portrait Gallery, London.

months longer and therefore on my knees I beg his sacred majesty would send a more vigorous Governor."[4]

Not only the Governor of the colony but the King himself was unable to prevent or control crises in the colonies.   The speed with which decisive events fol- lowed one another in Virginia required that adequate forces be available in the threatened colony and sub- ject to the direction of officials on the spot.   Average passage time for ships from Virginia to England was a month and a half,[5] but it could be shaved to about a

[4] William Berkeley to Henry Coventry, June 3, 1676, Long- leat, vol. 77, folio 103.

[5] Arthur Pierce Middleton, *Tobacco Coast: A Maritime History of Chesapeake Bay in the Colonial Era*, Newport News, Virginia, 1953, p. 8.

month. Added to this delay was the time consumed by the writing of letters and getting them aboard ship, and by the slowness of the King and his ministers in coming to a decision in England—particularly when the monarch was enjoying the pleasures of Newmarket. Consequently, six months often elapsed before answers to burning questions were forthcoming.

The royal decisions concerning the rebellion were made directly by the King and his closest advisers on the Committee for Foreign Affairs, not by the Committee for Trade and Plantations or by the Privy Council. The documents at Longleat (the estate of the Marquis of Bath in Wiltshire), which contain Secretary of State Henry Coventry's minutes of the meetings of the Committee for Foreign Affairs, commonly known as the "cabinet council," demonstrate conclusively that all vital decisions concerning the rebellion were made by this informal group of top advisers. The Privy Council and the Lords Committee for Trade and Plantations tended to be agencies that gave their stamp of approval to policy already decided.[6] The exact composition of the cabinet council is uncertain, but no doubt it changed from time to time. During the period of Bacon's Rebellion this council probably included the King; the Duke of York; Thomas Osborne, Earl of Danby, the Lord Treasurer, then assuming a new and more powerful role;[7] Sir Heneage Finch, the Lord Chancellor; and either or both of the Secretaries of State, Coventry and Williamson.

At the meetings of the King and his close advisers, which often took place on Sunday, pertinent information received from Virginia by Secretary of State Coventry would be presented. Unfortunately—principally through the instrumentality of Giles Bland, the King's collector of customs in Virginia, who had the last viewing of all ships leaving the colony—too few letters were received from the loyalists and too many from Bacon's supporters. The King and his council also considered letters and petitions from the three Virginia agents in England: Francis Moryson, Thomas Ludwell, and Robert Smith. These men had been sent by the colony to obtain a new charter guaranteeing land titles and personal liberties of the settlers against infringement by grants that the King had carelessly made to some of his court favorites. The Crown did not ignore these representatives. Moryson was once even commanded to present his views and those of his fellow agents directly to the King.[8]

Early in July of 1676 King Charles II decided to send 300 troops to Virginia. This decision was partly taken on the advice of the Virginia agents who had informed him that 300 would be a sufficient number of soldiers to put down the rebellion while more would be burdensome to the country. When the agents belatedly discovered that the King intended the colony to be responsible for supporting the soldiers, they boldly asserted that the charge would be "insupportable" and that they had no power to commit the colony to any such obligation. They begged the King to defer his decision until he had heard the opinion of the Virginia Assembly. When later in the summer news of the rebellion became worse and Charles II again made plans to send troops, the agents, who were by that time plunged in gloom, urged him to wait until more troops could be raised. By November, when about 1,000 troops finally did leave England bound for Virginia, they were too many and too late.[9]

[6] Wilcomb E. Washburn, "Bacon's Rebellion, 1676–1677," Harvard University, doctoral dissertation, 1955, ch. 7; Longleat, vols. 77, 78, *passim*.

[7] Stephen B. Baxter, *The Development of the Treasury, 1660–1702*, Cambridge, Massachusetts, 1957, pp. 262–263. We are indebted to Andrew Browning's *Thomas Osborne, Earl of Danby and Duke of Leeds, 1632–1712* (Glasgow, 1944–1951, 3 vols.) for detailed knowledge of the powerful role played by Danby. That the members of the cabinet council varied in number at this time is indicated by the statement of Secretary of State Henry Coventry to John, Lord Berkeley, Sir William's brother, December 26, 1676, that "The Truth is either Sickness, busyness or Devotion have made the Meetings of the Committee of forreigne Affaires so rare, and those that Compose it so few, that I have not had the opportunity of speaking to the King, and the Lord Treasurer together since the writing my last to your Excellency" (Letter-Book of Coventry, British Museum, Additional MS. 25119, p. 75, quoted in Edward Raymond Turner, *The Cabinet Council of England in the Seventeenth and Eighteenth Centuries, 1622–1784*, Baltimore, 1927–1928, vol. 1, p. 70).

[8] Francis Moryson to "My Lord," September 7, 1676, Longleat, vol. 77, folio 208.

[9] Henry Coventry draft letter, July 10, 1676, Longleat, vol. 91, folio 17; notes taken at the July 12 and July 13, 1676, meetings of the "Committee of Forreign Affairs," *ibid.*, vol. 77, folios 150, 152; Henry Coventry, "Heads of dispatches for Virginia," August 22, 1676, *ibid.*, folios 187–191, 297–298; memorandum endorsed "Instructions Given at the Committee for Forrain Affaires September 1, 1676 Concerning Virginia," *ibid.*, folios 195–196; Francis Moryson to "My Lord," *ibid.*, folio 208; "Particulars to be considered in the dispatch of Sir John Berry to Virginia," October 3, 1676, Pepys Papers, Rawlinson MSS., Class A, vol. 185, folios 259–260, Bodleian

The fact that Bacon's Rebellion took up the time and thought of England's greatest men for such a considerable period of time had an effect on the King's attitude toward the colonies. The monarch saw how little he knew of colonial affairs and, in the words of Secretary Coventry, determined "to be a little better acquainted with those that bear offices in his Plantations than of late he hath been . . . and let them know, they are not to govern themselves, but be governed by him." [10]

Yet the King's new interest in the colonies did not automatically result in their better administration. The King's attempt to enforce order was almost hopelessly inadequate. Governor Berkeley was as much inconvenienced by having royal troops in Virginia after the rebellion as he had been by not having them there during it. The soldiers' failure to arrive in time to help against the rebels increased the Governor's wartime difficulties. Their arrival after the rebellion complicated the Governor's supply and shelter problems. The troops were to a large extent dependent on the populace. Their pay, which was supposed to come from England, rarely arrived, and as a result even greater burdens fell upon the Virginians. Thus the soldiers' presence weakened rather than strengthened the royal authority. In 1678, after exhausting all local resources for support of the royal troops, the Virginia Council was forced to beg the English government to take quick action in order to prevent the redcoats from either starving or raising a mutiny. [11] Thus, in 1677 and in the following years, Virginians were experiencing the difficulties brought about by the presence of a standing peacetime army. These inconveniences were similar to the difficulties that American patriots were to suffer in the following century.

Effect on Judicial Branches

In the judicial branches of the English government, Bacon's Rebellion caught administrators dozing. The King's Governor was not clearly authorized to institute martial law and wage war against fellow Englishmen. He was empowered to wage war against the Indians but not against rebel colonists. [12] The Governor assumed, however, that he had the right to put down rebellion, if not by the positive authority of his commission, at least by the natural law of self-preservation. [13] The English authorities were uncertain as to the judicial powers the King's Governor actually possessed in an emergency, and they prepared orders and commissions specifically authorizing Berkeley to apply martial law and to try and convict rebels. The most important document in which this authorization appeared was the so-called "Virginia Charter" of October 10, 1676, which promised security to Virginia landholders threatened by royal grants of parts of Virginia to court favorites. This charter gave the Governor and Council of Virginia "full power and authority to hear and determine all treasons, murders, felonys and other offences committed and done within the said government so as they proceed therein as near as may be to the laws and statutes of this kingdome of England." [14] There has been much confusion

Library, Oxford; Thomas Ludwell to Henry Coventry, October 5, 1676, Longleat, vol. 77, folio 231; Samuel Pepys to Sir John Berry, November 14, 1676, in J. R. Tanner, ed., *A Descriptive Catalogue of the Naval Manuscripts in the Pepysian Library at Magdalene College, Cambridge*, vol. 3, in *Publications of the Navy Records Society*, 1909, vol. 36, no. 3443.

[10] Henry Coventry to Sir Jonathan Atkins, governor of Barbados, November 21, 1677, in Letter-Book of Coventry, British Museum, Additional MS. 25120, p. 120.

[11] Thomas Ludwell [to Henry Coventry] in letter dated June 28, 1678, Longleat, vol. 78, folio 264; Herbert Jeffreys to Henry Coventry, July 4, 1678, *ibid.*, folio 269; Philip Ludwell to Henry Coventry, June 16, 1679, *ibid.*, folios 386–387.

[12] Wilcomb E. Washburn, "The Humble Petition of Sarah Drummond," *William and Mary Quarterly*, ser. 3, July 1956, vol. 13, pp. 366–367 and footnote 45. See also the King's commission to Governor Berkeley, July 31, 1660, in The *Southern Literary Messenger*, 1845, vol. 11, pp. 1–5. Matters of war and peace were discussed in terms of the Indians, but the King also authorized the Governor "to direct and Governe, correct and Punish our Subjects now inhabiting or being, or which shall hereafter inhabit or be in Virginia, or in Isles, Ports, Havens, Creeks, or Territories thereof, either in time of Peace or Warr . . . ."

[13] In October 1676 Attorney General Jones asked Francis Moryson, one of the Virginia agents and later King's commissioner, whether a commission from England to declare martial law in Virginia should be issued to Berkeley. Moryson answered that the Governor already had as much authority as the attorney general could give him: "all places will naturally have as much of that, as they need in time of warr: For martiall Law is (as I take it) but a branch of the Law of Nature, by whose impulse wee are commanded to defend ourselves, and if opposed by multitudes, then to resort to multitudes to defend us." (Colonial Office Papers, ser. 5, vol. 1371, pp. 6–12, Public Record Office, London).

[14] William Waller Hening, *The Statutes at Large . . . A Collection of All the Laws of Virginia . . .* , New York, 1823, vol. 2, pp. 532–533.

FIGURE 3.—The Great Seal of England. This fourth seal of Charles II was used between 1672 and 1685. On the night of February 7, 1677, an attempt was made to steal the Great Seal from the house of Lord Chancellor Finch. The thief, Thomas Sadler, missed the seal, which was lying under the Lord Chancellor's pillow; however, he made off with the mace and the purse for the seal, and, attended by his confederates, made a mock procession with these items near the Lord Chancellor's house. The escapade cost Sadler his life by hanging. The seal and counterseal are described in A. B. Wyon, *The Great Seals of England* (London, 1887, nos. 143, 144, and pl. 37). Photos courtesy of the Department of Manuscripts, British Museum, London, Seal lxxvi.1.

concerning the charter.[15] A more generous charter had been drafted and authorized by the King on November 19, 1675, and again on April 19, 1676, to pass under the Great Seal of England.[16] This earlier document had, however, despite the importunities of the Virginia agents, mysteriously failed to be put into effect. Finally, on May 31, 1676, the King directed the Lord Chancellor *not* to put the Great Seal on the Virginia patent.[17]

The reasons for the initial delay and final disapproval of the original charter are obscure, but Bacon's Rebellion was not responsible. Probably the tobacco merchants, the farmers (collectors) of the Virginia customs, the lords who would be deprived of the full fruits of their grants, and a few of the more

[15] Edward Channing, *A History of the United States*, New York, 1936, vol. 2, p. 64, footnote 3; Thomas Jefferson Wertenbaker, in an introduction to a printing of the original unsuccessful charter, *Virginia Magazine of History and Biography*, 1948, vol. 56, p. 264; George Bancroft, *History of the United States*, Boston, 1856, vol. 2, p. 211 (final revised edition, New York, 1883, vol. 1, p. 454).

[16] Hening, *op. cit.* (footnote 14), p. 531; John Daly Burk, *The History of Virginia*, Petersburg, Virginia, 1804–1805, vol. 2, p. 249; Minutes of the Court at Whitehall, April 19, 1676, Longleat, vol. 77, folio 70.

[17] W. Noel Sainsbury, ed., *Calendar of State Papers, Colonial Series, America and West Indies, 1675–1676*, London, 1893, no. 935.

FIGURE 4.—Heneage Finch, Earl of Nottingham, holding the purse in which the Great Seal was carried. He was Lord High Chancellor from 1675 to 1682 and Lord Keeper of the Great Seal from 1673 to 1682. The attempt of the Virginia agents to have their charter passed quickly under the Great Seal in 1676 was frustrated. This painting, after Michael Wright, is reproduced with permission of the owner, the Marquis of Bath. Photo courtesy of the Courtauld Institute of Art, London.

suspicious members of the King's council got together to resist the decision.

A totally new situation was created, however, when news of Indian troubles and rising discontent among the English colonists reached England. The Virginia agents appealed for reconsideration. The King and his cabinet council, justly worried by the bad news that arrived in early August concerning Bacon's actions in June, determined to allow the Virginians a new charter, which was finally issued on October 10. There can be little doubt that part of the reason for the passage of this charter was to assure Virginians that they did, indeed, own the land they were defending against the Indians and the rebels. The charter was a declaration of immediate dependence on the Crown (barring the possibility of an intermediate lord proprietor) and confirmed all land titles. It is true that the final charter was less liberal than that originally authorized, but it hardly deserves William Waller Hening's description of it as "a miserable skeleton . . . containing little more than a declaration of the dependence of the colony on the crown of England." [18] It granted many of the original demands of the colony, omitting only those which may have been considered detrimental to the King's prerogative or inexpedient in the existing circumstances. A promise not to tax Virginia but by her own consent, and a promise to consult the Virginia authorities before any more prejudicial land grants were made, might, if granted, have given the colonists the idea that they could bind the King's arms by rebellion. Similarly the colony's incorporation, which the Virginians had requested so that they could negotiate the purchase of the land that had been granted to the King's favorites, might have been considered an encouragement to the sort of intransigency practiced

---

[18] Henry Coventry (in "Heads of dispatches for Virginia," August 22, 1676, Longleat, vol. 77, folios 190, 297) notes "My Lord Chancellour to passe their Patent, according to the Heads allowed at the Foreigne Committee" and "To vacate the other two Patents complained of"; see also Hening, *op. cit.* (footnote 14), p. 519.

By the King.

A PROCLAMATION

For the Suppressing a Rebellion lately raised within the Plantation of Virginia.

...bing Subjects, That they do use their utmost endeavour to Apprehend and secure the persons of the said Nathaniel Bacon, and of all and every the said Complices, in order to the bringing of them to their Legal Tryal. And for the better encouragement of His Majesties said Loving Subjects to Apprehend and bring to Justice the said Nathaniel Bacon (who hath been chief Contriver and King-leader of the said Rebellion) His Majesty doth hereby Declare, That such person or persons as shall Apprehend the said Nathaniel Bacon, and him shall bring before His Majesties Governor, Deputy Governor, or other Commander in Chief of His Majesties forces within the said Plantation, shall have as a Reward from His Majesties Royal Bounty, the sum of Three Hundred Pounds Sterling, to be paid in Money by the Lieutenant Governor. And because it may be probable that many of the Adherents and Complices of the said Nathaniel Bacon may have been seduced by him into this said Rebellion, by specious, though false pretences; His Majesty out of His Royal Pity and Compassion to His seduced Subjects, doth hereby Declare, That if any of His Subjects who have or shall have ingaged with, or adhered to the said Nathaniel Bacon in the said Rebellion, shall within the space of Twenty days after the publishing of this His Royal Proclamation, submit himself to His Majesties Government, & before the Governor, Deputy Governor, or other Commander in Chief of His Majesties forces within the said Plantation, take the Oath of Obedience mentioned in the Act of Parliament made in England in the Third year of the Reign of His Majesties Royal Grandfather, and give such security for his future good behaviour, as the said Governor, Deputy Governor, or Commander in Chief shall approve of, That then such person so submitting, taking such Oath, and giving such security, is hereby pardoned and forgiven the Rebellion and Treason by him committed, and shall be free from all punishments and forfeitures for or by reason of the same. And His Majesty doth hereby further Declare, That if any of His Subjects who have engaged, or shall engage with, or have adhered, or shall adhere to the said Nathaniel Bacon in the said Rebellion, shall not accept of this His Majesties gracious offer of Pardon, but shall after the said Twenty days expired, persist and continue in the said Rebellion, That then such of the Servants or Slaves of such persons so persisting and continuing such Rebellion, as shall render themselves to, and take up Arms under His Majesties Governor, Deputy Governor, or other Commander in Chief of His Majesties forces within the said Plantation, shall have their Liberty, and be for ever Discharged and free from the Service of the said Offenders. And to the intent His Majesties Loving Subjects within the said Plantation may understand how desirous and careful His Majesty is to remove from them all just Grievances, His Majesty doth hereby make known to all His said Subjects, That he hath not only already given particular Instructions to His Governor, to reduce the Salaries of the Members of the Assembly to such moderate rates as may render them less burthensom to the Country, but hath also appointed and sent into the said Plantation, Herbert Jeffreys Esq; Sir John Berry Knight, and Francis Morison Esq; His Majesties Commissioners, to inquire into, and report to His Majesty all such other Grievances as His Majesties Subjects within the said Plantation do at present lie under, to the end that such relief and redress may be made therein, as shall be agreeable to His Majesties Royal Wisdom and Compassion. And although the pretended Acts or Laws made in the said Assembly of June last (being in manner aforesaid obtained) are in themselves null and void, yet to the intent no person may pretend ignorance, His Majesty hath thought fit hereby to Declare and Publish His Royal pleasure to be, That all and every Acts and Act, made or pretended to be made by the said Governor and Assembly in the late said Assembly held at James City in the Moneth of June last past, shall be taken and held as null and void, and shall not for the future be observed or put in execution.

Given at Our Court at Whitehall this Seven and Twentieth day of October, 1676. In the Eight and twentieth year of Our Reign.

GOD SAVE THE KING.

LONDON, Printed by the Assigns of *John Bill* and *Christopher Barker*, Printers to the Kings most Excellent Majesty, 1676.

FIGURE 5.—King's proclamation of pardon. From Henry Coventry Papers at Longleat, vol. 77, folios 263, 265. Reproduced by permission of the Marquis of Bath.

Figure 6.—Jeffreys' Regiment of Foot (1676–1682). Reproduced with permission of The Company of Military Collectors & Historians, *Military Uniforms in America*, 1961, pl. 199.

by publishing rather than suppressing a printed proclamation in the King's name that had been designed to induce active rebels to surrender. Furthermore, the commissioners took up the defense of rebels whose property had been confiscated by the loyalist forces in the last stages of the war.

Berkeley refused to accept the commissioners' interpretation of his authority on grounds that appear to this writer to be justifiable. Not only on the issues mentioned above but also on numerous smaller matters involving the legal relationship of the victorious loyalists to the defeated rebels, Berkeley and the commissioners clashed. Finding the commissioners adamant, Berkeley appealed to the King, to the Privy Council, and to "the learned judges of the law." He failed, however, to get support from these sources. Attorney General Jones' opinion was evasive, and Charles II was in no mood to let his father's course of action in the English civil wars—to which precedent Berkeley particularly appealed—serve as a justification for the Virginia governor.[19]

The result of these disagreements in matters of law was operational chaos. The Virginia Governor issued his own proclamation of pardon jointly with the King's printed proclamation even though Berkeley's proclamation modified that of the monarch. Flagrant rebels went scot free. Plundered loyalists found the courts closed to their pleas for justice. The Assembly's act allowing recovery of stolen property was disregarded by a new Governor who complained that Virginia's representative body, "instead of making an Act of Oblivion, have made a Statute of Remembrance, to last and intayle trouble from one Generation to another. . . ." [20]

Effect on Legislative Branches

The fact that Bacon's Rebellion occurred in the same year that Parliament, contrary to custom, failed to meet has at most only symbolic significance. The management of colonial affairs was still entirely in the King's hands. Parliament was, except in its passage of occasional legislation such as the Navi-

by the corporation of The Governor and Company of Massachusetts Bay in New England. So, although it was in one sense responsible for limiting the charter's scope, Bacon's Rebellion was also responsible for the charter's final approval.

Partly as a result of the confusion concerning the facts of the difficult Virginia situation and the uncertainty as to where authority lay in the colony, the English government decided to create a new commission consisting of three men who were to determine what had caused the rebellion in the colony and to aid in correcting any abuses found. This move resulted in further uncertainty concerning the rebellion and the lines of authority in Virginia. Immediately on their arrival in Virginia the commissioners began to question many of the legal procedures that Berkeley had adopted. The commissioners induced Berkeley to switch from courts martial to civil trials for captured rebels. They also tried to persuade him to grant the defeated rebels full pardon

[19] Wilcomb E. Washburn, *The Governor and the Rebel: A History of Bacon's Rebellion in Virginia*, Chapel Hill, 1957, pp. 107–113; also, *op. cit.* (footnote 12), "The Humble Petition of Sarah Drummond," pp. 354–375.

[20] Herbert Jeffreys to Henry Coventry, May 4, 1677, Longleat, vol. 78, folio 44.

gation Acts, as yet not an active factor in colonial government, and therefore colonial matters did not find much place in its debates. Its attention was directed towards the King and towards England's European neighbors.

On November 22, 1675, Charles II prorogued his Long Parliament for 15 months—until February 15, 1677. During these 15 months the King relied heavily for funds on a secret agreement that had been made with Louis XIV of France to pay the English monarch £100,000 a year while Parliament was not sitting.[21] The interests of the French king were served so long as the hostile English Parliament was unable to align England actively with the continental allies resisting Louis XIV's campaigns of aggrandizement in the Low Countries and elsewhere.

While Parliament was in recess, financial disaster struck the English government. A look at the revenue figures for 1675, 1676, and 1677 tells the story better than can words. In 1675 the yield from customs was £727,769. In 1676 this yield dropped to £565,675; by 1677 it had climbed to £683,192. Excise fell from £499,177 in 1675 to £301,785 in 1676 before it climbed somewhat in 1677 to £373,367. Thus in 1676 the total income from customs and excise dropped to a low point of £867,460 from the £1,228,946 that was received in 1675 and in contrast to the respectable £1,056,559 collected in 1677.[22]

The situation was particularly critical in the fall of 1676. Secretary Coventry wrote to the Earl of Essex on October 2, 1676:

Virginia is what taketh up our thoughts now where one inconsiderable man one Bacon of a mean or no fortune and of a Lesse Reputation as to any good qualitye hath made himself head of a Rebellion and with that Successe that in a few months he hath made himselfe Master of all that Colony, possesseth and disposeth every mans Estate as he pleaseth and how Long his Rule will Last I know not but I feare he will have time enough and desperatenesse . . . to put that Colony past recovering it selfe in many years. His majesty is sending away 1,000 men immediately with good Officers. I hope it may turne the Tide before it is become too strong for us but at the best we can hope it will be a great blow to the revenue.[23]

Antoine Courtin, the French ambassador to the English court, reported that during the latter stages

FIGURE 7.—Bronze bust of Louis XIV. This bust is based on the marble bust of the French king that was created by Lorenzo Bernini in 1665 and is now at Versailles. In National Gallery of Art, Samuel H. Kress Collection. Reproduced, with permission, from National Gallery of Art photo.

of preparation for the expedition to subdue the rebellious colony, "every day" the English monarch pressed him to hurry the payments of the subsidy from Louis XIV.[24] William Harbord in a letter to the Earl of Essex, December 17, 1676, wrote that "ill news from *Virginia and New England* [then recovering from King Philip's War] doth not only *alarm us* but extreamly *abate* the *customs* so that notwithstanding *all the shifts Treasurer can make this Parliament or another must sitt. . . .*"[25] This extreme drop in revenue

[21] Browning, *op. cit.* (footnote 7), vol. 1, pp. 166, 184, 189–190.
[22] William A. Shaw, ed., *Calendar of Treasury Books, 1676–1679,* London, 1911, vol. 5, pt. 1, p. xiv.
[23] Longleat, vol. 84, folios 47–48.

[24] Antoine Courtin to King Louis XIV, November 9 and 30, 1676, and King Louis XIV to Antoine Courtin, December 8, 1676, in Correspondance Politique, Angleterre, vol. 120, pp. 174, 244. (In Foreign Office Archives, Paris; microfilmed by Colonial Records Project of Virginia 350th Anniversary Celebration Corporation.)
[25] Clement Edwards Pike, ed., *Selections from the Correspondence of Arthur Capel, Earl of Essex, 1675–1677,* in *Publications of the Royal Historical Society,* London, 1913, Camden Series, ser. 3, vol. 24, p. 87.

may well have been one of the factors that undermined Lord Treasurer Danby, whose power was greatest in 1675 when income was most plentiful and weakest when the King's financial problems became intolerable.

The role played by Virginia in creating the financial disaster of 1676 has never been adequately considered, partly because of the secondary consideration normally given colonial occurrences by the mother country. Detailed analysis of the precise economic loss occasioned by Bacon's Rebellion has yet to be made. A thorough study of the effect of Bacon's Rebellion on English finances should take into account not only the fact that imports from Virginia declined drastically at the time of the uprising but that in the fall of 1676 exports from England were reduced because of the embargo placed on ships sailing for Virginia ports. Because of the nature of the American trade routes this embargo had an adverse effect on English trade with the West Indies as well as with English colonies on the North American mainland. The drop in West Indian customs receipts was, indeed, spectacular. Between Michaelmas (September 29) 1675 and Michaelmas 1676, the returns of the 4½ per cent duty in Barbados and the Leeward Islands amounted to £5,993. In the following 12-month period the returns of this duty fell to £800. In the 1677–1678 period the proceeds from the West Indian duty jumped to £3,650.[26]

Whatever the exact figure may be, Virginia's unsettled condition resulted in a disastrous financial loss for the Crown. On December 3, 1676, Charles II complained to the French ambassador that Virginia would cause him a loss of £80,000 on tobacco duties and that furthermore an expenditure of £120,000 would be required to put down the rebellion.[27]

Careful husbanding of resources by Treasurer Danby, involving reductions in expenses for almost every branch of the government, failed to solve the financial problem.[28] In February 1677 Charles II recalled Parliament and asked for a money bill to supply his many needs. Parliament was more recalcitrant than it had previously been in granting the King's requests for funds. The long adjournment was deemed illegal by many members who asserted that Parliament was thereby automatically dissolved. The King's reluctance to enter a formal alliance against the French and a suspicion that the monarch was secretly wedded to French interests made Parliament reluctant to grant the Crown large sums of money. In vain did the King plead with the House of Commons; in vain did he cite his extraordinary expenses of 1676 caused by "those contingencies which may happen in all kingdoms, and which have been a considerable burden on me this last year."[29] Parliament wanted proof that his intentions matched its own; until such proof was forthcoming, Charles II must manage his affairs as best he could. The plight of the King is shown in the instructions he gave to the Earl of Feversham, who was sent to the court of Louis XIV in the winter of 1677. Charles pointed out:

. . . we shall be necessitated to call a Parliament in April, by reason of a very great Branch of our Revenue that will determine at Midsummer next . . . . How far the irresistable temper of the House did necessitate us to a peace

---

[26] Thornton, *op. cit.* (footnote 3), pp. 258–259.

[27] Antoine Courtin to King Louis XIV, December 3, 1676, Francois Auguste Marie Alexis Mignet's *Négociations relatives à la succession d'Espagne sous Louis XIV ou Correspondances, mémoires, et actes diplomatiques concernant les prétentions et l'avénement de la Maison de Bourbon au trone d'Espagne accompagnés d'un texte historique et précédés d'une introduction*, Paris, 1835–1842, vol. 4, p. 430. The figure of £80,000 yearly accruing to the Crown from the Virginia tobacco duties is cited in the debates of the House of Commons, March 7, 1670 (Basil Duke Henning, ed., *The Parliamentary Diary of Sir Edward Dering, 1670–1673*, New Haven, 1940, pp. 92–93). In an undated petition to the King (Colonial Office Papers, ser. 1, vol. 40, no. 110, Public Record Office, London), Governor Berkeley reported that the Virginia trade brought in £100,000 annually.

Berkeley's figure is matched in a petition entitled "The Virginia Trade Stated" submitted by the merchants and traders in tobacco to the House of Commons in 1677 (Colonial Office Papers, ser. 1, vol. 40, no. 142, Public Record Office, London). Summaries of these petitions are contained in W. Noel Sainsbury and J. W. Fortescue, eds., *Calendar of State Papers, Colonial Series, America and West Indies, 1677–1680*, London, 1896, nos. 304, 552.

[28] Browning, *op. cit.* (footnote 7), vol. 1, pp. 186–187ff.

[29] Speech of King Charles II to both houses of Parliament, February 15, 1677, in *A Collection of Kings' Speeches; with the Messages to and from both Houses of Parliament, Addresses by the Lords and Commons, and the Speeches of the Lords Chancellors and Speakers of the House of Commons; From the Restauration, the Year One Thousand Six Hundred and Sixty, to the Year One Thousand Six Hundred and Eighty-five*, London, 1772, pp. 135–136. In his speech of January 28, 1678, to both houses (*ibid.*, pp. 141–142, and *Journals of the House of Commons*, vol. 9, p. 427), Charles II specifically mentioned the heavy charge of "a Rebellion in Virginia." In the debate of March 12, 1677, on the King's request for more funds, Sir John Ernly pointed out that "the rebellion of *Virginia* has cost the King £100,000," and that a

with Holland, is well known to the most Christian King; and they having the like advantage now upon us in respect of our Revenue as they then had in respect of our Expences, to what streights they may, and are like to drive us, is not hard to guess.[30]

The influence of Virginia on the policy of Charles II has never been fully assessed. Could it be that the falling off of customs from Virginia and the plantations during 1676 and the expenditures involved in putting down Bacon's Rebellion placed Charles in a financial quandary from which it proved impossible to emerge except by radical alterations in policy? It seems possible that the situation in Virginia may have been a decisive factor in subsequent English relations with both France and Holland. In any case Charles II, perhaps consciously influenced by events in Virginia, broke his tenuous agreement with France and, by marrying his niece, Mary, to William of Orange, allied himself with Holland. After these changes in foreign policy were in effect, the King again confronted Parliament with a request for funds. The fact that Charles II remained unsuccessful in dealing with Parliament does not of course mean that the situation in Virginia did not exert a significant influence on his changes in policy. Charles II reigned in the dim beginnings of a new era; his difficulties with Parliament and with the colonies could be resolved only by political expedients that had not yet evolved.[31]

Bacon's Rebellion and its aftermath caused a distinct change in the relationship between the Virginia Assembly and the Crown. The King's failure to reward those who had supported the Governor's authority caused a reversal of sentiment in both houses of the Assembly. What "anti-imperialist" feeling was created in Virginia in 1676–1677 can truly be said to have derived not from the rebels who fostered the rebellion but from the loyalists who put it down.

It is customarily thought that the Assembly of June 1676 represented a democratic reform movement aimed directly at the royal government of the colony. Although historians may represent its legislation as "radical," nothing the Assembly of June 1676 did— with the possible exception of passing a law allowing all freemen, rather than property-holders only to vote—was such as to upset either King or Governor. Moreover, Berkeley had already allowed freemen to vote in the elections to the June Assembly, and all freemen had had the vote in Virginia up until 1670 when the law was altered to bring it into conformity with English practice. The King did not object to the "reform" character of the laws of June 1676 but to the pressure exerted on the Assembly by Bacon and 500 armed men. Furthermore, all evidence suggests that this pressure was exerted not in behalf of reform legislation but to obtain clear authority for Bacon to fight the Indian war as he pleased.[32]

The June Assembly can in fact appropriately be thought of as having resoundingly endorsed the principle of royal authority in the colony as represented by the King's lieutenant, Sir William Berkeley. The June Assembly went on record that:

Whereas the Right Honourable Sir William Berkeley Knight our good Governour hath for many yeares most wisely, gratiously Lovingly and justly governed this whole Country, and still continues to governe the same with all possible prudence Justness and mercy, this house in a deep Sence of the premisses doth humbly intreate and request his honor that he will please still to continue our Governor.[33]

Having passed this action, the burgesses begged the King not to accept the Governor's resignation.

war with Algiers and "other things make his Revenue fall short . . . ," Anchitell Grey, ed., *Debates of the House of Commons, from the Year 1667 to the Year 1694*, London, 1763, vol. 4, p. 224. Although we know the King and his ministers were concerned with the rebellion, it is hard to find evidence of Parliamentary interest. Andrew Marvell wrote to Sir Henry Thompson, November 14, 1676, giving an account of Bacon's Rebellion as received from a ship just arrived from Virginia (Huntington Library, San Marino, California, HM 21813); nevertheless, in *An Account of the Growth of Popery, and Arbitrary Government in England. More Particularly, from the Long Prorogation, of November, 1675, Ending the 15th. of February, 1676, till the Last Meeting of Parliament, the 16th. of July 1677* (Amsterdam, 1677) Marvell makes no mention of the rebellion. There are few references to the rebellion in the journals of the two Houses or in official proclamations. Nevertheless, it is dangerous to suppose that the Virginia colony was out of mind. European affairs were central to the thought of Englishmen at the time, especially in official circles. Colonial affairs were on a lower level of consideration and, indeed, merited attention only when they erupted in violence or in loss of revenue. Like many problems of the modern day, however, their importance was significant in fact though insignificant in theory.

[30] Charles II, "Instructions to our Right Trusty and well beloved Cousin Louis Earl of Feversham sent by us to the Court of France," November 10, 1677, in Letter-Book of Coventry, British Museum, Additional MS. 25119, p. 8.

[31] Mr. K. H. Haley has written the most detached account of "The Anglo-Dutch Rapprochement of 1677" (*English Historical Review*, vol. 73, October 1958, pp. 614–648), but he finds no overt evidence of a Virginia connection.

[32] Washburn, *op. cit.* (footnote 19), ch. 4.

[33] *Ibid.*, p. 56.

It was in the postrebellion assemblies of February and October of 1677 that dissatisfaction with imperial domination really arose. Not only Berkeley and the Council but also the burgesses of the February Assembly found the attitude of the King's three commissioners mistaken and insulting. The commissioners told the burgesses how to perform their duties as they told the Governor how to do his. The burgesses and the Governor reacted similarly; they all ignored the commissioners' directives, suspecting that these representatives of the Crown were exceeding their instructions, as indeed they were.[34] Governor and burgesses proceeded in their accustomed courses, trusting that the King would eventually support their actions and repudiate the commissioners. They were mistaken in this belief. Partly through ignorance and partly through poor administration, the King upheld these recently delegated commissioners rather than his long-established authorities. The possibility of one royal authority arraigning another—a situation that had been feared by Francis Moryson, one of the commissioners, and by Samuel Pepys, of the Navy Board—had become a reality.[35]

We have now arrived at a more valid starting point than Bacon's Rebellion for the conflict between the people's representatives and the King's Governor that culminated a hundred years later in the expulsion of Lord Dunmore. The crisis began on April 27, 1677, when Lieutenant Governor Herbert Jeffreys, one of the three commissioners and commander of the troops sent by the King, proclaimed himself Governor. Berkeley, already on his way back to England but not yet aboard ship, reacted angrily, accusing Jeffreys of having an "irresistable desire to rule this Countrey" and asserting that his action could "neither be Justified by your [Jeffreys'] Commission, nor mine nor any visible Instructions you [Jeffreys] have from His most sacred Majestie. . . ." "And no [know] Sir," Berkeley admonished the Colonel, "that I may not conceale my owne imperfections and pride of hart from you I will confesse to you that I beleeve that the inhabitants of this Colony will quickly find a difference betweene your managment and mine . . . ."[36]

As Berkeley had foretold, the people did soon notice a difference in the two administrations. The disenchantment of the House of Burgesses with the King's vicegerent was manifested in a bold action of October 23, 1677. Under the leadership of their clerk, Robert Beverley, one of Berkeley's fiercest supporters, the burgesses formally protested to Jeffreys, calling the seizure of their journals by the commissioners in the previous April "a Great Violation of our Priviledges." The Assembly declared:

This House doe Humbly Suppose his Majestie would not Graunt or Command [such a power in the Commissioners] for That They find not the same to have been Practized by Any of the Kings of England in The Like Case. And Because This Commission was Never yett Published or put upon record this House doe Humbly pray your Honor will Please to Grant them a Veiw of the same, and that your Honor as his Majesties Governor and Representative here, will Please to give this House such satisfaction that they may be assured noe such violations of their priviledges shall be offered for the Future.[37]

Jeffreys, sick and near death, retorted weakly that he could not produce a copy of the commission.[38] King Charles II, in considerably better health than Jeffreys, exploded with rage when he was informed of the protest and directed Lord Culpeper, Jeffreys' successor, to signify his "high resentment" of the Assembly's "Seditious declaration," which he ordered expunged from the Virginia records.[39]

The rights of the Council were as vigorously defended as those of the House of Burgesses. One of the first controversies centered around fiery Philip Ludwell, Berkeley's right-hand man during the rebellion. Lieutenant Governor Jeffreys had prevented Ludwell from suing rebels for property they had stolen from him. One night, heated by drink, Ludwell denounced Jeffreys as "a pitiful Little Fellow with a perriwig" who had "broke more Laws in Six Months time than Sir William Berkeley Did in 35 Years Government . . . ." If the courts allowed Jeffreys to protect the rebels, said Ludwell, "they must allow and own the said Governor to rule by an Arbitrary power." Jeffreys ordered Ludwell tried for "scandalizing the

---

[34] *Ibid.*, pp. 94, 101, 128–129.

[35] Francis Moryson to Henry Coventry, September 6, 1676, Longleat, vol. 77, folio 204; "Particulars to be considered in the dispatch of Sir John Berry to Virginia," *loc. cit.* (footnote 9).

[36] William Berkeley to Herbert Jeffreys, April 28, 1677, Longleat, vol. 78, folio 34, quoted in Washburn, *op. cit.* (footnote 19), pp. 132–133.

[37] Longleat, vol. 78, folio 123.

[38] Jeffreys' answer to the assembly was made on the same day as the protest, October 23, 1677 (*ibid.*, folio 124).

[39] Order of King in Council, December 21, 1681, as reported in Virginia Council proceedings, *Virginia Magazine of History and Biography*, 1910, vol. 18, p. 245, and in Hening, *op. cit.* (footnote 14), p. 560.

Louis, running after Charles
　　Calls, stay, O King, do stay.
If you'll stop running after peace
　　I've lots of gold to pay,
And pow'r to trample Holland down
　　Until in ruins she lay.

But King if you desert me
　　My nerve and plan will fail.
De Ruyter on my open coast
　　His wooden horse will sail.
And the brass of the Fearsome Tromp
　　Will descend in a deadly hail.

FIGURE 8.—Cartoon depicting Charles II, Louis XIV, and the states of Holland on the matter of peace or war (1677?). From *Catalogue of Prints and Drawings in the British Museum*, Division I (1870), no. 1055. Printed at right is the poem as translated by Mrs. Juliette S. Bevis. Photo courtesy of the Trustees of the British Museum.

Governor by saying that he was perjured and had broke several Laws." When Ludwell admitted the scandalous nature of his charges but pleaded their truth as a defense and asked for a jury to decide whether in fact Jeffreys had broken the laws of the colony, the Governor became enraged. Ludwell's defense was so far ahead of its time that it could not be accepted by the other members of the Council, who were sitting as a general court. However, the court, in accordance with "the Laws and Constant known proceeding of this Colony," did allow Ludwell to appeal from its decision to the Assembly.[40] This concession caused Jeffreys, who wanted the case referred to the King, to denounce the councilors for showing themselves to "Vallue the Power and lawes of A few Ignorant Planters mett in An Assembly for this Government to be of greater Authority, then his most Sacred Majesty and his Councill."[41]

In another case Jeffreys found himself opposed by James Bray, one of four councilors whom the Governor had highhandedly dismissed without formal charges. Bray, in a written statement presented to the Council on September 26, 1677, stated:

Cheifly in defence of the Rights Priviledges and Honor of the Kings Councill of State in this Country I have Thought it Necessary to make my Addresse to This Honorable Court and without Arrogancie Ambition or Other Ill meaning to Demand my Place and Priviledge in This Seat of Judicature being a Court Appoynted by Law where the Councellors of State are Injoyned to give their Attendance without Lawfull Occasion Preventing them, not but that I most Redily Comply and submit to be Ousted Degraded and Rejected being Lawfully Convicted by this Honorable Court of Crimes merriting such Indignities and Dishonor.

---

[40] Washburn, *op. cit.* (footnote 19), pp. 134, 233–234.

[41] Herbert Jeffreys to Henry Coventry [?], April 2, 1678, Longleat, vol. 78, folios 216–217, quoted in Washburn, *op. cit.* (footnote 19), p. 134.

My Demands I Request may bee Committed to Record with your Honors Resolve thereto.[42]

Despite this entreaty, Jeffreys and the Council ordered Bray suspended until his Majesty's pleasure might be known.[43] The Governor forwarded the papers on the Bray case to Secretary of State Coventry, noting Bray's "Insolent Behaviour in Comeing to Claime his Seat in the Council in Open Court."[44]

The restrictions placed upon representative government in Virginia through measures taken against the House of Burgesses, the Council, and the courts occurred after the rebellion, not before it, and were opposed by the loyalists, not supported by them. There is little evidence to show that the rebels were concerned with representative institutions either during the rebellion or in the postrebellion period, but it is abundantly clear that the loyalists were. The battle for democratic rights in Virginia was waged after and not during the rebellion; consequently, it is to the postrebellion period that we must look for knowledge of the evolution of representative government in the colony of Virginia.

The effect of Bacon's Rebellion on the development of representative institutions in England is more difficult to assess. The rebellion was immediately effective in that it gave support to the King's opposition in the House of Commons by cutting off a significant portion of the King's income and thus forcing him to go begging to Parliament to replace it. (The aid given by the rebellion was accepted without comment by the members of the House of Commons because, as a colonial matter, it required no thanks and no acknowledgement.) A more lasting result of the rebellion was that it drew attention to the inability of the English constitution satisfactorily to comprehend within its terms the growing numbers of Englishmen "without the Realm." The problems brought on by the rebellion revealed that the political relationship of colonist to King was evolving too haphazardly. What could have been a warning, however, was seen merely as an annoyance, and the opportunity to re-establish the loyalty of the colony by fair and intelligent treatment was lost.

---

[42] Longleat, vol. 78, folio 89.

[43] Order of a General Court, September 27, 1677, Longleat, vol. 78, folio 85.

[44] Herbert Jeffreys to Henry Coventry, February 11, 1678, Longleat, vol. 78, folio 207.

U.S. GOVERNMENT PRINTING OFFICE: 1962

Contributions from
The Museum of History and Technology
Paper 18

Excavations at Rosewell
in Gloucester County, Virginia, 1957–1959

Ivor Noël Hume

An artist's conjectural reconstruction of Rosewell as originally planned. From Thomas Waterman's *The Mansions of Virginia*, Chapel Hill, University of North Carolina Press, 1946, p. 106.

ACKNOWLEDGMENTS

I am vastly indebted to Miss Nellie Deans Greaves, Maj. Fielding Lewis Greaves and the late Col. G. A. Greaves for permission to excavate at Rosewell and for their generosity in agreeing to present the finds to the Smithsonian Institution.

My gratitude and commiserations go out to my wife Audrey Noël Hume and to John Van Ness Dunton, who suffered through snow, frost, rain, heat, and mosquitoes to help me with the excavation, an operation that was really too large for three people to handle. I am further indebted to them for their assistance in assembling the glass and ceramics, and particularly to Mr. Dunton for his work on the chemical treatment and cleaning of the metals.

I am also indebted to the department of architecture of Colonial Williamsburg, Inc., Williamsburg, Virginia, for its assistance in the construction of this report and for generously carrying the cost of preparing the illustrations.

Among the many persons who have given freely of their council and guidance are Frederick M. Bayer, associate curator of marine invertebrates, Smithsonian Institution; R. J. Charleston, assistant keeper in the department of ceramics, Victoria and Albert Museum, London; Philip H. Dunbar, curatorial assistant at Colonial Williamsburg; John Gloag;

by Ivor Noël Hume

Excavations at
ROSEWELL
in Gloucester County, Virginia, 1957-1959

In the fall of 1957 excavations were undertaken in the vicinity of the ruins of Rosewell, an 18th-century mansion in Gloucester County, Virginia. The deposit, which was in a trash pit, yielded artifacts that should be of significant interest to archeologists and historians concerned with the excavation of colonial sites.

This article describes and analyzes the important Rosewell finds, which have been given to the Smithsonian Institution by the present owners of the mansion.

THE AUTHOR: *Ivor Noël Hume is chief archeologist at Colonial Williamsburg, Inc., and an honorary research associate of the Smithsonian Institution.*

John M. Graham II, vice president and curator of collections, Colonial Williamsburg; J. C. Harrington, chief of interpretation, Region I, U.S. National Park Service; Edward P. Henderson, associate curator of mineralogy and petrology, Smithsonian Institution; J. Paul Hudson, U.S. National Park Service curator at Jamestown, Virginia; A. Edwin Kendrew, senior vice president, Colonial Williamsburg; Dr. Ben McCary; Ralph Merrifield, assistant keeper, Guildhall Museum, London; Eric P. Newman; John L. Pope, assistant director, Freer Gallery of Art, Washington; Dr. E. M. Riley, director of research, Colonial Williamsburg; Thad Tate of the research depart-ment, Colonial Williamsburg; and C. Malcolm Watkins, curator of cultural history, Smithsonian Institution.

I am further indebted to Mr. Mann Page and Mr. and Mrs. Hugh Dabney of Gloucester County, Virginia, for their valued assistance in tracing the genealogy of the Page family and the history of Rosewell. Finally, I wish to express my appreciation to Mr. and Mrs. A. E. Kendrew for providing space in their home for the initial treatment of the artifacts, and to Ann D. Parish and J. Ricks Wilson for help-ing in the initial and supplementary surveys of the site.

FEBRUARY 1962. I. N. H.

EXCAVATIONS IN THE VICINITY of the ruined mansion of Rosewell in Gloucester County were undertaken not to gain information concerning the plantation house and its dependencies but to recover stratified and closely dated groups of artifacts that would be of value as comparative material for archeologists and historians concerned with the excavation of colonial sites. This paper relates to a single trash deposit, the main filling of which is believed to have taken place between the approximate years 1763 and 1772. The deposit was found by Mr. J. V. N. Dunton while searching through the woods for the site of Rosewell's icehouse. Oyster shells and wine-bottle fragments had been thrown up from the pit by the burrowing of a groundhog that had made its home deep in the refuse. Although the discovery was made in October 1956, it was not until the autumn of 1957 that the writer sought permission of the owners of Rosewell for excavations to be carried out on the site.

History of Rosewell

Rosewell stands on the west bank of Carter's Creek at the point where it enters the York River, thus its lands are bordered on the southwest by the river and on the southeast by the creek. The tract was said by some authorities to have been willed by John Page, the emigrant, to his son Mathew in 1692. But others claim that the land came into Page hands through Mary Mann whose family won the land in a game of push-pin.[1] Mary Mann was the wife of Mathew Page, of the King's Council, who built a frame house on the land in the late 17th century. After the death of Mathew Page in 1703 the land passed to his son Mann Page I, who, after the destruction of the Page home in 1721,[2] began to build himself a mansion of such grandeur that it rivaled the palace of the Royal Governor in Williamsburg, and has since been described as the finest example of domestic architecture in Colonial America.

In 1730, with Rosewell apparently still far from completed, Mann Page I died, leaving to his widow Judith "his dwelling house, with all out houses thereto belonging, where he then lived, and the mansion house then building, with all the land thereto adjoining . . . ."[3] It is perhaps significant that his wife was the daughter of Robert "King" Carter, who had built Corotoman on the Rappahannock, then one of the wonders of Virginia. It was not impossible that Mann Page I embarked upon the building of Rosewell at the instigation of, or to keep pace with, his father-in-law.

The bulk of the Page estates passed to Mann Page II when his elder brother, Ralph, died intestate. Mann Page II continued to work towards the completion of Rosewell, but he soon found that he possessed insufficient funds to pay the immense debts incurred by his father that were compounded by his own efforts to finish the mansion. In 1743 Mann Page II married Alice Grymes, and in the following year he petitioned the Assembly to break the entail on 27,000 acres scattered over nine counties.[4] It has been assumed that until this land was sold Rosewell remained unfinished, but there is, in fact, no mention of the house in the plea to the Assembly, only a desire to pay existing debts. It is perhaps reasonable to suggest that the house was actually finished on credit before Page's marriage and that the necessity to pay the resulting bills occasioned the land sale in 1744. The history of the mansion throughout the remainder of the 18th century is one of gradual decline, the Page family having too little money to maintain it, to entertain in it, or to enjoy it as its opulence demanded.

April 1744 saw the birth of Mann Page II's son John, who was destined to become the most influential of his clan. Educated in England, he became master of Rosewell about 1765, by which time, for some uncertain reason, his father had moved out of the house. During the decade 1761–1770 the father built for himself another imposing residence, Mannsfield,

---

[1] A. Lawrence Kocker and Howard Dearstyne, *Shadows in Silver*, New York, 1954, p. 66. Miss Nellie Deans Greaves was kind enough to contribute the following information: "Mathew, son of John Page, married Mary Mann, sole heir and daughter of John Mann, and thus became master of the Rosewell tracts. John Mann had purchased the property on September 24, 1680, 'by virtue of an indenture of bargain and sale,' from Elizabeth Coggs and Mary Perry, heirs and granddaughters of George Minifree (sometimes spelled 'Menefee'). George Minifree had come into possession of the tract when he received an original grant in 1639."

[2] William Byrd, *The London Diary, 1717–1721*, edited by Louis B. Wright and Marion Tinling, New York, 1958, entry for

March 12, 1721, p. 506: "After dinner I put some things in order and then took a walk to Mrs. Harrison's who told me Colonel Page's house was burnt to the ground, which I was much concerned to hear." Robert Carter, writing on March 8, 1721, reported that Colonel "Cage's" house and barn had burned to the ground (Louis B. Wright, ed., *Letters of Robert Carter 1720–1727*, San Marino, California, 1940, p. 90).

[3] William Waller Hening, *Statutes at Large . . . A Collection of all the Laws of Virginia . . .* , Richmond, 1819, vol. 5, p. 278.

[4] *Ibid.*

FIGURE 1.—Location of Rosewell, where Carter's Creek flows into the York River. From map made by Joshua Fry and Peter Jefferson in 1751 and revised, with place names, by J. Dalrymple in 1755. Photo courtesy Library of Congress.

in Spotsylvania County near Fredericksburg.[5] As a result of his father's departure, John Page, then a very young man, unexpectedly found himself the master if not the owner of Rosewell and faced with the unenviable tasks of running a plantation that had not shown a profit in years and of maintaining a house that was rapidly falling apart. Although the records are far from explicit, it would also seem likely that John Page had to contend with a father who did not entirely see eye-to-eye with him.

The relationship between John Page and his father, Mann Page II, is of prime importance in the consideration of the material excavated at Rosewell, for it all belongs to the period of transition when the son had taken the place of the father. The exact date of the departure of Mann Page II is uncertain,

[5] Thomas T. Waterman, *The Mansions of Virginia*, Chapel Hill, University of North Carolina Press, 1946, p. 418. Miss Nellie Deans Greaves explains the departure of Mann Page II by the fact that John Page was his eldest son by his first marriage and so would inherit Rosewell. His eldest son by his second marriage, Mann Page III, had no such inheritance, and therefore Mann Page II moved to Spotsylvania County and built Mannsfield for Mann Page III. Mr. Mann Page of Shelly has suggested that Mann Page II's departure from Rosewell may have been occasioned by his marriage to Anne Corbyn Tayloe, but this event took place in about 1748 according to Edmund Jennings Lee (*Lee of Virginia*, Philadelphia, 1895). In any case it would seem that the Pages never learned that mansion-building was an expensive undertaking. In 1796 Mann Page III was forced to sell Mannsfield because of financial difficulties. Mannsfield was destroyed during the War Between the States. The site was excavated by the National Park Service in 1934.

but in a letter of May 27, 1769, to John Norton from Rosewell, John Page makes the following excuse for delaying payment of his debts:

. . . no Body hates the Thoughts of being in Debt more than I do: but the Great Scarcity of Money here, the Shortness of my Crops for four Years past, & the necessary Expences of an encreasing Family joined to the Commencement of Housekeeping in a large House, have forced me to submit to it for a while . . . .[6]

It might therefore be construed that John Page had been farming the Rosewell lands for four years prior to 1769 and that he may have been master of Rosewell during much of that time.

In a letter to John Norton dated February 22, 1770, Mann Page requested that certain goods be shipped from England "to be landed where I live near Fredericksburg." It is apparent from the same letter that Mann Page was growing tobacco there and that he had been doing so for at least one year previously.[7] In a letter from London in 1773 John Norton mentions Mann Page's tobacco in the following terms:

. . . the quality of the Crop is amazingly inferior to what it us'd to be, the same may be said of Mr. Mann Page's, I delivd. a hhd of his M P aday or two ago that had a large part of the hhd dry rotten, perish'd and stunk like a dunghill and is not worth a farthing pr cwt if I think of it you shall have a sample of it with the mark and no. his Rappa. Tobo. is likewise Trash.[8]

This reference is important in that it indicates the nature of Mann Page's tobacco mark, the same mark that appears on a wine-bottle seal (fig. 16, no. 9) found during the excavations at Rosewell.

John Page's tribulations at Rosewell have become known to us only in scraps of evidence culled from the *Norton Papers;* unhappily, few records of Page life at Rosewell survive, and no contemporary descriptions or inventories of the house have come to light. It is known, however, that John Page had little success with his tobacco and was constantly forced to stave off his creditors. In a letter to John Norton written at Rosewell on October 11, 1771, he described a scheme to increase his tobacco yield:

. . . they [his friends] advised me to rent some Land in Frederick (where exceedingly fine Land may be rented on very good Terms) break up my Cheescake Quarter, lease it out, send the Hands to Frederick & draught about 10 or 12 from Rosewell (where there are 27 in the Crop) & send them up which would make up a Gang of 16 or 17, which Gang say they will produce you from 30 to 40 Hhds. pr Anm. & you make within 3 or 4 Hhds. as much Tobo. in Gloster as you do now; for I never made but 3 Hhds. at Cheescake nor more than 15 at Rosewell.

He goes on to express his hopes for the success of the plan and to excuse himself for not having sold some of his slaves to pay his debts, a course that he had previously promised to take:[9]

. . . I shall be better able to sell Negros a few years hence, if there should be Occasion for it then, when a great Number of young ones will be grown up, than I am now, I am determined to adopt this Plan.

Later in the same letter John Page gives some indication of Rosewell's appearance less than 30 years after it was completed:

As my House is very much out of Repair, I have engaged a Man to put it in a saving Condition next Spring. I shall therefore be much obliged to you if you will send me the articles mentioned in the inclosed Invoice early in the Spring . . .

100 lb of White Lead	2 lb of white Coperass
20 lb Yellow Ochre	A Glaziers Diamond of 20/
A Bar.l of Oyl	Value [10]
20 Lb of Venetian Red	10 M 8d Nails
2 Gallons of Spt. of	10 M 10d Do
Turpentine	5 M 6d Do
5 lb Red Lead	2 M 20d Do
3 lb Lamp Black	2 M 4d Do

Although John Page's financial affairs were never in the best of order, his status in the colony and subsequently in the State of Virginia rose steadily throughout his life. In 1774, as a member of Lord Dunmore's Council, he made his political position clear by

---

[6] Francis Norton Mason, ed., *John Norton & Sons: Merchants of London and Virginia*, Richmond, 1937, p. 94, hereinafter referred to as *Norton Papers*.

[7] Mann Page to John Norton, February 22, 1770, *Norton Papers*, pp. 123–124.

[8] John Norton to Hatley Norton, March 20, 1773, *Norton Papers*, p. 309. It is suggested in the *Norton Papers* that the Mann Page of this letter and the one cited in footnote 7 was not Mann Page II of Rosewell but the son of John Page of North End. However the accumulative evidence from other sources strongly suggests that the letters refer to Mann Page II, formerly of Rosewell but then of Mannsfield.

[9] *Norton Papers*, p. 199. It is not known how many slaves John Page owned at this time, but he is recorded as possessing 160 in Abingdon Parish in April 1786 and 27 in Petsworth Parish in October 1782. In Hening (*op. cit.* footnote 3, p. 283) Mann Page is shown to have applied, in September 1744, to the Assembly for the ownership of 76 slaves left by his father to his deceased brother Ralph. Of these, 17 were at the Scotland Quarter, 12 at Clements Quarter, 19 at Clay Bank, and 28 at Rosewell, all in Gloucester County.

[10] Many fragments of window glass were found in the excavation, and a number of the pieces bore evidence of having been cut with a diamond.

refusing to censure Patrick Henry for his verbal retaliation following the Governor's removal of the powder from Williamsburg's magazine. He subsequently became a member of the Committee of Safety, and a member of the First Council in 1776. During the Revolutionary War he saw active duty in the campaign against Benedict Arnold. In 1789 Page became a Member of Congress, retaining the seat until 1797, and in 1802 he became Governor of Virginia. He died in 1808 leaving a widow, Margaret (Lowther), whom he had married in 1789 and who had borne him eight children in addition to the twelve born to his first wife, Frances (Burwell), who had died in 1784 at the age of 37.

John Page was not only a plantation owner and a politician but a man of science. He was president of the Society for the Advancement of Useful Knowledge, an organization formed in Williamsburg in 1773 which, in the course of its life, had such illustrious members as George Wythe, Bishop Madison, Benjamin Franklin, and Dr. Benjamin Rush of Philadelphia. Page gained some fame as an astronomer after successfully calculating an eclipse of the sun. We know that he spent much time on the flat roof of Rosewell studying the heavens through a telescope. It would appear, by and large, that the roof of the great house made greater contributions to history than did the fine rooms beneath it. It was there that Page made the first American experiments in the recording of annual rainfall. In a letter to John Norton penned July 21, 1773, at Rosewell, Page gives a long account of his experiments and of an instrument he had devised that would measure 1/300 of an inch of rain.[11] He ends the letter by explaining his reasons for writing it, saying he believed the experiments were:

. . . the first that ever were made of this Kind in America, & I may say, with such an Instt in the World; & . . . I must beg the Favour of you to endeavour to procure me another, as I have unfortunately broke mine.

It was hoped that some evidence of John Page's scientific interests might be unearthed during the course of the excavations, but unfortunately all that was found was a single fragment of glass tubing (fig. 14, no. 9).

Rosewell's, and perhaps John Page's, principal claim to historic immortality lies in the fact that one day in June 1776 Page's close friend Thomas Jefferson visited him and, in a cupola on the roof, read over and discussed the first draft of the Declaration of Independence.

After the death of John Page his widow continued to live at Rosewell until she too died, whereupon the mansion was sold in 1838 to one Thomas Booth, whose name, it has been said, "should rank high in the annals of vandalism."[12] No sooner had Booth bought Rosewell for the sum of $12,000 than he began to tear it apart, ripping off the famous leaden roof, stripping the paneling from the walls, and removing the marble mantels as well as the marble that paved the magnificent entrance hall. Not content with this he went on to tear down and remove the bricks from the family graveyard walls and to cut down the stately avenue of cedars, all of which he sold as scrap for the princely sum of $35,000. In 1855, having sold everything except the shell of the mansion he disposed of that to the Deans family of Gloucester for $22,000, thus making a profit of $45,000 for having destroyed one of the finest examples of American colonial craftsmanship then surviving.

The new owners did all they could to salvage what was left of the great house and to make it into a pleasant home. But some who still remember staying in it recall that it resembled a gigantic mausoleum, cold, bleak and forbidding.[13] In March 1916, nearly 200 years after the first Page home had been destroyed by fire, Rosewell burst into flames and was gutted before help could be summoned. The four walls, which survived more or less intact until the 1930's, have since fallen prey to hurricanes and vandalism. The south wall has collapsed, and the west wall is (in 1961) in danger of following it, an event that will inevitably herald Rosewell's final eclipse. The lawns and floral gardens have long since been lost beneath the jungle of fast-growing vegetation that now surrounds and climbs over the walls of the house like a shroud. It was amid this wilderness that the recent excavations were conducted.

---

[11] John Page to John Norton, July 21, 1773, *Norton Papers*, p. 339.

[12] Kocher and Dearstyne, *op. cit.* (footnote 1), p. 68.

[13] Miss Greaves remarked that this opinion is not shared by all of those who remember the mansion as it was in the early years of the present century. However, Thomas Allen Glenn (*Some Colonial Mansions*, Philadelphia, 1899, p. 171) gives the following description: "Dismantled now and scarcely habitable, with a dismal 'flavor of mild decay' pervading its halls and passageways, as if the sickly malarial damp creeping up from the river had bored to the very marrow of its wooden bones, this relic of Colonial Virginia, once the pride of its fair lords, shivers out the last years of the span of life allotted it, neglected and forgotten."

Rosewell's Architecture and Topography

The exact size of the Rosewell estate as inherited by the first Mann Page is uncertain, but we know that when he died his three sons inherited a total of 70,000 Virginia acres, most of which must have been in the vicinity of the home plantation. As mentioned earlier, the Page home was built on the western shore of Carter's Creek where it enters the York River, and it is supposed that the first house stood in this general area, although no traces of it have yet come to light.

It would appear that the huge number of bricks needed in the building of Rosewell were fired on the site from clay dug nearby. There is some indication that Mann Page II, who completed the house, also provided brick used in the building of Carter's Grove on the James.[14] The digging of clay could readily explain the existence of numerous trash-filled pits that exist on the Rosewell property—pits too large to be explained away merely as repositories for domestic refuse.

The bricks were laid in Flemish bond with random glazed headers, no attempt being made to use the glazed bricks in decorative patterns. Such a simple and common device was unnecessary in a building that boasted so many ornamental features. All the corners and window jambs were of rubbed bricks, their vermilion color carefully selected and matched, while gauged bricks were used for the belt courses, window arches, panels beneath the sills, and, most dramatically, for the great doorways in the centers of the north and south walls. The window sills, keystones, doorway caps, and pilaster bases were of Portland stone, with the latter carefully and elaborately fluted to match the remarkable brick pilasters above.

The house stood a full three stories above an English basement, the windows in each story being less tall than those of the floor beneath, and the windows above the main doors being of greater width to balance the breadth of the doors themselves. A parapet of uncertain form surrounded the flat roof, traces of which can still be seen in the stone cornices set into the chimneys at the height of the original parapet caps. This feature was removed during the Booth era in the mid-19th century, as also were the two cupolas. A fanciful engraving of Rosewell with the cupolas intact is to be found in Bishop Meade's *Old Churches, Ministers and Families of Virginia,*[15] but it is obvious that the picture bears little resemblance to Rosewell as it was in the colonial or any other period. Lucy Burwell Page Saunders, who knew the place well, gave the following description of Rosewell in her story *Leonora and the Ghost,* published in 1876:

. . . a wall of bricks, surmounted by large flagstones, surrounded the top of the building. At each end was a turret, within which were small apartments and on the roof of each, large weather cocks whirled mournfully. Into one of the rooms you ascended from the winding staircase, leading from the basement to the roof. From the other, called the summerhouse, you beheld from its four fine windows beautiful views of the winding Carter's Creek, and the majestic York River.[16]

The 19th-century alterations saw the removal of the deck on hip roof and the construction of a low hip roof with pediments added at east and west, pediments which were constructed of brick laid in informal bond, contrasting unfavorably with the uniformity of the Flemish bond beneath.

The splendor of the ornamental brick doorways at north and south was rivaled by the great arched windows at east and west that cast cathedral-like shafts of light into the stair hall. The hall, which was entered from the north, was the mansion's principal room and, when occasion demanded, was used as a ballroom. It is probable that originally the hall was richly paneled in mahogany, but all that remained of the woodwork after Booth had departed were the balustrade and stringer of the great staircase. Photographs of the staircase taken in the 1890's and in the early years of the present century show that it was undoubtedly the finest in America, being wide enough for eight persons to ascend abreast. The principal features of the staircase were the immense newel and the fascia board around the well with its carved floral and foliate scrolls and baskets of fruit, a style so similar to that of surviving fascia at Tuckahoe that the two probably were made by the same hand. The treatment of the balusters is also paralleled at Tuckahoe as well as at Sabine Hall and Westover, although these are all lighter and more delicate.

---

[14] Waterman, *op. cit.* (footnote 5), p. 112.

[15] William Meade, *Old Churches, Ministers and Families of Virginia,* Philadelphia, 1857, opposite p. 332.

[16] Lucy Burwell Page Saunders, *Leonora and the Ghost,* Baltimore, 1876, p. 3. Mrs. Saunders was a daughter of Governor John Page.

Little is known about the other rooms of Rosewell, said to have been no fewer than 40 in number. The principal source is again Mrs. Saunders, who states that "All the rooms were wainscoted with wood of different colors, and had marble mantels, the ceilings were also of great height." [17]

The description of the house given in the paragraphs above is by no means complete, but it perhaps indicates the splendor of the structure as originally conceived and draws attention to features that have some bearing on finds made during the recent excavations.[18]

Of great importance from an archeological point of view are the sites of the outbuildings, which played a major part in the life of the plantation if not of the mansion itself. Of these little or nothing remains above ground. A circular icehouse, with its shingled roof intact until the 1930's, stood at some distance to the southwest of the house. Today, however, the roof has fallen into the pit and only part of the wall still stands—a wall which probably dates from the 19th rather than from the 18th century. A colonial well encircled by thick underbrush remains open a few yards to the east of the mansion, but it is filled with rubble to within ten feet or so of the top. No attempt has yet been made to excavate the contents.

The principal outbuildings were the east and west dependencies, which flanked the north approach to the house and which were originally intended to be linked to it by brick-walled passages similar to those that survive at Mount Airy (1751). Although the walls of the house were carefully keyed so that the passage walls could be bonded into them, and regardless of the fact that doors actually opened into the places where the passages should be, it is doubtful whether such passages were ever actually built. Only careful archeological excavations can solve this problem, and the dangers of working so close to the crumbling ruin will prevent such an investigation until the walls finally collapse.

An insurance policy (fig. 5) issued by the Mutual Assurance Society of Virginia in 1802 that related to five buildings—the mansion itself, its two dependencies, a brick stable and a wooden barn—set the value of the property at $9,900. A comparison between the sketches on the policy with the site plan (fig. 2) clearly shows that the former were not drawn with much regard for the relationships between the five buildings. The kitchen (c) and the dwelling (b) sketched on the policy represent the two dependencies of the same size that stood on a north-south axis. However, it does seem likely that buildings b, c, d would have been shown correctly to east and west of the main house. The positioning of the barn (e), on the other hand, may have been dictated only by the space remaining on the policy.

The presence of the well to the east of the house supports the belief fostered by the insurance policy that the kitchen was at the east. But the trash pit—with which this paper is principally concerned—is to the west of the house, and it contained large quantities of refuse that one would have expected to be associated with a kitchen. On the grounds that it would be unlikely that the kitchen trash pits would normally be dug where it would be necessary to carry the refuse across the front of the house, the present anomaly may be explained by the need to fill a large hole that was dug for another purpose.

Archeological evidence will later be used to indicate that the policy is correct in situating the massive (120 by 24 feet) brick stable (d) to the west of the mansion. A careful search through the jungle of vines and underbrush in the area revealed a short stretch of colonial brickwork northwest of the trash pit with a number of cobble stones and bricks around it, these perhaps having served as part of a roughly paved yard. Scattered about to the east of the wall fragment are a number of architectural items of Portland stone, including nosings and a large semicircular piece that may have formed part of the base of a column or, more probably, the newel from a balustraded flight of steps.

Probing and minor exploratory digging have revealed the site of the east dependency, which seems to have disappeared before the close of the 19th century. An area approximately 56 by 45 feet was littered with bricks, shell mortar, and huge quantities of oyster shells, amid which were a few fragments of crockery that could be attributed to the second half of the 19th century.

The west dependency was doubtless the twin of the kitchen, but its purpose is unknown. Photographs taken in the late 19th century show standing on this site a 1½-storied brick building with a wooden

---

[17] *Ibid.*, p. 4.

[18] For a commentary on the ground plan of Rosewell, see Marcus Whiffen, "Some Virginia House Plans Reconsidered," *Journal of the Society of Architectural Historians*, 1957, vol. 16, no. 2, p. 17ff.

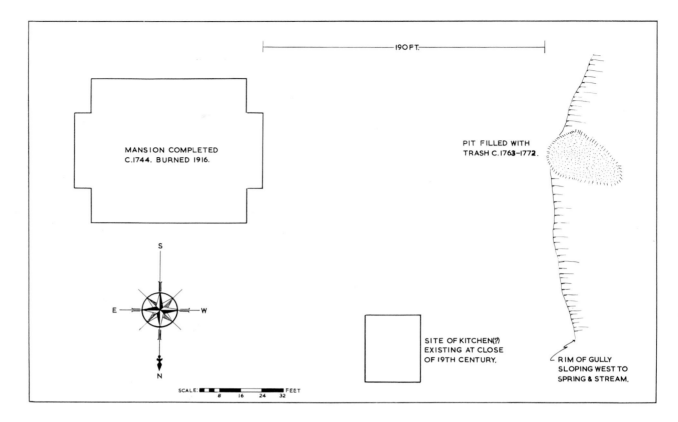

190 FT.

MANSION COMPLETED
C.1744. BURNED 1916.

PIT FILLED WITH
TRASH C.1763–1772.

SITE OF KITCHEN(?)
EXISTING AT CLOSE
OF 19TH CENTURY.

RIM OF GULLY
SLOPING WEST TO
SPRING & STREAM.

SCALE: FEET
         8   16   24   32

FIGURE 2.—Plan showing pit in relation to the mansion.

lean-to at the rear,[19] but it seems unlikely that this was the original colonial dependency. An examination of the surviving foundations revealed the use of large pieces of dressed stone, some with moldings; but whether these were used as repairs or were in the original construction of the building is not yet clear. No careful excavation has been undertaken in this area, but souvenir hunters have apparently dug holes here and there within the confines of the walls and have unearthed small quantities of domestic trash that appear to date to the late 19th century or early 20th century.

The site of the Page barn has not been identified, but it is possible that it stood to the northwest of the house and that its foundations spanned the track now leading to the ruined mansion. In the course of deep ploughing in 1958 and 1959 traces of shell-mortared colonial brick foundations were found running north and south. The same operations also revealed two large domestic trash deposits. The contents of these deposits have not been investigated but they are known to be of colonial date.

There is no doubt that John Page possessed other structures in the vicinity of Rosewell that did not feature in the 1802 insurance policy—buildings such as smokehouse, dairy, lumber sheds, icehouse, and so forth. No reference is made to a slave quarter, and one can only wonder whether the slaves were housed in unsightly shacks unworthy of insurance or whether some were allowed to reside in the west dependency.

The 1957–1959 Excavations

In the course of its own excavations of the trash pit, the burrowing ground hog had thrown out large quantities of oyster shells, brickbats, and bottle fragments. The site of the pit lies 190 feet west of the plantation house (see fig. 2) on the edge of a natural slope that runs into a small valley. Through the valley winds a stream fed by a spring popularly known as Pocahontas' Spring—a reminder that Powhatan is said to have had a settlement in the

---

[19] Kocher and Dearstyne, *op. cit.* (footnote 12), pl. 111.

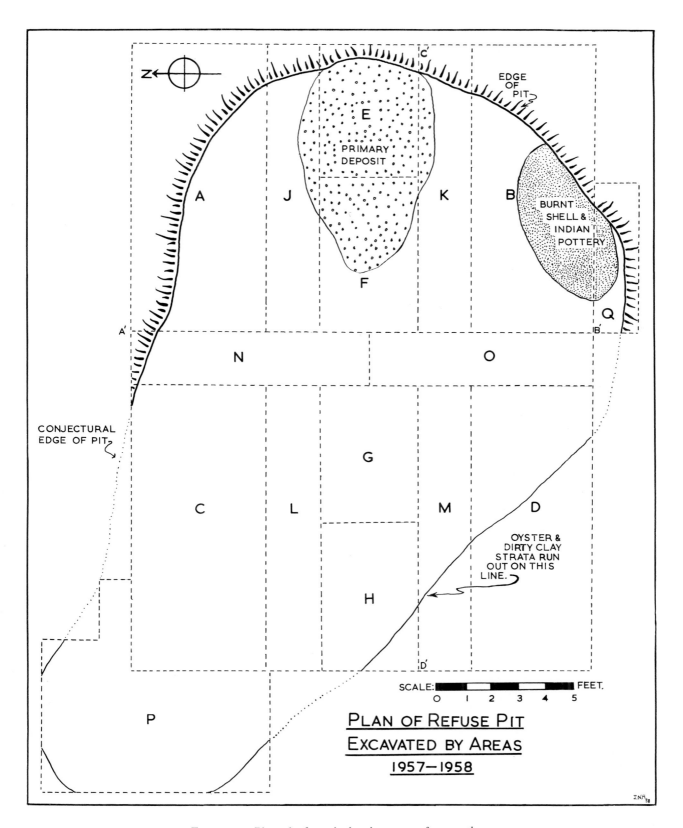

FIGURE 3.—Plan of refuse pit showing areas of excavation.

vicinity of Rosewell. The spring is also said to have inspired the name of the house, but for this information we have only the fanciful pages of *Leonora and the Ghost* to rely upon.

When marked on a plan, the ground hog's five entrances to his burrow create a circle some 12 feet in diameter. The majority of the artifacts were found in the westerly holes—those farthest down the slope towards the stream. The approach to the northerly segment of the circle was impeded by a large tree that the excavators did not remove because of an agreement with the owners that the excavations were not to do any permanent damage to the property.

To ensure that the excavation should include the entire trash deposit, an area 20 by 28 feet was hacked out of the undergrowth. After initial clearance of matted underbrush, many artifacts were recovered from the surface and from the top 6 inches of humus that had been disturbed by the removal of vines and other vegetation. All the artifacts from this part of the excavation are described as surface finds and cannot be used as dating evidence.

PLAN

Since the colonial deposit would in all probability measure between 5 and 10 feet in diameter and 4 or 5 feet in depth, it was estimated that the area would take less than a week to clear. In order to locate the pit an exploratory trench 3 feet wide was dug in an east-west direction from the top of the slope to the western edge of the cleared area, a total length of 28 feet.

The trench revealed that its eastern extremity was excellently placed on the eastern rim of the colonial pit but that its western end stopped short of extending through the pit. The original estimate of the depth was reasonably accurate for it was found that the deposit was 5 feet 3 inches in depth at its deepest point. The completed work revealed that the pit was pear-shaped, with its ends lying southeast to northwest, and was 34 feet long and 18 feet wide at its widest point. The excavation took some 360 man-hours to complete.

The first trench was divided into four sections (E–H in fig. 3) arranged so as to leave a 2-foot balk running north and south across the center of the pit (fig. 4). Subsequently four area excavations were laid out to cover the rest of the prepared area within the right angles created by the trial trench and the projected north-south balk. These area excavations (A–D in fig. 3) were dug so as to leave balks

flanking either side of the first trench, thus preserving north-south and east-west sections through the filling. Eventually the balks (lettered J–O) were removed. The final stage of the excavation was the extending of the excavated area to the northwest (P in fig. 3) in the hope of reaching a westerly edge. Unfortunately, this part of the work was completed in some haste as the presence of chiggers and swarms of mosquitoes that breed in the valley made it abundantly clear that the excavating season was over.

STRATIFICATION

The stratification of the pit (see fig. 4) was quite simple. The top layer, of brown soil, was only some 2 inches thick at the top of the slope but it increased to a depth of more than 2 feet at the west. This layer contained very few artifacts other than those left in the ground hog's burrow passages.

The second stratum, consisting almost entirely of oyster shells, bones, and artifacts, was the principal source of finds. It commenced close to the top of the slope but thickened rapidly towards the center of the pit; unlike the first stratum, it dwindled to practically nothing at the west, causing the first and third layers to merge together at that end.

The third stratum, of varying thickness, was created by water-eroded clay from the sides of the pit, into which many artifacts had sunk. It rested on natural clay at the west but became confused with a variety of intrusions at the east.

The fourth layer in area B was a localized deposit of wood ash, burnt oyster shells, and fragments of Indian pottery; it had been cut into the side of the pit at the southeast. Considerable reddening on the pit side as a result of fire suggests that Indians had built a cooking fire in the pit and probably had used the side as protection from the wind. The fact that the burning overlay washed clay containing colonial artifacts dating from the first half of the 18th century clearly indicates a terminus post quem for this occurrence.

The primary filling was confined to the central area of the pit, accumulating against the steep east bank and spreading out thinly towards balk N–O. This stratum contained fragments of early 18th-century wine bottles and three thin glass flasks (fig. 29, no. 6), tobacco-pipe fragments, and the stem of a wine glass (fig. 32, no. 7) of a type that could date no earlier than about 1740, which provides the earliest date for use of the pit as a repository for trash.

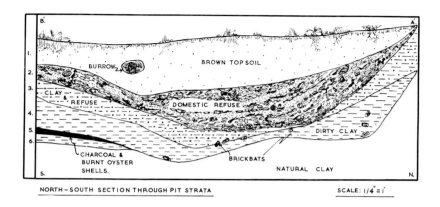

NORTH-SOUTH SECTION THROUGH PIT STRATA   SCALE: 1/4" = 1'

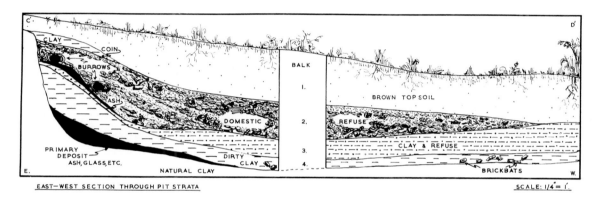

EAST-WEST SECTION THROUGH PIT STRATA   SCALE: 1/4" = 1'.

FIGURE 4.—North-south and east-west sections through the pit.

DATING EVIDENCE

The earliest possible date for the primary filling, 1740, does not necessarily indicate the date of the digging of the pit. The presence of numerous brickbats, with shell mortar attached, in the lower eroded clay stratum suggests that a brick structure had been altered or demolished at the same time or soon after the pit was dug. In view of the facts that the pit was much too large to have been dug solely as a trash repository and that it received very little refuse for some time after the digging (indicated by the clay silting), it is reasonable to suggest that it was dug as a borrow pit for clay needed in brickmaking.

If this theory can be accepted, it only remains to establish the dates at which building or alterations were in progress on the Rosewell Plantation to learn the date at which the pit was dug. The principal construction years, as stated previously, occurred between about 1720 and 1743 or 1744. The date of the pit's primary filling could conceivably indicate that it was

dug during the last spate of building when Mann Page II was completing the mansion. On the other hand, it seems extremely unlikely that the pit would have been left open until the late 1760's, when the bulk of the trash was deposited. Furthermore, after the archeological excavations had been completed it was found that the re-dug pit silted to a depth of 18 inches in the course of three winter months. It is reasonable, therefore, to infer that the pit was dug and filled with trash within one year.

On the evidence of the artifacts recovered from the various strata, it would be possible to create a slow progression from the 1740's to the late 1760's; however, the absence of later material in the lower levels provides only negative evidence that can be readily disputed. Since there were comparatively few items of late date in the upper layers, and there were many more items in those layers than in the lower ones, it is quite reasonable statistically for later items to be missing altogether, thus creating false dating evidence.

Under the circumstances, the dating of the digging of the pit must rely upon the evidence of nature (silting) and upon historical data. Since there are few surviving written records of Rosewell and there are no data relating to the building or maintenance of the house and no accounts of day-to-day life there,[20] we must fall back on elementary deductions—deductions that can very easily be wrong.

The presence of mortar-surfaced brickbats in the early silting of the pit indicates that there was a period of remodeling at Rosewell. It seems possible that such a change could have been occasioned by the advent of John Page as master of Rosewell in the mid-1760's. If, as has been suggested, the pit was dug to obtain clay for brickmaking, we have evidence of both construction and destruction side by side. On the other hand, we have John Page's own words to show that he had little money to spare for house repairs and that in 1770 he was forced to do something to Rosewell to put it in "a saving Condition." It could therefore be argued that the pit was dug at that time. The presence of fragments of cut window-glass and a bullion from a crown is clearly indicative of glazing and might coincide with the advent of the "Glaziers Diamond of 20/Value" ordered in October 1771.[21] Also to be taken into consideration is a small group of six English creamware sherds of good quality, one of them coming from the first layer and the others from the top of the second. Generally speaking, one does not expect to find much creamware—or "Queen's ware" as Josiah Wedgwood called it—in use in the colony before about 1770. Nevertheless, there is evidence to show that the Pages knew of creamware and owned some by that date. Mann Page II's order requesting that goods be shipped from England "to be landed where I live near Fredericksburg" included "1 Dozn. Tea Cups 1 Dozn. Saucers, 1 Dozn. Coffee Cups & 1 Dozn. Saucers, 1 Slop Bowl of Queen China."[22] Consequently, it need not be surprising to find creamware in use at Rosewell by 1770 or that sherds of such ware should be present. But if the ante quem and post quem dates for the pit are very close together, then the creamware fragments are strong evidence in favor of a date close to 1770 or even 1772 for its filling.

The principal post quem dating is provided by a pewter shoe buckle, found at the bottom of the second layer, that is decorated with a pair of molded barrels at the middle and with the legend "NO EXCISE" at either end (fig. 7). This is almost certainly an English political memento produced in the 1760's, when the slogan was shouted by the same radicals who cried out so loudly for "Wilkes and Liberty." Use of the slogan can be traced back as far as 1733 when Walpole's Excise Bill was abandoned and the public took to wearing badges and cockades adorned with the words "Liberty, Property and No Excise." It reappeared in 1763 following the passing of the so-called Cyder Act, which became law in March of that year. Hartshorne's *Old English Glasses* shows an English cider glass with "NO EXCISE," a barrel, and a cluster of apples engraved on the bowl.[23] Discussing this and another glass of its type Hartshorne states that "These words are part of the old popular cry which had been revived by the conduct of Wilkes and the appearance in 1763 of No. 45 of the *North Briton*, and, as to cider, by the excise regulations of the same year touching it." The blending of the "Wilkes and Liberty" and the "No Excise" slogans is to be seen in a ledger entry of August 1763 from a Bristol glasshouse which reads: "To 6 Enamelled p^t Canns wrote *Liberty and no Excise*." [24]

If, as Hartshorne and others have inferred, the "No Excise" slogan can be associated with Wilkes, then its presence on a shoe buckle found in Virginia makes sense. Cast in the rough-and-ready mold of Patrick Henry, John Wilkes was looked upon by many colonists as the wind of freedom blowing through the halls of Parliament. On April 23, 1763, Wilkes published the 45th edition of his radical newspaper, the *North Briton*, in which he attacked the King's speech to the House of Commons claiming that the recent Treaty of Paris had the full support of England's ally, the King of Prussia. Wilkes, contending that the Prussian monarch had, in fact, been sold up the river, condemned both the treaty and the government of the Earl of Bute. It was Lord Bute and his Scots colleagues who had instituted the levy on cider, a tax bitterly resented by the English on the grounds that their Scots cousins neither made nor drank cider. A broadside published in March 1763 contained a vicious cartoon lampooning both the King and Lord Bute and a sketch of a happy Scotsman crying "By the Laird, this is a brae sight: I sal be Commissioner of Exceese in Time."

---

[20] Other than the brief references previously quoted from the *Norton Papers*, op. cit. (footnote 6).

[21] *Norton Papers*, op. cit. (footnote 6), p. 199.

[22] *Ibid.*, pp. 123, 125. The order was dated February 15, 1770.

[23] Albert Hartshorne, *Old English Glasses*, London, 1897, p. 312.

[24] *Ibid.*, p. 311.

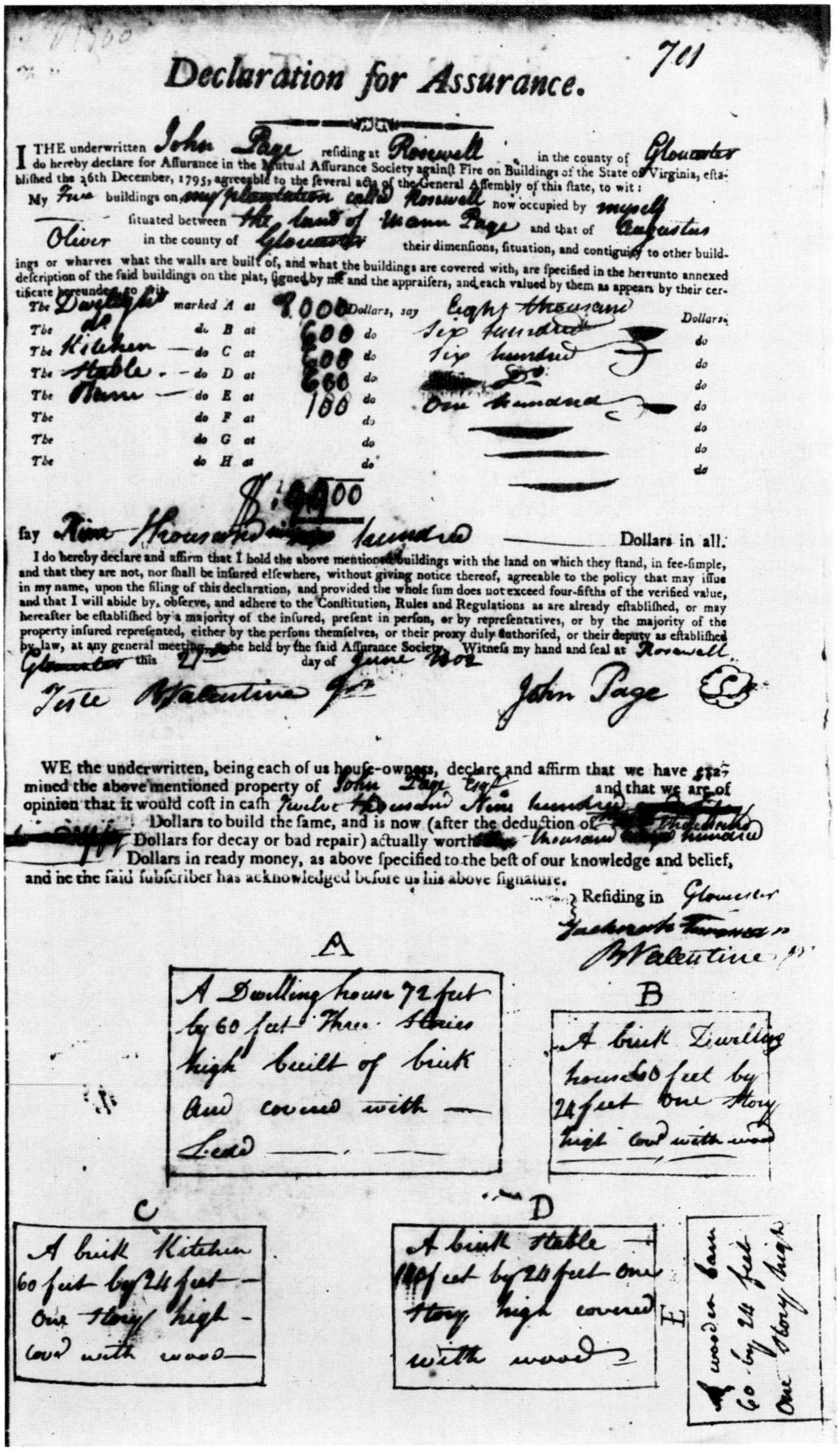

Declaration for Assurance.

I THE underwritten *John Page* residing at *Rosewell* in the county of *Gloucester* do hereby declare for Assurance in the Mutual Assurance Society against Fire on Buildings of the State of Virginia, established the 26th December, 1795, agreeable to the several acts of the General Assembly of this state, to wit:
My *Five* buildings on *my plantation called Rosewell* now occupied by *myself* situated between *the land of Mann Page* and that of *Augustus Oliver* in the county of *Gloucester* their dimensions, situation, and contiguity to other buildings or wharves what the walls are built of, and what the buildings are covered with, are specified in the hereunto annexed description of the said buildings on the plat, signed by me and the appraisers, and each valued by them as appears by their certificate hereunder, to wit:

The *Dwelling*	marked A at	8000	Dollars, say	*Eight thousand*	Dollars.
The *do*	do B at	600	do	*Six hundred*	do
The *Kitchen*	do C at	600	do	*Six hundred*	do
The *Stable*	do D at	600	do	*do*	do
The *Barn*	do E at	100	do	*One hundred*	do
The	do F at		do		do
The	do G at		do		do
The	do H at		do		do

$9900

say *Nine thousand nine hundred* — Dollars in all.

I do hereby declare and affirm that I hold the above mentioned buildings with the land on which they stand, in fee-simple, and that they are not, nor shall be insured elsewhere, without giving notice thereof, agreeable to the policy that may issue in my name, upon the filing of this declaration, and provided the whole sum does not exceed four-fifths of the verified value, and that I will abide by, observe, and adhere to the Constitution, Rules and Regulations as are already established, or may hereafter be established by a majority of the insured, present in person, or by representatives, or by the majority of the property insured represented, either by the persons themselves, or their proxy duly authorised, or their deputy as established by law, at any general meeting to be held by the said Assurance Society. Witness my hand and seal at *Rosewell Gloucester* this *27th* day of *June 1802*

Teste B Valentine Jr   *John Page*

WE the underwritten, being each of us house-owners, declare and affirm that we have examined the above mentioned property of *John Page Esq* and that we are of opinion that it would cost in cash *Twelve thousand Nine hundred* Dollars to build the same, and is now (after the deduction of *three tenths* Dollars for decay or bad repair) actually worth *thousand* Dollars in ready money, as above specified to the best of our knowledge and belief, and he the said subscriber has acknowledged before us his above signature.

Residing in *Gloucester*

Zachariah Florence
B Valentine Jr

A

A Dwelling house 72 feet by 60 feet Three stories high built of brick And covered with — Lead —.

B

A brick Dwelling house 60 feet by 24 feet one story high covd with wood

C

A brick Kitchen 60 feet by 24 feet One story high covd with wood —

D

A brick stable 100 feet by 24 feet one story high covered with wood

E

A wooden barn 60 by 24 feet One story high

FIGURE 5.—An 1802 insurance policy for Rosewell.
Microfilm copy courtesy of Virginia State Library.

A disgruntled Englishman mutters "This Rascally Scotchman is going to pick the Nation's Pockets with his infamous Excise Scheme."

A week after his newspaper appeared, Wilkes was arrested and thrown into the Tower of London. In November 1764 he was outlawed, and he fled to the Continent where he remained for four years. Then, still an outlaw, he returned to England and campaigned for the Parliamentary seat of Middlesex, winning by a large majority. He then surrendered as an outlaw, but received a sentence of only one year in prison. After being expelled from Parliament on February 4, 1769, he was quickly re-elected by his constituents on February 16, and just as quickly was expelled again. On April 13 he stood again and soundly defeated his opponent, Col. H. L. Luttrell, but regardless of Wilkes' massive majority, the Commons insisted on seating Luttrell. It was at this time that the "Wilkes and Liberty" cries were loudest.

During the following decade Wilkes became an outspoken champion of the colonial cause. After he returned to Parliament in 1774 he gave no fewer than ten speeches urging the cessation of hostilities between Britain and her American colonies. It is not clear exactly when Wilkes became associated with the discontented colonials, but there is no doubt that his stormy Parliamentary career was being followed with interest in America at least by the time of his repeated expulsions from Parliament in 1768/9. Wilkes was a forthright if crude radical who became the champion of peoples' rights, and as such he had much to commend him among the more hot-headed colonials. The following extract from a letter written to a Londoner in July 1770 by Roger Atkinson of "Mansfield," near Petersburg, expresses the feelings of a typical colonial radical of that time:

. . . ye Britons are a corrupted—I am sorry to say it—a very corrupted People. I hope you will mend as you grow older—I trust you will—I think you are in a very fair way to be mended now. Follow Mr. Wilkes, he will show you.

Pray send me the Newspapers & Magazines & Political Registers regularly. Everything that relates to my old friend J.Wilkes, Esq're.—for I never desire to read anything else except an Almanack, a Prayer Book & a Bible.[25]

Although John Page's letters do not mention Wilkes by name, a letter to John Norton written at Rosewell in August 1768 mentions with horror the news of the rioting (in favor of Wilkes) in London:

I hope long before this your terrible Riots are over. In what an unhappy situation was Great Britain! Unsteadiness in her Councils, Confusion, Riots & Tumults, little short of Rebellion in her very Metropolis; Discontent in all her colonies, each, & every one justly complaining of the Arbitrary Proceedings of Parliament; and many of them provoked at the Severe Restrictions on their Trade, are ready to give a Stab almost vital to the Trade of G-t B-n.[26]

Enthusiasm for Wilkes in Williamsburg is indicated in an engraving of 1775 in which a gathering of citizens on a Williamsburg street is busily signing a petition, using a makeshift table formed by hogsheads similar to those depicted on the Rosewell buckle. One of the hogsheads bears the inscription "TOBACCO A PRESENT For JOHN WILKES Esq. LORD MAYOR OF LONDON." [27]

The foregoing digression is relevant in regard to establishing a relationship between the "No Excise" slogan and the Pages so that the date span for the Rosewell pit might be narrowed. If it could be shown that the buckle bearing the slogan was made or came to Virginia not in 1763 but when Wilkes was at the height of his flamboyant career after his return from Europe in 1768, then it could be deduced that the relevant repairs to Rosewell took place after that date, as also did the deposition of the contents of the pit. Although there is every reason to believe that the pit was dug in the autumn of 1771, became silted during the winter, and was filled with trash while repairs were in progress at the mansion in the spring of 1772, the evidence of the buckle is not sufficiently clear to provide an incontrovertible terminus post quem of 1768. Consequently, the date brackets must embrace the years between the late winter of 1763 (Treaty of Paris and Cyder Act) and the spring of 1772.

---

[25] Roger Atkinson to Robert Bunn, July 30, 1770, *Virginia Magazine of History and Biography*, 1908, vol. 15, no. 4, p. 349.

[26] John Page, Jr., to John Norton, August 26, 1768, *Norton Papers, op. cit.* (footnote 6), p. 64.

[27] Rutherford Goodwin, *A Brief and True Report Concerning Williamsburg in Virginia*, Williamsburg, 1940, p. 65. Some measure of the popularity of Wilkes in America can be seen in Paul Revere's famous "Wilkes and Liberty" punch bowl of 1768 and in an advertisement for swords with hilts decorated "either with the heads of General Washington, General Lee, Lord Chatham, John Wilkes, Esq.; with shells pierced and ornamented with mottoes; for Pitt's head, Magna Charta and Freedom; for Wilke's head, Wilkes and Liberty . . ." (*New York Gazette and Weekly Mercury*, April 1, 1776, as reprinted in *Virginia Magazine of History and Biography*, 1929, vol. 37, no. 1, p. 60).

The Artifacts

It is not to be inferred that all the items represented by the artifacts, or finds, were made in the period 1763–1772, but merely that they were thrown away at that time. It can be assumed, however, that most of them were in use contemporaneously and thus, together, they represent an important insight into the possessions of a late colonial plantation owner. But in considering the finds in this light it is necessary to remember that the objects that were broken and thrown away were generally those that were in common use, not the items which were more decorative than useful and which would have been preserved with care. Consequently the absence of such objects does not necessarily indicate that they did not exist at Rosewell.

The finds fall into six main classes, (1) ceramics and glasswares, (2) personal and domestic possessions representing such things as buttons, pins, scissors, curtain rings, etc., (3) stable relics and metal tools such as spurs, harness buckles and fittings, horseshoes, locally made hinges, knives, and iron- and brass-working waste; (4) animal and bird bones, (5) marine specimens, and (6) architectural items comprising fragments of worked marble, Portland stone, bricks, iron nails, window glass and painted plaster.

CERAMICS AND GLASSWARES

This is by far the largest group. In addition to tablewares it includes ceramic and glass items that were used in the kitchen and in the bedroom. In general, it may be said that the quality of the tablewares was good, that Chinese export porcelain was much used at Rosewell, and that the Pages owned at least one set of matching cups and saucers of varying sizes. Plates and bowls were numerous and of varying quality. The best of them, decorated in underglaze blue as well as in overglaze enamel, were on a par with the best examples from the Governor's Palace in Williamsburg.

English white saltglaze wares, also plentiful and generally of good quality, included tankards, teapots, cups, saucers, bowls, and plates. Only one small fragment was found to be ornamented with applied enamels. Of considerable interest is a small fragment of a molded teapot in the shape of a house with a shield of arms and lion and unicorn supporters over the doorway. Teapots made in the shape of early Georgian houses were not uncommon; it is popularly believed that they were presented by friends to people

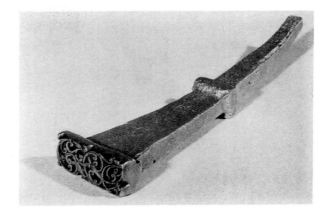

FIGURE 6.—Brass die, used in bookbinding, that was found near Rosewell graveyard subsequent to the dig. Face of die, enlarged in lower figure, is 1 inch wide.

who had recently moved into or built a new house. Although no evidence has been found to confirm or deny this story, it would be pleasant to be able to associate the Rosewell fragment with Mann Page II's completion of the mansion. (See fig. 8.)

There is a three-storied-house teapot in the Burnap Collection that is attributed to about 1740;[28] another appears in Griselda Lewis' *Picture History of English Pottery* and is given the same date.[29] However, Bernard Rackham, in his *Early Staffordshire Pottery*, indicates that molded wares of this and other types were not in production before about 1745.[30] Nevertheless it does seem possible that the teapot could

---

[28] *Frank P. and Harriet Burnap Collection of English Pottery in the William Rockhill Nelson Gallery of Art*, Kansas City, 1953, hereinafter referred to as *Burnap*.

[29] Griselda Lewis, *Picture Book of English Pottery*, London, 1951, p. 24.

[30] Bernard Rackham, *Early Staffordshire Pottery*, London, 1951, p. 24.

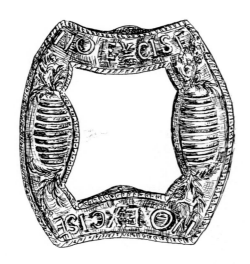

Figure 7.—Pewter shoe buckle with the inscription "no excise." Enlarged.

have reached Rosewell soon after the mansion's completion. An article in *The Antiquarian* has an illustration of a house teapot that looks remarkably like Rosewell, rising as it did three stories above an English basement and with the top-story windows being much smaller than those beneath.[31] Unfortunately it has not been possible to discover the present whereabouts of this pot.

Since most authorities estimate that white saltglaze had almost ceased to be manufactured by about 1770,[32] the presence of saltglaze fragments and the absence of creamwares in an excavation encourages dating prior to that date. It is of interest, therefore, to note the request in Mann Page II's invoice of that year for the purchase in England of "4 White quart stone Cans" and "4 pint . . . Do." Bailey's English dictionary of 1749 describes a can or cann as "a wooden Pot to drink out of." It is reasonable therefore to assume that Mann Page was ordering white stoneware tankards. While this assumption in no way alters the accepted dating for the Rosewell pit, it indicates that some of the white saltglaze items need not be as early as one might think.

Descending the scale of domestic wares, we come next to the English tin-glazed earthenwares or delftwares, which by the mid-18th century had lost much of their appeal as tablewares, having been largely superseded by white saltglaze and imported porcelain. By 1770 English delftware was generally used only for chamber pots, closestool pans, wash basins, and ointment pots—the principal roles that it played at Rosewell. The Mann Page II invoice quoted earlier in this report requests the acquisition of "1 Dozn. white wash Basons" and "1 Dozn. white Chamber Pots" to be sent in 1770 to his home near Fredericksburg. The marked preponderance of these items over delft tablewares at Rosewell suggests that his son made similar purchases.

The use of German stonewares, which in the 16th and 17th centuries had been among the most impressive products of the potter's art, declined in the 18th century, quantity being considered more important than quality, grace, or ingenuity. Gone were the Knutgens and the Emmens, the great masters of Siegburg and Raeren, gone the fine signed pieces still prized as the creations of individual potters and workshops. In their place we find the mass-produced tankards, jugs, and chamber pots so lacking in distinction that they can be attributed to no particular factory but only to the Westerwald district of the Rhineland where most of the factories were located. The finds from Rosewell do nothing to soften this sorry picture, being confined to jug, tankard, and chamber-pot fragments as might be expected. Pieces of two jugs ornamented with "G. R." medallions serve only as reminders that Rhenish potters were among the first to appreciate the sales value of manufacturing specifically for foreign markets. But this was not something that they had learned in the 18th century. In the second half of the 16th century "Bellarmine" jugs had been decorated with the arms of Tudor England, and in the 17th century we find others adorned with arms and crests of patrons, towns, and wholesale exporters.

Although no such examples were found in the Rosewell pit, it may be here noted that many of the worst blue and gray tankards, jugs, and chamber pots found in the northern American colonies probably were the products of emigrant potters who set up their kilns in New York and New Jersey. These factories first produced only the accepted Rhenish forms; but when the results proved to be coarse, clumsy, and poorly colored, the potters began to develop new styles and so created the ubiquitous cobalt-decorated gray stonewares so characteristic of the American scene in the 19th century.

---

[31] Elma Allee Weil, "Salt-Glaze," *The Antiquarian*, New York, February 1926, vol. 6, no. 1.

[32] W. B. Honey, *English Pottery and Porcelain*, London, 1952.

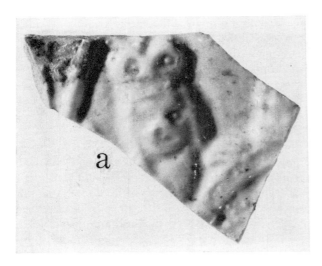

FIGURE 8.—Saltglaze "house" teapots. *a*, Fragment (enlarged) from the Rosewell refuse pit; *b*, teapot resembling the design of Rosewell.

The emigration to the colonies of potters from the Rhineland, the Netherlands, and England has added immeasurably to the archeologist's problems, for it is often extremely difficult to distinguish between wares produced by the same men before and after they moved to America. The arrival at Yorktown, Virginia, of an English potter who was almost certainly trained in London or Bristol has resulted in the utmost confusion in the identification of brown stonewares hitherto attributed to factories in or near London.

Although his kilns have not yet been located in Yorktown, there is little doubt that the English potter was in business there. Wasters and broken kiln furniture found on most Yorktown sites apparently were used as hard-core in the repairing of roads. This is in keeping with similar practices in England where kiln waste from stoneware and delftware kilns was used in the stabilizing of the foreshore of the Thames at Queenhithe and on the Bankside, as well as in the lining of drains and in filling around foundations.[33] Sagger fragments from Yorktown are identical in appearance to those used in London, and so too is the style of the tavern tankards, which were among the principal products of the English kilns. It would seem, however, that the Yorktown potter was less successful in maintaining the correct kiln temperatures than were his English counterparts, for many of the Yorktown pieces are badly overfired, with the result that the brown slip became almost purple instead of ginger brown and the gray body became dark and greenish. These features are to be found on a high percentage of the Yorktown wasters as well as on products which were actually sold to the public.[34] In contrast, the thousands of wasters from the London kilns that have been examined rarely exhibit these characteristics.

The foregoing discussion serves to indicate that an element of doubt exists in the identification of brown stonewares from the Rosewell pit. Among such items found are two large pitchers—one of which is likely to be of English origin—a small tankard of unusual size and doubtful origin, a large storage jar probably from Yorktown, and another storage jar that may be English.

Coarse kitchen pottery is not strongly represented among the finds from the pit, the majority of these sherds coming from the ploughed top of a deposit to the east of the mansion that, as yet, is unexcavated. Recovered fragments of such items include sherds from simple lead-glazed cream pans probably imported from England and other utilitarian pans of

[33] Adrian Oswald, "A London Stoneware Pottery, Recent Excavations at Bankside," *The Connoisseur*, London, January 1951, vol. 126, no. 519, pp. 183–185.

[34] J. Paul Hudson, "Early Yorktown Pottery," *Antiques*, May 1958, vol. 73, no. 5, pp. 472–473.

smaller size, a rim sherd from a jar of Buckley ware[35] from North Wales, and a rim from a pan of a type made at Yorktown. The latter should not be confused with previous references to Yorktown brown stonewares. Although invariably present in the same contexts, it is uncertain whether both were products of the same factory. There is, however, no doubt that they were in production contemporaneously at Yorktown, probably between about 1730 and 1770.

The Indian wares can be divided into two groups—those made by Indians for Indians and those made by Indians for colonists. Reference has already been made (p. 162) to the legendary association between Rosewell and Pocahontas and Powhatan, and numerous fragments of so-called late Woodland and early Contact pottery have been found in ploughed fields to the east of the house. It is also possible that quantities of oyster shells found 6 inches below the surface on a promontory overlooking the creek to the southwest of the house might have Indian associations.[36] Nevertheless, the only stratified Indian artifacts yet found at Rosewell came from area B of the excavated pit, where they were found in a secondary deposit (described on p. 164) apparently representing the site of an Indian cooking fire built in the lee of the pit's southeast face. The sherds found therein are of considerable significance in view of the fact that they came from a strictly Indian deposit overlying 18th-century colonial refuse, yet are of a type normally attributed to the pre-Contact or early Contact eras. On this evidence it may be suggested that truly native forms continued in use throughout the colonial centuries and cannot, at this time, be readily pinned down to any particular phase of the period.

More readily identified are the Colono-Indian products that were made in pseudo-European shapes in the traditional manner—that is, hand-worked, shell-tempered, and stick- or pebble-burnished. Many fragments of these wares have been found in excavations at Williamsburg in dated contexts ranging between about 1740 and about 1770. Shapes copy English delftware porringers, bowls, and cups, Westerwald chamber pots, metal, triple-legged, and triangular-handled cooking pots, and flat-handled

skillets. Fragments of vessels of comparable shapes have been found in an 18th-century context at Jamestown, Yorktown, Tutter's Neck, and Greenspring Plantation. One leg of a cooking pot was found in the second layer of the Rosewell pit, and a large part of a bowl was recovered from layer B5. Small sherds from no fewer than five other vessels were also recovered, most coming from the second and third layers.

Fragments of these Colono-Indian wares have been found on the Pamunkey Reservation along with European sherds dating from the second half of the 18th century, and there is little doubt that the former were made there. It has been suggested that the wares were produced by the Pamunkey Indians for use among slaves,[37] for it is thought unlikely that any European, however poor, would be reduced to making use of such inferior wares. The slaves, on the other hand, would not be used to eating in European style and with European kitchen utensils and tablewares. There can be no denying that the presence of the Colono-Indian wares in Williamsburg, at Jamestown, and on the great plantation sites must be occasioned by a common denominator—and that can reasonably be represented by the presence of slaves on each and all of the sites.

The presence of true Indian wares in the Rosewell pit can hardly be accounted for in the same way. There is evidence that in the 17th and 18th centuries Indians were used as servants and hired to act as hunters and to rid plantations of unwelcome beasts of prey. It is possible, though not proved, that John Page hired them for some such purpose and that they camped in the vicinity of the pit.

Glass from the Rosewell pit can be divided into three unequal groups: beverage bottles, jars, and pharmaceutical phials; fine glass wares such as wine glasses, decanters, mirror plate, and cupping glasses; and window glass.

Glass wine bottles represented approximately two-thirds of all the artifacts found in the pit and ranged in date from around 1700 into the 1760's. Although it was not possible to divide up the thousands of body fragments into their respective bottles, a count of the bases and necks showed (at a conservative estimate) that no fewer than 351 were represented and that the

---

[35] K. J. Barton, "The Buckley Potteries II, Excavations at Prescot's Pottery 1954," *Flintshire Miscellany*, 1956, no. 1, reprinted from *Flintshire Historical Journal*, vol. 16.

[36] A minute fragment of brick found with the shells in the only trial hole dug does not support this possibility.

[37] In a paper prepared by the present author and delivered by C. Malcolm Watkins at the Ethno-Historic Conference on the American Indian, Washington, D.C., 1958.

majority belonged to the years between about 1725 and 1750. Most of the bottles had the appearance of being of English manufacture, although there is as yet no method of identifying unmarked 18th-century bottles of American colonial manufacture. A small number of the bottles are of French origin, notably the three ovoid flasks found in the primary deposit, and others may be of Dutch or Rhenish manufacture. Well represented were the bottles made specifically as containers for Pyrmont mineral waters; five seals were found bearing this information.

Only one personal seal was found in the pit; it bears the initials "M. P." (Mann Page II) on a bottle fragment of the 1760's. This seal is surprisingly simple. Most gentlemen of the 18th century possessed carefully executed bottle seals that often bore their full names, dates, crests, and shields of arms or rebus. It might therefore be expected that the Pages would have possessed wine bottles bearing expensively engraved seals befitting the cellars of so opulent a mansion as Rosewell. That they did not has consequently been construed as evidence of their penury. However, the scarcity of sealed bottles is perhaps a clearer indication of this than is the simplicity of the seal, for there is ample precedent to show that many colonial gentlemen used their tobacco marks on their bottles, and we know that Mann Page's mark comprised only his initials.[38]

Of greater interest in its own right is a seal (fig. 16, no. 1) that was uncovered by ploughing in the field east of the mansion. This seal bears the initials $\begin{smallmatrix} & O & \\ T & & A \end{smallmatrix}$ and is clearly of the late 17th century. The arrangement of initials in the pyramidal form was generally used to indicate a husband and wife combination, the initials of first names of the husband and wife being capped by their surname initial. This arrangement was accepted practice in England as early as the 16th century, and it appears on thousands of English wool bale seals in the 17th century; in the second half of the same century it appears on many beverage bottles made for taverns, indicating the initials of both the licensee and his wife. In the 18th century Virginia planters and merchants often used the triple initials as shipping marks. However, some confusion creeps in when it is realized that these men sometimes varied the long-established arrangement by putting the initial of their middle name at the apex

of the triangle. Thus, on the same page of a tea account of 1769 we find the shipping marks $\begin{smallmatrix} & N & \\ R & & A \end{smallmatrix}$ for Robert and Ann Nicholas and $\begin{smallmatrix} & L & \\ N & & S \end{smallmatrix}$ for Nathaniel L. Savage.[39] Further confusion resulted when some men used different marks for the produce being sent from or to different plantations, the individual properties being indicated by a symbol such as a diamond or a mullet above two initials, or even an additional identifying letter above them—thus creating again the apparent triple initial triangle.[40]

The practice of making cheap bottle seals by employing stock letters and setting them up in pairs to order was common in the second half of the 17th century but seems to have been rarely used in any other period. Until the Rosewell seal was discovered no example of the triple initial had ever been found to have been set up in this way. For want of evidence to the contrary, this seemingly unique seal is read in the conventional manner, indicating perhaps some such names as Thomas and Ann Osborne.

Other glass items from the Rosewell pit included fragments of square-sectioned bottles of the type frequently identified as gin or case bottles. The illustrated section through one of the examples from the pit shows that, in the absence of their necks, such bottles could just as easily be called pickle jars (fig. 31, no. 13). Also present were fragments of large, globular, thick-necked bottles; some of these fragments probably came from wicker-encased carboys. Of value as dating evidence were fragments from two octagonal wine bottles (not illustrated) whose shapes are comparable to examples bearing the name of John Greenhow and dated 1770 that have been found in Williamsburg excavations.

The table glasswares from the pit are predominantly of good quality and speak for themselves. However, the straight-stemmed and trumpet-bowled example from the primary filling (fig. 32, no. 7) is valuable as dating evidence; it is of a type not in use prior to about 1740, but this item probably dates somewhat later. Other finds of table glassware included fragments of an early lead glass decanter and pieces of two rare bag-shaped cupping glasses.

---

[38] *Norton Papers, op. cit.* (footnote 6), p. 309.

[39] *Ibid.*, opposite p. 81.

[40] C. Malcolm Watkins, "The Three-Initial Cypher: Exceptions to the Rule," *Antiques*, June 1958, vol. 73, no. 6, pp. 564–565.

This category embraces all small items of a personal nature that do not fit into a specialized category. As a collection, these objects might be expected to contribute something to the portrait of life at Rosewell as revealed by the contents of the pit; unfortunately, however, they serve only to raise more questions.

The first small find to be recovered from the excavation was a Louis XV silver half-écu (fig. 18). It was found on the first day of digging in the first trial trench (E) and in the top of the principal artifact-bearing layer (2). The coin was minted at La Rochelle (H mint mark) during the period that John Law was handling French finances and when the Mississipie Companie was the object of substantial investment both by the government and by private individuals. Much French coin came to America to promote the development of the Mississippi Valley, and as a result French silver coins were not uncommon in the British colonies in America. Spanish-Colonial was the most prevalent silver coin in the colonies; French coin was in second place and was far more common than English silver coin.

A series of proclamations and laws regulated the value at which silver coins should circulate in the American colonies. A proclamation of Queen Anne on June 18, 1704, provided that French écus should pass at 4s. 6d. each, and fractional coins in proportion. This ruling was disobeyed and avoided from time to time but was the law after 1709 and remained in effect until the Revolution. There is no doubt that French écus were in circulation in Virginia in 1750 and 1760. Such specie was much more likely to be obtained when tobacco markets were prosperous, than when times were financially dull. [41]

The coin found at Rosewell was in excellent condition, and the team of excavators became excited at the prospect of unearthing a hoard of silver treasure. While such thoughts are generally quickly suppressed by professional archeologists, there is no denying that the recovery of such a fine specimen at the top might lead one to hope that it was but a sample of a hoard lying deeper in the ground; however, this was the only coin recovered. Furthermore, its early date

had absolutely no bearing on the dating of the rest of the finds in the pit.

The recovery of the coin raised the rather obvious question of how it came to be in the Rosewell pit. With an exchange value of an English half-crown (a higher denomination than any coin found in the excavation of the whole city of Williamsburg) and on the site of a plantation known to have had a large slave population, it is inconceivable that the coin could have been carried to the pit along with refuse. It can only be suggested that it was lost by someone who had been tipping trash into the pit.

The coin was not the only silver item found in the pit. Also uncovered was one pair of a set of silver sleeve buttons (fig. 19, no. 4) of a type common in the mid-18th century. Here again, one is left to wonder why such an item was in the pit. Had a servant seen the buttons they would certainly have been salvaged and sold for their silver value. But one of the curious features of the pit was that it contained a number of unbroken objects that could have seen further service. Even if they were no longer needed at Rosewell, there would surely have been many hands ready to salvage them for barter or sale. Among such items are the miniature padlock and key (fig. 19, no. 11), brass buttons (in fig. 19), brass weight (fig. 20, no. 4), and the fine harness buckle and silvered brass harness ornaments (in fig. 22).

A number of relics relating to firearms were found in the first exploratory trench, but here again the early promise was not fulfilled as the excavations progressed. Indeed, it was later shown that the first trench (areas E–H) had cut through the heart of the pit and that most of the artifacts were scattered on that line but became less frequent towards the west, indicating that the contents of the pit had been tipped from the east. Among the firearm fragments and associated items were an iron pistol barrel (fig. 36, no. 1), a brass ramrod thimble (fig. 20, no. 5), two gun flints (fig. 20, nos. 8, 9), and two strips of lead waste from shot and bullet molds, one of which had manufactured at least six balls at a time (fig. 20, nos. 11, 12). Of particular interest was part of a bullet mold made from the local, shell-tempered, Colono-Indian pottery (fig. 21, no. 19).

Relics of children's items were surprisingly lacking, being confined to two pottery marbles, part of a slate pencil (fig. 20, no. 14), and a roughly made brass "buzz" (fig. 20, no. 3). The last two items, however, were not necessarily associated with children. Buzzes have been found on British military camp sites in the

---

[41] Information supplied by Mr. Eric P. Newman of St. Louis, Missouri.

New York area;[42] apparently they were a common source of amusement in the 18th century.

STABLE RELICS AND METAL TOOLS

Among the metal finds, items grouped under this heading are the most numerous. The presence of so many objects of an equestrian nature leads one to believe that the stables were situated in the vicinity of the pit, that is, west of the mansion. The indications of iron-working can reasonably point to the existance of a smithy in the same area. If the stables were there it would seem a natural corollary that the forge should be there too. It seems probable that the Rosewell forge undertook repairs to carriages and farm tools, shod horses, and may even have made simple tools and hinges. The evidence for the last activity is derived from three crudely made knives (fig. 23, no. 10; fig. 36, nos. 2–4) and two apparently home-made hinges (fig. 38, nos. 1, 2). But in accepting these items as local products, one must bear in mind the fact that John Page is known to have ordered his nails from England. However, this can, perhaps, be explained by the size of the order, a quantity that would be as cheap to import from England as it would be to try to make on the plantation. The belief that there was a forge there at all is based only on the evidence of the many fragments of waste iron (examples in fig. 23) that were found in the pit.

It has often been suggested that the absence of paved streets and of hard, rocky roads in the Tidewater area made it unnecessary for horses to be shod. Archeological evidence is scant. The majority of the horseshoes found in Williamsburg excavations are unstratified and could easily be of 19th-century date. Nevertheless, in recent years a few shoes have been found in dated contexts, the earliest belonging to the decade 1740–1750. Research in this direction in England has resulted in the identification of certain trends; for example, the absence of toe-caps before the 19th century, the presence of more than four nail holes per side on shoes from the 18th century onward. Unfortunately, the number of horseshoes found so far in Virginia has been insufficient either to support or disprove these rules, but the presence of only four holes on either side of the Rosewell shoe does nothing to promote confidence in them.

There are no written records to indicate whether the Pages possessed a carriage, although it might reasonably be assumed that they did. Here archeological evidence is more helpful, for the recovery of the handsome brass harness buckle (fig. 22, no. 1) and the harness ornaments (nos. 6–8) clearly indicate that there was at least some coach harness at Rosewell. Another ornament (no. 3) and a fragment from a decorative brass mounting (no. 9) point to the same conclusion. Also, the base of a brass terret (no. 2) is more likely to have been associated with a coach or carriage saddle rather than with a vehicle of lesser stature. A purely utilitarian farm harness would normally have had fittings of iron, and relics of such fittings include four iron buckles (fig. 38, nos. 9–12) and fragments from two iron hub sleeves (one is shown in fig. 38, no. 7). No bits or stirrups survived as relics of the horseman at Rosewell, but two broken spurs—one of iron (fig. 38, no. 8) and the other of brass (fig. 22, no. 12)—were found.

The number of brass and copper items recovered proved to be surprisingly large compared to the small quantities found in the average trash deposit in nearby Williamsburg.[43] Many of the items were nothing more than scraps of waste metal, trimmings from objects whose identity cannot be deduced (fig. 24, nos. 1–3, 5, 8). However, these trimmings are of considerable interest because they definitely indicate that the Rosewell workshop or shops could handle metals other than iron. Perhaps the most significant of all the finds with such associations was a lump of unshaped stone streaked with veins of copper ore, a combination of malachite and hematite. The recovery of this item caused a good deal of speculation. It certainly was not indigenous to the area, and it seemed highly unlikely that the Pages would have transported or imported ore simply to obtain enough metal to supply their needs at Rosewell, needs which could well have been met by the purchase of scrap.

---

[42] W. L. Calver and R. P. Bolton, *History Written with Pick and Shovel*, New York, New York Historical Society, 1950, p. 80, pl. 4.

[43] In the summer of 1960 after this report had been completed, an important brass bookbinder's tool was found by a student in the vicinity of the Page graveyard. The object was used to impress into leather bindings a foliate device incorporating the head of a fox. The shape of the tool, with its T form and long cast tang, was comparable to a number of such objects found on the printing office site of the 18th-century *Virginia Gazette* on Duke of Gloucester Street in Williamsburg. There is no doubt that this new find is of colonial date, and it may be assumed that bookbinding (or at least leather decorating) was among the crafts practiced at Rosewell. (See fig. 6.)

In this connection the following information from the *Virginia Magazine of History and Biography* is pertinent:

In 1728 "King" Carter, his sons Robin and Charles, and his son-in-law, Mann Page of Rosewell, organized the Frying Pan Company to mine copper in the cupreus sandstone formation on the present boundary of Fairfax and Loudoun.[44]

Also, a notice in the *Virginia Gazette* stated that the ship *Sally* was cleared on January 13, 1767, bound for London with a cargo that included, among other items, five casks of copper ore.[45] It is not intended to imply that ore was taken to Rosewell for smelting. Such a major undertaking would require very much more evidence, either archeological or historical, before it could be established as so much as a likelihood. In the absence of this evidence, one lump of ore must be explained away as a sample sent down or perhaps brought from the mines by John Page, possibly as part of some experiment or even as an exhibit presented before members of the Society for the Advancement of Useful Knowledge.

From areas and levels B4, O3 and Q3 came fragments representing five crucibles of small and medium size, all save one of the fragments bearing traces of copper on the insides. Since the crucibles are of a coarse, sandy pottery—a ware favored for this purpose certainly as early as the 15th century—and their shapes (small circular bases and triangular mouths) are of similar antiquity, they are extremely difficult to date. However, the Rosewell crucibles are of sizes comparable to numerous examples recovered from the cellar floor of a house in Williamsburg occupied by the goldsmith John Coke from about 1740 until his death in 1767.

It may be significant that most of the waste brass and copper that was uncovered came from the north side of the pit, suggesting that metalworking may have been carried out in the vicinity of the foundations north of the deposit.

ANIMAL BONES

As might be expected in a pit containing a predominance of domestic trash, animal bones were plentiful but generally so splintered and broken that it was impossible to identify all of them.[46] In bulk the bones weighed 70 pounds, but this, of course, gives no indication of the number of animals represented. Beef bones were plentiful, but only one ox skull was included, this represented by a single horn core. Pig bones also were common, and the mandibles and disassociated canines were readily identified. Deer were also identified by mandibles, but in neither pig nor deer did skulls survive intact.

Among the smaller bones were the mandible of a squirrel, the skull and incomplete skeleton of a cat (E primary), part of the plastron from a Carolina box tortoise, vertibrae and ribs from a small fish (attached to the copper pan, fig. 24, no. 9), numerous chicken bones, and a few bones that came from either turkey or goose.

MARINE SPECIMENS

Under this heading must be grouped the huge quantity of oyster shells of all sizes that comprised the bulk of the finds from the second stratum. These shells were clearly kitchen debris and were not retained. Of greater interest were a single cowrie shell and a small number of coral fragments, most of the latter in an extremely worn condition. Sample pieces of the coral were submitted to Frederick M. Bayer, associate curator of marine invertebrates at the Smithsonian, who provided the following information:

Specimen from stratum O2. — *Diploria strigosa* (Dana). A reef coral widely distributed in the West Indies, including the Bahamas and Florida Keys north to Miami; also Bermuda.

Specimens from strata C2, D2. — Too worn for accurate identification, but both probably West Indian.

ARCHITECTURAL ITEMS

The architectural finds included fragments of worked stone, builders' hardware, plaster, and window glass. Had all such pieces been found in the ruins of the mansion itself, one would be on reasonably safe ground in associating them with the building and in using them—as was done at the Governor's Palace in Williamsburg—as the basis for the reconstruction of

[44] "The Will of Charles Carter of Cleve," annoted by Fairfax Harrison, *Virginia Magazine of History and Biography*, 1923, vol. 31, no. 1, p. 48, note 18. See also "Carter Papers," *Virginia Magazine of History and Biography*, 1898, vol. 6, no. 1, p. 18.

[45] *Norton Papers, op. cit.* (footnote 6), p. 22.

[46] For a study of the identification and significance of excavated animal bones, see J. W. Cornwall, *Bones for the Archaeologist*, London, 1956.

individual features. The Rosewell finds, however, do not come from the building but from a hole in the ground 190 feet away from it, closer to various outbuildings than to the mansion itself. Having made this reservation it may seem contradictory to immediately proceed on the assumption that most of the stone fragments *did* come from the house. However, the quality of the stone and of the workmanship thereon indicates that they belonged to a more imposing structure than a kitchen, office, or stable.

Fragments of two marble flooring slabs—one white Purbeck measuring 10¾ by 1¼ inches and the other black Belgian measuring 10¾ inches square—almost certainly came from Rosewell's main hall. These slabs immediately remind one of the entrance or Middle Room at the Governor's Palace in Williamsburg where similar black and white slabs were used. No pictures of the Rosewell floor exist, and it is generally assumed that the marble was removed during the Booth occupancy in the mid-19th century. However, it is now apparent that repairs to the floor or the replacement of the floor became necessary as early as the period 1763–1772. Any possibility that these slabs were left over after the laying of the marble floor is removed by the evidence of shell mortar clinging to the sides and backs.

Among the other finds are a piece of white marble that may well have come from the base of a fireplace mantel, a fragment from the base of a Portland stone column, and numerous pieces of Portland nosings of various sizes. Builders' hardware was surprisingly poorly represented, comprising only a vast collection of old nails ranging in length from 1¼ inches to 5+ inches and a brass keeper (fig. 21, no. 1) from a rim lock of medium size. It could be construed from the latter find that brass locks were used on some of Rosewell's smaller doors as well, presumably, as on the large ones.

Window glass was plentiful in the Rosewell pit, and its presence can reasonably be used to add weight to the belief that the pit was open at a time when extensive repairs were in progress either at the mansion or at its dependencies.

Window glass was manufactured by two separate methods, the results of which were known as "broad" glass and "crown" glass. Broad glass, also known as Lorraine glass, was made by blowing a long bubble, opening the ends to create a cylinder, cutting the cylinder down one side, and opening out the resulting sheet onto an iron plate covered with sand. The final product was frequently marred by distortion, varying

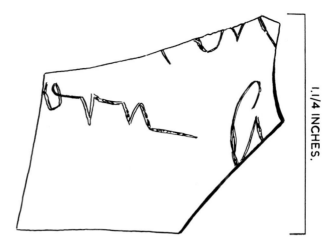

FIGURE 9.—Inscription scratched on fragment of window glass. For possible interpretation see page 178.

thickness, and rough surface, and was limited to sheets that rarely exceeded 4 square feet in area. The crown glass, often termed Normandy glass, was created by transferring a bubble to a pontil iron and rotating it so that the open mouth left by the removal of the blowing iron opened out to create a disk which, as the pontil iron rotated, grew larger and larger. This type of window glass offered much greater brilliance than the older broad glass, but the size of panes derived from each crown was limited because of the thickening towards the central "bull's-eye" or "bullion" to which the pontil iron had been attached. The outer edges also were of little value as they were too curved to be useful.[47] An edge fragment and a bullion (fig. 17) from the Rosewell pit show that John or Mann Page had purchased glass by the crown as well as, or instead of, by previously cut panes, the more normal practice. It is not difficult to envisage the possible relationship between this discovery and the "Glaziers Diamond of 20/ Value" purchased by John Page in 1771.[48]

The need to produce a glass of even thickness and extreme brilliance was constantly in the minds of 18th-century glassmakers. In the late 17th century English makers were producing what they called "blown-plate," which was simply broad glass made

---

[47] H. J. Powell, *Glassmaking in England*, Cambridge, Cambridge University Press, 1923, p. 105.
[48] *Norton Papers, op. cit.* (footnote 6), p. 199.

sufficiently thick so that it could be ground and polished on both sides. This glass was used primarily for mirrors. Whereas the English continued throughout the 18th century to improve their crown glass, the French and Germans devoted their researches to making finer broad glass, which was known as German glass or sheet glass.

The fragments from Rosewell vary considerably in thickness and would seem to be predominantly of crown type. There are, however, a small number of thicker pieces that can be identified as plate. But the most important fragments are molded with raised diamond and lozenge patterns, and are of a type for which no records have been found and which no glass historian has yet been able to identify. The glass varies in thickness, is a pale straw in color, and presumably was made initially in the broad glass manner and then rolled and impressed into a mold. The purpose of the glass is uncertain, for it is only semitransparent and is reminiscent of the molded and frosted panes used in bathroom windows and the like in the 19th century and in the early years of the present century. However, it is possible that it was used in a decorative manner, for sunlight striking the raised patterns causes them to sparkle and glow. It is conceivable that such glass was used in one or both of the great stairhall windows on the east and west sides of the mansion.

The only dating evidence yet found for glass of this type was provided by fragments found in a trash pit excavated by the writer on property owned by Messrs. Price Waterhouse & Co. in Frederick's Place and Old Jewry in the City of London. The pit, containing a quantity of tin-glazed wall tiles and clay tobacco pipes, was considered to have been filled in the period between about 1725 and 1750.[49] Also, a fragment of molded glass, purple in color, was picked up on the site of an early 17th-century glasshouse at Sydney Wood in Surrey, England, but there is no proof, or even likelihood, that the piece is of that date. Nevertheless, on the Old Jewry evidence it may be suggested that the molded glass found in the Rosewell pit was installed when the mansion was under construction in the second quarter of the 18th century and that the recovered fragments were removed during repairs to the house in the 1760's or early 1770's.

---

[49] Contents of this pit are in the collection of Guildhall Museum, London.

In conclusion, notice should be taken of a small fragment of conventional window glass (fig. 9) on which had been scratched an inscription, most of which is missing. Beneath a line of which nothing can be made are the letters "orn A." Four letters hardly make either sense or a sentence, but it is recalled that John Page was [b]orn A[pril] 1744.

Conclusions

The preceding summaries of the history of Rosewell, its architecture, the methods of excavation, and of the most significant finds appear to support the following conclusions:

(1) The pit may have been dug to obtain clay required for brickmaking.

(2) The digging and filling of the pit were probably no more than a winter apart.

(3) The filling was thrown into the pit sometime between about 1763 and 1772, with the latter as the most probable date.

(4) The finds include relics of repairs or alterations to the mansion as well as domestic trash thrown away by the Page family.

(5) The finds are to be associated with John Page and his family and not with Mann Page II, who had moved to Mannsfield near Fredericksburg in the mid-1760's.

(6) Rosewell possessed a blacksmith's shop as well as the 120-foot brick stable described in the 1802 insurance policy, and both were situated to the west of the house.

Illustrations

The objects illustrated in figures 10–38 are representative of the principal artifact types found in the Rosewell excavations. They do not, by any means, show all the finds that were recovered.

LOCATIONS

The presence of a capital letter and arabic numeral after the description of each stratified find indicates the area and stratum from which the item comes. Where two or more sets of letters and figures occur, fragments of the object were found scattered over the areas and through the strata listed. Where more than one fragment was recovered from a single location, no additional letter or figure is included. For the identification of areas and strata see figures 3 and 4, respectively.

DATING

Where available, published parallels are quoted as dating evidence. In addition, unpublished evidence derived from Colonial Williamsburg excavations is used. Unfortunately, however, the majority of the finds are without support in either of these directions; in such cases the stated dates are only the writer's opinion based on his own experience. However, the accepted sealing date for the filling of the Rosewell pit provides a terminus ante quem of 1772 for all strata other than the top (no. 1 in fig. 4), which was considered slightly disturbed and may have included items dating as late as about 1800.

Some of the more common items are described as "18th century" or "second half of 18th century," indicating that they represent *types* of relics that cannot be closely dated on stylistic grounds. However, providing the items were found below the pit's top level, these particular examples must date before 1772. It should be remembered that all other quoted dates are those of manufacture and do not indicate the length of time during which the objects would or could have been in use.

SCALE

Unless otherwise stated, all photographed items are depicted against a 1-inch-square grid and can be scaled accordingly. Scales for the drawn items are indicated on the drawing or in the legend. Where the illustrations do not indicate the object's thickness, internal diameter, or any other pertinent feature, this data is included in the description.

UNSTRATIFIED ITEMS

Included in this report are a number of objects considered to be of interest but which were not found in the vicinity of the pit. These come predominantly from the large trash-strewn area revealed by deep ploughing south of the Page graveyard and east of the mansion. Most of the material from this area belongs to the first half of the 18th century, but this time span is made worthless by the presence of a small number of items of the late-18th and 19th centuries that, as a result of the ploughing, became mixed with the earlier material. Two iron items from other ploughed areas are also included— an iron ice skate found to the northwest of the Page graveyard (an area that yielded more 19th-century

than 18th-century refuse) and an 18th-century hoe found in the vicinity of the foundations of the colonial barn (?) close to the path northwest of the mansion (see p. 162). These items appear as nos. 7 and 4, respectively, in figure 37.

Figure 10

1. Plate, Chinese porcelain. Base slightly raised; underglaze floral decoration in cobalt; no footring. Second half of 18th century. C2. Reconstructed drawing, fig. 25, no. 3.
2. Plate, Chinese porcelain. Rim sherd only; decoration in roughly painted underglaze blue. Style is reminiscent of the Canton willow-patterns of the early 19th century, and for this reason is thought to date no earlier than the 1760's. E2.
3. Plate, Chinese porcelain. Base slightly raised; floral decoration in underglaze blue, good quality; no footring. Fragments much scattered over the northeast area of the pit. 18th century. A2, J1, J2, E2. Reconstructed drawing, fig. 25, no. 1.
4. Plate, Chinese porcelain. Wide, somewhat sloping rim; small incurving footring; elaborate floral ornament in underglaze blue. Second half of 18th century. L2. Reconstructed drawing, fig. 25, no. 2.
5. Soup plate, Chinese porcelain. Narrow rim; heavy footring; celadon edge to rim; decoration in underglaze blue; ornament of rim is somewhat Imari in style, that of the center is floral with *ju-i* border. Second half of 18th century. D2, F2, G1, G2, N2, O2. Reconstructed drawing, fig. 25, no. 5.
6. Plate, Chinese porcelain. Rim sherd only; decoration in underglaze blue. Probably third quarter of 18th century. E2.
7. Plate, Chinese porcelain. Rim sherd only; decoration in underglaze blue, in technique similar to no. 2. Third quarter of 18th century. D2.
8. Plate, Chinese porcelain. Rim sherd only; willow tree decoration in underglaze blue. 18th century. Surface.
9. Small soup plate, Chinese porcelain. Rim and wall sherd only; decoration in underglaze blue, the lattice pattern rather similar to that of no. 5. Third quarter of 18th century. C2.
10. Plate, Chinese porcelain. Rim sherd only; edge with iron oxide wash; carefully painted floral decoration in underglaze blue. 18th century. E3.

Figure 10.—Chinese porcelain.

Figure 11.—Chinese and English porcelain.

Figure 11

1. Group of cup and saucer fragments, Chinese porcelain. All fragments appear to be from the same set. Stylized lotus design in underglaze blue. Interior of cup is decorated with an unidentifiable flower on the bottom surrounded by a single ring and with another ring slightly below the lip. 18th century. E3, K2, D1, D2. Reconstructed drawing, fig. 25, no. 7.

2. Saucer, Chinese porcelain. Has small, slightly incurving footring; decoration as in no. 1. 18th century. E3, K2. Reconstructed drawing, fig. 25, no. 8.

3. Saucer, Chinese porcelain. Slightly flaring rim; small footring; elaborate floral decoration of medium quality in underglaze blue. 18th century (?). C2, L2. Reconstructed drawing, fig. 25, no. 10.

4. Saucer, Chinese porcelain. Slightly flaring rim and small footring as in no. 3; loose floral decoration and paneled scenes in underglaze blue. E2 and surface. Reconstructed drawing, fig. 25, no. 11. The treatment of the flowers and the use of dividing panels are paralleled in a Chinese porcelain saucer found in excavations at St. Benedict's Gate, Norwich, England, where it was attributed to the period 1650–1700.[50]

5. Cup, Chinese porcelain. Small cylindrical; iron oxide on rim; decoration in underglaze blue with deep blue band below rim and elaborate floral ornament in pale blue on the body. Second half of 18th century. O1.

6. Cup handle, Chinese porcelain. Oval-sectioned; spinal floral decoration in underglaze blue. Second half of 18th century. J2, P3. These locations provide a good example of the degree of scattering.

7. Cup, Chinese porcelain. Small, cylindrical, body very white; decoration in underglaze blue. The hatched zone below the rim may be compared to a similar device surrounding the central ornament in fig. 10, no. 1. Second half of 18th century. B1. Dating for nos. 5–7 is based on the fact that cylindrical coffee cups were made in China to conform to a European fashion not appearing before second half of the 18th century. It will be noticed that two of the pieces come from layer 1, and therefore need not be as early as the finds recovered from the sealed strata of the pit.

8. Saucer, Chinese porcelain. Gently curving wall; small footring; decoration in underglaze blue with a butterfly-and-lotus motif as the central ornament. The open-weave borders may be compared to the less carefully executed varieties that appear on the soup plate in fig. 10, no. 5, and to the smaller example in fig. 10, no. 9. E3, K3. Reconstructed drawing, fig. 25, no. 9. A very close parallel, illustrated by Jenyns,[51] is stated to have been in the famous collection, now in Dresden, that was formed by Augustus the Strong, King of Poland and Elector of Saxony. The collection was built up principally during the short period from 1694 to 1705. The piece comes from one of the Ching-tê Chên factories, and there is little doubt that the Rosewell example comes from the same source, though perhaps a little later.

9. Plate or shallow bowl, Chinese porcelain. Wall markedly curved; small footring orange at the bottom; rim with iron oxide beneath gilding. The body of this fine quality piece is decorated on the wall with floral motifs in pale blue underglaze, but most of the ornamentation is created in overglaze enamels. The zone below the rim is decorated in red with scrolls and petals filled with gold and with leaves in green outlined in black. Traces of the latter technique are visible in the center of the piece, which is framed in a ring of ju-i heads outlined in red and filled with gold. This border motif is less common than the simpler spearhead form seen on so much overglaze-decorated Chinese export porcelain.[52] Third quarter of 18th century. E3, F2, J2, and surface. Reconstructed drawing, fig. 25, no. 4.

10. Vase or bottle fragments, Chinese porcelain. Interior markedly ribbed; exterior decorated in underglaze blue; design a typical boat with lake and willow motif from which the willow pattern was later derived. 18th century. G2, M2.

11. Teapot stand(?), Chinese porcelain. Corner sherd only. Unglazed on the back; tile slightly raised within a collar whose upper edge shows traces of iron oxide. Decoration in underglaze blue; design of individual lotus blossoms within the lattice border—seen also in fig. 10, nos. 5, 9, and fig. 11,

[50] See J. G. Hurst and J. Golson, "Excavations at St. Benedict's Gates, Norwich, 1951 and 1953," *Norfolk Archaeology*, vol. 31, pt. 1, 1955, p. 85, pl. 156.

[51] Soame Jenyns, *Later Chinese Porcelain*, London, 1953, pl.12, fig. 1.

[52] John G. Phillips, *China-Trade Porcelain*, Cambridge, Harvard University Press, 1956, p. 58.

no. 8—was created by confining diamonds of decreasing size within squares or, as in this case, within ovals and circles. The identification of this item as a teapot stand is merely a tentative suggestion, for no parallels have yet been found. 18th century. P2.

12. Cup, Chinese porcelain, European style. Thin-walled with the lip slightly everted; floral pattern in underglaze blue on the exterior, a wide band in herringbone style below the lip on the inside. Second half of 18th century. D1, F2. Drawn, fig. 25, no. 16.

13. Cup, Chinese porcelain. Similar to above; exterior floral decoration in underglaze blue, but with curious "flowing-blue" foliate ornament below the lip on the inside. Second half of 18th century. E3, K1. Reconstructed drawing, fig. 25, no. 15.

14. Cup, Chinese porcelain. Presumably hemispherical, in Oriental style; decoration in underglaze blue. 18th century. E primary.

15. Saucer, Chinese porcelain. Gently sloping wall; small footring; decoration in polychrome overglaze decoration with bamboo motif on wall, the leaves in red and the stems green outlined in black. The green has become covered and partially destroyed by a brown incrustation, a phenomenon invariably associated with overglaze green after long contact with the soil. The central floral decoration makes use of the aforementioned colors and is surrounded by a belt of red "basket" ornament. The underside of the base bears a double ring in a rich underglaze blue and part of an unidentifiable mark in a deeper blue. Probably mid-18th century. E2, F2. Drawn, fig. 25, no. 13.

16. Cup, Chinese porcelain. From same set as the above saucer; wall fragments only; overglaze bamboo ornament on the exterior and red basket zone below the lip on the inside similar to that on the saucer. Probably mid-18th century. A2. Drawn, fig. 25, no. 14.

17. Cup, Chinese porcelain. Same type and decoration as no. 16 but with the brushwork neater, the lines wider apart, and the hatched zone on the interior wider. Probably mid-18th century. C2.

18. Cup, Chinese porcelain. Wall fragment only, underglaze blue ring above the foot and base both inside and out; elaborate exterior decoration in overglaze polychrome enamels with flowers in red and gold and in white and gold outlined in red, and the leaves green, outlined in black. Mid-18th century. J3.

19. Saucer, English Bow porcelain. Small footring; the body pale straw in color with underglaze blue decoration of uncertain design. Third quarter of 18th century. N2.

20. Cup, English Bow porcelain. Lip and wall fragments only; pale straw-colored body; underglaze blue decoration in Chinese manner with bamboo and huntsman(?) motif and a narrow ring of blue on the interior below the lip matching that on the exterior. Third quarter of 18th century. F1, J2, and surface.

21. Bowl or slop-basin, English Worcester porcelain. Molded foliate ornament below the rim and molded cartouche surrounding underglaze blue ornament of uncertain form; a hatched zone below the rim and another, slightly wider, on the interior. Early Doctor Wall period. About 1751–1765. F2.

Figure 12

1. Plate, Chinese porcelain. Base and wall fragments only, the former curving and the latter with footring unglazed on the bottom; pastoral(?) decoration in underglaze blue. 18th century. C2, L2, N2.

2. Bowl, Chinese porcelain. Rim sherds only; elaborate underglaze decoration in blue and with iron oxide on rim; two narrow rings of blue below the rim on the inside; a wide ornamented band on the outside above a floral motif. The wall of the bowl is thin but the surface is somewhat pitted. First half of 18th century. E2, F2, J2, G2.

3. Soup plate, small, Chinese porcelain. Rim slightly flaring; small footring with the base raised within; iron oxide around rim; decoration in underglaze blue with central floral motif of uncertain form. Second to third quarter of 18th century. F1, F2, N2. Reconstructed drawing, fig. 25, no. 6.

4. Bowl, Chinese porcelain. Basal fragment only; tall footring slightly incurving; foliate decoration on exterior in underglaze blue; single line around base on interior. 18th century. J3.

5. Bowl, large, Chinese porcelain. Rim and body sherds only; elaborate floral decoration in underglaze blue. 18th century. F2, J2. See also nos. 6, 7. Reconstructed drawing, fig. 25, no. 17.

6. Bowl, large, Chinese porcelain. Rim sherd only, probably part of same bowl as nos. 5, 7. 18th century. F2.

7. Bowl, large, Chinese porcelain. Body sherd only, probably part of same bowl as nos. 5, 6. 18th century. N2.

8. Saucer, Chinese porcelain. Curving wall; small footring; poor quality ornamentation in underglaze blue and overglaze red, with landscape motif spreading from base onto the wall and ceasing below the rim in a pale blue line. The two fragments have the appearance of being part of the same saucer, but their positions in the pit make this unlikely. Probably third quarter of 18th century. E primary, C2.

9. Saucer, Chinese porcelain, rather similar in style to no. 8. Rim slightly everted; small footring with base raised within; decoration in underglaze blue and overglaze red; floral motif with blue stems and flowers and some red leaves; similar decoration on exterior of wall. Probably third quarter of 18th century. J2, O1. Reconstructed drawing, fig. 25, no. 12.

10. Cup, Chinese porcelain. Rim sherd only; landscape decoration in underglaze blue and overglaze red in style similar to that of no. 8 with a thin blue line around interior below rim. Probably third quarter of 18th century. E3.

11. Saucer, Chinese porcelain. Wall fragment only; human figure in underglaze blue; vigorous painting of pleasing quality. 18th century. A3.

12. Bowl, Chinese porcelain. Body fragment only; floral decoration in pale finely-drawn underglaze blue. 18th century. K1.

13. Bowl, Chinese porcelain. Upper body sherd only; underglaze lily-pad decoration on interior below the rim in underglaze blue and with butterfly in flight on exterior. 18th century. N2.

14. Blanc de chine figurine. Back of head and fragment of ear only.[53] 17th or 18th century. H1.

15. Bowl, London or Bristol delftware. Floral ornament in cobalt. Second to third quarter of 18th century. Surface.

16. Bowl, Bristol delftware. Hemispherical, stylized foliate ornament in cobalt; ring of same color 1¼ inches below rim on interior. Second to third quarter of 18th century. F2, K2.

17. Bowl, similar to or perhaps part of no. 15. Second to third quarter of 18th century. Surface.

18. Bowl, probably Bristol delftware. Decorated in Chinese style; exterior decoration in cobalt with

red rim. Second to third quarter of 18th century. G3.

19. Bowl, probably Bristol delftware. Foliate pattern on exterior in cobalt; red-edged rim; single broad line below rim, double line above foot, and double line around interior ⅝ inch below rim. Second to third quarter of 18th century. K2.

20. Basin, London or Bristol delftware. Everted rim with cobalt decoration on upper surface. Probably second quarter of 18th century. E primary.

21. Bowl, probably Liverpool delftware. Body sherd only; floral decoration in pale, somewhat speckled cobalt with black highlighting, gray interior surface, probably a second. Second to third quarter of 18th century. Surface.

22. Bowl, London or Bristol delftware. Cobalt decoration of uncertain form. Second to third quarter of 18th century. S1.

23. Bowl, London or Bristol delftware. Small rim sherd only; rich blue cobalt decoration of uncertain form. First to second quarter of 18th century. Surface.

24. Bowl, Bristol delftware. Lower body fragment only; foliate ornament in deep blue cobalt, leaves created in "spade" brushwork; single line around base on interior. Second quarter of 18th century. B3.

25. Plate, Bristol delftware. Base fragment and rim fragments, damaged by fire; cobalt decoration with "spade" brushwork as in no. 24. Second quarter of 18th century. Q2.

26. Cup or small bowl, probably Bristol delftware. Foliate decoration in deep cobalt neatly applied; thin body. First half of 18th century, perhaps first quarter. A2, N1.

27. Bowl or porringer, English delftware. Everted rim and plain white tin-glaze; belongs to same class as the many chamber-pot and wash-basin fragments found in the pit. Third quarter of 18th century. C2. Reconstructed drawing, fig. 25, no. 24.

28. Ointment pot, English delftware. Everted rim and somewhat bulbous body; white tin-glaze.[54] 18th century. Surface.

29. Ointment pot, English delftware. Thin-walled; rim slightly everted and wider than base (a characteristic that became more pronounced as the 18th

---

[53] See Jenyns, op. cit. (footnote 51), pl. 120, no. 2.

[54] F. H. Garner, English Delftware, London, 1948, pl. 11a, right.

FIGURE 12.—Chinese porcelain and decorated delftware.

600873—62——3

century progressed); base thick and slightly concave within the foot; white tin-glaze. Second to third quarter of 18th century. C2, N2. Drawn, fig. 25, no. 21.

30. Drug jar, English delftware. Body sherd only; decorated in cobalt. 18th century. M2.

31. Drug jar, English delftware. Base thin and somewhat concave; exterior glaze almost lost, but traces of cobalt bands remain. 18th century. A2. Drawn, fig. 25, no. 23.

32. Drug jar, English delftware. Small body sherd only. Chain ornament in deep cobalt. 18th century. Surface.

33. Handle fragment, tin-glazed earthenware. Probably continental European; body somewhat pink. Presumably 18th century. A2.

35 Bowl, tin-glazed earthenware. Probably continental European; decoration in cobalt overlaid with antimony with a narrow cobalt band around the interior; pink body. Presumably 18th century. A2.

35. Ointment pot, English delftware. Small, slightly everted rim; body slightly bulbous and constricted above base, which has a diameter approximately the same as that of the rim; base thin and slightly concave. First half of 18th century. J3. Reconstructed drawing, fig. 25, no. 22.

Figure 13

1. Westerwald chamber pot, gray saltglazed stoneware. Rim thickened, flattened, and everted; cordoning beneath rim ornamented with single band of cobalt, similar cordoning and cobalt band above slightly concave base; typical body ornament in form of applied, molded lions, rampant and crowned, alternating with impressed rosettes; all ornamentation highlighted and surrounded with cobalt. Because a template was used in making it, the body shows evidence of chattering, a characteristic that generally appears on chamber pots and storage jars, but not as often on other German gray stoneware forms. Handle incomplete but characteristically heavy and markedly reeded. Chamber pots of this type were in production by around 1720 and seem to have remained popular until about 1760; however, like pots of other wares, they became slightly taller and less pleasingly shaped towards the end of the period. It may be significant that in 1770 Mann Page ordered white chamber pots for use at Mannsfield,[55] but makes no mention of the German blue and gray. This example seems to belong to the second quarter of the 18th century. C2, C3, P2, P3. Reconstructed drawing, fig. 26, no. 7.

2. Westerwald tankard, gray saltglazed stonewares. Rim and upper body sherds only; rim somewhat V-sectioned with heavy cordoning beneath it highlighted with two bands of cobalt; body apparently decorated with hatched diamond motif, alternate diamonds being filled with cobalt. Mid-18th century. J2, K1. Reconstructed drawing, fig. 26, no. 8.

3. Rhenish, possibly Grenzhausen, jug, gray saltglazed stoneware. Neck fragment only; rim V-shaped with broad band of cordoning offset beneath with two bands of cobalt; body bulbous and decorated with cobalt, no evidence of design. Jugs of this type were popular during the last decade of the 17th century and the first of the 18th. The pieces were generally ornamented with the cypher of William III or Queen Anne. The poor quality of this specimen suggests that it belongs to the latter reign or perhaps a little later.[56] First quarter of 18th century. G3. Reconstructed drawing, fig. 26, no. 9.

4. Westerwald jug, gray saltglazed stoneware with cobalt decoration. Neck fragment and part of handle. Probably second quarter of 18th century. F3.

5. Westerwald jug, gray saltglazed stoneware. Body sherds only; ware thinly potted and pale brown on interior; stylized foliate decoration on exterior incised and filled with cobalt surrounding a central medallion molded with a wreath around the "G. R." cypher of King George of England with a crown flanked by two birds above and a winged angel beneath. The initials of the moldmaker, "S. W.," beside the right wing and beneath the tail of the R. Another example of this maker's work has been found in excavations in Williamsburg.[57] The "G. R." cypher was made for export to England during the reigns of George I and George II, and it is uncertain to which reign this jug belongs. Probably second quarter of 18th century. B2, F2.

[55] *Norton Papers, op. cit.* (footnote 6), p. 125.
[56] See *Catalogue of the Guildhall Museum*, London, 1908, pl. 72, no. 4.
[57] Adalbert Klein, *Rheinisches Steinzeug Des 15. Bis 18 Jahrhunderts*, Darmstadt, 1955, pl. 22.

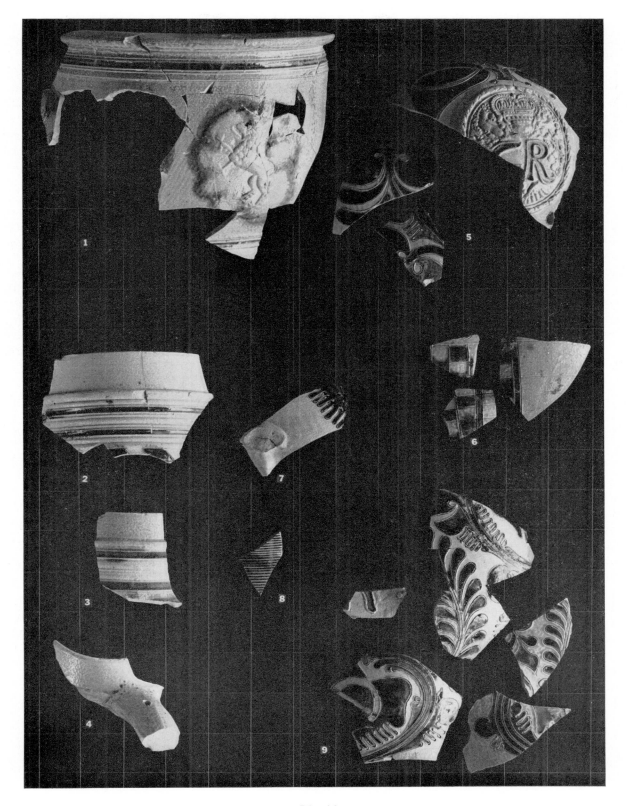

FIGURE 13.—Rhenish stonewares.

6. Westerwald jug, gray saltglazed stoneware. Thin body sherds only; decoration includes girth zone of incised checker-pattern with alternate squares cobalt filled. A jug with similar ornamentation was found on the site of the Printing Office in Williamsburg but was unfortunately unstratified. Probably second quarter of 18th century. A2, N2.

7. Westerwald jug, gray saltglazed stoneware. Body fragment with tail of handle only; incised foliate decoration filled with deep cobalt. Probably mid-18th century. C2.

8. Westerwald jug, gray saltglazed stoneware. Neck fragment only; decoration in form of multiple horizontal grooving, the whole coated with manganese; probably comes from a jug of the same type as nos. 5–7. Probably mid-18th century. C2.

9. Westerwald jug, gray saltglazed stoneware. Lower body fragments only; pale brown ware with pronounced potting rings on interior; exterior decoration stylized foliate ornament surrounding "G. R." medallion of quality inferior to that of medallion in no. 5; handle fragment, no. 7, may be part of same vessel. Probably second quarter of 18th century. B1, B2, C2, C3, E2, F1, F2, K1, K2, and surface.

Figure 14

1. Dish, Staffordshire slipware. Bat-molded; pale yellow body; notched rim; swirled marbleized slip decoration in yellow and light and dark brown; back unglazed. Two dishes of this type have been found in Williamsburg excavations. Second to third quarter of 18th century. B2, F2, K2. Drawn, fig. 25, no. 19.

2. Posset cup, Staffordshire or Bristol slipware. Pale yellow body; somewhat flaring rim; body bulbous and incurving to a foot unglazed on exterior; small looped handle, oval in section; yellow glaze with brown dots around rim, brown combing on body. First half of 18th century. C2, E2, H2, L2. Reconstructed drawing, fig. 25, no. 18.

3. Posset cup, ware as above. Basal fragment only; pale yellow glaze on interior, no glaze on exterior; small foot spreading below the incurving body and base thinning towards center. First half of 18th century. F1, F2, and surface. Reconstructed drawing, fig. 25, no. 18.

4. Dish, Staffordshire slipware. Small, circular, bat-molded with raised bird design; notched rim; slightly pink ware with yellow glaze over white slip. Mid-18th century. B2. Drawn, fig. 25, no. 20.

5. Coffeepot (?), Whieldon pineapple ware. Cream colored earthenware; green molded leaf with yellow fruit on either side. About 1760–1770. F2.

6. Teapot or teapoy, English white saltglaze. Molded in shape of house with shield of arms and lion and unicorn supporters above door (recovered fragment shows only head of lion and edge of shield).[58] About 1745. J2.

7. Body fragment from vessel of uncertain form, English white saltglaze. Ornamented with dots of overglaze enamels in red, green, pink, and yellow. Third quarter of 18th century. G2.

8. Wine glass, English lead glass. Fragment of bowl of bell or waisted type; engraved with tall-stalked flowers with narrow leaves, their heads hanging on either side of a central stem (possibly bluebells).[59] Third quarter of 18th century. B surface.

9. Short length of thin, lead glass tubing with internal bore of 3.5 millimeters. 18th century. E primary.

10. Tobacco pipe, clay. Mouthpiece only; coated with red wax; stem-hole diameter $\frac{1}{16}$ inch. 18th century. E3.

11. Tobacco pipe, clay. Stem section close to mouthpiece; mouthpiece coated with black slip; stem-hole diameter $\frac{5}{64}$ inch. 18th century. N2.

Figure 15

1. Bag-shaped vessel, native Indian pottery. Rim sherd only; wall has average thickness of $\frac{1}{4}$ inch and narrows to V-shaped rim; finger smoothed on interior; cord-marked exterior; shell-tempered ware fired in a reducing atmosphere to gray-brown. Had this sherd been found elsewhere, it might be attributed to the late Woodland or early

---

[58] For further details see p. 169 and fig. 8. See also *Burnap*, *op. cit.* (footnote 28), p. 34, no. 93; Rackham, *op. cit.* (footnote 30), p. 24.

[59] For possible shape parallel see E. Barrington Haynes, *Glass through the Ages*, London, 1948, pl. 55c.

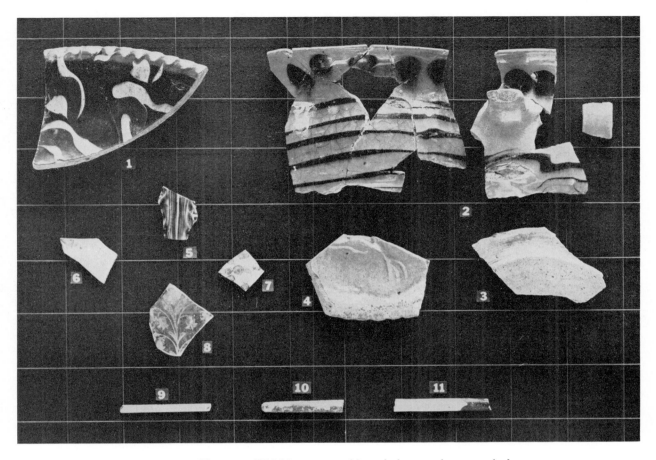

FIGURE 14.—Slipwares, Whieldon ware, white saltglaze, and engraved glass.

Contact period,[60] but it (and nos. 2–5, 8) came from the secondary deposit in the Rosewell pit and was undoubtedly deposited after about 1730 and probably as late as 1771 (see p. 164). B4.

2. Body sherd, native Indian pottery. Wall thickness ⅜ inch; heavily shell-tempered; no obvious decoration; fired in reducing atmosphere to black interior and gray-brown exterior. B4.

3. Body sherd, native Indian pottery. Wall thickness ³⁄₁₆ inch; shell-tempered; fired in reducing atmosphere to black interior and gray-brown exterior. B4.

4. Body sherd, native Indian pottery. Wall thickness ³⁄₁₆ inch; shell-tempered; scraped outer surface; fired in reducing atmosphere to gray or gray-brown. B4.

5. Rim sherd, native Indian pottery. Roughly flattened along rim; wall thickness ⁵⁄₁₆ inch; clay containing small flecks of red ochre; fired in oxidizing atmosphere; faint purple on interior, sandy brown on exterior. B4.

6. Rim sherd, native Indian pottery. Wall thickness ¼ inch, narrowing to slightly flaring V-shaped rim; shell tempered; scraped interior; exterior ornamented with overlapping crisscross design stamped with thong or root-wrapped paddle; fired in reducing atmosphere to gray interior and gray-brown exterior. The decoration is described by Evans as the "Roanoke Simple Stamped" style and attrib-

[60] The following dated cultural sequence was prepared by Dr. Ben C. McCary and printed in his book, *Indians in Seventeenth-Century Virginia*, Williamsburg, Virginia, 350th Anniversary Celebration Corporation, 1957, p. 90.

Period	Probable Time
Paleo-Indian	8000 B.C.–3500 B.C.
Archaic	3500 B.C.–500 B.C.
Early Woodland	500 B.C.–A.D. 500
Middle Woodland	A.D. 500–A.D. 1000
Late Woodland	A.D. 1000–A.D. 1600
Historic (Contact)	A.D. 1600–Present

uted to the Chickahominy Series; dating late Woodland to early Contact eras.[61] O2.

7. Body sherd, native Indian pottery. Wall thickness 3/16 inch; shell tempered; scraped interior; exterior fabric impressed and ornamented with hatched incised lines (slight shell tempering); fired in reducing atmosphere to gray-brown. K1.

8. Body sherd native Indian pottery. Wall thickness 3/16 inch; shell tempering shows only on interior; stamped decoration (see no. 6); fired in reducing atmosphere to gray interior and gray-brown exterior. B4.

9. Body sherd, native Indian pottery. Broken on coil line; wall thickness 1/4 inch; coarsely shell-tempered; exterior fabric impressed; fired in oxidizing atmosphere to pale orange. Surface.

10. Body sherd, native Indian pottery. Broken on coil line; wall thickness 1/4 inch; coarsely shell-tempered; scraped interior; exterior fabric impressed; fired in oxidizing atmosphere to pale orange, same type as no. 9. Surface.

11. Body sherd, native Indian pottery. Wall thickness 1/4 inch; shell-tempered; exterior fabric impressed; fired in poorly controlled oxidizing atmosphere, pale gray-brown interior, brown to pink exterior. Chickahominy Series.[62] E1 (top 6 inches).

12. Body sherd, native Indian pottery. Wall thickness 1/4 inch; temper leached out; some scraping internally; fabric-impressed exterior; fired in reducing atmosphere to an even gray. 01.

13. Bowl or dish, Colono-Indian pottery. Rim sherd; wall thickness, 3/16 to 4/16 inch; rim everted and tooled up from beneath; flattened on top; wall sharply sloping; characteristic buff; shell-tempered ware with gray core; stick or pebble burnishing inside and out. See p. 172. J2.

14. Cooking pot leg, Colono-Indian pottery. Diameter 3/4 inch; leg made in separate roll to be luted to pot with smeared clay; stick or pebble burnished; foot flat at bottom; ware buff to pink over gray core; slight shell-temper. See p. 172. A2.

15. Bowl, Colono-Indian pottery. Rim sherd; rim flattened on top and slightly everted; body somewhat bulbous; wall thickness 3/16 inch; shell-tempered; buff with slightly darker core; some burnishing inside and out. See p. 172. B2.

Figure 16

1. Beverage bottle seal with initials "T.A.O." Impressed from separate matrices. For further details see p. 173.[63] From field surface south of graveyard, unstratified.

2. Bottle seal in olive-green glass. Bears the legend "PYRMONT WATER"[64] around a crowned shield of arms. "Quarterly of nine. Overall, in the 5th or an eight-pointed Star, sa. (Waldeck). In the 1st and 9th ar. a Cross ancrée gu. (Pyrmont). In the 2nd and 8th ar. three Shields gu. (Rappolstein). In the 3rd and 7th ar. three Crows Heads sa. tongued gu. crowned or (Hoheneck). In the 4th and 6th ar. semy of Billets couchées az. a Lion gu. crowned or."[65] Second to third quarter of 18th century. J2.

3. Bottle seal, olive-green glass. Bears incomplete legend ". . . E PYRMONT WATE[R]" around crowned shield of arms as in no. 2; seal attached to a shoulder fragment indicating bottle is of same shape as sealed example shown in fig. 31, no. 6. Second to third quarter of 18th century. Surface.

4. Bottle seal, glass much decayed. Bears legend "*PIERMONT [W]ATER" around an eight-pointed star. This is an early form of the Pyrmont water seal. Two examples of this seal were found in a coffee-house trash pit in London that has been dated to the second quarter of the 18th century. From field surface south of graveyard, unstratified.

5. Neck of Pyrmont water bottle, pale amber glass. Round-sectioned string-rim trailed around neck and pressed to it with same tool used to apply "Piermont" seal; letter "N" impressed into string-rim. Use of seal matrix for this purpose is not uncommon and encourages belief that matrix was mounted close to furnace mouth and that bottles were pressed against it and not it against them. An identical

[61] Clifford Evans, *A Ceramic Study of Virginia Archeology*, Smithsonian Institution, Bureau of American Ethnology Bulletin 160, Washington, 1955, p. 47.

[62] *Ibid.*, pl. 7, example "h" for closest parallel.

[63] See also Ivor Noël Hume, "A Century of London Glass Bottles," *The Connoisseur Year Book 1956*, London, 1955, p. 103.

[64] Pyrmont was the capital of Waldeck, in Germany; it was noted for its mineral springs, the waters of which were widely exported.

[65] The heraldic description of the arms is quoted from the late Lady Ruggles Brise's book *Sealed Bottles*, London, 1949, p. 78.

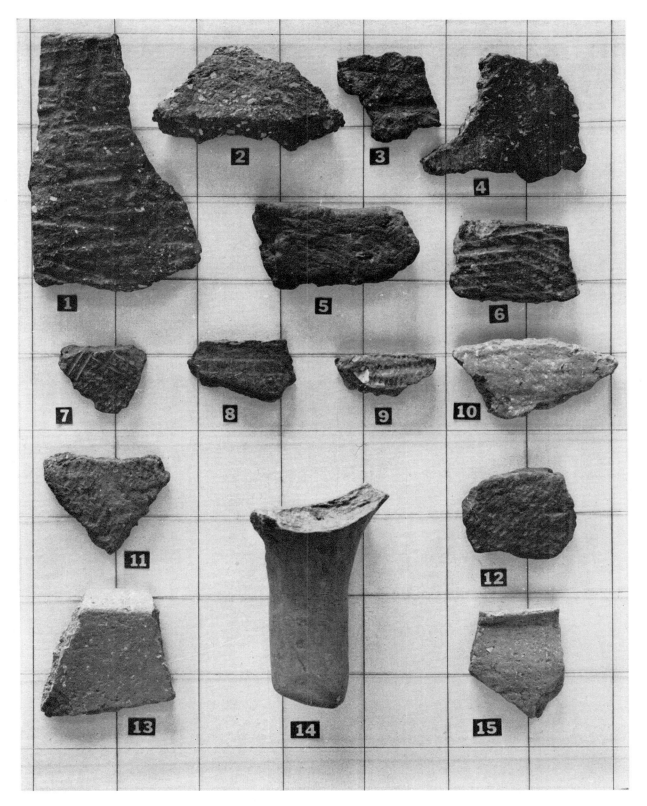

Figure 15.—Indian and Colono-Indian pottery.

FIGURE 16.—Bottle seals and neck of Pyrmont water bottle.

neck found on Dr. Gilmer's lot in Williamsburg [66] is limited in date by Gilmer's span of ownership to

the decade 1735–1745. The same use of the seal matrix is apparent. There is a clear impression of the letter "P" preceded by a large period and by what is believed to be the point from a star en-

[66] Colonial Williamsburg, cat. no. 163–29A2.

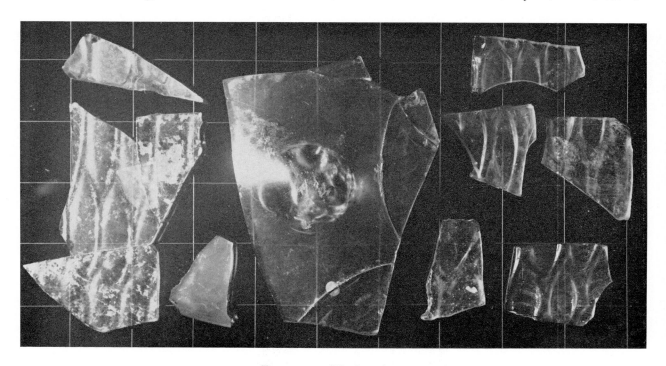

FIGURE 17.—Window glass.

FIGURE 18.—Reverse and obverse of Louis XV silver half-écu. Enlarged.

closed within a raised circle. There is little doubt that this impression is part of a seal comparable to that in no. 7. Probably second quarter of 18th century. J3. Drawn, fig. 31, no. 4.

6. Bottle seal, decayed olive-green glass. Bears legend "PYRMONT WATER" around a crowned shield of arms as in no. 2; lettering somewhat smaller than on preceding examples. Second to third quarter of 18th century. A2.

7. Bottle seal, pale olive-green glass. Bears legend "PIERMONT WATER" followed by a large period surrounding an eight-pointed star. Second quarter of 18th century. C2.

8. Bottle seal, glass blackened and soapy with decay. Bears conjectured legend "PIERMONT WATER" surrounding sharply molded, eight-pointed star; probably from unusual squat bottle illustrated in fig. 30, no. 4. First quarter of 18th century. C3.

9. Bottle seal, olive-green glass gilded by irridescence. Bears initials "M:P" (for Mann Page). This seal was attached to a cylindrical-bodied bottle of a type unlikely to date before about 1760; this fact, and the context, precludes it from belonging to any member of the Page family other than Mann Page II. About 1760–1770. L2.

Figure 17

Center: Bullion or bull's-eye from a crown of window glass, the metal a pale blue-green becoming more pronounced towards the center. Thickness ¼ inch at left edge close to center, narrowing to ⅛ inch at the farthest measurable distance from center. Probably second half of 18th century. D1. To the left of the bullion is an edge fragment from another crown: metal is pale green; the edge thickening on both sides and rounded; thickness is ¼ inch at the outer edge, and ¹⁄₁₆ inch at about 1½ inches in from the outer edge (see p. 177). Probably second half of 18th century. C1.

Left and right: Fragments of molded window glass. Clear to straw metal; all decorated with embossed lozenge patterns. Lozenges vary in length from pane to pane, the shortest measuring 1¼ by ⅜ inches and the longest 1¾ by ½ inches. The thickness and height of the molded lines vary considerably, those at the botton left being the lightest and those at the bottom right being the heaviest. Of the joined fragments at the left, only the upper pair belong together; the lower fragment has been attached merely to illustrate the shape of the complete lozenges. Glass of this type appears to be unique in Virginia but is paralleled by fragments found in a trash pit on the site of a tenement that stood on the corner of Old Jewry and Frederick's Place in London. These date from the second quarter of the 18th century and are now in the Guildhall Museum in London (see p. 178). Surface, B1, D1, E2, E3, K2, O1.

Figure 18

Silver half-écu. Reverse: Bourbon shield of arms beneath crown and legend "SIT. NOMEN. DOMINI. H. (mint mark) BENEDICTVM" (Blessed be the Name of the Lord) followed by the date 1719. Obverse: Lauriate head of Louis XV in right profile with legend reading "LVD. XV. D.G. FR. ET. NAV. REX"; edge inscription, "DOMINE **** SALVVM FAC **** REGEM." (See p. 174.) E2.

Figure 19

1. Shoe buckle, pewter. Surface molded in relief with two barrels flanked by flowers and the words "NO EXCISE" at either end (see p. 166). 1763–1770. A2. Enlarged drawing, fig. 7.

2. Shoe buckle fragment, and tongue and tines. The buckle is silver-plated brass with ridged and notched ornamentation. The iron tongue and tines came from the same pit area as the buckle fragment but they are not necessarily from the same buckle. 18th century. H2.

3. Button, silver-plated brass. Back slightly conical with a U-shaped brass wire thrust into the apex; diameter $^{15}/_{16}$ inch. Second half of 18th century. K2.

4. Sleeve buttons or links, silver. Octagonal; engraved with stylized flower within a diamond; small, somewhat flattened loops with single oval link; small oval on back of one button may be an illegible maker's mark.[67] Probably second quarter of 18th century. E3.

5. Button, gilded brass. Shell type; embossed with rosette in thread style; originally possessed bone back similar to no. 10. 18th century. F2.

6. Boss or large button, brass with iron nail or shank mounted within small collar on the hollow reverse. Diameter 1⅜ inches. Size and shape suggest that it may have been a harness ornament. 18th century. J2.

7. Button, pewter. Back missing; front decorated with molded rose; probably a British naval button; diameter $^{15}/_{16}$ inch. First half of 18th century. L2.

8. Button, brass. Hollow-cast type; small brass shank, the wire rectangular in section; casting hole on either side of shank; diameter ⅝ inch. Buttons of this type found in the Revolutionary cemetery at the Governor's Palace in Williamsburg have been described as French military buttons.[68] 18th century. F2.

9. Button, silver-plated brass. Flat with round-sectioned wire loop; front surface somewhat scratched, which might indicate a rough attempt at decoration; diameter $^{11}/_{16}$ inch. Second half of 18th century. Surface.

10. Bone back for button of type illustrated by no. 5. Carefully made; somewhat convex with edge tooled to take rim of brass front; central hole drilled to take a wire shank; diameter $^{9}/_{16}$ inch. 18th century. C2.

11. Miniature padlock with brass key. Iron mechanism and brass casing; probably from a jewel box. The height is ¾ inch and the thickness 5 mm. The key protrudes ¾ inch. Because the mechanism was so rusted, no attempt was made to extract the key. 18th century. E3.

Figure 20

1. Curtain ring, brass. Rolled metal, a method of manufacture considered to be later in date than that used in making no. 2. 18th century. Surface.

2. Curtain ring, hammered brass with filed edge. 18th century. F2.

3. Buzz or whirligig, brass or copper. Roughly serrated edge; two holes through center. 18th century. (See p. 174.) N2.

4. Ounce weight, bronze. On opposite sides of a small collared lug in the center of the upper surface are the mark "V^8" and the figure "16"; thickness of disk 5.5 mm. 18th century. F2.

5. Ramrod thimble, ribbed brass. Made from strip of brass curved to form circular tube ⅜ inch in diameter; ends of strip flattened together and pressed

---

[67] See Faith Russell-Smith, "Sleeve-Buttons of the Seventeenth and Eighteenth Centuries," *The Connoisseur*, London, 1957, vol. 139, no. 559, p. 36ff; and Ivor Noël Hume, "Sleeve Buttons: Diminutive Relics of the Seventeenth and Eighteenth Centuries," *Antiques*, April 1961, vol. 79, no. 4, pp. 380–383.

[68] Calver and Bolton, *op. cit.* (footnote 42), p. 228.

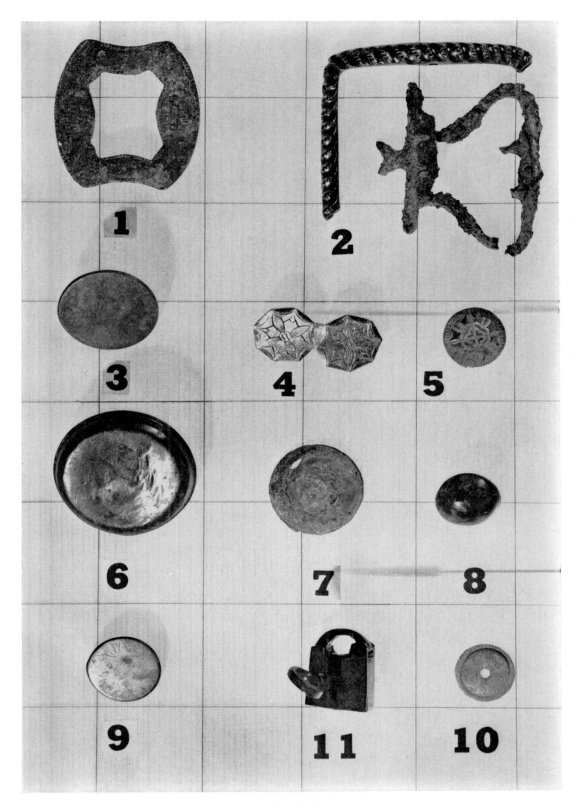

FIGURE 19.—Buckles, buttons, etc.

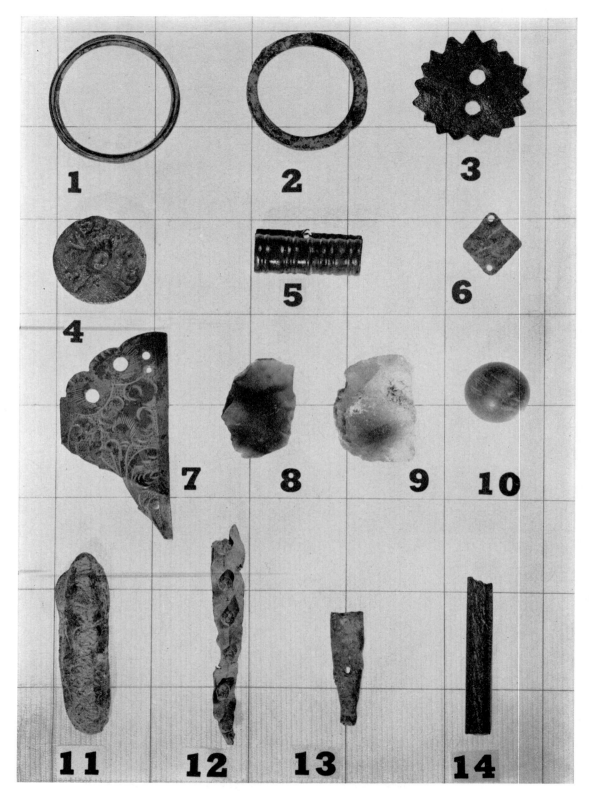

FIGURE 20.—Curtain rings, gun flints, brass weight, etc.

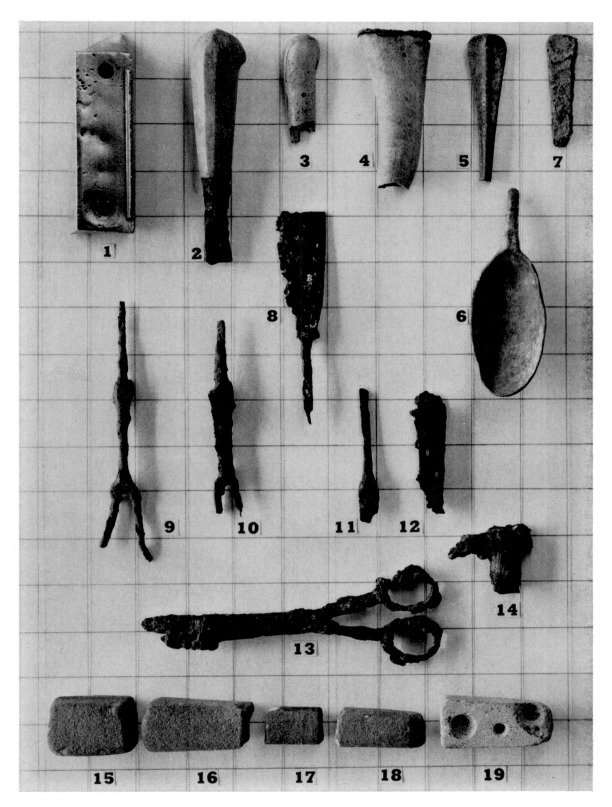

FIGURE 21.—Cutlery, hones, bullet mold, etc.

into a slot in woodwork of weapon and held in place by single nail or rivet. 18th century. F2.

6. Brass plate. Diamond-shaped; very thin with small hole at base and apex; possibly harness ornament. 18th century. E2.

7. Fragment of brass with engraved foliate ornament. Three round holes stamped in the making of the piece and a fourth hole (at lower right) hammered through at a later date. It has been suggested that this piece may have come from the face of an ornamental clock; however, at the time it was thrown away it probably was waste metal, for it had been roughly cut at the lower lefthand side. 18th century. O2.

8. Gun flint showing bulb of percussion. Thin, brown; trimmed along striking edge. 18th century. C2.

9. Gun flint. Thick; white; trimming on three sides. 18th century. N2.

10. Toy marble of polished brown clay. 18th century. E3.

11. Waste fragment from bullet mold, lead. Pouring shanks from four balls partially filed off. 18th century. J2.

12. Waste fragment from shot mold, lead. Pouring shanks from six shot attached. 18th century. K3.

13. Fragment of shaped lead pierced by small hole. Uncertain purpose. Surface.

14. Slate pencil. Filed to an oval section; greatest width ¼ inch. 18th century. J2.

Figure 21

1. Brass striking plate for rim lock. Two holes for retaining bolts or screws; depth ⅞ inch; metal thickness 1/16 inch. 18th century. J2.

2. Table knife. Bone pistol-grip handle octagonal in section; solid iron shoulder much corroded but probably also octagonal. Shank length 1 inch. 18th century. G2.

3. Cutlery handle. Bone; pistol-grip type; incomplete. 18th century. F1.

4. Knife handle. Made from antler; oval iron cap at top; remains of iron tang within. 18th century. O2.

5. Handle of pewter spoon. Flaring terminal; spinal ridge; diameter at broken section ¼ inch. This type of spoon was common in Virginia in contexts of the mid-18th century (see also no. 6). C2.

6. Bowl of pewter spoon. Rat-tail from handle extends onto back of bowl; faint, rouletted scratches within bowl may have been mark of identification but are no longer legible. This spoon originally possessed handle similar to no. 5, and it is possible that the two fragments are parts of the same spoon. Mid-18th century. Q2.

7. Handle of pewter spoon. Much decayed; spreads slightly at top; probably square-ended; thickness, 4 mm. It is possible that handle was stamped with initials "M.P.," but metal too decayed to be certain. 18th century. L2.

8. Kitchen knife, steel. Good-quality metal; short, hipped shoulder, square-sectioned tang; blade back measures 3 mm. at greatest thickness; cutler's mark "R" on left side of blade 1⅛ inches below shank. 18th century. K2.

9. Fork, iron. Two-tined; thin shoulder spreads and becomes octagonal (?) at junction with handle; rectangular-sectioned tang. 18th century. Surface.

10. Fork, iron. Two-tined; unusually flat-sectioned; octagonal shank; incomplete. 18th century. C1.

11. Table knife. Tang and squat-hipped shoulder only. 18th century. B1.

12. Folding handle from small pocket knife, iron. Originally bone-plated on either side, incomplete. 18th century. J2.

13. Scissors, iron. Loops centrally set above baluster-shaped handles; junction of loop and stem ornamented with quadruple horizontal ribbing; narrow blades, one possibly pointed, other rounded at end. Much decayed, but a reasonable reconstruction was made possible by fragments that were revealed, though destroyed, in the course of cleaning. 18th century. A3. Reconstructed drawing, fig. 37, no. 6.

14. Quillon sleeve from small sword, iron. Pas d'anes curve downward towards missing shell guard. A single quillon extends to the rear while part of the knuckle bow shows at the front. Probably third quarter of 18th century. N2. A slightly larger example of the same type was found in an unstratified Williamsburg deposit and was used in reconstruction (fig. 38, no. 15).

15. Hone, sandstone. Fragment only; section approximately 1⅛ inches square. 18th century. J2.

16. Hone, sandstone. Fragment only; section approximately 1 inch square. 18th century. N2.

17. Hone, sandstone. Fragment only; section approximately ¾ inch square. 18th century. A2.

18. Hone, sandstone. Fragment only; section approximately ¾ inch square. 18th century. E2.

19. Bullet mold, shell-tempered Colono-Indian pot-

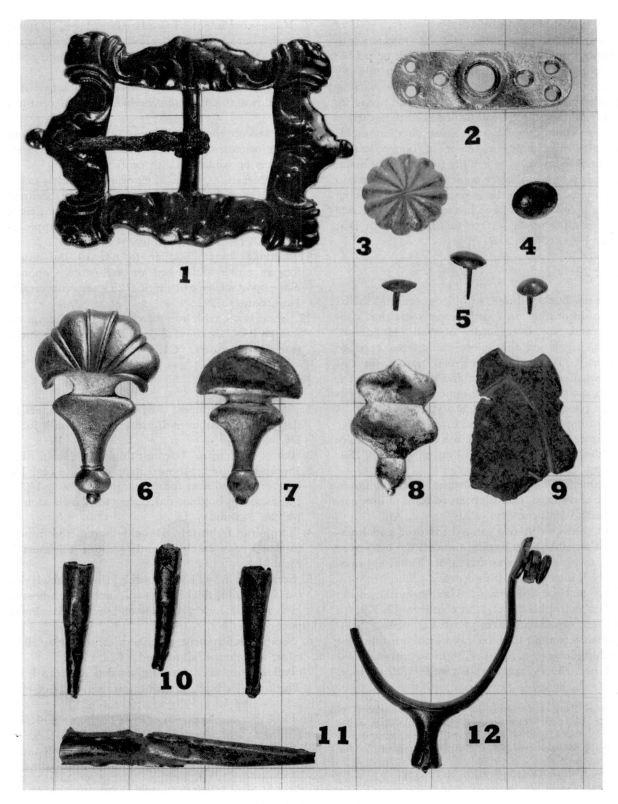

Figure 22.—Harness buckle, ornaments, spur, etc.

tery. Probably made by the Pamunkey. Half of mold only; greatest thickness 22 mm.; width narrows from 1 to ¾ inch; curved; stick or pebble burnished on back; single groove runs up midway along one side but does not continue across back or up other side; two similar grooves ¼ inch apart up broad end, and three small drilled holes of uncertain purpose; pouring slot runs into circular mold; conical drilled hole in center of upper surface presumably intended to key the two halves of mold. There is a larger, slightly conical hole, of uncertain purpose, towards left edge at narrow end; the drilling of this hole seems to have broken through the side mold, causing upper surface to flake away in that area. 18th century. B2.

Figure 22

1. Harness buckle, brass with iron tang. Molded foliate decoration on face; reverse somewhat concave and rough-surfaced; over-all length 4½ inches, suggesting that piece came from carriage harness.[69] The pale, olive-green patina on this item was found to be stable and was not removed, which accounts for the dark appearance of the item in the photograph. 18th century. B2.
2. Mounting for harness terret, brass. Central collar with internal screw thread; three nail or screw holes at either end; evidence of filing on back.[70] 18th century. B2.
3. Ornamental boss, silvered brass. Small collar in center of concave back supports remains of iron nail or shank. 18th century. P2.
4. Stud, brass, with two tangs bent over and hammered together after passing through the leather or wood to which stud was attached. Tangs approximately ⅛ inch thick. 18th century. B2.
5. Three tacks or studs, brass. Used for ornamenting saddles and upholstery. 18th century. J2, K2.
6. Harness ornament, silver-plated cast brass. Scallop shell terminal; back concave with four tangs for attaching object to leather;[71] three tangs around shell and fourth tang at bottom.[72] 18th century. E2.

---

[69] Colonel Paul H. Downing in his "Carriage Report" of 1957 (MS, Colonial Williamsburg, Virginia, vol. 12, p. 538a) describes buckles smaller than though somewhat similar in shape to the Rosewell example as "Believed to be sword baldric or belt buckles."

[70] For parallel see Downing, *op. cit.*, pl. 5, no. 4

[71] A scrap of leather *in situ* when found.

[72] See Downing, *op. cit.* (footnote 69), pl. 1, nos. 9 and 10.

7. Harness ornament, silver-plated cast brass. Similar to no. 6 but slightly smaller and without the scalloped shell. 18th century. K (in lining of ground hog's nest).
8. Harness ornament, cast brass. Three tangs in a row down slightly concave back.[73] 18th century. H2.
9. Harness ornament, cast brass. Fragment cut from larger ornament for scrap; probably once used on blinkers or winkers. 18th century. A2.
10. Three ferrules, brass. Left example crudely made with no provision for retaining nail; center specimen has two nail holes and wood still in position; right item still has iron nail; diameter of each, approximately 8 mm. 18th century. C3, H3, N2.
11. Ferrule, brass. Similar to no. 10 but much longer; either unfinished or deliberately opened along most of length; original diameter uncertain. 18th century. N2.
12. Spur, brass, with iron rowel. Heel width approximately 2 inches; rowel apparently small five-pointed star. 18th century. C1.

Figure 23

1. Scrap-iron fragment. Slightly waisted; tapers to sharp edge at either end; greatest thickness ⅜ inch. D1.
2. Bar of scrap iron. Greatest thickness ¾ inch. P3.
3. Scrap-iron, wedge-shaped item. Possibly rear leg from crude andiron; measures approximately 1½ by 1¾ inches at bottom, narrowing to ⅞ inch at top; weight, 3 pounds. J2.
4. Scrap-iron fragment. Roughly hammered; tapers to sharp edge at either end; greatest thickness ¼ inch. L1.
5. Scrap-iron fragment. Possibly rim of bowl; incurving at top, thickening to 9/16 inch; much beaten and split at lower, broken end, which is almost paper-thin. N2.
6. Scrap-iron fragment. Deliberately cut along right edge; sharp edges all around. B2.
7. Poll of axe, presumably discarded as scrap iron. Thickness 7/16 inch, tapering towards walls of eye. E2.
8. Fireback, cast iron. Fragment only; probably intended as scrap iron; molded foliate (?) decoration along right side; thickness, approximately ⅜ inch. Surface. Drawn, fig. 37, no. 2.

---

[73] For massive example in same shape, see Downing, *op cit.*, pl. 1, no. 1.

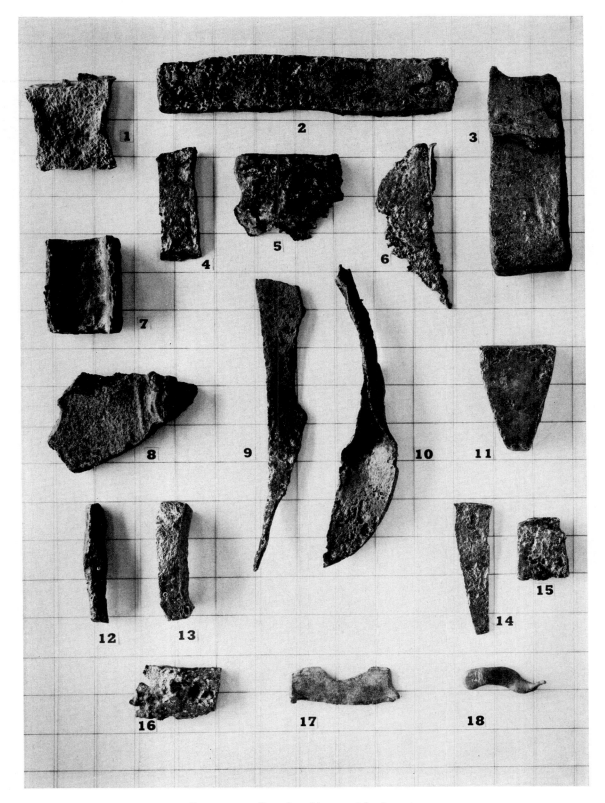

Figure 23.—Samples of iron and lead waste.

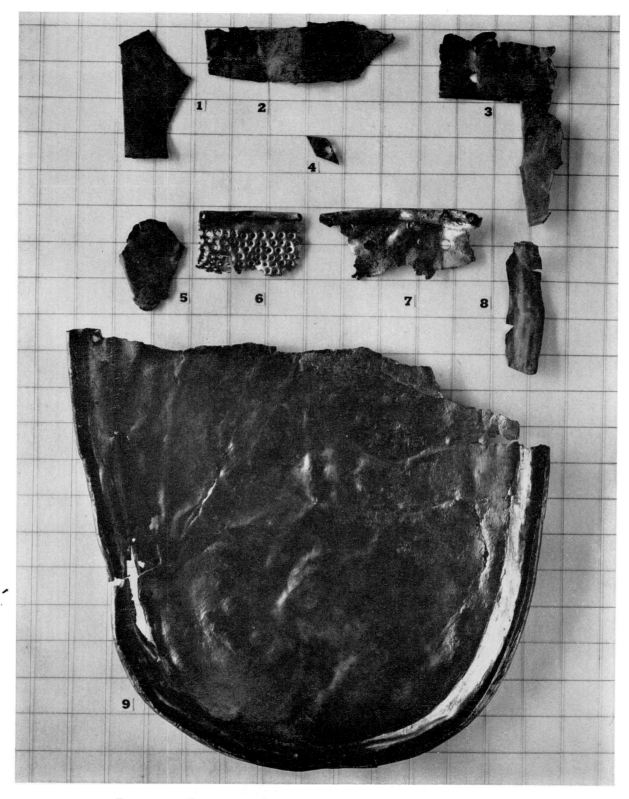

Figure 24.— Copper pan or tray, strainer fragments, copper and brass waste.

9. Scrap-iron fragment. Trimmed on all sides; possibly tang and part of blade from unfinished knife or sickle. M2. Drawing cf rather similar item, fig. 36, no. 3.

10. Iron tool of uncertain purpose. Made from flattened piece of iron; handle fashioned by turning up sides at one end, heating them, then beating and rolling them together; thickness of blade approximately ⅛ inch; no cutting edge on blade. There is little doubt that this object was made on the plantation. L2. Drawn, fig. 36, no. 2.

11. Block of scrap iron shaped like miniature smoothing iron. Possibly heater for small box iron; thickness ¹¹⁄₁₆ inch; weight, 10 ounces. E2.

12. Rod of scrap iron. Thickens in middle where sides are flat; diameter at ends ⅜ inch; thickness at center ½ inch; possibly an unfinished small hammer of type used by brass-workers and silversmiths. A2.

13. Scrap-iron bar. Slightly curved; measures ¾ by ½ inch at one end and ⁹⁄₁₆ by ⁹⁄₁₆ inch at the other. F2.

14. Iron wedge. Possibly used to split and hold handle of axe within eye. L2.

15. Scrap-iron fragment. Thickness ³⁄₁₆ inch. G2.

16. Strip of iron slag. Much bubbled. B1.

17. Scrap of waste lead. Trimmed along three edges. J2.

18. Run of waste lead. Apparently ran along or down a flat surface. E2.

Figure 24

1. Scrap of waste brass. Deliberately cut along left and right edges; smooth upper surface; rough at back. N2.

2. Scrap of waste copper. Roughly trimmed on all sides. G2.

3. Scrap of waste brass. Very thin; has deliberate right-angled cut at left; other edges roughly broken. N2.

4. Washer, brass. Diamond-shaped; roughly made; hole diameter ³⁄₁₆ inch. K1.

5. Scrap of waste copper. No obvious shaping. J2.

6. Colander, copper. Rim fragment only; rim rolled inwards over iron wire; holes for straining hammered through with nails from inside; rough exterior surface caused by breaking of metal around holes suggests that fragment may have come from a grater rather than from a strainer. H2.

7. Colander, copper alloy with high percentage of lead. Metal apparently was in a fire, causing lead to melt out; rim rolled inwards but no evidence of an iron wire; holes are from ½ to ¾ inch apart and stamped out; diameter of holes ¼ inch. N2.

8. Scrap of waste brass. No obvious shaping.

9. Pan, tray or billy lid, copper. Wall shelves to a depth of ⅝ inch below internally rolled rim, which embraces a thick iron wire; crudely made, may be of local manufacture. 18th century. J2.

Figure 25

1. Chinese porcelain plate. See fig. 10, no. 3.
2. Chinese porcelain plate. See fig. 10, no. 4.
3. Chinese porcelain plate. See fig. 10, no. 1.
4. Chinese porcelain bowl. See fig. 11, no. 9.
5. Chinese porcelain soup plate. See fig. 10, no. 5.
6. Small Chinese porcelain soup plate. See fig. 12, no. 3.
7. Chinese porcelain cup. Reconstructed from fragments from same set. See fig. 11, no. 1.
8. Chinese porcelain saucer. From same set as no. 7. See fig. 11, no. 2.
9. Chinese porcelain saucer. See fig. 11, no. 8.
10. Chinese porcelain saucer. See fig. 11, no. 3.
11. Chinese porcelain saucer. See fig. 11, no. 4.
12. Chinese porcelain saucer. See fig. 12, no. 9.
13. Chinese porcelain saucer. See fig. 11, no. 15.
14. Chinese porcelain cup. See fig. 11, no. 16.
15. Chinese porcelain cup. See fig. 11, no. 13.
16. Chinese porcelain cup. See fig. 11, no. 12.
17. Chinese porcelain bowl. See fig. 12, no. 5.
18. Posset cup, English Staffordshire slipware. See fig. 14, nos. 2, 3.
19. Dish, English Staffordshire slipware. See fig. 14, no. 1.
20. Dish, English Staffordshire slipware. See fig. 14, no. 4.
21. Ointment pot, English delftware. See fig. 12, no. 29.
22. Ointment pot, English delftware. See fig. 12, no. 35.
23. Drug jar, English delftware. See fig. 12, no. 31.
24. Bowl or porringer, English delftware. See fig. 12, no. 27.

Figure 26

1. Basin, English delftware. Rim everted and slightly downbent; slightly flaring footring, base flat within

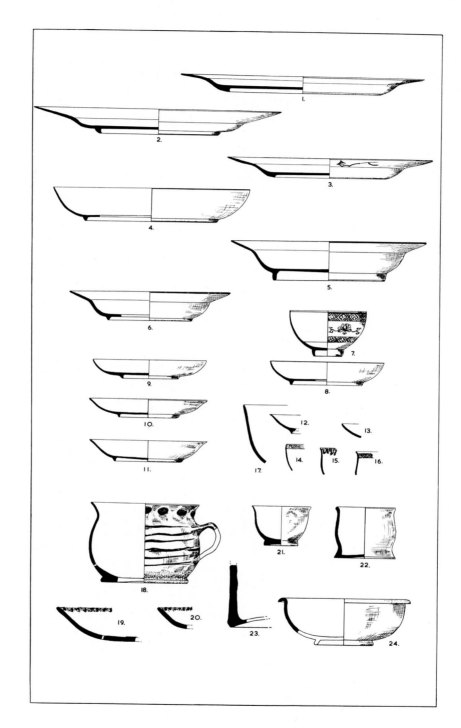

FIGURE 25.—Chinese porcelain, slip, and delftware. One-fourth.

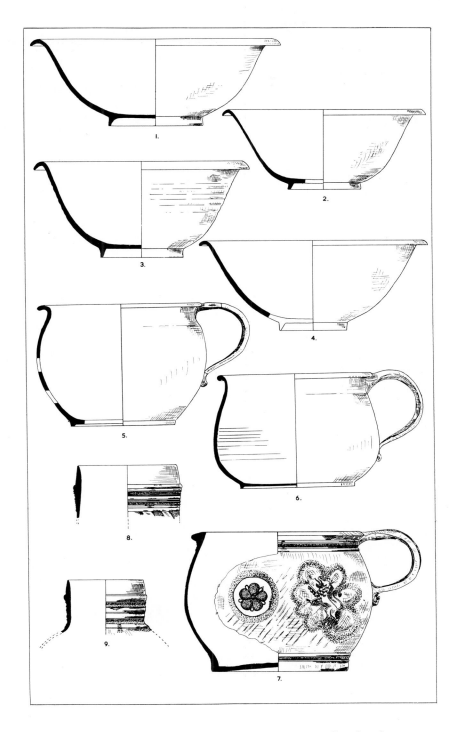

FIGURE 26.—Delftware and Rhenish stoneware. One-fourth.

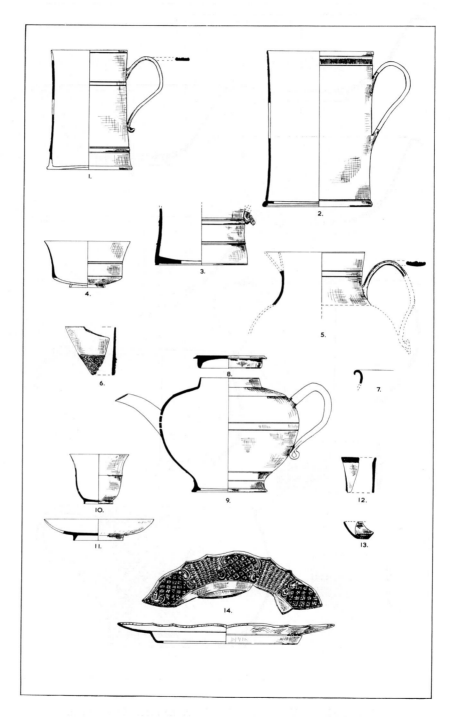

FIGURE 27.—English white saltglaze. One-fourth.

it; white glaze with hint of blue.[74]   Third quarter of 18th century.   F2, N2.

2. Basin, English delftware. Smaller than no. 1; rim small and rolled outwards; V-shaped footring; base much thicker than walls; white glaze with hint of green.   Third quarter of 18th century.   J2, J3.

3. Basin, English delftware. Walls taller than either no. 1 or no. 2; rim everted and downbent; pronounced potting rings on body; angular footring that is rather light for weight of body; thick white glaze with slightly pink appearance along crests of potting rings.   About 1740–1770.   E2, E3, K3.

4. Basin, English delftware. Rim and body sherds only; rim everted and slightly downbent; wall slopes at slightly wider angle than no. 3; same glaze as no. 3.[75]   About 1740–1770.   E3.

5. Chamber pot, English delftware. Perhaps from Bristol. Disassociated fragments only; rim everted and slightly downbent; vestigial footring with base slightly raised within; strap handle slightly concave on outer surface; rolled lower terminal thickly glazed; pale blue glaze; no glaze on bottom of foot.   Second to third quarter of 18th century.   K2, O2.

6. Chamber pot, English delftware. Rim everted and rolled; pronounced potting rings on body which spreads towards vestigial footring; base thin and slightly raised within foot; good white glaze appearing slightly pink where thin; accidental cobalt spots on interior of base; no glaze on bottom of footring; no joining handle found. This is an earlier shape than the uniformly bulbous-profiled no. 5. Probably second quarter of 18th century. G3. Reconstruction based on example, now in the Guildhall Museum, London, found in a refuse pit at the Church of St. Olave, Hart Street, London, and dating about 1720–1730.

7. Chamber pot, gray Westerwald stoneware. Impressed and molded ornamentation highlighted in cobalt. Surviving body fragments do not join to handle, which has been added only to show its relationship to the body form and not to the positioning of decoration. Ornament normally comprises three stamped rosettes—one opposite handle flanked by single sprigged lions facing towards it, the others to the left and right of lions.   See fig. 13, no. 1.

8. Tankard, gray Westerwald stoneware. Rim sherds only; cobalt decoration.   See fig. 13, no. 2.

9. Rhenish jug, possibly from Grenzhausen. Rim sherd only; cobalt decoration.   See fig. 13, no. 3.

Figure 27

1. Tankard, English white saltglazed stoneware. Handle and body fragments only; incised lines around upper body which pass beneath upper handle terminal. Above the slightly spreading base there is a pronounced ridge beneath two grooves.[76]   About 1740–1760.   C2, N2.

2. Tankard, English white saltglazed stoneware. Rim, handle terminal, and base fragments only; simple cylindrical form, rouletted zone below rim; rolled foot with base slightly raised.   Mid-18th century.   B2, C2, J2, K1, K2.

3. Tankard, English white saltglazed stoneware. Base and lower terminal of handle only; body somewhat constricted above base; narrow groove close to lower edge with pronounced ridge 2 centimeters above it; base slightly raised; reeded handle with characteristic pad terminal at bottom; smooth, glossy surface in contrast to pebbly surfaces of nos. 1 and 2.   Mid-18th century.   B1, F2, K2, and surface.

4. Carinated bowl, English white saltglazed stoneware. Wall and rim sherd only; extremely thin ware, flaring at rim; double girth groove around body. The base has been reconstructed from an example found in the pit (E2, F2), but it is uncertain that it is part of the same bowl, so the base is shown only in outline.   About 1740–1760.   C1.

5. Pitcher, English white saltglazed stoneware. Neck and handle fragments only; sharply molded spout; two pairs of grooves around neck on line of spout base; multiple-reeded handle; neck flares to bulbous body.   About 1750–1770.   C2, E2, F2, K1, K2, N2.

6. Tankard, English white saltglazed stoneware. Rim sherd only; matt surface; double groove 1¼ inches below rim; body rusticated with applied chips of white clay.   Probably about 1730–1750.   C2.

7. Chamber pot, English white saltglazed stoneware. Everted rim sherd only.   Mid-18th century.   B2.

8. Teapot lid, English white saltglazed stoneware. No indication of knob; body thick and coarse.   Third quarter of 18th century.   K2.

9. Teapot, English white saltglazed stoneware. Thin ware of good quality; glossy surface; rim is straight-

---

[74] See Graham Webster and K. Barton, "An Eighteenth Century Rubbish Pit, Trinity Street, 1953," *Chester and District Archaeological Society Journal*, 1957, vol. 44, fig. 2, no. 14, where basins of this type are recorded in a context apparently dating prior to about 1730. It is considered unlikely, however, that the Rosewell examples are as early (see p.170 of this report).

[75] *Ibid.*

[76] See Rackham, *op. cit.* (footnote 30), pl. 36.

walled collar inclining slightly inwards at top; flat shoulder ridged at outer end; bulbous body with double girth grooves incurves to ridge matching that below shoulder; rolled and flaring foot with raised bottom; traces of round-sectioned handle remain, but no evidence for spout; spout has been reconstructed from examples in Colonial Williamsburg's archeological collections. It is not to be inferred that lid no. 8 belongs to this teapot. Second quarter of 18th century. A2, E2, J2, K1, K2, and surface.

10. Cup, English white saltglazed stoneware. Conjectural reconstruction; small footring with raised base; girth ridge around body with wall flaring somewhat above it (see fig. 28, no. 14). Two cups of this type were found in excavations in a cellar of Robert "King" Carter's mansion, Corotoman, which burned in 1729. About 1720–1740. A2, E2.

11. Saucer (?), English white saltglazed stoneware. Base only; V-shaped footring; thick bottom. Probably third quarter of 18th century. E3.

12. Tankard, English gray-cored and white-slipped saltglazed stoneware. Rim sherd only; lip slightly everted and coated on outside with band of iron oxide. This coating, generally found on early examples, was a device to cover a falling away of the slip that tended to mar the appearance of the rim—an imperfection that is said to have been overcome by about 1720.[77] About 1710–1720. J2.

13. Saucer, English white saltglazed stoneware. Rim sherd only; body ornamented with molded basket motif. About 1745–1765. J2.

14. Plate, English white saltglazed stoneware. Rim molded with dot, diaper, and basket pattern; wall sharply angled inside and out; no footring; good quality molding. About 1745–1760. B2, D2, and surface.

Figure 28

1. Cylindrical mug or small tankard, brown stoneware—probably English. Strap handle; small groove below slightly everted rim; body ornamented above base with double ridge, cordon, and single ridge; foot flares slightly to resemble lip; base slightly rising; tight-grained ware; exterior gray, interior pale brown. Probably mid-18th century.[78] D1, F2, G2, J2, and surface.

---

[77] For parallel see Webster and Barton, *op. cit.* (footnote 74), fig. 2, no. 2.

[78] Were it not for the evidence of brown saltglazed stoneware manufacture at Yorktown (see p. 171), there would be no hesitation in claiming an English origin for all the Rosewell stonewares of this type.

2. Handle and body fragment from large brown stoneware storage jar, unevenly fired gray core and the interior surface pink. The handle is of the inverted cup type and roughly luted to the body, the exterior points of contact having been punched into the body with a flat-ended stick or some comparable tool. While this may have been intended as a decorative feature, it also served to bind the body and handle together. Probably Yorktown. Second to third quarter of 18th century. B1 and surface.

3. Large storage jar of brown stoneware. The rim thickened, outbent and shelved on the inside to take a lid, the walls thick and scored with decorative grooves at the shoulder and girth, the base thick and slightly rising. The exterior is coated with a thick, treacly and mottled green-brown glaze while the interior possesses an overall chocolate brown glaze. On the evidence of the paralleling of the exterior glaze among the Yorktown kiln refuse, it is considered that the Rosewell jar comes from that source. Second or third quarter of 18th century with the emphasis towards the latter. F3 and surface.

4. Bulbous storage jar of brown stoneware in the Lambeth or Fulham style. The outbent rim shelved on the inside to take a lid, the walls thin and scored with decorative grooves around the shoulder and girth, the base slightly rising. Mottled purplish glazing on the upper body but marred by yellow streaks running down from rim to base. A lump of excess clay (perhaps from touching an adjacent pot in the kiln), thickly vitrified, is attached to the body above the base, indicating that this vessel was probably a second. The ware is a tightly grained gray and the interior surface a pale brown (see also fig. 29, no. 1). Probably second or third quarter of 18th century. C2, C3, F3, J3, P3.

5. Rim of large lead-glazed earthenware storage jar of a type generally described as Iberian, examples of which were recovered from wrecks of vessels sunk in 1781 at Yorktown. The rim of the Rosewell example is much decayed but has been reconstructed for the drawing from examples in the Colonial Williamsburg collection. The rim is thickened and channeled around the inner edge to take a lid. The ware is pale pink and has a purplish brown glaze on the interior only. It should be noted that the glaze was clear but acquired its color from contact with the pink body. H2. Jars of this type possessed two vestigial lug handles luted to the

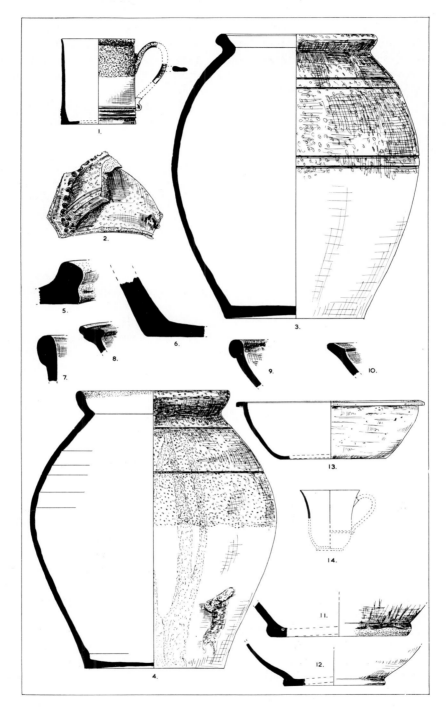

Figure 28.—Brown stonewares, coarse earthenwares, Colono-Indian bowl, and fragment of early white saltglaze cup. One-fourth.

wall above the girth, had an interior rim diameter of approximately 8 inches, and stood some 2 feet 9 inches. For a basal fragment see no. 6. A photograph taken in the hall at Rosewell in the late 19th century shows one such jar standing beside the fireplace.[79] There is a single restored example in the Colonial Williamsburg archaeological collections; another, privately owned, is in Captain Orr's Dwelling in Williamsburg; two restored examples are exhibited in the National Park Service ship exhibit at the Yorktown Visitor Center, and yet another is displayed at Mount Vernon. This last is believed to be one of "8 Soap Jars ($) 25" in the inventory of George Washington prepared by his executors after his death. The earliest date for these jars yet located by the writer is 1757, where an example appears in a painting of London's Custom House Quay, painted by Samuel Scott in that year. The painting is in the possession of the Worshipful Company of Fishmongers in London, but a reproduction can be seen in *The American Heritage Book of the Revolution*.[80]

6. Basal fragment from storage jar similar to the above. Thick pink body, leadglazed on the interior only. J1.

7. Folded rim from vessel of large flowerpot type. The surface much decayed, the ware yellow to pinkish orange slightly flecked with quartz, the surface a bright orange. Possibly Yorktown. Second or third quarter of 18th century. J3.

8. Wide-rimmed cooking bowl of Buckley ware from North Wales, United Kingdom. A pink body flecked with small intrusions of yellow clay, a thick black glaze on the interior, the body burnt to a light purple on the outside. The rim is thickened and outswept, markedly shelved below, the upper surface slightly reeded and on the inside incurving above the wall of the bowl—a characteristic Buckley technique.[81] Second or third quarter of 18th century. G3,

9. Rolled rim from cream pan or wide mixing bowl. Yellow to orange pink body slightly flecked with fine quartz, orange-brown glaze on the interior and in a stripe on the exterior at the junction of rim and wall. Provenance and dating as no. 7. F2, F3.

10. Upswept and everted rim from cream pan or wide mixing bowl. A small ridge on the interior at

the junction of rim and wall. Ware, glaze, provenance and dating as nos. 7 and 9. E3.

11. Basal fragment from lead tortoise-shell-glazed bowl or chamber pot. The body yellow with traces of pink on the surface showing on the worn foot below the glaze, and with slight traces of quartz in the clay. This might also be from Yorktown, although no parallels for glaze have yet been found. 18th century. N2.

12. Lower body and basal fragments from wide bowl or chamber pot. Highly fired pink to purplish body with a treacly brown glaze both inside and out. The glaze possesses innumerable small yellow flecks, a characteristic often found at Buckley. However, none of the fragments from the Buckley kilns in the writer's possession are as highly fired. 18th century. M2 and surface.

13. Bowl of Colono-Indian pottery (see p. 172). Shell-tempered and stick- or pebble-burnished, the ware largely pink but unevenly fired at one side, producing colors from yellow to blue-black. The rim is flat and undercut beneath. This incomplete bowl was found in a thin burnt stratum in association with no. 14, a white saltglazed sherd. Probably third quarter of 18th century. B5.

14. Rim sherd from small white saltglazed cup or possibly from a capuchine, a late-17th-century form that was first produced in brown stoneware. See James Morley's Nottingham trade card of around 1690, also the well known Place Cup made about 1680–1690 by Francis Place of York and which is now in the Victoria and Albert Museum.[82] For further details see description of figure 27, no. 10 (p. 208). About 1720–1740. B5.

Figure 29

1. Jug of brown stoneware. Bulbous body above small foot, base thin and slightly rising. Reeded cylindrical neck pinched and drawn out at the fore-edge to form a spout. Strapped handle with single deep spinal groove terminating at the base in a thumb-impressed rat-tail. The ware gray and tight-grained, the interior surface pale brown. The exterior above the girth a mottled purplish brown in the Fulham and Lambeth style.[83] Although it cannot be proved that this jug comes from one of the above sources, there is little doubt that it is a product of the same factory as no. 4

---

[79] Kocher and Dearstyne, *op. cit.* (footnote 1), p. 76, pl. 6.
[80] *The American Heritage Book of the Revolution*, New York, 1958, p. 33. (Narrative by Bruce Lancaster.)
[81] Barton, *op. cit.* (footnote 35).

[82] See Lewis, *op. cit.* (footnote 29), p. 85; and *Transactions of the English Ceramic Circle*, London, 1951, vol. 3, pt. 1, pl. 24, p. 65.
[83] Oswald, *op. cit.* (footnote 33).

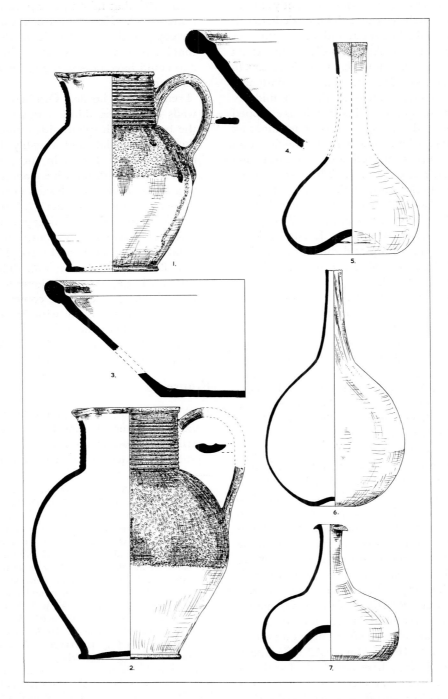

FIGURE 29.—Brown stonewares, coarse earthenwares, and glass bottles. One-fourth.

in figure 28. Probably second or third quarter of the 18th century. E2, E3, F2, F3, J2, and surface.

2. Jug of brown stoneware. Bulbous body above small foot, base slightly rising. The reeded neck is represented by a pinched spout and a small number of other fragments too few to indicate the exact shape of the opening. However, there is reason to believe that the fore-edge was somewhat flattened, thus creating a sharp angle to the rim midway between spout and handle. The handle is strapped and has a deep and wide spinal groove terminating in a finger impression. The clay at the junction of handle and body is smeared down and not tooled into the rat-tail form of no. 1. The ware a hard gray and the interior surface the same color; the exterior above the girth a dappled ginger-brown, becoming yellow in localized patches. This jug is certainly in the same style as no. 1, but lacks the refinement of workmanship and differs in coloring. Second or third quarter of 18th century. D1, F2, G2, G3, L2, M2, N2, O2.

3. Cream pan of coarse earthenware. Rim seemingly thickened and folded with a deep groove above the interior wall; the base flat. Red ware with ginger-brown glaze on the interior only.[84] There is no joining section through this pan, and the reconstructed height is based on examples in the Colonial Williamsburg archeological collections. To conserve space the full pan has not been drawn, but it is estimated to have had a rim diameter of 1 foot 4½ inches and a base diameter of 7¼ inches. Pans of this type were common throughout the 17th and 18th centuries and are consequently almost impossible to date with accuracy. A2, E2, K1, O2.

4. Large cream pan of coarse earthenware. The rim thickened and rolled with a deep groove or trough above the interior wall. A curious feature of this pan is a group of three-scored grooves running around the rim on the exterior face. Red ware with greenish brown lead glaze worn thin through use on the potting ridges of the interior, the exterior unglazed. Although the shape of the pan demands the same dating reservations noted for no. 3, the greenish brown glaze is more often found on pottery of the 17th than of the 18th century. A2 and surface.

5. Decanter of lead glass, base and body fragments only. The principal characteristics are the extremely weak shoulder and the conical basal kick.[85]

It will be seen that the reconstructed drawing of the Rosewell decanter incorporates a ground rim fragment (B1) that might perhaps have come from the same vessel. However, when using this decanter for comparative purposes it should be remembered that it may have been without grinding at the mouth and could have possessed a string-rim. E3, F2, J2, and surface.

6. French wine bottle. Originally wicker-encased, walls of extreme thinness turned black by decay, the body oval in plan with diminutive basal kick, the neck tubular and roughly broken from the blowing iron.[86] Found in the primary deposit of area E along with the wine glass (fig. 32, no. 7) and fragments of two other bottles of the same type, one of them with a shorter neck (3¾ inches).

7. Wine bottle of much-decayed olive-green glass. Possesses a remarkably domed basal kick, an unusually waisted neck, and a roughly applied string-rim flush with the mouth. This bottle is an anomaly but apparently belongs to the period about 1700–1720. The example comes from the primary deposit in area E along with fragments of no fewer than eight other wine bottles, none dating later than around 1730 and at least four of them belonging to the period about 1690–1720.

Figure 30

1. Wine bottle.[87] Olive-green glass; squat form with short neck and shallow basal kick; a V-sectioned string-rim close to the lip. N3. This form is generally attributed to the first two decades of the 18th

---

[84] See p. 208, fig. 28, no. 5 for comment on glaze.

[85] A close parallel for this shape is to be found in *The Connoisseur*, London, April 1929, p. 202, no. 7(a), where it is

attributed by W. A. Thorpe to about 1730. This early decanter had only recently graduated from the handled serving-bottle, still retained the old string-rim, and was made without a glass stopper. Consequently, the interior of the mouth was not ground. Thorpe was of the opinion that this form was in vogue during the decade about 1730–1740 and that during the second half of this decade the ground glass stopper made its appearance, although the balloon decanter with glass stopper and no string-rim did not reach its full prominence until about 1745. (See also *Apollo*, November 1947, p. 113ff.)

[86] Several examples of this bottle form are illustrated in William Hogarth's *Midnight Modern Conversation* (engraved 1733) and in *The Orgy* (engraved 1735). Other varieties of this basic "wanded" bottle shape have a shorter neck and a rigaree trail below the lip to form a string-rim. For a discussion regarding these wicker-encased bottles, see *Country Life*, June 16, 1955, p. 1575f; also Raymond Chambon, *L'Histoire de la Verrerie en Belgique*, Brussels, 1955, pl. T, no. 11.

[87] The accepted term "wine bottle" is used in preference to the more clumsy though more accurate "beverage bottle." But it is not to be inferred that all these bottles contained wine.

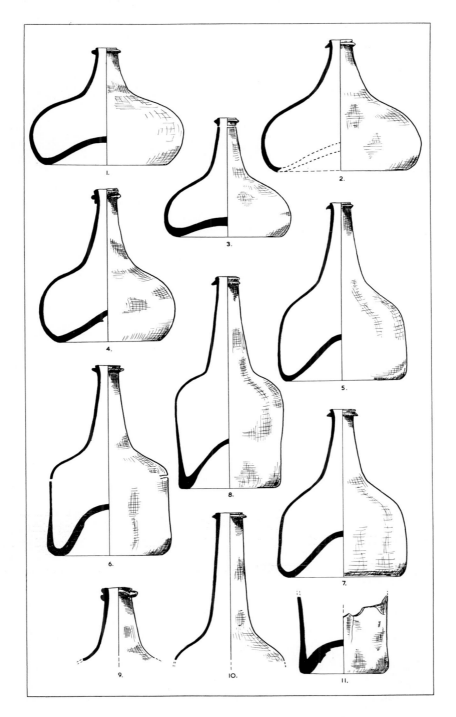

Figure 30.—Glass beverage bottles. One-fourth.

century, but a close parallel was provided by a bottle recovered from the wreck of the Dutch vessel *Huiste Craigenstein* that foundered off the Cape of Good Hope on May 27, 1698.[88] However, it is not suggested that this is a Dutch bottle.

2. Wine bottle. Olive-green glass; squat form with neck rather taller than that of no. 1 and the body slightly thinner in the wall; V-shaped string-rim; base missing. About 1700–1720. E3.

3. Wine bottle. Half-bottle size; olive-green glass appearing black in reflected light; weak shoulder and shallow basal kick; neck missing. About 1700–1725. Neck conjectured on the basis of another of characteristic form from deposit J2; body from K3.

4. Pyrmont water bottle. Early continental European form; the glass much decayed, soapy to the touch, and a matt black in color; tall tapering neck with a roughly trailed string-rim V-shaped in section; a conical basal kick with rough pontil mark. The "PIERMONT WATER" seal illustrated as no. 8 in fig. 16 is probably from this bottle. First quarter of 18th century? F2, L2.

5. Wine bottle. Deep olive-green glass appearing black in reflected light; weak shoulder; deep, domed basal kick; V-shaped string-rim ⅛ inch below the lip. C2. This is a transitional form between the squat varieties and the early cylindrical shapes. Examples of this type were plentiful in the cellars of Robert "King" Carter's mansion, Corotoman, which burned in 1729.

6. Wine bottle. Olive-green glass turned brown by decay; substantial neck crudely cut at the lip with a flat string-rim approximately ³⁄₁₆ inch below it; angular shoulder; body almost cylindrical; pronounced, domed basal kick. This bottle is reconstructed from fragments that do not represent a section through it. J2. The type may be attributed to the years 1730–1745 with the emphasis on the latter years.

7. Wine bottle. Olive-green glass much iridesced; weak shoulder; V-shaped string-rim approximately ¼₁₆ inch below the lip; pronounced domed basal kick. This bottle is comparable to no. 5. Date range about 1725–1735. F3.

8. Wine bottle. Olive-green glass turned brown by decay; short cylindrical body but slightly waisted; the shoulder spreading and angular; the neck substantial with a thin and flat string-rim with the mouth tooled outwards above it; a high conical basal kick. 1750–1765. B2.

9. Bottle neck. Olive-green glass turned brown by decay; angular shoulder; crudely trailed string-rim wrapped around the neck at the same level as the very roughly snapped mouth. No parallel has been found for this unusual neck, but the color of the glass and the nature of the decay might suggest that it is a contemporary of no. 8. N2.

10. Wine bottle neck. Amber-green glass appearing black in reflected light and extremely well preserved; neck unusually tall with a small V-shaped string-rim close to the evenly cut mouth; shoulder angular and apparently was attached to a cylindrical body. The bottle might be compared with no.1 of fig. 31. It is unlikely to date any earlier than about 1760; it could date as late as the 1790's, but in the present context it cannot, of course, do so. J2.

11. Bottle base. Rich emerald-green glass, thick walls; shallow domed basal kick with rough pontil mark on the base. This is almost certainly of French origin and must presumably date somewhere between about 1750 and 1772. C2.

Figure 31

1. Wine bottle. Olive-green glass appearing black in reflected light; cylindrical body with pronounced shoulder; tall neck and V-shaped string-rim close to the smoothly trimmed lip; shallow domed basal kick. This type could have been made at any date between about 1760 and the 1790's, but in the present context is limited to the bracket between about 1760 and 1772. O2.

2. Wine bottle. Rich olive to emerald-green iridescent glass; broad cylindrical body; angular shoulder; V-shaped string-rim approximately ³⁄₁₆ inch below the lip: lip tooled outwards above the constricting string-rim; shallow basal kick, which, having been thrust upwards, stuck to the pontil iron and was drawn down again when the tool was removed. Third quarter of 18th century. O2.

3. Wine bottle neck. Olive-green glass appearing black in reflected light; string-rim applied as a thick trail and tooled upwards toward the lip; lip tooled outwards so that it and rim together blend into a single collar; neck somewhat constricted below the string-rim. Examples of this type have been recovered from wrecks of vessels sunk off Yorktown in 1781. The form is late and would be surprising in any context prior to about 1770.

---

[88] See Ivor Noël Hume, "Bottles from beneath the Sea," *Wine and Spirit Trade Record*, June 1956, pl. 2.

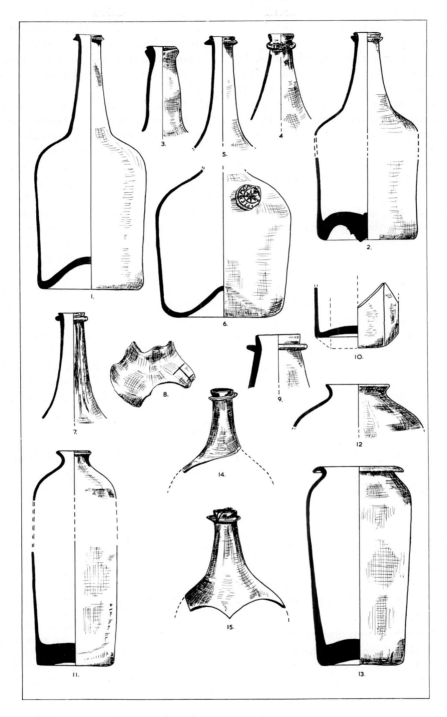

Figure 31.—Glass beverage bottles. One-fourth.

Coming as it does from stratum D1 it might be construed that the fragment does not belong to the pit.

4. Neck of "Piermont" water bottle. Impression of seal matrix on the string-rim. J3. For details see p. 190 (fig. 16, no. 5).

5. Bottle neck. Olive-green glass turned brown by decay; neck markedly tapering towards a flat string-rim approximately ³/₁₆ inch below the lip; lip tooled outwards above rim. This is a continental European shape and may well come from a Pyrmont water bottle with a body shaped like no. 6. Mid-18th century. A3.

6. Body of Pyrmont water bottle. Pale olive-green glass; butt-shaped with weak shoulder wider than the base; base with pronounced conical kick and rough pontil mark. The seal on the shoulder has an eight-pointed star in the center surrounded by the legend PIERMON[T WATER]. Mid-18th century. B3.

7. Neck of wine bottle or spa water bottle. Deep olive-green glass turned brown by decay; thick-walled; vertical stress grooves up the neck; roughly trailed round-sectioned string-rim approximately ³/₁₆ inch below the flat lip. Probably French. Third quarter of 18th century(?) K2.

8. Shoulder of wine bottle. Olive to amber-green glass turned brown by decay; possible graffito "E" or crossed "I" scratched on glass. Around 1740–1760. K1.

9. Neck fragment of large storage bottle or carboy. Olive-green iridescent glass; much decayed; oval string-rim ⁷/₁₆ inch below tapering lip. It is possible that the thinness of the lip was unintentional and resulted from chipping while in use. First half of 18th century. C3.

10. Base of snuff or blacking bottle. Olive-green glass turned brown by decay; octagonally molded; the base slightly rising. An intact bottle of this type was recovered from the wreck of a vessel that sank at Yorktown in 1781; others have been found in dated deposits in Williamsburg dating from the period about 1760–1770. B2, K2.

11. Case bottle. Pale olive-green glass much marred by decay; square body section; weak shoulder; short neck; everted lip; base thick, slightly rising, and with traces of a pontil mark. The bottle is reconstructed from fragments, though there is no section through it; the height was conjectured on the basis of intact examples in the collection of Colonial Williamsburg and elsewhere. Probably second or

third quarter of 18th century. Neck from C2, rest from J2.

12. Jar neck. Olive-green glass much decayed; probably from square-bodied vessel; shoulder broad and weak; rim everted. A jar of this type was found in a context attributed to the period 1740–1750 to the northeast of the Public Gaol in Williamsburg. C2.

13. Pickle jar(?). Olive-green glass much decayed; square-sectioned body broader at shoulder than at base; shoulder weak; mouth wide and with a sharply everted and down-tooled rim; base extremely thick and slightly rising. Second or third quarter of 18th century. F2, F3, G2, N2.

14. Wine bottle neck. Glass almost entirely destroyed by decay; large flat string-rim unevenly applied below the roughly out-tooled mouth. About 1720–1730. This fragment is of importance in that it was found in clay sealed by the secondary Indian deposit in B4.

15. Wine bottle neck. Olive-green glass turned brown by decay; similar in form to no. 14. Although many such necks were recovered, this example is of interest in that it still retains its original brass wire. Bottles with this shoulder form are known with dated seals from 1722 to 1727, indicating an over-all range of around 1720–1730 with the emphasis on the later years. K2.

Figure 32 [89]

1. Wine glass, lead metal.[90] Three-piece construction; waisted bowl with solid base; cushioned, inverted baluster stem; domed foot; a circular bubble in base of bowl; a squat, inverted tear in the baluster;[91] rough pontil mark in center of basal dome. The lip of the glass is missing and has been

[89] Dating and nomenclature used in these descriptions of wine glasses are derived from E. Barrington Haynes, *Glass through the Ages*, London, 1948.

[90] When discussing wine and other glasses, archeologists use the word "metal" to refer to the substance from which the vessel is made, thus avoiding confusion between "glass" as a shape and "glass" as (in the present instance) a mixture of silica, alkali, and lead oxide.

[91] All tears shown in this and the following drawings are drawn to indicate their exterior appearance. It is realized that the actual cavity is very much smaller than it appears. However, as the exact measurements could not be determined without breaking open the stems, and as any attempt to indicate the true size in the section would give an imperfect impressoin of the tear's appearance, the cavity is incorrectly drawn to the same size in both section and profile.

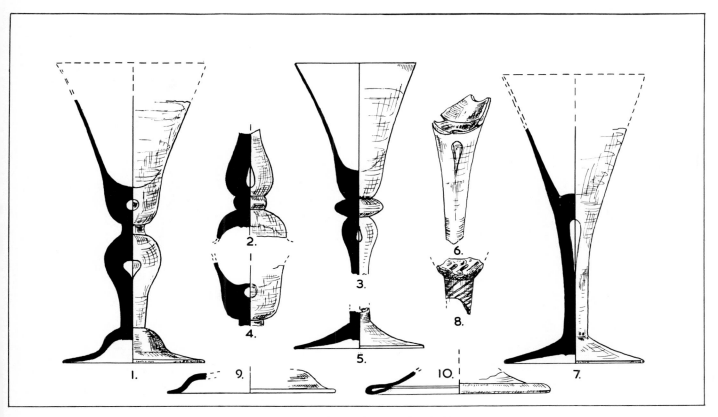

FIGURE 32.—Wine glasses. One-half.

conjecturally reconstructed in the drawing. About 1720–1730. P3.

2. Baluster stem, lead metal. Cushion knop; thick-domed foot with traces of pontil mark in center; a single tear in the stem. About 1715. Surface.

3. Wine glass, lead metal. Apparently three-piece construction; bell bowl welded above an angular knop that surmounts a light, inverted baluster containing a small tear; foot missing. After 1750. J3.

4. Solid base of waisted wine glass bowl, lead metal. Single tear; apparently with plain straight stem. After about 1740. J2.

5. Wine glass foot, lead metal. Plain conical form with base of light stem attached; pontil mark on base. Probably mid-18th century. G3.

6. Wine glass stem, lead metal. Two-piece construction; trumpet bowl; plain stem with elongated tear; foot and upper bowl wall missing. After about 1740. C3, D3.

7. Wine glass, lead metal. Two-piece construction; trumpet bowl; plain stem with elongated tear; plain

conical foot with pontil mark on base. After about 1740. This glass is important to the dating of the Rosewell pit in that it comes from the primary deposit in area E.

8. Straight stem fragment, lead metal. With air twist ornament, single multiple spiral (nine tubes), and apparently with heavy shoulder knop below the bowl. Around 1750. J2.

9. Domed foot fragment from large goblet, lead metal. 18th century. A2.

10. Folded conical foot from large goblet no less than 8 inches high; lead metal. Probably first half of 18th century. N2, N3.

Figure 33

1. Pharmaceutical bottle. Pale blue-green glass; short tubular neck with everted and flattened rim; conical base with rough pontil mark. Since there is no join between the neck and body fragments, the elevation has been conjectured on the basis of examples in the writer's collection. 18th century. E2, E3, F2, J2, J3, K2.

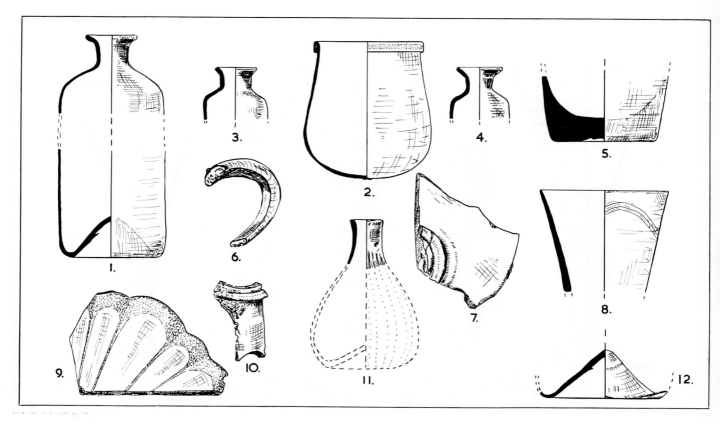

Figure 33.—Pharmaceutical bottles, cupping glass, and other glass items. One-half.

2. Cupping glass, lead metal. Folded rim; bulbous body; probably traces of a pontil mark on base. The drawing is reconstructed from fragments of two examples found together in the same stratum.[92] 18th century. A4.

3. Pharmaceutical phial. Pale green glass; neck and upper body fragment only; short tubular neck; angular shoulder; lip only slightly everted. Probably mid-18th century. A2.

4. Pharmaceutical phial. Pale blue-green glass; neck and upper body fragment only; short tubular neck; angular shoulder; rim everted. Probably of the same period as no. 3, although the wider lip often is indicative of an earlier date. F2.

5. Tumbler base, heavy lead glass. Base slightly rising with an unground pontil mark; interior wall sloping sharply inwards towards the bottom. Perhaps first half of 18th century. Surface. The bases of two other tumblers were among the finds from the pit, but neither is illustrated. These differ

from the base shown in that they are much lighter, the interior walls do not slope inwards towards the bottom, and the glass is more transparent. Perhaps third quarter of 18th century. A2, J2.

6. Lead glass handle from vessel of uncertain form. 18th century. H2.

7. Lead glass fragment from object of uncertain purpose. A double collar or perhaps an annulated knop above a flat piece of glass, more scratched on the underside than on the upper; metal transparent and of good quality. It has been suggested that the fragment may be from a lid or, if inverted, might be part of a pedestal-based dish. P3.

8. Wine glass bowl, lead metal. Possibly from glass of trumpet form (see fig. 32, no. 7). A group of three scored lines creating a wavy pattern around the bowl was caused by decay in stress marks created during manufacture. Probably after about 1740. J3.

9. Fragment of lead plate glass. Scalloped edge, and the same motif ground onto the upper surface. Mr. John Gloag, the English furniture expert, has ex-

---

[92] For parallels see *Country Life*, August 12, 1954.

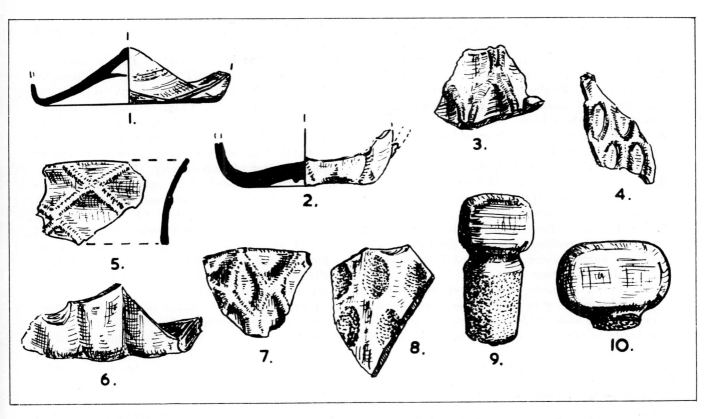

FIGURE 34.—Fragments from molded jelly glasses, perfume flask, and glass stoppers. Same size.

amined this fragment and has suggested that it comes from a mirror of the period 1690–1720. A2.

10. Neck fragment from wine bottle. Glass apparently calcined, possibly through having been inadvertently included in the burning of oyster-shell mortar. The presence of shell mortar attached to all the sides and broken edges of the fragment tend to support such a conjecture. Third quarter of 18th century. D2.

11. Neck fragment from perfume (?) bottle. Pale blue-green glass; lip slightly thickened but not everted. A series of striations towards the lower edge of the fragment are comparable to those on the neck of a bottle of similar glass found in a sealed deposit in Williamsburg. The latter bottle (E.R. 140.27B) has an oval body and conical base, both decorated with molded vertical ribbing; the neck possesses the same striations at the top of the ribs but is tooled outwards at the mouth to provide a flaring lip. It is suggested that the mouth of the Rosewell item would have been the same had it been tooled, thus expanding and, at the same time, thinning the

wall. In consequence a conjectural reconstruction has been indicated, using this neck atop the Williamsburg body, which comes from a sealed deposit with a terminal date of about 1745. A2.

12. Base of pharmaceutical bottle. Clear lead glass; conical kick with traces of pontil mark. Clear bottles of this type gradually took the place of the green and blue-green forms during the second half of the 18th century. F2.

Figure 34

1. Base of pharmaceutical bottle. Clear lead glass; conical kick with rough pontil mark (see fig. 33, no. 12). B2.
2. Base of small handled cup. Clear lead glass; base slightly rising with rough pontil mark; wall ornamented with widely spaced molded vertical ribbing. 18th century. C2, F1.
3. Bowl fragment. Clear lead metal; possibly from spirit glass; wall ornamented with raised ribbing in

lozenge patterns. This pattern would appear to be in the "Nipt diamond waies" tradition of the late 17th century.[93] F1.

4. Bowl fragment close to flaring rim. Perhaps from dwarf ale or jelly glass; clear lead metal;[94] molded decoration of small, highly ridged lozenges. No earlier than about 1730. B2.

5. Rim fragment, possibly from wide-mouthed jelly glass, lead metal, molded diamond decoration. No earlier than about 1730. O2.

6. Basal fragment from tumbler or cup, clear lead glass, the wall decorated with molded fluting or ribbing. 18th century. D1.

7. Rim fragment. Probably from jelly glass; brilliant lead metal; molded diamond decoration; rim slightly angled where the molded lines touch it. No earlier than about 1730. O2.

8. Fragment. Probably from body of perfume flask; pale blue-green glass with some lead content; ornamented with molded lozenges. Possibly from a bottle in the same class as no. 11 in fig. 33. Surface.

9. Bottle or decanter stopper. Solid lead glass; rectangular knob; the body ground below the shoulder; bottom diameter $\frac{1}{2}$ inch. 18th century. E2.

10. Knob from bottle or decanter stopper. Solid lead glass; oval form. 18th century. K2.

Figure 35

1. Tobacco-pipe bowl. Clay; of English manufacture; cylindrical bowl terminating at the base in a flat heel; stem-hole diameter $\frac{7}{64}$ inch. This item may be compared to Adrian Oswald's Type 7a,[95] although it lacks the slight in-curve above the fore-edge of the heel. Oswald dates the type to the period about 1670–1710; however, this writer has found numerous examples in debris from the Great Fire of London in 1666, but few in contexts dating much later than about 1680. Whatever the true date of the Rosewell specimen, there is no doubt

that it is a stray in the present context. Around 1660–1680. C2.

2. Tobacco-pipe bowl. Clay; of English manufacture; thin-walled; small heel; stem-hole diameter $\frac{5}{64}$ inch. First half of 18th century. K3.

3. Tobacco-pipe bowl. Clay; of English manufacture; small heel; walls thicker than in no. 2 and the bowl with slightly more thrust on the fore-edge of the rim; stem-hole diameter $\frac{5}{64}$ inch. Second or third quarter of 18th century. F2.

4. Tobacco-pipe bowl. Clay; of English manufacture; wall 3 mm. thick; pronounced heel with maker's initials "I.D." (the "I" is considerably smaller than the "D" and could perhaps be read as "T"); stem-hole diameter $\frac{5}{64}$ inch. Two examples from this mold were recovered, both from the primary filling in area E. Second or third quarter of 18th century.

5. Tobacco-pipe bowl. Clay; of English manufacture; wall approximately 2 mm. thick at rear but appreciably thinner at the fore-edge; somewhat squat heel with maker's large initials "A.S."; stem-hole diameter $\frac{5}{64}$ inch. Second or third quarter of 18th century. E4 (another example from C2).

6. Tobacco-pipe heel and stem fragment. Clay; of Irish manufacture (?); narrow heel with crowned harp molded on either side in place of the more common maker's initials; stem-hold diameter $\frac{4}{64}$ inch. Probably third quarter of 18th century. K2 (another example from J1).

7. Tobacco-pipe bowl and section of stem. Clay; of English manufacture; bowl wall 2.5 mm. thick; the heel long and of small diameter; maker's initials "R.M.," molded on either side, are thick and cleanly cut, though weak in the first stroke of the "M"; stem-hole diameter $\frac{4}{64}$ inch. Probably third quarter of the 18th century. E2, G2.

8. Tobacco-pipe bowl. Clay; of English manufacture; neither heel nor spur;[96] wall of somewhat un-

---

[93] A possible parallel for the style of the Rosewell fragment appears in *Country Life*, January 25, 1946, p. 169, no. 7. This fragment is attributed to about 1685; however, it is unlikely that the Rosewell fragment is as early.

[94] Haynes (*op. cit.* footnote 89) stated that some examples of mold-ornamented jelly glasses are of soda metal. All the Rosewell fragments were tested for lead and gave positive results.

[95] *Archeological News Letter*, April 1951, vol. 3, no. 10.

---

[96] It has been suggested that these pipes were specially manufactured for the American colonies, for examples without heel or spur are extremely rare in England but are common on American sites. However, the explanation that pipes with these plain bowls were less liable to be damaged in shipping does not bear scrutiny, for a pipe rarely breaks at the heel. It might, however, be suggested that pipes were made in this style to parallel the forms made and used by the Indians. A painting (in the Historical Society of Pennsylvania) by Gustavus Hesselius in 1735 of the Indian chief Tishcohan (He-who-never-blackens-himself) shows one of these pipes

even thickness but measuring 2 mm. at thickest point. Probably third quarter of 18th century. N2. [Four other slightly smaller bowls of this same basic type were recovered from the pit, two of them with stem-hole diameters of $\frac{5}{64}$ inch and the others without measurable stems surviving. All second or third quarter of 18th century. E4, F1, K2, N2.]

9. Tobacco-pipe bowl. Clay; of English manufacture; neither heel nor spur; larger than no. 8; stem-hole diameter $\frac{4}{64}$ inch. Probably third quarter of 18th century. Surface.

10. Tobacco-pipe. Clay; of English manufacture; end of stem missing; wall thickness 2 mm.; heel with maker's initials "H.S." on the sides, the "H" smaller than the "S"; stem-hole diameter approximately $\frac{5}{64}$ inch. Most pipes of this type seem to have a stem length of a little under 13 inches (measured from behind the heel). However, the diameter of the fractured stem of this example could suggest a missing section of as much as 4½ inches, giving a total length of approximately 1 foot 3½ inches. Second or third quarter of 18th century. E3.

NOTE: While most of the mouth-piece fragments recovered from the Rosewell pit were without glazing or coating of any kind, a few possessed one or other of these characteristics. Examples illustrated as nos. 10, 11, in fig. 14 are coated with a post cocturam

red wax and with an ante cocturam black slip, respectively. Other specimens have a treacly brown glaze or a bluish green glaze flecked with light brown or orange.

For students of Mr. J. C. Harrington's stem-hole theory the following statistics will be useful:

Stratum	4/64″	5/64″	6/64″	7/64″
2........	(124)26%	(327)67%	(32)6.5%	(2)0.5%
3........	....	(15)83%	(3)17%	....
Primary [97].	....	(3)50%	(3)50%	....

It should, however, be remembered that it is believed that all three strata were deposited within a few months. For this reason, and in view of the small number of fragments from the two lower levels, only stratum 2 is of any statistical value.

Mr. Harrington was kind enough to examine the above statistics and to make the following observations:

Stratum 3: (485 fragments): Based upon my charts [98] (which I still insist are not intended for such use, but only to illustrate a suggested technique), I would have to date this collection 1740–1760, and call the 2 with $\frac{7}{64}$ holes family heirlooms.

Stratum 3: Too small a sample, but if forced, I would say 1730.

Primary: Ditto; 1710.

Figure 36

1. Pistol barrel. Iron; tang with screw-hole in top for attaching barrel to stock; a small loop beneath the barrel for pinning to the lower housing; barrel octagonal at rear and tapering towards muzzle; two ornamental grooves $3\frac{13}{16}$ inches from rear; priming hole on right side $\frac{7}{16}$ inch from rear; total length

---

hung around the subject's neck. Excavations beside the colonial gaol in Williamsburg (Excavation Register 140) resulted in the recovery of 16 pipes of this type from a context attributed to the decade 1740–1750. Each of these pipes had a stem-hole diameter of $\frac{5}{64}$ inch but none was marked with the maker's initials. Such marks are rare, but the most common is that of R. Tippet, whose name appears in a cartouche on the right wall and with the initials "R. T." impressed on the wall above the stem. The name is generally written in three lines R/TIP/PET, but in some cases only the initials "R. T." are molded in the cartouche. One example from Williamsburg was found in a post-1770 context, and another came from a group dating from between 1720 and 1740 (Colonial Williamsburg site no. 28F4, Excavation Register 150D). The stem hole of this last example measures $\frac{5}{64}$ inch. Tippet also made pipes with heels. Adrian Oswald in his article "A Case of Transatlantic Deduction" (*Antiques*, July 1959, vol. 76, no. 1, pp. 59–61) shows that the Tippet pipes were manufactured in Bristol, England, and that members of the Tippet family were working there as early as 1660. An earlier form of the heelless-spurless pipe is occasionally found in Tidewater Virginia with the maker's initials molded on the base. If read from left side to right from above (as the heeled varieties are), the initials are "S. A." On the other hand it is possible to turn these pipes bottom up and read the letters as "A. S." An example from

Skimino Plantation, south of the York River, was found in a ploughed field with other artifacts of the period around 1680–1710 (Colonial Williamsburg Collection, cat. no. 195). Such an early date for the marked pipe is supported by the $\frac{5}{64}$-inch diameter of the stem hole. As noted above, the Rosewell example (no. 8) has a stem-hole diameter of only $\frac{4}{64}$ inch.

[97] Additional items subsequently recovered from this deposit would make the $\frac{5}{64}$″ column read "(16) 76.2%" and the $\frac{6}{64}$″ column read "(5) 23.8%."

[98] J. C. Harrington, "Dating Stem Fragments of Seventeenth and Eighteenth Century Clay Tobacco Pipes," *Quarterly Bulletin of the Archaeological Society of Virginia*, September 1954, vol. 1, no. 9.

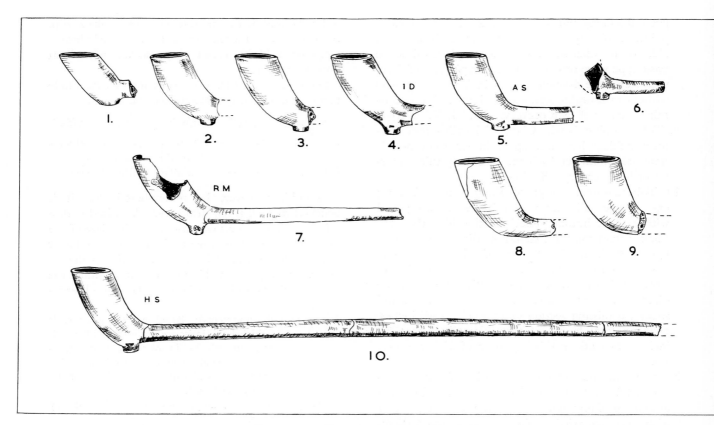

FIGURE 35.—Clay tobacco pipes. One-half.

of barrel 8⅜ inches; .60 caliber. Possible traces of an armorer's touch mark, a cross within a square, are to be seen on the lower left facet, 1 inch from rear. The barrel is too short for this pistol to have been a standard military weapon. 18th century. E3.

2. Tool, locally made, of uncertain purpose. See fig. 23, no. 10.

3. Sickle (?). Roughly made and probably unfinished; square-sectioned tang; blade broken; traces of a cutting edge close to the break on the lower edge; rectangular impression, ½ inch by ⅜ inch, on the reverse side of the blade 1¼ inches below the tang might be the remains of crude mark of maker. P2.

4. Knife. Iron; single edge; flat tang pierced by three holes for riveting bone or wooden plates to it to provide the handle; extremely crudely made, the tang being roughly folded and beaten into shape without any effort having been made to remove surplus metal; likely to have been of local manufacture. G2.

5. Axe blade. Narrow, thickening to ¾ inch below

socket; socket broken and appears to be unfinished, suggesting that this item is another product of the nearby forge. B2.

6. Wedge-shaped item of uncertain purpose. Iron; somewhat bowed in section with greatest thickness of ⁵⁄₁₆ inch narrowing to approximately ⅛ inch at either end; a rectangular hole at one end; the other end blade-shaped. J2.

7. Chisel. Iron; hollow octagonal socket for wooden handle; interior diameter ⅝ inch; blade slightly waisted above the cutting edge; sides of blade crudely beaten and spreading to form ridges along the edges; end of socket has been beaten until it has spread, split and curled, indicating that the chisel was used without the intended wooden handle. This tool, probably a forming chisel or firmer,[99] was perhaps a product of the local forge. J2.

---

[99] The closest parallel encountered is to be found in Henry C. Mercer, *Ancient Carpenters' Tools*, Doylestown, Pennsylvania, The Bucks County Historical Society, 1951, fig. 148, no. 20633.

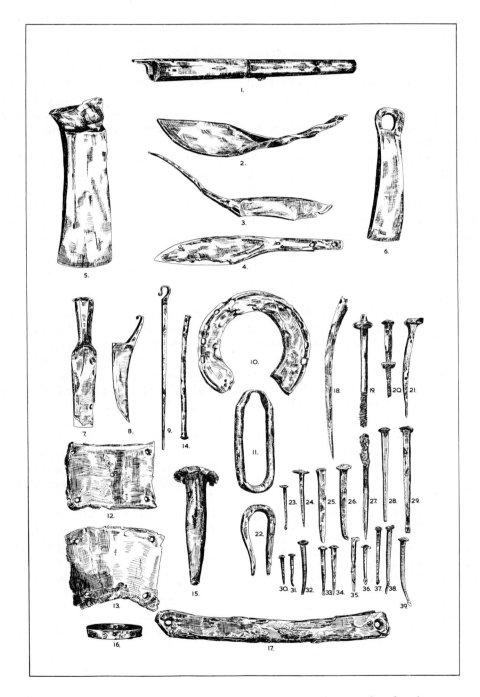

FIGURE 36.—Iron pistol barrel, tools, horseshoe, nails, etc.   One-fourth.

8. Tool of uncertain purpose. Iron; small, slightly curved blade with no cutting edge, flat on one side and slightly convex on the other; rectangular-sectioned handle or tang extending from one corner and narrowing to a thin strip that is bent over into an angular hook.[100] It has been suggested that this tool may have been used by bricklayers for scoring the mortar between the bricks. N3.

9. Skewer. Iron; rectangular-sectioned, ⅛ inch thick; drawn out at top and shaped into a scroll-like hook. J2. Skewers of this type were common in the 18th century, and were sold in sets, suspended from an ornamental, wrought-iron hanger.

10. Horseshoe. Iron; keyhole type; the heels slightly rising; four nail holes on either side, fullered. N3. The presence of this shoe in the Rosewell pit is of interest in that it fails to support the often heard contention that in Tidewater Virginia it was unnecessary for horses to be shod because there were no stony or paved roads to damage their hooves.[101] It should be noted that the keyhole form of the Rosewell shoe was not the only shape favored in the 18th century and was, in fact, less common than the more narrow conventional type. A shoe of this form was found in a refuse pit of about 1740 at Tutter's Neck near Williamsburg during excavations in 1960.

11. Link from large chain. Carefully worked lap-joint at one end; the other end so worn by friction from the next link that the iron is practically worn through; diameter ⅜ inch at widest point. C1.

12. Plate. Iron; rectangular; roughly trimmed at the edges and pierced by five nail holes, one at each

corner and the fifth in the center; measures 3¾ by 2¾ inches; slightly down-curved at the shorter sides; of uncertain use.[102] The workmanship on this item closely allies it with the fragments of iron waste illustrated in fig. 23 and indicates that it, too, comes from the local forge. C2.

13. Plate. Iron; rectangular; roughly trimmed at the edges and pierced by four nail holes, one at each corner; measures 4¼ by 3⅜ inches; markedly curved at its shorter sides, suggesting that it may have been some kind of protective plate, perhaps from an axle hub. Comparable to the smaller example (no. 12). A2.

14. Rod. Iron; probably a curb from a Pelham or curb bit. 18th century. Surface.

15. Punch. Iron; the head spread and curling from constant use; the shaft round-sectioned at the top, tapering and four-sided towards the end; the point of percussion somewhat concave; weight 1 pound 7 ounces. This is almost certainly a farrier's punch.[103] B2.

16. Band. Iron; circular; ½ inch in width and slightly tapering; pierced by three small nail holes, two opposite each other and the third midway between them. The object presumably was used to encircle the end of a tapering pole. N2.

17. Bar. Iron; with countersunk nail or rivet holes at either end; slightly bowed; metal much decayed, but original thickness probably about ½ inch; of uncertain purpose. E2.

18. Tine from agricultural fork. Rectangular-sectioned towards the top; ⅜ by ⁵⁄₁₆ inch; tapering and becoming round-sectioned towards the point. The curvature at the top is inherent in the object, suggesting that the fork was of the dished variety. K2.

19. Bolt. Iron; a washer welded to the shaft ⅜ inch below the top to form the head; shaft square-sectioned beneath the head, quickly becoming round-sectioned; threaded length 1⁹⁄₁₆ inches; diameter approximately ⁵⁄₁₆ inch. F2.

---

[100] Another example was found by this writer in the destruction of a house on Duke of Gloucester Street, Williamsburg, that burned in February 1776. Until shortly before the fire the building had been the house or shop of Peter Scott, a cabinet-maker. Three further specimens have since been found—one at Tutter's Neck, James City County, in a context of about 1725–1735, and two others at Clay Bank, Gloucester County, in a deposit of about 1700.

[101] There is, however, literary evidence that such was the case in the early 18th century. Hugh Jones in *The Present State of Virginia*, London, 1724 (edited by Richard L. Morton, Chapel Hill, 1956), p. 14, when describing Governor Spotwood's celebrated ride over the Appalachians, made the following statement: "For this Expedition they were obliged to provide a great Quantity of Horse-shoes (Things seldom used in the lower Parts of the Country, where there are few Stones:) Upon which Account the Governor upon their Return presented each of his Companions with a golden Horse-Shoe."

[102] A vague parallel is illustrated by Kenneth E. Kidd (*The Excavation of St. Marie I*, Toronto, University of Toronto Press, 1949, p. 100 and pl. 37, top). That piece measured 6½ by 5¾ inches and may have been a part of a box or cupboard. It came from the site of a Jesuit mission, in Canada, that existed only during the years 1639–1649. An almost exact parallel was found in Williamsburg excavations in 1961 (Excavation Register 384C.15A) in a context of 1750–1765.

[103] See tool illustrated in Diderot's *Encyclopédie*, vol. 7 (Paris, 1769), pl. 4, fig. 19.

20. Bolt. Iron; smooth and convex head forged from the shaft; shaft square-sectioned and tapering; threaded length 1½ inches; diameter approximately ³⁄₁₆ inch; nut, still in position, measures ⁹⁄₁₆ by ⁹⁄₁₆ by ⅛ inch. K2.

21. Spike. Iron; four-sided; tapering to flat blade point; heavy square head approximately ¼ inch thick. C1.

22. Staple. Iron; round-sectioned at top, showing evidence of hammering; becoming rectangular-sectioned at the tapering sides, which bend towards each other above the blade-shaped points. Surface.

23. Nail. Iron; flat head, rectangular-sectioned; flattened point. This nail and all the following examples come from stratum 2, but are not identified by area.

24. Nail. Iron; rose head (?), rectangular-sectioned; normal point.

25. Spike. Iron; rectangular sectioned; vestigial round head; point lost.

26. Planching nail. Iron; round head flattened on either side to form T-shape, rectangular-sectioned; chisel point. Such nails were generally used for flooring and were punched below the surface.

27. Nail. Iron; head missing; round shank becoming "four square," that is, equi-sided; sharp and narrow point.

28. Spike. Iron; rose head; rectangular sectioned; blunt end.

29. Spike. Iron; rose head (?), rectangular-sectioned; flattened point.

30. Lath nail. Iron; rectangular head, shank "four square" and tapering to a point.

31. Lath nail. Iron; small round head; rectangular-sectioned; flattened point.

32. Planching nail. Iron; T-shaped head; rectangular-sectioned; blunt end. See no. 26.

33. Nail. Iron; rose head; rectangular-sectioned; flattened point.

34. Nail. Iron; rose head; rectangular-sectioned; tapering to point. This type is sometimes described as "Rose-sharp," while the flat-pointed variety can be called "Flat-point-rose."

35. Nail. Iron; L-shaped head; rectangular-sectioned; blunt point.

36. Nail. Iron; T-shaped head, possibly broken; rectangular-sectioned; spear point.[104]

37. Nail. Iron; vestigal rectangular head; rectangular-sectioned and the point flattened.

38. Nail. Iron; possibly with L-shaped head; rectangular-sectioned, tapering to point.

39. Nail. Iron; roughly square rose head; rectangular-sectioned; flattened point.

All the foregoing nails are hand wrought and are illustrated as representative of the sizes and types included among the hundreds recovered from the Rosewell deposit. For a list of nails ordered by John Page in 1771 see page 158.

The first machine for making "cut-nails" was patented by Ezekial Reed of Bridgewater, Massachusetts, in 1786, and by about 1800 cut nails were rapidly taking the place of the old wrought varieties. Cut nails were made from sheets of iron cut to appropriate lengths, the heads being beaten in a vice by hand. Such nails can be identified by the fact that the shank tapers only on the two cut sides, the front and back being parallel as was the sheet from which they were cut. The first English patent for a machine to manufacture cut nails was granted to John Clifford in 1790. In the first half of the 19th century the French manufactured wire nails by hand and developed a machine for producing them in the second quarter of the century. Sample machines were imported into America soon afterwards. The first handmade wire nails with round-sectioned shanks and heads were made by William Hersel of New York City in 1850.

Figure 37

1. Cauldron. Iron; body fragment only; decorated with two encircling ridges; the beginning of one of the triangular, ear-type handles appears at the upper edge; wall thickness ³⁄₁₆ inch. Such vessels had tripod legs and a pair of handles; they owed their origins to the bronze cooking vessels of the 14th and 15th centuries. P2.

2. Fireback. Iron; ornamented fragment only. See fig. 23, no. 8.

3. Hoe. Iron; large size; D-shaped blade; socket thicker at base than at top. Diameter 2¼ inches; height 2⅝ inches. The form is typical of the 18th century. E3. This example was found in wet clay, an environment unsuited for the preservation of iron; in consequence, the blade is too decayed for it to undergo chemical cleaning without drastic loss of shape. Without cleaning it is impossible to tell whether the hoe possesses a maker's mark—a feature generally stamped on the V-shaped spine. A comparable, unstratified example found in Williamsburg

---

[104] See Mercer, *op. cit.* (footnote 99), fig. 201, B3.

is stamped three times with the initials "W.D." [105] The socket and spine of another hoe of similar type was also recovered. The spine bears traces of illegible maker's stamps. The socket is somewhat unusual in that it had been flattened at the back and differed from the illustrated example by a wider angle between the socket and the rear edge of the blade. It was too decayed to merit illustration. J2;

4. Warren hoe. Iron; heavy socket; V-shaped spine extending along most of blade; blade convex on upper surface and concave behind; maker's stamp "IM" stamped on blade on either side of the spine; socket tall and narrowing towards the top, thickness at base approximately $\frac{1}{4}$ inch; diameter approximately $2\frac{1}{2}$ inches; height $2\frac{3}{4}$ inches; forge welded down the back. It has been suggested that hoes of this type were used for cutting drainage gullies. This example was found after ploughing in the field north of the mansion in the vicinity of the barn(?) foundations. But the character of the workmanship and the style of the lettering in the maker's stamp leave no doubt that this is a colonial instrument. Unstratified.

5. Grub hoe. Iron; flat blade with narrow V-shaped spine triple-stamped with maker's mark "W.M."; socket tapers slightly towards the top, is $\frac{3}{8}$ to $\frac{3}{16}$ inch thick at base, approximately $2\frac{3}{8}$ inches in diameter, and $2\frac{1}{2}$ inches long. Examples of this type have been found in Williamsburg excavations and in a cache of agricultural tools at Greenspring Plantation near Jamestown. [106]

6. Scissors. Iron (see fig. 21, no. 13, p. 198).

7. Ice skate. Iron; fluted blade; the toe flattening and curving gracefully upwards; screw fitting beneath heel for mounting into wooden patten, and a notched lug close to the ball of the foot for a similar purpose. From field north of Page Graveyard. The skate was tied to the sole of the wearer's shoe by leather thongs or with ribbons. In 1709 William Byrd records that he took a group of house guests for a walk and "slid on skates, notwithstanding there was a thaw." [107] In 1769 the shop of Sarah Pitt in Williamsburg was offering fluted and plain

skates, with or without leather. [108] Skates of the Rosewell type are to be seen in numerous pictures of the late 18th century, notably the engraving *Winter Amusement*, 1782, printed and sold by Carington Bowles of London, and in a mezzotint from a painting by John Collet entitled *The Pleasures of Skating—or, a View in Winter*, 1780, also published by Bowles. [109]

Figure 38

1. Hinge or hasp. Iron; crudely made; with butterfly terminal; a rivet punched through the broken arm; the other arm without any holes for nailing or riveting; metal approximately 1 mm. thick. See no. 2. 18th century. J2.

2. Hinge or hasp. Crudely made; with butterfly terminal at one end and no evidence of nail holes; the other arm broken and much decayed. In the course of cleaning it was found that the broken arm was riveted to a fragment of iron of the same thickness as itself. Unfortunately, there was insufficient metal surviving for chemical cleaning to be possible. 18th century. J2. [110]

3. Hinge (?). Scroll terminal at bulbous end and nail attached $\frac{1}{2}$ inch from it; part of another nail hole at the break; metal slightly convex and 1 to 2 mm. thick. 18th century. C3.

4. Hinge. Iron; one arm almost entirely missing; end of other arm lost; [111] latter arm pierced by two nail holes, one with diameter of 3 mm.; metal 1 mm. thick; length of surviving arm 2 inches. 18th century. A2.

5. Hinge or ornamental strap. Iron; blade-shaped with two rivets attached and a hole for a third rivet at the broken end; metal 1 to 2 mm. thick. 18th century. L2.

6. Plate from interior of rim lock. Iron; shaped to enable key to pass beneath it; metal 1 to 1.5 mm. thick; heavily brazed; probably comes from a brass lock. Surface.

---

[105] Colonial Williamsburg archeological collection. No. 2–287–OC.

[106] See Louis R. Caywood, *Green Spring Plantation*, archeological report, Washington, D.C., U.S. National Park Service, 1955, pl. 9.

[107] William Byrd, *The Secret Diary of William Byrd of Westover, 1709–1712* (edited by Louis B. Wright and Marion Tinling, Richmond, 1941), entry for December 29, 1709.

[108] *Virginia Gazette*, October 26, 1769, p. 2.

[109] For further details concerning skating in the 18th century, see Jane Carson, *Colonial Virginians at Play* (multilithed research report), Research Department, Colonial Williamsburg, 1958, pp. 190–192.

[110] A fragment of a third hinge of this type was found in stratum M2.

[111] When found, this hinge appeared to spread at the end into the butterfly form of nos. 1 and 2. Unfortunately the end disintegrated during cleaning.

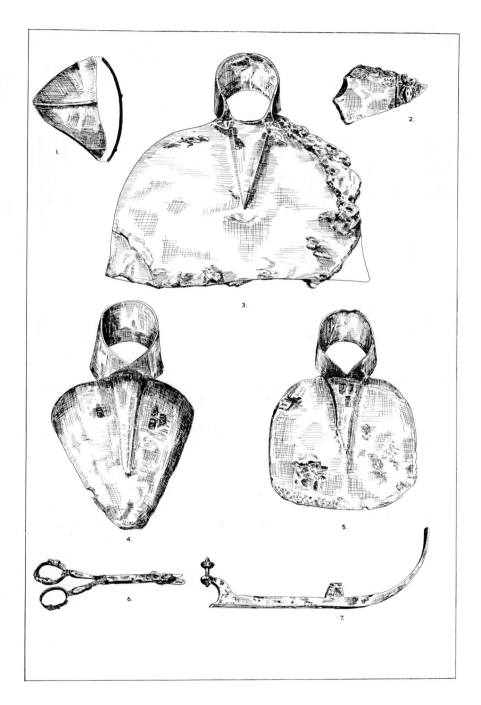

FIGURE 37.—Hoes, scissors, iron ice skate, etc.   One-fourth.

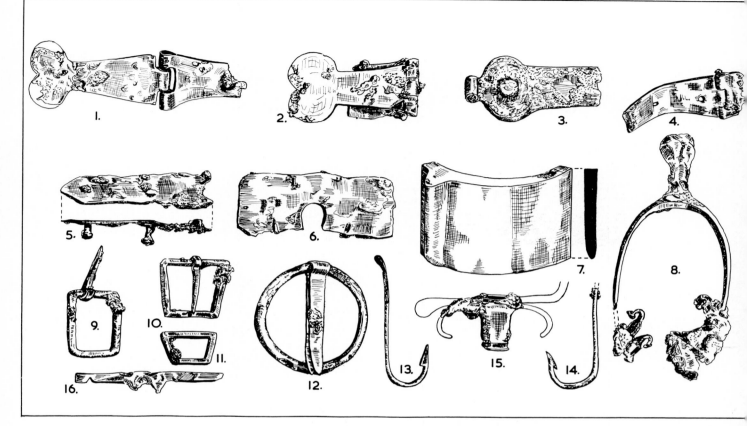

FIGURE 38.—Iron hinges, buckles, fish hooks, etc. One-half.

7. Nave-sleeve from wheel. Iron; fragment only; internal diameter 3 inches; wall $5/16$ inch thick at one end, tapering to a weak V at the other; retaining lug flush with the thick end and curving before reaching the tapered end. 18th century. C1. Another example, without the tapering wall, had an internal diameter of $3\frac{3}{4}$ inches. 18th century. G2.

8. Spur. Iron; rowel and T-shaped fastenings much decayed; the sides flat on the inside and convex on the outside; width of heel approximately $2\frac{1}{8}$ inches. 18th century. E4.

9. Harness buckle. Iron; s q u a r e - s e c t i o n e d; the pointed tang flattened at the junction end and wrapped round the frame; frame thickness approximately $3/8$ inch. 18th century. P2.

10. Harness buckle. Iron; the frame round-sectioned at the tang side, the other sides of frame flattened and slightly angled; the tang pointed, flattened at the junction end, and wrapped round the frame. Surface.

11. Harness buckle or leather junction. Iron; four-sided; one side round-sectioned and the others square. Surface.

12. Harness buckle. Iron; the ring round-sectioned; tang fashioned from a strip of iron pinched round the frame with its ends of equal length and both cut to a point, the two ends springing apart after passing through the hole in the leather. Surface.

13. Fish hook. Iron; single barb at the point; end of shank flattened and spreading but without any pierced hole; much decayed, but the shank probably was about 3 to 4 mm. thick. 18th century. L2.

14. Fish hook. Iron; similar to the above, but the point and barb more gracefully curved; top of the shank missing; surviving portion approximately 4 mm. thick. 18th century. L2.

15. Quillon sleeve from small sword. See fig. 21, no. 14.

16. Bolt from light cabinet lock. Iron; 2 mm. thick. 18th century. N2.

U.S. GOVERNMENT PRINTING OFFICE: 1962

Index

234